D0428776

ON BRAVE OLD ARMY TEAM

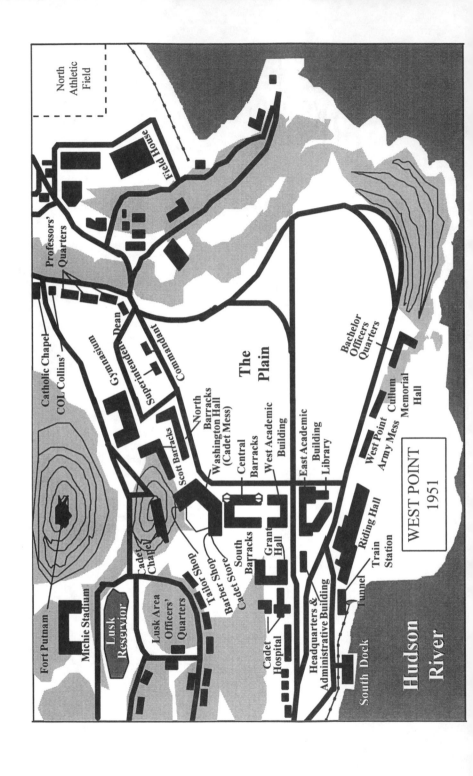

WEST POINT
1951

ON BRAVE OLD ARMY TEAM

THE CHEATING SCANDAL THAT ROCKED THE NATION
WEST POINT, 1951

James A. Blackwell

PRESIDIO

Published by Presidio Press
505 B San Marin Dr., Suite 300
Novato, CA 94945-1340

Library of Congress Cataloging-in-Publication Data

Blackwell, James.
    On brave old Army team : the cheating scandal that rocked the nation : West Point, 1951 / James A. Blackwell.
        p.   cm.
    Includes bibliographical references.
    ISBN 0-89141-553-X
    1. United States Military Academy—Football—History—20th century. 2. Sports—Corrupt practices—New York (State)—West Point—Case studies.   I. Title.
    GV958.U5285B53   1996
    796.332'63'0974731—dc20   96-7174
                                                                                     CIP

Frontispiece map by Evan Ellis.
All photos courtesy USMA West Point special collections except where noted.
Printed in the United States of America

Contents

Preface

Of all human virtues, integrity is most revered at West Point, the U.S. Military Academy. Honor is sacred there. Cadets, faculty, and alumni treat their honor code as gospel, entrusted to them in their time for interpretation, education, and enforcement.

Of all human endeavor, football is most prized at West Point. The Army team is a living symbol of the academy's commitment to winning at all costs. The cadets of West Point consider themselves corporately to be an inseparable part of the team—a twelfth man. It is a way to demonstrate their commitment to winning the nation's wars.

Honor and winning at West Point are meant to be coequal, perfectly complementary moral contributors to the development of America's Army leaders. Usually they are; but once in a while they collide, sometimes destroying careers and lives. This book will tell the story of perhaps the biggest—and at the same time least discussed—such collision, which occurred in 1951, when nearly ninety cadets, mostly football players, were summarily dismissed from West Point for cheating.

Acknowledgments

This book would not have been possible without the cooperation of several of those involved, one way or another in the cheating of 1951 and its resulting impact on West Point. Bill Jackomis has been especially generous in this regard. Special thanks to former USMA superintendent Gen. Dave Palmer for all of his valuable assistance. In the many months of research and preparation their willingness to bare their own souls waxed and waned, but in the end they proved to be the real heroes of this story. They have allowed us to look into their private lives in a way that most of us ordinary people would never contemplate doing. Their willingness to lay transparent all their strengths and weaknesses is testimony to their courage and honor.

Several of those involved in the cheating provided me with much material but asked that their identity not be revealed in this book. I have kept their confidence in this regard and where they were important to the story I have used pseudonyms to hide their real names. As they occur in this book the following names are fictitious but apply to real people who are still alive and asked that I not reveal their true name, or I felt that it would be best not to mention them explicitly: Fred Jones, Bill Johnson, Ralph Martin, Richard Hunt, James Jackson, Michael Kelly, John McDonald, Charles Mitchell, Harry James, George Williams, James Davidson, Jeffrey Rich, William West, Randy Ford, Eugene Lawrence and Bruce Wilson. No one by these names was involved in the scandal itself, and no USMA graduate or former graduate who may have these or similar names was involved in the cheating incident in any way.

Most of the sources employed in this book are in the public domain or are accessible. Many of West Point's official records are available in the Pentagon Library. Especially useful in this regard are the annual Official Register of Officers and Cadets, and the Report of the Superintendent. Less readily accessible but still available are a few special sources that were vital to unraveling this story. Mr. Richard Sommer, the archivist at the U.S. Army Military History Institute at Carlisle Barracks, Pennsylvania, was particularly helpful. At West Point, much material was made available by Alan Aimone of Special Collections in the USMA Library.

In the National Records and Archives Administration two sources proved to be quite useful. Mr. Richard W. Peuser of the Military Reference Branch, Textual reference Division, spent many hours digging through Army staff files on my behalf. The USMA Archives at West Point, which is also part of the National Archives system, provided some critical documents.

My brother Jeff served as my research assistant and part-time sleuth in helping me to track down leads and resolve the many issues and questions that arose as I uncovered this story piece by piece. He also provided much of the legwork of getting to and from West Point to collect documents and photographs. He also assisted in early composing, indexing, and editing.

A number of people helped by reading early drafts and providing ruthless criticism, including Donna Carpenelli, Larry Donnithorne, Perry Smith, and Tony Hartle. The staff at Presidio Press, including Dale Wilson, E. J. McCarthy, and Bob Kane, were especially helpful, as was my literary agent, Ed Novak.

In many cases recollections and records are incomplete and sometimes conflicting. I have resolved these to the best of my ability and present in this book my best understanding of what happened.

Prologue

Bill Jackomis looked at his watch again. I was now fifteen minutes late. Typical, thought Jackomis. In the five years he had come to know me I was nearly always at least a few minutes late. Fifteen minutes was about normal. He knew I was not too far away and would be down soon.

Jackomis had arranged to meet me for dinner at the hotel where we were staying for the strategic planning workshop held by Allied Signal Aerospace Corporation every year in the spring. The Torrance, California, Marriott was a nice place and the food was good, especially the breakfast, Bill Jackomis's favorite meal. This was the second year Jackomis had managed to talk the Center for Strategic and International Studies into sending me to the annual strategic planning seminar. Allied Signal was a big donor to CSIS, and Jackomis exploited the company's contribution to extract from the center's staff as much help as he could get in his own work as director for strategic planning in the Washington office. Jackomis had moved to Allied Signal in 1985 from Williams International and quickly developed a reputation with his boss for getting critical market intelligence by exploiting the resources and assets available from corporate headquarters, such as the relationship with CSIS.

At the time I was the director for political military studies at CSIS, and what Jackomis needed was the access we could provide him to senior Pentagon planners who were mapping out the broad future course for the Department of Defense. Allied Signal's problem with strategic planning was that its marketing people were in contact with program managers who were still optimistic, even in 1990, that the defense budget was going to keep going up and their business would follow suit. Jackomis had been a budget planner in the Air Force and knew that the guys at that level in the Pentagon were always the last to get the word when things were about to get cut. Jackomis could read the political winds of change and sensed that big defense cuts were coming and we were one of the few Washington think tanks that shared such predictions. In 1990 we had been fairly accurate in forecasting the size of the cuts that the Bush administration ultimately announced.

The only problem now was that we were in high demand by all of our donors and the media, and it was hard to get us to focus on Allied Signal's needs. During the Persian Gulf War CSIS was launched into worldwide prominence providing media commentators on the war as it unfolded. The military experts from the Political Military Program were in constant demand and frequently went on fund-raising trips on behalf of the center, a non-profit research institution. But then that was how it was easy to get us to focus on Allied Signal's problems; it just took a friendly reminder as to how much the annual gift from the company was.

So Bill Jackomis had managed to schedule me to come out to Allied Signal's West Coast facility in Torrance, a Los Angeles suburb, for the 1992 planning workshop, where we were to meet with the company's strategic planners, market analysts, and other consultants to draw up the forecast for the next decade. I was late for dinner, but Bill knew I was not going anywhere else either because at the moment Los Angeles was under a total curfew; no one was allowed out on the streets. That morning the jury in the trial involving Rodney King had returned a "not guilty" verdict on charges against the Los Angeles Police Department officers who had arrested King; the charges alleged that the officers had violated his rights with the brutal beating he had taken during his arrest, a beating captured on videotape and broadcast all around the country. Regardless of the legalities of the trial, people in Los Angeles could not understand how such a beating could be justified, and they took their case to the streets that night.

Los Angeles was in flames, and it was not at all certain that Allied Signal was going to be able to complete its strategic planning session tomorrow. Jackomis and I were stuck at the hotel and had planned to get better acquainted over dinner. I finally arrived at the table, making my usual apologies.

"That's okay, Jim, I didn't mind waiting; I had nowhere else to go anyway. I've already ordered. Here, take a look at the menu. How are things going for you, anyway?"

"Nothing has slowed down at all, Jake. Our president, Dave Abshire, has me on the road a lot, maintaining contact with donors. I'm actually glad to be able to work with you guys at Allied Signal for a while because it involves real analytical work, which I don't get as much time to do anymore." As I sat down and reached to pick up the menu, my West Point ring clanged on the dinner plate.

Typical West Pointer, thought Jackomis. "You know, I went to West Point, too," he said to me, the ring-knocker.

"No, you didn't, you were an ROTC graduate, you told me so yourself," I said to the retired Air Force officer, thinking that Jackomis was pulling one of those straight-faced jokes he was so good at. I thought smugly that I sure had called Jackomis' bluff on that one and decided to rub it in a little. "Besides, if you went to West Point, where's your ring?"

"I didn't get a West Point ring: I have a Notre Dame ring."

"You couldn't have flunked out, you're one of the smartest men I know." It was true. Jackomis sometimes came across as a big oaf, but that was deceptive; he was brilliant. In fact, I was convinced that he cultivated that image as part of his business intelligence-collecting strategy to lure you into a false sense of intellectual security. All the while Jackomis was carefully logging away every detail of what you told him and always getting just a little bit more out of you than you had intended to give him.

"I didn't flunk out, I was thrown out in 1951 along with ninety others who were accused of violating the honor code," said Jackomis without a hint of emotion.

Suddenly I realized that I had discovered a side of Bill Jackomis that I had never seen before, probably one that few if any others had ever seen. That night, as Los Angeles went up in flames, Bill Jackomis began to relate the incredible story of the cheating incident of 1951 at West Point and how he and others got caught up in it. His story was captivating and has never been told.

I followed up with Jackomis in the following months, meeting or speaking with others who had been dismissed in the 1951 affair (no one involved in the matter on any side of the issue likes to call it a "scandal," although that is exactly what it was at the time). Letters and calls followed for nearly three years. Then I decided it was a story that had to be told.

In this book I have attempted to tell that story as accurately as possible in as readable a style as I can. There are few footnotes. I have also chosen not to reveal the identity of any cadet involved in this story who has not already chosen to do so. Therefore, no index is included. Two former cadets, Bill Jackomis and Jim Pfautz, have been especially generous in providing me with their own recollections of these events. Some, such as Robert Blaik, chose not to respond to my request for their assistance, but their involvement has been revealed elsewhere and has been widely known for years. Still others made their involvement know beginning in August 1951 when cadets such as Gene Filipski, Al Pollard, Vinnie Vergara, Don Beck ,and Ray Malavasi spoke to reporters or provided information to newspapers on their post-West Point plans. Some former cadets provided me with a wealth of information on their experiences but asked me not to use their names. I have respected their requests and have used aliases to protect their identities. Many other cadets and former cadets appear in this account in the guise of aliases.

Part One

New Cadets

One

R Day

Bill eased into his seat on the 7:35 A.M. Greyhound bus that was soon to depart from Manhattan's Thirty-fourth Street bus station. It was a special bus, just for men admitted to the incoming West Point class, and in about two hours it would arrive at the academy's train station, where it would discharge its passengers to join up with trainloads of other new arrivals to begin their first day in the U.S. Corps of Cadets. It was already hot and muggy, even for the first of July. He was not ready for the weather to be this sticky. Why did everyone smoke on humid days? The air was too thick to walk through, and those clouds of cigarette smoke soon formed cumulonimbus thunderheads inside the bus. Bill hated it. He had to puke; it made him choke. He sat next to the side of the bus and slid the window open. At least the early morning city atmosphere was a little fresher than the air inside the bus.

He had not slept very well the night before. It had been a long ride on yet another bus from his hometown of Gary, Indiana; an all-night affair. Bill had worked hard at several odd jobs during the summer months of his junior and senior years in high school and had saved enough money to pay for his initial uniform cost. The letter notifying him that he had been selected to come to the academy told him that the tuition was paid by the government, but that all newly arriving cadets had to pay three hundred dollars for their first issue of uniforms. That was a lot of money then, and Bill closely guarded his wallet, especially in and around New York City.

Bill had spent the night on the bus from Gary trying to sleep, but it was futile. He had closed his eyes and thought about what it might be like at West Point, and what it would be like being an officer, and a paratrooper, in the Army when he graduated four years from now. He thought about how he, the son of poor, hardworking, but proud parents, could be so fortunate. Bill was confident of his abilities to measure up, both academically and on the athletic field. He thought about what the Army's airborne corps would be like and about how many touchdowns he would score for the Army team.

His thoughts were interrupted in the early morning hours as the bus from Gary arrived in New York City and pulled in to park at the bus terminal. Bill was hungry, so he treated himself to a hearty breakfast. It was expensive, but it made him feel better. Bill Jackomis always got up early and ate a big breakfast no matter what had happened the night before. That's just the way he was raised.

Now he was on another Greyhound bus, getting ready to pull out. This would be the last leg of his trip, and a rush of adrenaline combined with the carbohydrates and fats of his three eggs, bacon, and pancakes kept him awake and alert. He felt the subtle movement of the bus's initial pull into motion. It was a very quiet move, almost imperceptible except that he could now detect any motion in any direction that morning. God must have made adrenaline the ultimate motion sensor. It made him feel a little light-headed. He knew he would soon suppress the wooziness and get his sense of balance back. He always did whenever he felt this way, whether from a lost night's sleep or a day of busting someone's chops on the football field or an afternoon of sprinting himself into exhaustion on the track. William Jackomis was a resilient man, even at age eighteen.

Now he was on his way to manhood and West Point. It had been his dream for nearly half a decade—a very long time for such a young man, more than a fourth of his entire time so far on the face of the planet. He had wanted for a long time to go to West Point and become a soldier. His uncle had gone off to World War II when Bill was barely ten years old and had come home a war hero. Bill would never forget the day his uncle returned; he stared at the stiffly starched khaki uniform with all those ribbons across his uncle's broad chest. What impressed him more than anything else was the highly shined boots with the trouser legs tucked sharply into the uppers. Bill's uncle was a tanker. He had served in one of General Patton's tank destroyer battalions in World War II and for months after his return told tales of combat that had captivated the family. Bill especially liked the story of how his uncle's section of three tank destroyers had encountered six German panzers and destroyed them all.

As a young teen Bill had dreamed of himself as an officer leading a dozen tank destroyer guns in battle. But when the West Point football recruiters came to talk to Bill at Tolleston High School, they told him that the Army was changing and the place to be was in the airborne divisions. Bill wanted to be an airborne trooper from that day on.

The Jackomis family, with four children, was a first- and second-generation immigrant family with roots in Greece and Russia. His uncle had been born in the United States, was his namesake, and served in the 2d Armored Division from its formation in the States, through the invasion of Normandy in 1944, and throughout the Allied advance on Europe. As the division moved forward into Normandy to attack the Germans he even had the opportunity to link up on the ground with the Free Polish Division that had participated in the Normandy operation with the Allies. Those poor expatriates had escaped the German invasion in 1939 and trained in England for the next five years for the opportunity to fight their way back home. They never got the chance; the Soviets beat them to Poland. At least some of them could return to families in America to a hero's welcome. Bill's uncle was among those in the first U.S. tank elements to link up with the Soviets at the Rhine River at war's end. During that short-lived linkup, Bill's uncle served as an interpreter for senior American officers. Bill respected his uncle. He hoped his own life could amount to something important like that.

The bus was out of Manhattan now, passing by street after street of suburban New York dwellings. He wondered about the families inside. Most were probably still sleeping. Some probably were just like his own family, and had been up for two hours already.

He thought about his own family back in Gary. There was not much of a home life there, actually. His mother and father had separated and would be divorced in a few months. His father was not even aware that he was on his way to West Point, and Bill wondered what he would say when he found out. Bill wondered when he would see his father again, if ever. Bill had been basically on his own for most of his teenage years, and he stayed out of trouble for the most part. His grades were pretty good, although studying was not the most important aspect of life back then.

What was really important to Bill Jackomis in those days was athletic competition. He loved to win. Most of the time he did. He was an awesome runner. In the eighth grade he had won the Gary City sprint championship. In high school he set new records in the 100-, 220-, and 440-yard dashes. He was the star running back for Tolleston High School. He thought about going to Notre Dame, but that was only a dream beyond the realm of reality. He held out hope for a football or track scholarship to Villanova or Purdue. But he did not want to go to Villanova or Purdue. He wanted to go to West Point.

As the bus crossed the George Washington Bridge over the Hudson River, he noted a sudden change in the surrounding terrain. Fading back onto the famous New York City skyline were the flat streets and tall buildings. Ahead lay the gray granite walls of the Palisades and the rocky, rolling, wooded hills of New Jersey.

Getting into West Point was hard to do for a guy like Bill Jackomis. You had to get an appointment from a congressman or a senator to go to one of the military academies. Bill's family was poor and had no political connections. The way to get connected in those days was to be close to a politician or close to the leadership in one of the steelworkers' unions. Bill's family just did not have the family connections to do that. He had tried to work sum-

mers in the mills, but no one in his family was high up enough to
pull the right strings for that, much less to get an appointment
to West Point. That appointment had gone to some guy named
David Mirisch.

Bill had to earn his way in. He had done that with his athletic
ability as much as with his brain. West Point's scouting coaches
had seen him run, and they were impressed. His high school
grades were good enough that he did not need to go to the football "monster" school to prepare for the entrance exam. He wondered how they could teach you in a week what it took guys like
himself to learn in four years. Bill wondered how they taught the
course; perhaps he would have to study extra hard on his own to
keep up with those guys. He had heard that some football players needed lots of extra help and that "monster" school instructors were very good at teaching just the right material.

For Bill, the coaches secured a spot for him to take the vali-
dating entrance examination in Chicago, and when he passed
with flying colors they also got him his appointment. As it turned
out, his congressman had an extra slot that year, and the football
coaches had somehow managed to use it for Bill. Bill Jackomis was
admitted from the First District of Indiana to the Class of 1953.

Now he was almost there. He wondered if he would get to meet
the famous Coach Blaik. He did not get to see him personally back
in Gary. He had met with some assistant coaches and with a National Guard officer in Gary who had initially scouted him at Tolleston High and reported him to Blaik's staff as a hot prospect.
Maybe the legendary Red Blaik would be there at the train station to meet the football players and take them up to Michie
Stadium. He wondered how the football arena got such a strange
name. He figured he would find out soon enough.

Bill also hoped that he would get to go through airborne training right away. He read in the academy's literature that Maxwell
Taylor was the superintendent and that Taylor had brought about
numerous changes in cadet military training. He hoped that the
famous airborne pioneer had put some jump training into the
program; Bill certainly wanted to do that right away. With the Soviets beginning to threaten in Europe, you never knew when the

country might need the airborne once again to jump in behind enemy lines. Bill Jackomis was ready to go.

The bus eased around the sides of mountains, now reaching upward to nearly a thousand feet above the river below. It was a little thrilling to look out the window and see the rocks below, stretching down to the fast-moving river. Occasionally there was a vessel of one type or another making its way downstream. He noted barges being tugged along headed south, toward New York Harbor, no doubt. He wondered where that cruise ship steaming north was headed.

A SOLITARY SERGEANT

About two hours after leaving New York City, the bus pulled into the West Point station. It was a smallish building, with a waiting room; a ticket office; a rest room; and a short, covered landing. Bill saw that it had a sharply pitched roof, probably so that falling snow and ice off the side of the mountain would run off quickly. There was barely room between the station and the rocky side of the mountain for the street leading up and onward to the academy grounds above. On the other side of the train tracks, a few hundred yards away, was the Hudson River, just a few feet below. A train had just arrived, and about a hundred men were already milling around at the station.

There was a solitary sergeant standing on the landing as the train eased to a halt. He had on a set of rumpled khakis and dull brown boots. His crunched-up, saucer-shaped cap apparently had been brightly white in color once; today it was yellow and frayed. This was not exactly the picture of starched and sparkling uniformity that his uncle had always displayed. The guy had a black armband on his left sleeve that bore the letters "MP." Bill knew that stood for "Military Police," but maybe it was also some kind of special designation for uniform purposes.

As the thirty or so men got off the bus, each with his one suitcase in hand, Bill heard the MP tell them to gather around him on the street across from the station. They kind of milled around a little, and before long the MP was leading them in a kind of gaggle, walking up the street. This was not much of a military formation, Bill thought. With the rumpled old sergeant in front, the whole thing seemed most out of place at West Point, at least compared to the pictures he had seen of the cadets on parade. He wondered how the academy was ever going to transform this bunch into some kind of military unit. They seemed to have a long way to go.

It got worse as they walked up the hill. It was a steep incline on a hot asphalt road. After a few steps they had to lean forward to maintain their balance. In the midmorning July heat they all soon broke out in a sweat. Before he was halfway up the hill Bill had already soaked his cotton shirt. He normally did not sweat much. But when he was exerting himself he sweated profusely. He hoped today's weather was abnormal. It would be a long summer if it was always this humid. Maybe that's why the sergeant's uniform was so disheveled. Maybe cadets were so sharply creased only before the parade. Maybe it was only in pictures that they could stay so sharp-looking.

Soon the road curved around to the left, and as the group reached the summit, about five hundred feet above the train station, Bill could see a building emerge into view. First to come into sight was the top of the building, a square, rocky watchtower made of gray granite. As they continued to walk up, Bill's eyes were fixed on the building as it rolled into view. The tower was sitting on top of a massive fortresslike structure with an imposing black wrought-iron gate raised over a wide opening to an inner square. He could now see through the gate, and he momentarily caught sight of a tallish figure dressed in some kind of gray-over-white outfit move quickly across the square.

When the group at last reached the top of the hill they were facing the building directly. It was just about the only thing they could see as they faced north at the entrance. To their left was a street and another gray granite building not quite as tall as this one. To the right was open sky and the opposite bank of the Hudson River, over a mile away. Bill guessed that the river must have been about seven hundred feet or so below and out of sight.

As the MP led the men through the gateway, nearly everyone craned his neck upward to look at the thick ironworks. The gate was raised about halfway to the top of the opening and was formed from crisscrossed flat iron bars. The points at the end of its eleven vertical bars were about twenty feet from the ground. Across the bars were seven horizontal bars, with a bolt fixing each point where the horizontal and vertical bars intersected. As he passed directly below the gate Bill could see that it could not actually be raised and lowered; it was permanently fixed in this half-raised position. Maybe that had some symbolic meaning about how cadets could come and go. Maybe it was just a cheap way of building a gate.

When the last man passed under the gate and the entire group was inside the square formed by the building, the MP herded them around a set of steps atop which was standing another soldier, this one an officer wearing a more military-looking uniform. He placed his hands on his hips as he spoke to them.

"Men, you are about to join the ranks of the Long Gray Line. Before you begin your life as a new cadet, however, we must take care of a few administrative details. You are in the central area of the Administration Building, which is, by the way, the largest free-standing granite structure in the world. You were told in your reporting instructions to bring one bag with a change of clothing and essential toilet articles only. Those of you who have brought more than that should turn them over to us now, and they will be returned to you later. You were also told to bring three hundred dollars as a deposit on the clothing and equipment you will be issued over the next several days. If any of you drop out, any damage to that equipment will be deducted from your deposit. Up these steps and directly behind me through these doors you will enter a large hall, where you will find desks with letters displayed. Find the desk for the first letter of your last name and report to the clerk there. He will have you fill out the necessary forms and take your deposit. Welcome to West Point. If you have any questions about the program you are about to enter, now is the time to ask. Later on this morning you will not have much of an opportunity to ask questions because you will be very busy."

The officer then motioned them to follow him up the steps and inside. As they stepped up the stone stairs leading into the building, Bill leaned over to the guy next to him, a lanky, tall guy, and said, "Sounds like he memorized that speech. I wonder what he meant by that stuff about asking questions now." The tall man replied, "I don't know, but I don't like the sounds of any of this. This ain't what they told me it was gonna be like."

"I'm Bill Jackomis," he said as he grabbed the guy's hand in a hearty grip accompanied by a wide grin. It was just about the first thing he'd said to anybody today, he realized. The light-headed-ness from lack of sleep must be wearing off. Bill was normally very friendly and quite verbal, except when he was very tired.

Bill's attempt at friendship was not returned; the guy didn't even offer what his name was. Bill thought he'd try to get the guy to warm up a little. Jackomis had never been all that outgoing, but he was at least friendly, and he thought it a little strange that this guy did not tell him what his name was. Bill tried to press him a little further. "What'd they tell you West Point was going to be like? So far it's pretty much what I expected," he said.

The guy had one of those weak, limp handshakes, and his palms were sweaty. "I only came here 'cause my folks wanted me to. I really wanted to go to the University of Kansas back home, but my old man wanted me to come to West Point so bad it woulda broken his heart if I told him I didn't really want to. I've heard that it's really rough here, they still have hazing, even though the books say it's been gone for years. I heard one old West Pointer back home tell me they wait until everyone is in bed, then they drag a few plebes out and really abuse them. I just know they're gonna get me. I hope I can take it long enough to survive plebe year."

That wasn't at all what Bill had heard about West Point. Sure, it was tough physically and even tougher mentally. But all the books about the academy said that the days of uncontrolled haz-ing were gone. The officers and men running the academy in the 1940s were supposedly all men of integrity and decency, most of them veterans of World War II. They knew what was required for battle and did not tolerate any of the foolishness that used to be part of the tradition of plebe year. The program was tough, but its purpose was to prepare men to be leaders in battle, not to harass them like in some fraternity. At least that was Bill's impression.

The athletic recruiters had also told him that football players—in fact, all athletes—would be treated the same as all other new cadets in the corps. The only exception was that new cadet athletes would be able to eat their meals in the dining hall with other athletes at training tables. That way—during mealtime, anyway—they would not be subjected to the rigors of the modern-day hazing at company tables. This would be an incentive to them to do well in football and remain on the team roster. The recruiters also told him that in the afternoons he would be attending football practice, and track practices in season. There he would be able to relax a bit from the tension of being a plebe and focus on preparing for competition. Bill looked forward to that, but so far this was not so bad either. He wondered where this beanpole had gotten his impression. Bill did not get a chance to ask him, for now they were dividing up to report to their assigned desk clerks.

The steps had led them through a dark passageway that opened into a huge medieval-looking hall. The desks were arranged around the edge of the outer perimeter of the large central hallway, and clerks were sitting at each desk just as the officer had said. Each desk had a placard with large block letters, such as "A–C." Bill looked all around the expansive room until he found the desk he was supposed to go to.

Bill shuffled over to the "J" desk and got in line. The soldier at the desk didn't even look up at him as he said, "Name?" "Bill Jackomis," he replied. "Last name first, and spell it out for me. I don't have the telephone book memorized," growled the clerk. Bill spoke slowly as he spelled it out, "J-A-C-K-O-M-I-S, Jackomis," he said. Bill was not used to this. Back in Gary it was not exactly the most popular family name, but most people did recognize such Greek names and could spell them fairly accurately. The clerk checked his name off of a list, asked for his money and his wallet, and told him that he would get it back at the end of the day. He also filled out a tag and tied it to Bill's belt.

While he waited in line, Bill could not help staring up and around at the massiveness of the Administration Building. He was also curious about the tag. He lifted it up and saw that it had his name on it, last name first, with a large bold-type "4th CO" printed on it. Bill wondered what that was for. There were also several blank spaces next to entries such as "waist," "shoulders," "shoes," and other such entries, apparently for writing in his measurements. The clerk looked up at him for the first time since Bill had gotten up to the desk. "You better enjoy that gazing around now, Jackomis. Pretty soon it will cost you a lot more than three hundred bucks if you get caught doing something like that." Bill wondered what that meant.

"Now take your bag and go over there to the other gate and wait for the officer to take you to the central area," said the clerk. "And go ahead and gaze around some more, look at all the buildings, be the tourist while you can, get it out of your system." Bill thought he was being sarcastic now. He wondered if all enlisted men treated cadets this way.

He looked over to the other gate. It was in the wall that ran perpendicular to the gate they had entered from the train station. It was constructed just like the other one and opened out into a street. On the other side of the street he could see another gray granite building, although he could see only a small part of the first floor of it from his vantage point inside the central square of the Administration Building. He made his way over to the group that was forming of the other men who had finished their sessions with the clerks.

THE MAN WITH THE RED SASH

Bill did not even try to find the tall guy he had met earlier. He just stood there shoulder-to-shoulder with a dozen other guys waiting for their next instructions. Soon another MP sergeant came up to them and said, "All right, you guys come with me. Keep together and don't wander off on your own. We're gonna go over to the central area for your official welcome into the United States Corps of Cadets."

With that he walked out the gateway and across the street. There was a sidewalk there, and the MP led the little group up across the road and onto the sidewalk. Then he turned up the road, taking his group past the building that Bill had seen through the Administration Building gate. Next there was another little street to cross—more of an alleyway, really—then another building on their left. This one was obviously older than the one just before it. It was four stories high and made of a brownish-gray block, rather than the cut gray granite of the other two buildings.

They walked about a hundred yards before the sergeant stopped and turned to the group again. "All right, men, hold up here." It seemed like a strange place to halt. It was getting really hot now. It was midmorning, and Bill was now dripping in sweat. He could have used a drink of water, but he had no idea how to go about asking for one. He figured the building they were next to must be the dorm, and they were about to go inside to pick out their rooms. There must be a water fountain there, at least in the hallway.

The sergeant now spoke in a louder voice. "Now I want you men to line up in a single file, one straight line, you should be looking at the back of the head of the man in front of you." Bill shuffled over and got himself in the middle of the twelve men in the line. There was a dull noise in the background now, kind of a low roar, in contrast to the animated babble of the hundred men he had marched up the hill with from the train station. He could not quite figure out what that sound was, but it reminded him of a steel mill in full shift from a distance.

"I'm gonna go ahead about ten yards," barked the MP. "When I get there I will motion to you one at a time to come forward. When I give you this hand wave, I want you to come up to where I'm standing, turn to the left, and walk forward into the sally port. There you will see a cadet in a gray coat over white trousers with a red sash across his chest. You will walk up to him and say the following words, 'Sir, Cadet Candidate so-and-so reports to the man with the red sash'. Don't say 'so-and-so', of course, state your last name. Now let's practice. Repeat after me. 'Sir, Cadet Candidate so-and-so reports to the man with the red sash'."

He paused, indicating he wanted them all to repeat his words. Bill thought this was silly, there was no need to rehearse this, it's not like it was some big speech. "Sir, Cadet Candidate Jackomis reports to the man with the red sash." It sounded funny to hear people say their own name all together. Now, that was a real melting pot, he thought. Some guys tried to be cute and said "so-and-so," instead of their name, drawing a look of disgust from the sergeant. Others said nothing. Apparently the MP was tired of such attempts at insubordination; he did not bother to correct them. Before he walked up to his position he said to them, "Good luck, men. You'll need it now."

As the sergeant walked ahead, Bill heard the low rumble of an engine come up from behind them. He turned and saw another big Greyhound bus come along the road, belching black fumes. That was a smell he enjoyed. It reminded him of Gary's streets back home, which were always filled with diesel smoke from trucks hauling raw materials into the steel plants or steel products out of town. He could make out the heads of about forty guys in the bus as it went by.

Gene Filipski was gazing out of the bus window as it entered the academy grounds. He could hardly believe he was finally here. From his earliest memories of childhood back in California he had dreamed of the day when he could go to West Point. He wanted to be a star on the Army football team just like Glenn Davis. Maybe they would even make a movie about him as they did for Davis and Doc Blanchard.

Now it was midmorning on the first of July 1949, and his bus eased into the academy grounds. The big windows let him see all the sights he had seen before only in pictures. The Hotel Thayer right at the entrance gate, the long row of big brick houses on the road to the Plain, the Administration Building, the Riding Hall, the academic buildings, and finally the parade ground known as the Plain, all passed in review through the big picture window in the bus. He could almost feel the presence of the thousands who had come this way before. He was about to become part of the Long Gray Line.

The bus was going along at no more than ten miles per hour, he guessed, as it passed a group of about a dozen men who were lined up single file on a sidewalk facing a solitary Military Police sergeant who was looking off into an entranceway into one of the old buildings. That sure looked strange, he thought. Maybe they were in some kind of trouble. That was hardly the way to start off at West Point. The bus made a right turn just past those men and went past the building he recognized from its rounded corners as the library. Then it turned again to the right to go down past the entrance of the riding hall, back to the right again, and up to the Administration Building.

An MP sergeant came in through the doors and told them to bring their bags and follow him through the gate into the central area of the big gray building ahead of them. Soon Filipski found himself standing before the "F" table explaining how to spell his name. Within a half hour he, too, was in a group of a dozen men lined up waiting to report to the man with the red sash. "Now I want you men to line up in a single file . . ." Gene Filipski wondered when Head Coach Red Blaik would come out to greet him.

Bill was next in line to go up to the MP sergeant. He watched while a half dozen other guys had walked up to him on the sidewalk about a hundred yards away. Each man had sauntered up to him, paused for a moment, apparently exchanging a few words, then turned to the left and disappeared into the arched entryway in the center of the old stone building. After that he had no clue about what was happening. He figured he'd find out soon enough. Some of the other guys in line had lit up cigarettes and were nervously puffing away. Bill wasn't nervous. Even though he had no idea what was in store for him, he figured he would come out okay. He had to. He was going to be an Army football player and eventually an airborne trooper. Whatever was going on in there had to be tough to make sure the academy produced only the finest officers possible. He knew he could make it.

The sergeant waved his arm for Bill to come up. As he walked, his bag seemed to get heavier. When he reached the sergeant he could see into the arch. There was a flurry of activity in there but he could not make any sense out of it. There were men rushing to and fro, lots of yelling and screaming, and a line of about four cadets stretching across the entranceway. The sergeant didn't even look at him and said, "Go on into the sally port." Bill turned to the sergeant and said, "What's a sally port?" For the first time that day, the sergeant stared him directly in the eye and said, "You're looking at it, sir. Say, what's your name anyway?"

"Bill Jackomis," replied Bill.

"Well, Jackomis, you're gonna do just fine. Now go on in and report to the man with the red sash." With that, the MP turned away and waved in the next man.

Bill strolled up to the second cadet from the left. By now it was about 11:00 A.M., and the sun was bearing down on him. There was not a cloud above, and it seemed to shine right into his left eye. He was sweating bullets now, and the yelling around him reached a deafening thunder. Every new man was being yelled at by a cadet. Suddenly Bill started to stiffen. He wasn't afraid or even confused, but he became nervous about what might be in store for him.

The cadet he faced didn't have a drop of sweat on him anywhere. He was only about five feet, four inches tall, and the bill on his saucer cap seemed to be aimed right at Bill's nose. His steely eyes glared straight ahead, boring a hole through Bill's brain. His arms were straight down at his sides, with his hands cupped along the crease of his trousers. Bill looked down at those shoes, spit-shined so bright they reflected the sun as if there were a mirror on top of the pitch black leather. Bill looked back up at the cadet, who had what appeared to be a thick silk cummerbund across his chest. The cadet had not moved. Bill lost all composure and forgot what he was supposed to say. He tried anyway, "Sir, I am Cadet Bill Jackomis, and I'm supposed to report to the sash with the red man."

"Try again, Mister Jackomis," said the pillar of stone across from him.

Bill could not imagine why it was so important, but this guy was dead serious. He could not imagine what would happen if he didn't get this right. Maybe this was some kind of final test. If you couldn't remember a simple sentence maybe they wouldn't let you in after all. He had to try again. "Sir, Candidate Jackomis reports to the man with the red sash."

"Wrong again. Repeat after me. 'Sir, *Cadet* Candidate Jackomis reports to the man with the red sash'." Still there was not a hint of emotion in that cadet's voice.

Bill tried again, "Sir, Cadet Candidate Jackomis reports to the man with the red sash."

As soon as he finished, Bill knew he had gotten it right. He gave himself a little smirk of satisfaction.

"Wipe that smirk off your face, Jackomis!" Suddenly the robot with a red stripe seemed to lose its temper; at least that's the way it sounded from the volume of the sound burst he just gave Bill. He reached down and looked at the tag that had been tied to Bill's belt back in the Administration Building. He let it go and said, "Now drop that bag!"

Bill bent down at his knees and set his suitcase on the concrete next to him. "I said drop that bag, mister! Now pick it back up and drop it."

Bill bent down and picked up his suitcase. When he straightened his legs up he let the bag go. He heard a "thunk!" as it hit the cement. He hoped it didn't break the hinges. That was an expensive bag, at least by Jackomis family standards. He did not want to break it.

The man in the red sash was obviously unhappy with this. "Mister Dumbjohn, I said drop that bag. When I say drop that bag I mean drop that bag. I don't mean ease it on down, I don't mean let it go, I don't mean bend down and let it go, I mean drop it! Now try that again, and this time you drop that bag so hard that it breaks the concrete you're standing on! Now DROP THAT BAG!"

Bill raised up his suitcase and threw it down on the concrete. It didn't break open, neither did the cement. "I'm sorry, sir. I didn't understand what you meant when you said drop—"

"Hey dumbjohn, did I give you permission to speak? Shut your trap and listen up. From now on you will speak only when spoken to. There are only four things you are authorized to say. They

are: 'Yes, sir'. 'No, sir'. 'No excuse, sir'. and 'Sir, I do not understand'. Now try it, Jackomis!"

The sweat was running down Bill's back now. It was trickling
down the crack of his butt. It dripped down in there and really
made him feel wretched. He wanted to reach down and scratch
himself but he knew he'd better not. He could hardly remember
his name much less what those four answers were. "Yes, sir. No,
sir. Sir, I have no excuse, and I don't understand."

Suddenly the man with the red sash lowered his voice to a
barely audible tone, almost a whisper. "Jackomis, you'll never
make it here if you can't get a few simple instructions straight.
That's 'Yes, sir', 'No, sir', 'No excuse, sir', and 'Sir, I do not understand'. Do not think about it, just spout it off!"

Bill disengaged his brain and said, "Yes, sir. No, sir. No excuse,
sir. Sir, I do not understand." There; he could function under pressure, it was just like remembering the plays out of the huddle.

"Very good, dumbjohn, now say it like you mean it, again," demanded the cadet, who had yet to take his eyes off of an imagi-
nary point somewhere in the back of Bill's head as he stared at
the son of proud and tough Greek and Russian immigrants from
Gary, Indiana.

"Yes, sir. No, sir. No excuse, sir. Sir, I do not understand," said
Bill loud enough to be heard around him but not so loud that he
might be yelling in this guy's face. Bill did not want his raunchy
forty-eight-hour breath to bowl this guy over.

"Come on, Jackomis, you have a pair of balls, bang them together and sound off with your four answers!" This time the cadet
seemed to find a volume dial that cranked his yelling up to a loud
thunder.

"YES, SIR. NO, SIR. NO EXCUSE, SIR. SIR, I DO NOT UN-
DERSTAND!" yelled Bill, louder than he had ever before in his life.
If he was going to have to yell like this he would soon lose his voice,
he thought. He hoped this would satisfy the man with the red sash.

"That's better, dumbjohn. Now I want you to pick up your bag
and double-time behind me to the desk in the central area
marked with the large number four, and do not gaze around while

you are moving. You keep your head and eyes straight ahead to your direct front. Do you understand, Mister Jackomis?"

THE ROOM

"Yes, sir!" seemed to be the only one of his four answers that fit the moment. He grabbed his suitcase and ran around to the desk, about ten yards away. There were two cadets there. One looked at his tag and read his name off. The other checked his name off on a list. He heard them talk to each other but dared not look down at them. "It's not lunchtime yet, this one goes up to his room first," said the one who looked at his tag. The other looked up at Bill and said, "Jackomis, you are going to go through that door directly in front of you and run up to the fourth floor. You will find your name over the door of one of the rooms up there. Go in and put your suitcase there and wait until someone comes to pick you up to go to the next station. Understand?"

"Yes, sir!" His second answer as a cadet was the same as his first. He could barely see the doorway ahead of him without moving his head. It was up a short set of steps that led to a stoop running across the entire length of the building. He could not tell how long the building was, and he was not about to look back and forth to judge its size, but he figured it was the back side of the building they had marched along just before the MP waved them in through the sally port. He wondered what the next station was going to be.

Bill dashed across the area, skipped half of the ten steps leading up to the stoop, and was just about to dart in the doorway when he heard someone yell, "Hey, mister, you there that just skipped those steps, halt right where you are!"

It had to be Bill he was yelling at. He could see no one else that had skipped any steps. Anyway, he was not gazing around to see if it was anyone else, for all Bill knew there might have been twenty other guys doing the same thing. He knew he had done it, and he'd better stop or something worse might happen.

Another cadet came up to him; this one did not have a red sash on but he looked just as spit-and-polished. He got right in Bill's face and yelled at him, "Who do you think you are, skipping my steps?" He was one of those guys who spit whenever he yelled, and he was sprinkling right into Bill's eyes. "Now you go right back down there and run up these steps again. This time you hit every one of them!"

"Yes, sir!" At least the part about what he was supposed to say was not getting any more difficult for Bill. Down he went, hitting every step. He turned around and hammered each one with his foot. "Again," said the cadet, "just to make sure you understand." This was getting to be a strain, thought Bill. He had run steps before in football practice, it was great conditioning, but this was ridiculous. It was hot, and he needed water. Maybe if he just could get inside the dorm he could find a fountain and get a drink.

"All right, Jackomis, you can go. But be careful, I'm watching you. I'll be your squad leader for Beast, so you'd better start doing things right, or you won't last very long."

"Yes, sir," said Bill as he raced up the stairwell. On the fourth floor, sure enough, there were four rooms, one on each corner of the stairway. Over each door was a metal rail with the names of two men on a white cardboard tape slid into the sides. One of the rooms had three names on it. There he saw his name, "Jackomis, W. N. 53." Right next to his name was another, "Filipski, E. I. 53." Bill supposed that was his roommate, and he wondered when he would get to meet him.

He was not going to meet him just now. He walked into the room and closed the door behind himself. He put his suitcase down—he did not drop it—and right away spied the thing he wanted most right then. There was a water pitcher in the room. He jumped over to it, held it up over his face, and emptied the vessel of its contents. It was the most refreshing thing he had ever experienced in his whole life. He let the water splash over his entire head for a moment, washing away all the sweat and salt that had dried on his skin. Then he cocked his head so he could get his mouth under the lip, opened wide, and let the water gush in. He gulped it as fast as he dared without choking. He was in heaven.

Two

Mister Dumbjohn

Bill Jackomis had never tasted such good water. He let his mind wander back to Tolleston High School, back home in Gary, Indiana, when he would drink just like this after a track meet. With his eyes closed to keep from getting them splashed he could almost see himself back home. Then, from behind him, he heard a loud Bang! Bang! Bang! from someone rapping something on his door. From the sound it must have been a baseball bat. Suddenly the door flew wide open and slammed against the wall with a crash. There in the doorway stood that same cadet from the stoop in that crisp gray-over-white uniform. He didn't sweat either. "Are you Jackomis or Filipski?" bellowed this intruder.

"Sir, I'm Bill Jackomis." Bill had no idea what he was supposed to say. His four authorized answers did not fit this situation, and he did not know if he was supposed to stick to them or try to answer the question directly.

"That's cadet candidate Jackomis, and just forget about your first name when I'm around. I'm your squad leader and you will call me Mister Jones." This guy was built just like Bill, about five feet nine-and-a-half inches tall, broad muscular shoulders, a barrel-shaped chest, and short legs with bulging thighs. He must be a football player, too, with a build like that, thought Bill.

"Yes, sir," said Bill. That answer so far never got him in trouble. Jones walked up to him and noticed that his head was soaked. "What the hell are you doing Jackomis, trying to drown yourself?"

"No, sir." That was a first. He wanted to explain how he was so very thirsty and how he hated to have sweat on his skin, but he figured he'd better not try to say too much.

"Oh, you're thirsty, huh, Mister Jackomis? Well, from now on you will not get a drink without permission from me or some other upperclassman, you understand?" Jones could really yell. He was even louder than the man with the red sash.

"In fact, Mister Dumbjohn, for the next eight weeks while you are in my squad you will not do anything without my permission. You won't drink, eat, shower, shave, or even shit unless I tell you to. Do you understand?"

"Yes, sir!" Bill smirked a little. He was trying to imagine how he was going to ask permission to take a shit. Then Jones got right in his face.

"What's so funny, Jackomis? Did I give you permission to smirk? You wipe that smirk off your face and never let me see it again. This is not some circus you came to, this is West Point. You better learn right now this is serious business. You better follow instructions to the letter. We are going to teach you what you need to know to become a cadet. We are going to teach you what you need to know to be a soldier. We are going to teach you what you need to know to be an officer. If you cannot follow instructions in combat you will be killed. This is a serious business so you better stop smirking right now, mister. Do you understand?"

"Yes, sir!"

"Now, Mister Jackomis, for your first lesson in becoming a cadet. You see, right now you're just a cadet candidate. If you make it through this day we will let you become a new cadet, and if you make it through Beast Barracks, we will let you become a plebe. And if you make it all the way through plebe year, then and only then we will let you become a cadet. It will be a long year, Mister Jackomis, and you will never make it if you do not get rid of that shit-eating grin of yours."

The speech from his squad leader continued.

"You must first learn the proper position of attention. Your heels should be together with your toes spread at a forty-five degree angle. Now lock your knees back so your legs are straight. Roll your hips back, suck your gut in, and pull your chest up."

Bill followed these instructions but he couldn't imagine that he would be able to hold this position all the time. He couldn't believe it when Jones told him there was more to it.

"Now, dumbjohn, with your head and eyes straight to the front, pull your chin back so that it is directly over your sternum."

Bill had no idea what that meant. He was beginning to get angry at being called "dumbjohn." He figured it was just one of those Army expressions, but he was not dumb and his name wasn't John. For a moment he thought he should correct his squad leader, but he quickly decided to let it pass.

"Here, Jackomis, let me help you." Jones took his right index finger and put it on Bill's chin and shoved it back as far as it would go. "Now, look at yourself in the mirror over the sink." Bill turned around and stared at himself. "See all those wrinkles under your chin?" Bill looked really stupid, he thought. "This is the proper position of attention that all cadet candidates and new cadets must maintain at all times when they are outside their rooms. Even inside, if a cadet orders you to "brace," this means to assume the correct position of attention. Do you understand, Mister Jackomis?"

"Yes, sir!" It was very difficult to speak with his chin pushed back like that. He sounded more like a garbled duck than an all-state halfback.

"Good," said Jones. "Now come with me. You need a haircut."

Bill followed him out the door. Jones turned to him and said, "Another thing, Jackomis. Anytime you are walking in my halls you will stay to the outside wall. At all times your sleeve must be touching the wall. Only upperclassmen are permitted to be on the inside of the hall or stairwell. Do you understand that?"

"Yes, sir!" Why did these guys always ask if he understood? If he didn't he would just say, "Sir, I do not understand." Bill hugged the outer wall as he ran down the stairwell. Keeping his sleeve against the wall made him square the corners as he rounded each turn. "You are not moving fast enough, Jackomis, move out smartly!" There were two landings for each floor and he almost got dizzy by the time he reached the stoop after turning eight times on his way down.

Bill double-timed down the stairs of the stoop, pounding each step on the way so Jones could see and hear that he hit every one of them. But now what? Jones said he had to go get a haircut, but Bill had no idea where the barbershop was. He could not ask where it was because not one of his four authorized answers covered this situation; he had to ask a question, not answer one.

FOLLOW ME

He stopped when he got down onto the concrete surface of the central area. He just stood there staring straight ahead, not daring to look around for a barber pole. He stood at a brace, figuring that's what Jones wanted him to do. Out of the corner of his eye he saw there were eight other cadet candidates standing there in a line, so Bill moved up next to the one on the end.

"Very good, Mister Jackomis. All right, you men, follow me," said Jones with a snarl. He stood to the left and just behind the front man in the line as they walked across the vast expanse of concrete that lay in the center of the large square building made of brownish-gray stone. Bill could see as they walked that it was actually three buildings joined at the corners, forming what must be what they had been calling the central area. You could have a parade in here, thought Bill.

Diagonally opposite the area from his stoop there was another one of those archways known as a sally port. They walked through this sally port and across another expanse of concrete toward yet another gray granite building that towered above them. He had no idea what that building was for, although he could smell the sweet fragrance of fresh-baked bread wafting out at him. Suddenly Bill was ravenously hungry. He wondered when they were going to have lunch. He hoped it would be right after this haircut.

Jones escorted them up five flights of stairs that led to a set of double doors that opened into a long corridor. After several feet of walking in this wide hallway, Jones turned the group into a set of double doors, and they emerged into the largest barbershop Bill had ever seen.

There must have been forty chairs there, each with a barber at work cutting the hair off of one of Bill's fellow cadet candidates. Jones had them stand single file to wait for a turn to go forward to the next available barber. "Filipski, you go over there and take that chair. Come back here and get in line with me when you are done. Jackomis, you go over there to the left."

So, his roommate had already been in line. Bill dared a look over at the guy who must have been Filipski, E. I. 53. Were these barbers part of the game here? Would they yell at him for gazing around? Apparently not. Filipski seemed to be a little bit bigger than Bill, slightly taller with longer legs. He looked like a football player. Bill hoped so.

Bill slid into the chair and let his chin ease out a little. The barber did not say a word as he pumped the seat up a few inches with the foot pedal at the base of the chair. The floor was already covered with at least half a foot of cut hair. Bill's contribution melded into the giant carpet of cadet candidate hair as the barber took all of two minutes to snip off all his hair save about half an inch right at the top. At least he would not have to worry about combing it for a while.

Jones was waiting by the door as Bill got up and brushed the snippets off his neck and face. He hated the way those little specks of hair stuck to his skin. As much as he was sweating, they just kind of plastered themselves to his face and neck. Bill could see by the impatience on Jones's face that he was not going to get time to wipe them off. He moved on over to the door and got in the line forming up next to his squad leader. Filipski was directly ahead of him. Bill wondered what the "E" in "E. I." stood for—Edward, probably.

"All right men, follow me," said Jones when the last man joined up. Again they moved into the corridor, and they walked down the stairs. Jones formed them up in a formation and marched them off behind the great gray building they had just come out of. The building towered above them on their right, while the rocky side of the hill the academy stood on reached above them.

Suddenly the stench of garbage caught their attention, and from the look of things they were apparently behind the dining hall.

They rounded another corner of the building and halted before another double-door entrance. Again they went up five flights of stairs and walked down a corridor. This time, as they entered a room that seemed to mirror the barbershop, there were about a dozen men with tape measures, each standing next to a footstool. "File around these footstools, men. Stand up tall and let the tailor take your measurements." Jones was barking his orders now. He seemed to be warming up to his new charges.

Bill stepped up on the stool. "Reach outa' you arms like-a this," said the apparently Italian tailor as he stretched out his own arms to show Bill which way he meant. As soon as Bill got them out, the tailor spread his tape measure from fingertip to fingertip and wrote a number down on Bill's tag, still tied to his belt. Then he said, "Now spreada' you legs just a leetle bit. That's-a good," and he stretched the tape from the inside of the arch of his left foot up to his crotch, then around his waist. It took only an instant, and again the tailor wrote down the numbers on Bill's tag. "Now step-a down on de floor." Bill stepped down, and the tailor stood up on the stool to measure his head and neck. That was it; all his measurements had been taken in less than a minute.

There was Jones. "Line up over here, men. Time to go to one more station before lunch." Bill was suddenly hungry again. He had forgotten that less than half an hour before, when he had gone into the barbershop, he first noticed his hunger. Now he felt famished at the mention of food. He remembered the smell of that bread and thought he could still detect it coming from somewhere outside this fitting room.

Jones took them out of the tailorshop to another set of double doors. They entered another large room, this one a supply room. There was a long counter facing them as they came in. Several men on the other side of the counter were grabbing things off of a wall filled with shelves and throwing the items across the countertop to about two dozen cadet candidates standing before them. Soon this group stuffed all the gear they had been handed into a green laundry bag they were holding and marched off to the right by their squad leader out another set of double doors. Apparently their squad leader was not the screamer that Jones was.

Jones told them to line up in front of the counter. Then he walked past them and tore off a perforated card from each of their tags. He lifted a hinged section of countertop and handed each of the clerks the card belonging to the cadet candidate standing opposite him. The clerks then disappeared into the jungle of shelves and began pulling things down into their arms and tossing them onto the counter in front of their men. Bill watched as T-shirts, boxer shorts, handkerchiefs, black socks, a robe, towels, and facecloths soon stacked up in front of him. The last thing to come off the shelf was that green laundry bag with a rope tie laced through the opening. Jones then told them to stuff the clothing issue into the bags and pull the draw rope taut.

CLASSMATES

When his entire squad had secured their bags, Squad Leader Jones ordered, "Now, men, sling your bag over your right shoulder and follow me." With that he led them out the doors, down the stairs, and back out into the bright sunlight. When they came up the steps into the central area, Bill could not see a thing. He had to squint tightly, the sun was so bright in his eyes. Then Jones yelled, "Okay, men, now we need to make up some time to get back to the mess hall before lunch is over. Does anyone want to skip lunch?"

Bill couldn't believe this question. "No, sir," he said, as did one or two others feebly. Everyone else must have been intimidated. Maybe he had given the wrong answer to that one.

"I can't believe you guys don't want to eat lunch!" retorted Jones. "Are Jackomis and Filipski the only guys who want to eat? Let me hear it again; Anyone want to skip lunch?"

"No, sir!" replied nine voices in unison.

"I can't hear you!" shouted Jones. Bill recognized this game from the Army movies he had watched back home. It meant the squad leader wanted them to yell louder.

"NO, SIR!" shouted the nine, about twice as loud.

"You men are weaklings. I guess we have our work cut out for us. All right, then, let's double-time back to your rooms. Come on, run." Jones took the lead man by the upper arm and pulled him into a trot. Jones ran beside him and looked back at the rest of them trying to keep up. "Let's go, every one of you. You better double-time back to your rooms so you can double-time to the mess hall and eat before it closes."

It wasn't easy running with a heavy bag on your shoulder. It wasn't the weight that made it hard, it was the imbalance caused by the uneven weight. To make it worse, some guys tried to switch shoulders to give their aching muscles a break. In the process, inevitably one guy's bag knocked into the guy behind him.

Suddenly, in front of him, Bill saw someone careen over and fall to the concrete. He heard a sickening "thud!" as the body hit the hard surface. Bill and the other men in the squad abruptly stopped running and circled around their squadmate. No one seemed to know his name, and he was perfectly still except for an occasional shallow breath.

No one seemed to know what to do. Jones pushed his way through them and bent down next to their fallen squadmate. It was getting hotter as the day wore on. Bill was not surprised someone had passed out. If things kept up at this pace he, too, would probably pass out before long. That had never happened to him before. He wondered what it felt like.

Their squad leader had lowered his own face down to that of this unknown classmate. He could not see what Jones did, but after a few seconds, the man on the ground came to and opened his eyes. Jones helped him to his feet, though he was obviously still groggy. "You, Filipski, Jackomis, come over here to either side of this man. He's your classmate. You carry him along. No one falls out in my squad unless everyone falls out. If someone starts to fall, you men pick him up and bring him along. You will stick together no matter what. Now let's double-time back to the barracks. Everyone, that means you, too, Jackomis and Filipski. Don't slow down a step just because you're carrying Smith."

So that was his name. Bill took Smith's left side while someone else grabbed his classmate's bag. Filipski took the right side. They lifted him up under his arms by the shoulders and ran along as best they could with their own laundry bags on their free arms. It was really awkward, but somehow they made it to their stoops. By then Smith could at least stand up on his own strength.

Jones ran them up to the stoop, then halted them at the door to their stairwell. "All right, you have thirty seconds to run upstairs, drop your bag in your room, and get back down here to march off to lunch. Smith, you stay here. Jackomis, you take care of his bag." He couldn't mean just thirty seconds, thought Bill; it would take that long just to get up half the steps.

"And I mean thirty seconds," added Jones, "not forty-five, not a minute. You have thirty seconds and you better stay to the outside of the stairway or you'll be doing push-ups instead of eating lunch. Now move out!"

Bill sprung into motion as hard and as fast as his legs would take him. He reached the doorway ahead of the two guys in line ahead of him and sprinted up the steps to the squad's rooms at the top of the four floors. Dodging past Smith's room, he tossed the injured man's bag in without even pausing. Then he tossed his own bag across his room next door without even going inside and passed Filipski still coming up as he raced back down. He was the first man to get back out and stood at attention waiting for the others to come out. Everyone else was still behind him; they had gone inside their rooms and tried to sort out whose bag was to go on top of which bunk. Bill didn't care about which bunk he got; he would worry about that tonight if they ever got that far. Right now he just wanted to comply with whatever Jones told them to do.

"Not bad, men," said Jones as the last man scrambled out about a minute after they had started this little footrace. Maybe Jones has a heart after all, Bill thought. That was the closest thing to a kind word he had spoken to them all morning. "Now let's go to lunch. Follow me."

They walked together, Jones in the lead, across the area back toward the building where they had gotten their haircuts and drawn their clothing. Instead of taking the steps up, they walked over to another set of stone steps leading upward to a set of large wooden double doors standing open in an arched entrance. Some mess hall, Bill thought.

LUNCHTIME
They climbed up the steps and walked in. "Wow!" Bill thought. They were in one of the largest buildings Bill had ever seen. It stretched out before him for more than a hundred, maybe two hundred yards, he estimated. It looked to be about the size of the airplane hangar he had been in once at Chicago's airfield. There were rows and rows of tables with cadets and cadet candidates seated in bow-backed chairs along the sides of each table and a uniformed cadet at one end.

Jones took them inside, past several rows to a wide center aisle, then turned them up to the head of the building. When they got to the last row, Bill could see that they were in just one wing of the mess hall, which had two more just like this one. The three sections were joined at the top; each one angled out from this central section. It was amazing. There were high windows along each outside wall, and at the end of each wing there was something unique. The center wing had a massive stained glass window. Bill could not make out what it depicted, but it looked impressive. The two wings that flared out from the center each had painted murals. He hoped to get closer to see what they looked like.

The squad leader took them to an open table in the far wing and told them to take a seat along the sides. Bill then realized why there were nine men in a squad; with the squad leader they exactly filled the ten seats at the table. He looked at the spread on the table and couldn't believe what he saw. There was a large white tablecloth covering the long and wide table. An oval silver plate held a pile of roast beef that was still steaming. There was a silver gravy bowl, a huge silver bowl of mixed vegetables, a round apple pie, and two pitchers of drinks at one end. Each place had been set with a china dinner plate, knife, fork, and spoon. Ten tall empty glasses were lined in two rows of five at the end by the drink pitchers.

Jones told the man nearest the beef to serve himself then pass the plate to his left. Likewise he got the other foods going around the table. Bill had taken the seat next to the end; he figured that way he would be least visible to Jones from the angle between that chair and the head seat. But Jones picked on him again, "Jackomis, you lucky man, you are at the seat that is reserved for the cold beverage corporal. You'll learn more about that later. For now grab one of those pitchers and start pouring drinks."

Bill wondered how he was going to get served food while he was pouring drinks, when Jones spoke out again, "Filipski, you serve Jackomis. Everyone make sure you take only one serving. If anyone takes more than his fair share, you're only hurting your classmates." Jones practically had to yell his instructions to be heard over the din of the mess hall activity. Everything seemed to echo off the high ceilings and walls, making it hard to hear anything.

Bill had never had such a good meal. Oh, he had eaten juicier beef before, but under the circumstances of this particular day, roast beef had never tasted so good. He gulped down the drink, some kind of orange-flavored beverage, probably Kool-Aid, he guessed. The other pitcher had milk, and after everyone had finished drinking down a glass of Kool-Aid Jones told them to pass their glasses to Bill and get a glass of milk. Bill had no idea how each man was going to get his own glass back. He didn't much care at that point, he just poured fast so he could get to his own glass of milk. He had the feeling that somehow this was not going to be a leisurely lunch.

Bill was right. "Cease work!" ordered Jones. Bill had just brought his glass of milk up to his lips when the squad leader bellowed out this demand. Bill wondered what he should do next. Should he bring the glass back down and leave that cool, nourishing liquid to spoil on the table? Or did the "Cease work!" order imply that he could finish whatever he had in motion at the time? In football the last play continued to completion even if time has expired after the ball is snapped. Surely Jones would want him to take that drink, if only to make sure that what had happened to Smith didn't happen to Jackomis.

He turned the bottom of the glass up as Jones was standing up out of his chair. "Jackomis! I said to cease work. Who do you think you are?" Bill slammed the glass down in the middle of his gulp. White liquid drooled out of the corners of his mouth, down his chin, and dripped onto the table. "Brace, Jackomis!" Bill had no idea how he was going to stand at attention at that point; Jones didn't give him the chance to say what he wanted to try, which at that point seemed most appropriately, "Sir, I do not understand." Jones addressed the entire squad. "Now men, Mister Jackomis has just volunteered to demonstrate something you will all get to know very well, how to brace at the table."

"Jackomis, remain seated, suck your stomach in, pull your chest out, and bang your chin in! Grab some wrinkles, mister, I want to see more! Now look down at your plate without turning your head. That's it, keep your head straight but look down at your plate." Bill's eyeballs hurt. It was a strain on muscles he didn't even know he had and that certainly weren't made to do this. "That, gentlemen, is the proper position to brace at the table," instructed Jones. "Now each of you, BRACE! Get your eyes off of me, Filipski, look down at your plate. No, don't turn your head down, keep it up, look down only with your eyes. That's better, mister." Bill had no idea what military value this had. He figured it must have something to do with combat. Maybe they would tell him later.

"All right, men, now let's move out to your first lesson in D&C," said Jones. That was evidently the end of the first of what was to be 3,518 meals he was programmed to eat in the mess hall. Bill had no idea what "D&C" was, but he suspected he would not like it any more than squaring corners, bracing, or being cold beverage corporal. He couldn't believe the day was only half over.

DRILL AND CEREMONY

Jones took them out a different door. This one led out to the wide parade field in front of the barracks. Out on the grassy plain, he lined them up in a squared-off U shape and placed himself at the center so they all could see him. "Head and eyes on me, men," said Jones.

For the next two hours they stood there in the hot sun facing their squad leader as he taught them the basics of drill and ceremony. At first they were stationary as he showed them how to salute, how to stand at attention and at ease. For each position there was a prescribed stance, every body part had a specified position, and after he demonstrated, Jones talked them into the same position. Then he had them hold there as he went to each man and corrected him, one at a time. "Do not bend the wrist in the hand salute, keep your fingers extended and joined, arms straight down at your sides in the position of attention, fingers cupped, thumbs behind the seam of your trousers." He had it all memorized.

There was a command for everything. In fact, there were two commands, a preparatory command and a command of execution. It took them about an hour, but they were all doing them in unison in the prescribed manner as a squad. Then Jones moved on to the drills that placed them in motion. "Right face, left face, about face." These took a while as some of them had some difficulty keeping their lefts and rights in the correct places. In about fifteen minutes they were turning and whirling in the same directions on command from Jones.

Then they started to march. Bill never realized how hard it could be to get nine men moving in the same direction at the same time. Just remembering to lead off with the left foot was hard enough. Thinking about making sure that your right arm was forward when your left foot was out took more coordination between his brain and his body than he realized. It reminded him of his freshman year in high school when he had to learn all those football drills, taking handoffs with his left forearm over his right and drawing the ball in to his body took a while to become automatic as well, he recalled. Soon he was marching without thinking, just like he ran the football without thinking. So this is D&C, he thought.

Jones marched the squad over to a green canvas bag held up by a rope hanging from a tripod made of wooden tent posts. Each man had a chance to hold his mouth open under a spigot that had been plugged into the bag and drink some warm, salty water. At least it was wet. Then Jones formed them up to go back into the barracks area.

It was a little past midafternoon, and they marched in step this time just as their squad leader had taught them. Jones led them through the central area and past the back of the mess hall. Here West Point's terrain resumed its steep, rocky incline. The mess hall butted up against a wall of granite. Jones led the squad up a set of stairs that took them back to the upper floors of the building that housed the mess hall's western wing.

Here there were more supply rooms and tailors. They must have gone into five different rooms over the course of the next hour or so. They were loaded up with more issue items: toiletries, shoes, uniforms of all different types. At the last station they received a single pair of pressed cotton white cadet trousers, a gray woolen long-sleeved coat with a zippered front and a stiff collar, and a cotton belt with their last name stamped on the back so they could be identified from the rear. They were also given a gray, saucer-shaped cap with a shiny black leather bill. Finally, they received a little green book called *Bugle Notes*. They dumped all this into two more green laundry bags and marched back to their rooms.

A PLACE FOR EVERYTHING

Jones had them all come in to Smith's room to show them where each item was to be stored in the bare furnishings available. Every item had a specified place and was never to be out of that place unless it was on their person or in the laundry. Bill had no idea how he was going to remember all that. Jones sent them up to their rooms and gave them five minutes to have everything stored properly for his inspection.

Bill and Filipski finally had a chance to talk as they dashed around their room putting things away.

"My name's Gene. Call me 'Flip'."

"I'm Bill. Do you play football?"

"Yeah, but I don't know if I'm gonna stick around for the season. I didn't sign up for this shit. The coaches told me we wouldn't be hazed. If this ain't hazing, I don't know what is!"

The two cadet candidates tried to remember which shelf the underwear went onto, what order the shirts were to be hung in the steel locker they had for a closet, and what order the shoes were to be arrayed left to right under the bed. When everything was somewhere, they stood at the foot of their beds in the "at ease" position as Jones had instructed them.

It took a while for Jones to make his way up to their fourth-floor room. He entered with a loud "bang!" on the door with his fist. Jones walked around the perimeter of the room once, his heels clicking sharply on the polished tile floor. He looked at every shelf of their lockers. He inspected every inch of their floors. Then he went into a rage. "You men can't get anything right!" Jones reached into their lockers and pulled everything off the shelves and hangers and swept it into a pile in the center of the room. Then he reached under their beds and kicked all their shoes out from under the bunks. He looked over at Jackomis's bunk. The mattress was supposed to be folded in half with his pillow and bed linens laid squarely on top. He had laid his mattress out, hoping to have an opportunity to try it out before the inspection started. Jones grabbed the mattress and tossed it out the window to the area below.

He turned away, pulling the door closed in front of him. Reaching back into his pocket he pulled a piece of paper out, unfolded it, and stuck it on the coat hook screwed into the door. "Since you dumbjohns don't seem to have much of a memory, here's a diagram of the storage location for everything you have been issued. You are to go through and stamp each item with your name and put them in their proper places. Since you slugs are so slow I'll give you fifteen minutes to get it done before I come back. And Jackomis, I want that bed squared away. Now move out smartly!"

Bill could not believe what he had just seen. What difference did it make if he had his T-shirts on the second shelf instead of the first? He soon realized he did not have time to wonder. Bill and Flip got busy sorting out their clothes, stamping them, and putting them away again. They got to know each other's moves pretty well over the course of the next fifteen minutes. This time they were more efficient and were standing "at ease" by their beds for about five minutes before Jones returned. From the noises they could hear outside in the other rooms, apparently everyone else in the squad was going through the same exercise.

This time Jones just went through quickly, barely glancing at where Bill and Flip had placed their things. Without saying a word about the orderliness of their room, Jones poked his head out their door and yelled, "All right, you beanheads, everyone over here in Filipski and Jackomis's room, on the double!" Now what? wondered Bill. Was he going to do it again, this time throw his fit in front of the rest of the squad? This was getting ridiculous, but Bill determined that he was not going to let it get to him. He could take anything Jones could dish out, if that was what it took to get to play football and be an airborne trooper. This can't go on for long, it must be just a test, like a fraternity initiation, he thought.

Soon all ten of them were crowded into Bill's room. "Now listen up, dumbjohns. You are about to march out onto Trophy Point to be sworn in as new cadets. I don't know if you are going to make it for the next four years, but you have made it this far, and you'll get to try to make it as plebes. You will wear your first cadet uniform, and you will march out with the rest of your seven hundred classmates to take the oath of office as a new cadet. You better make your mind up now if you really want to be a West Point cadet, because if you don't think you want it, or if you don't think you can make it, you better quit right now. I don't want to be embarrassed by anyone changing his mind out there in front of the Supe and my classmates. Anyone want to quit?"

Bill didn't dare look around. He had no doubts about this, but he wondered if Flip was going to stick it out. No one budged or even batted an eyelash.

"Good," said Jones, for the first time today in a normal tone of voice. "Now pay attention while I instruct you in the proper wear of the uniform." Jones talked them through the items they were to put on in the order they were to put them on. First go the black socks, then pull on the white trousers, with suspenders attached.

Next come the black shoes. Put your sleeves into your gray coat and zip up the front all the way, then hook the collar closed. Place the cap squarely on the head and pull the bill down so that you can fit two fingers between it and your nose.

"Any questions?" They knew by now that he really did not want them to ask, so no one said anything. "Good. Men, you have three minutes to get this uniform on and report downstairs ready to form up." The squad quickly scuffled out of their room, and Bill and Flip went to get their uniforms together.

AN EVENING TO REMEMBER

Bill felt a warm, sensual glow come over him as he zipped up his gray coat. It felt a little like the first time he had sat behind the wheel of a car and began to believe that he was turning into a man. It was almost like that time he first kissed a girl and felt the rush of hormones through his body. This was it. He was on his way to becoming a cadet, an Army football player, an officer, an airborne soldier. He was going to make it no matter what Jones dished out.

Flip and Bill finished at about the same time and double-timed down the stairway, then the stoop, and then fell in line in the formation that had started. All nine of them were in a row facing Jones, who was carefully checking each man to ensure that the uniform was properly worn. Most of the guys had to run back up into their rooms to change something or adjust themselves. Bill and Flip were squared away and just stood there, bracing.

Soon all nine of Jones's cadet candidates were properly turned out. Bill watched as the central area filled with dozens of other squads just like his. They were arranged in four large sections, one in front of each side of the central barracks building. In front of each was a cadet holding up a gray and gold flag with lettering on it. On Bill's side the flag bore the marking "4th CO." That must mean Fourth Company, Bill figured. So he was in Jones's squad in 4th Company. That suited Bill just fine.

Suddenly things got very quiet all across the area. Squad leaders began to report to platoon leaders. Bill heard Jones report, "Sir, Fourth Squad is all present." Platoon leaders then reported to company commanders, and the four company commanders, standing before their section of the area, reported to a cadet standing in the center, with four others in line behind. Then a remarkable thing happened.

Out of seemingly nowhere, a band struck up a march. Bill didn't recognize it, he didn't know much about music anyway, but it was stirring. His heart leaped. This was about as thrilling as it got. After a few John Philip Sousa favorites, the music abruptly stopped. He heard some commands being shouted; he could not make out the words. Then he heard his squad leader echo the platoon leader's command, "Right face, forward march!" They were on their way.

It was a marvelous formation, four men across, ten deep. Five such platoons in each of the four new cadet companies. They marched out of the sally port they had first been in when they reported to the man with the red sash. The parade then went onto the road, then turned left up toward Trophy Point.

Trophy Point stands at the north end of the Plain, a promontory overlooking the Hudson River in majestic splendor. Planted in the ground there is a huge solid marble obelisk towering 150 feet above the ground. At the base of this monument are inscribed the names of all the regular Union Army soldiers who died in the Civil War. Surrounding the monument are captured trophies of previous wars, mostly cannon, but some other memorabilia as well.

In step to the stirring bars of the band, the eight-hundred-man formation moved steadily toward Trophy Point. As each company arrived, the company commander issued the order to pull it up abreast of the one before it until all eight hundred men, cadets and candidates, were arrayed before the monument. At the steps were several distinguished-looking officers who took a series of salutes from the cadets in charge of the formation.

Then they were ordered to salute while the band played the national anthem. Then they were placed at ease, and a general stepped forward to speak to them. "Gentlemen, I am Major General Bryant E. Moore, superintendent of the United States Military Academy." He proceeded to give one of those forgettable speeches about how they were embarking on a great adventure.

Bill was disappointed; he thought Maxwell Taylor was the supe. He wanted to see and hear the famous airborne general who had parachuted with his 101st Airborne Division into Normandy in 1945. He must have gone on to something else.

The supe led them in swearing the oath of office. When the ceremony was over, General Moore told them they were no longer cadet candidates, they would henceforth be called "new cadets." They marched to the mess hall for dinner. This time they had to brace nearly the entire meal, and Bill had messed up his cold beverage corporal duties so badly that the entire table was punished. The punishment was severe: no food for anyone, except Jones, that is.

It was a sullen group that marched back to the barracks. But it was still light in the early evening and there was more to be done. Jones instructed them how to polish their shoes and shine their belt buckles. This time when they got things wrong they had to do push-ups as well as tolerate the verbal berating and the incessant references to "dumbjohn." Well after dark, Jones instructed them on the proper method of taking a shower at West Point.

In the central barracks the showers were located in the basement of each stairwell. The stairwell was in fact to be called, he informed them, a "division." They were to wear only their cadet bathrobe, with a single towel folded in thirds and draped over their left forearm, holding their soap in a soap dish as they marched down the stairs to the showers, lathered, rinsed, and returned promptly to their rooms.

Bill had forgotten all about those flecks of hair that had pasted themselves to his skin during the day. It was a relief to wash off all that salty residue from his sweat and those hair flecks. As he double-timed back up the stairs to the fourth floor, he broke out in a sweat again. Oh, well, at least it was bedtime. Maybe tomorrow would be different.

Jones told them he would come through waking them early and that they had one more duty to perform before turning in. Each of them was to take out a piece of the stationery that had been issued and write a letter home, seal it in an envelope, address it, and hand it over to Jones. He would mail it for them. He explained that over the next eight weeks they would be so busy that many of them would probably not think to write home and let their folks know they were alive and well. It was therefore a squad leader's custom to make each man write a mandatory letter home on this first night as the last thing to be done before lights out.

Bill finished his letter and handed it to Jones at the door. Then he climbed onto his bunk and stared at the dark ceiling above. He was exhausted. He fell asleep without a word to Flip.

Three

Beast

Bill awoke to a horrendous banging sound. Something was pounding, it seemed, on his brain. He sat up straight, staring at the solitary lightbulb shining down from its fixture in the ceiling of the room. He looked to the doorway, and there was Jones banging on the metal wall lockers with his fists.

"Get up, you beanheads! You gonna sleep all day? Out of the rack, smackheads, let's go, dumbjohns, time to become new cadets." What a way to wake us up, thought Bill as he rolled himself over the side and landed on the floor. "Both of you, put these on," said Jones as he pulled uniform parts off of Filipski's shelf. "I want you formed up outside in two minutes!"

Bill looked at his watch. It was five-fifteen in the morning. So this was West Point. After yesterday, Bill knew it was going to be a long day. The uniform Jones had extracted was gym shorts, T-shirt, white socks, and sneakers. It looked like they were in for some prebreakfast conditioning.

On this second day of beast barracks they started well before breakfast with "physical training," or "PT." Jones marched them out onto the Plain, where all the others were also forming up. There in front of them on a raised wooden platform was an older man, obviously an officer, standing tall and erect. When all the new cadets were formed up, he spoke.

"Men, I am Colonel Paul D. Harkins, your commandant of cadets. I will lead you in your first session of West Point PT." Now, this is something else, thought Bill. He had never seen a colonel lead a formation before in the movies. His uncle always spoke of senior officers as rear-echelon bureaucrats. Except for George Patton, of course. Patton was his uncle's hero. Bill remembered the tales his uncle used to tell back home about the general who was always at the front, aggressive, but always a winner in battle, and always looking out for the troops. Bill wanted to be like that.

Jones had told them on the way over to the PT formation that Harkins had served with Patton in World War II. The commandant was tall and slim, and from the way he did his PT this morning, he was in excellent shape for an old man. Bill was impressed. He led them through the army's standard twelve exercises, the "daily dozen," by the book. They marched straight from PT over to the mess hall for breakfast. It was going to be a great day, Bill thought.

It was certainly going to be a long day. More uniform fittings, more D&C, more yelling and screaming. Over the next two days they were issued rifles, belts, field gear, and helmets. Now this was beginning to look to Bill like it was real soldiering.

Six more meals. Other guys in the squad had their chance to be the cold beverage corporal; they did no better than Jackomis had done. They learned about more duties as well. That second night one of them was assigned to be the "minute caller," whose duty it was to be prepared before everyone else at each formation and to stand under the clock in the hallway and yell out the number of minutes remaining until assembly time. "Sir! There are fifteen minutes until assembly for drill formation! The uniform is khaki under arms. Fifteen minutes, SIR!" The caller had to stand at the fourth-floor landing and yell it at the top of his lungs so everyone in the division, all the way down to the first floor, could hear. Then he had to call it out again at ten minutes, and every minute thereafter. After calling out one minute before assembly, the minute caller would be the last man down the stairs and into the formation. At least they wouldn't have Jones banging on their lockers.

The book titled *Bugle Notes* turned out to be a storehouse of information about West Point's traditions and customs. The words to all the football fight songs were in there, as were those for other tunes such as the "Alma Mater." Jones told the squad they would have to memorize them all before they would be accepted into the Corps of Cadets as plebes, and every night they had to recite some new portion of the book perfectly to their squad leader's satisfaction. There was also a large section of facts, figures, and other sayings called "Plebe Poop."

Bill didn't mind having to recite; he was pretty good at memorizing things quickly. He would get his own "poop" checked off and help Filipski with his. Old Flip was a little slower in the brains department. Bill especially liked the football fight songs. These were great. He wondered where they got the words for "Sons of Slum and Gravy." He liked reciting it because at the beginning it went, "Sons of Slum and Gravy, will you let the Navy take from us the victory? HELL, NO!" Jones demanded that they yell out the swear words really loud, and Bill was beginning to enjoy doing that.

MASS ATHLETICS

On Sunday in the afternoon they had another surprise formation. This one was called "mass athletics." Out in the 4th Company area there were about twenty upperclass cadets standing in gym uniforms and holding a placard over their heads. Each placard had a sport printed on it: baseball, track, swimming, soccer, football, and others. Jones read their names off and assigned them to one of these sports squads. Bill and Flip went to the football squad. At last, thought Bill, they would get to do what they had come to the academy to do.

Bill stood at ease in line behind a plebe from 1st Company, Ray Malavasi. Ray was a big guy, a lineman. They had met on the first day of Beast in the Administration Building. Bill looked to his left at the guys in the swimming squad. He looked up at the head of the line. The man up in front was obviously an upperclassman and most likely a football player, judging by his build.

He watched their leader come down the line and walk right next to Ray. Bill heard him say, "You look like a dumb football player, kid—if you have any trouble in academics, remember that the people in the other regiment have instruction before you do. Get the poop. Then you'll get by." Bill was quickly learning that "poop" was cadet slang for any information of importance. He had already discovered what "plebe poop" was. Now there was "*the* poop." He figured from the comment that it had to do with academics.

"What was that all about, Ray?" he whispered.

"I don't know, Bill. Maybe he'll tell me more when we get to football practice. Do I look that dumb?"

"You don't look dumb, man. You look like a great football player to me," Bill replied.

Before long they marched off across the Plain just as all the other lines did. The upperclassman marched the little plebe football squad across the Plain, around Trophy Point, and down to some athletic fields near an expansive track and field arena. Then they learned who the upperclassman leading them was. It was the football team captain, John Trent!

Trent told them to fall out and gather around him as he spoke. "Men, I'm John Trent, your mass athletics cadet-in-charge for football players, and cocaptain of the 1949 Brave Old Army Team. Welcome to Army football. From now on, any time we are down here, below the level of the Plain, you can call me John." He went to each of them and shook their hands, asking their first names. He said that he had just "recognized" them, meaning that they were now on a first-name basis. Trent explained that soon all the upperclass football players would recognize them so that practice would not be hampered by the new-cadet system.

Then Trent spoke to them in an easy manner, "During Beast barracks you will be brought into the Army football system. You will meet your coaching staff for the plebe team, you will undergo special conditioning drills, you will go through position drills and tryouts, and you will scrimmage. This is mostly for us to get a closer look at you and to begin your development as a collegiate football player. All of you were high school football stars, but you are in the big time now. You have a lot to learn."

Then, it seemed like out of nowhere, a coach came up to the group. He was about Bill's height and build. Trent told them to make way as he passed through to the center of their group. "Men, I'm Vince Lombardi. I'll be helping to coach you during Beast barracks as we go through your introduction to Army football."

Bill didn't know quite how to size up this coach. He looked like he was a powerful man. But his voice was not all that strong. Maybe he was one of those guys who got loud only when he was mad. Maybe he was new and uncertain. Maybe he was the junior coach and was assigned to coaching plebes because none of the other coaches wanted the job.

Coach Lombardi had about ten other upperclassmen with him to help in the coaching chores. There were also four other coaches. They soon were split into groups by position: linemen, running backs, passers, and receivers worked together, as did defensive backs and linebackers. It was a light workout, no hitting, just a few easy drills and a lot of talking among themselves.

Bill welcomed the opportunity to "fall out" a little with his classmates. He had not had a chance so far to meet hardly anyone except Flip. Bill quickly warmed up to his fellow running backs. He soon realized that he was going to be one of the fastest men on the plebe squad. That made him feel good about his chances of making the team.

It was also his first chance to see upperclassmen in a completely different light. These varsity players helping Coach Lombardi were decent men. None of them yelled, even when you made a mistake. It was very hard not to call them "sir," after all that Jones and the others had put them through, but that was what they wanted. In fact, if you did call them "sir," some of them did get a little steamed and raise their voice a little in telling you not to do that. They even gave Bill a nickname: Jake. They often gave such one-syllable nicknames to guys who had long last names if they did not already have a nickname from home or from some exploit during Beast.

Lombardi was everywhere. He must have checked in with each group six times. He talked, he demonstrated how to do things, he even showed the proper technique for tackling by taking down several of the upperclassmen. And it was obviously not a big show; Lombardi really banged into those guys. Wow! thought Jake. He had never seen a high school coach do that. He hadn't even heard of a college coach doing it. This was going to be some football program.

The end of the practice session came far too soon. Trent lined them up and walked them all back up the hill to the area. As they got to the level of the Plain, Trent told them they now had to brace like everyone else and march in formation the rest of the way. "Look sharp, men. Don't give the detail or the tacs an excuse to write you up. They will be looking especially closely at you from now on, now that you are marked as a football player. Keep yourself in line. If someone gives you a really hard time, just let me know and we'll straighten it out through the football office."

Jake couldn't see how that would be necessary. Jones seemed to be fair with them so far. Maybe other football players didn't have it so good.

THE GRAND TOUR

Saturday brought a welcome change of pace. After the usual morning formations for reveille, PT, breakfast, and drill and ceremony, new cadets were taken on a tour of the West Point grounds. Jones led the squad on a hike all around the immediate area of the academy and its surrounding hills, stopping at dozens of sites where history was commemorated.

Jake was glad to see in full color, depth, and panorama all the things that West Point's literature could show only in black and white on a half-page cropped photograph. It was indeed an inspiring campus. But the really fascinating sites were those not normally seen in the books and movies.

They hiked up into the hills above the Plain and crawled through the ruins of Fort Putnam. Built in 1778 to fire cannon down to the Hudson River below to protect one of America's major waterway lines of communication, it commanded a wide view of the academy grounds below the river, and of the Hudson highlands beyond to the east.

Jones was reading a script, and Jake could tell that he was not enthusiastic about this history lesson for his plebes. "Men, this is Fort Putnam, named for General Israel Putnam. It was built during the Revolutionary War to prevent the British from taking further territory up the Hudson after they had captured New York City," read Jones disinterestedly. "The fort was built from plans left by Polish-American patriot and soldier Count Tadeus Kosciuszko." Now, that is very interesting, thought Jake. Imagine that—a Polish guy planned the fort that defends West Point from the Redcoats.

"This is one place where you will not often be permitted to visit," continued their squad leader. "You can come here only on weekends when you have privileges. Most of you guys won't see privileges for a long time, so take a good look now; it may be your last for a long time. This place is called "Plebe flirty." Let me warn you now that alcohol is not permitted here. During the academic year you may hear of cadets getting caught up here drinking or messing around. Don't do it. You'll be on the area forever if you are not kicked out."

As Jake looked around it did seem to be a suitable spot for a late Saturday night date. The tops of the parapets were flat and had long ago grown over with a thick carpet of grass. On a warm summer night it could easily become a huge bed. All along the stone walls of the gun emplacements and ammunition storage magazines, iron gates swung wide open, offering their enclosed spaces for privacy. No doubt a whole squad of guys could hole up in one of those rooms for a night of drinking and debauchery that any college fraternity would envy.

As the squad made its way back down the hill they passed the Cadet Chapel, the Catholic Chapel, and more famous monuments, to West Point heroes George Washington and Sylvanus Thayer. They saw the last remaining links of the great chain that had stretched across the Hudson River to prevent British boats from getting up the river, and the Battle Monument at Trophy Point.

Along the way they stopped off at the old Cadet Chapel and the West Point cemetery on the chapel's grounds. Inside the chapel, Jones pointed out the Benedict Arnold tablet. "Here inside the chapel the names of Revolutionary War generals are carved on such wooden plaques," Jones related, "but Arnold's name does not appear on the tablet, nor does it even have his date of death. Those who put it there were so disgusted with the fact that Arnold, who commanded the West Point garrison during the Revolutionary War, had tried to turn West Point over to the British, that they would not dishonor the academy's sacred ground with his name."

Elsewhere in the cemetery, Jones pointed out to them the grave sites of dozens of famous West Pointers who had served their country honorably. One of the largest markers was that of Sylvanus Thayer. There were many odd shapes close to the chapel, but as the markers radiated outward, they became more simple and consistent in the familiar white stone cross or flat granite ground stone. Jones explained that with so many West Pointers wanting to be buried there, policies after World War I required all graves to be added in a circle on the outside of the perimeter and to be small and unassuming. Jake noted that there was some space remaining next to the chapel and wondered if they would eventually have to come back and fill those spots.

Finally, the squad's tour guide took them to the side of the academy's grounds overlooking the Hudson River. On the far corner of the grounds Jones halted them at yet another statue of a nineteenth-century general holding a sword. "Men, this statue is in honor of a great man who fought with Washington's troops, Count Tadeus Kosciuszko. It was erected on the Fort Clinton parapet by a group of Polish Americans in 1913."

Then Jones took them down the rocks below a ways to Kosciuszko's rock garden, which was directly under the walls of Cullum Hall. Jones explained to them that Kosciuszko had built a little retreat for himself, away from his labors on the fort, in the European style of the day. Captain Joseph G. Swift, the first man to graduate from West Point, rescued the garden from ruin in 1802 when he became superintendent, and it has been preserved in its original condition ever since.

On Sunday they had their first experience with mandatory chapel at West Point. After breakfast as usual, the company formed up in the area by religious group. There was one formation for Catholics, one for Jewish cadets, and another for Protestants. They marched off to their respective chapels for services. Jake was impressed with the Catholic chapel; it was about the same size as the churches back home in Gary, but it wasn't anywhere near the size of the huge churches in Chicago or New York City where he had occasionally attended Mass.

Flip told him all about the Protestant chapel, with its huge arched entrance, stained glass windows, and cavernous sanctuary area. It sounded to Jake more like a cathedral. It certainly looked like a cathedral the way it towered above the Plain in great Gothic splendor. Jake told himself he would go see it sometime when they got privileges; he especially wanted to see all those army flags from previous wars he had heard were hanging from the walls inside the chapel. He had not seen enough of them on their brief Saturday afternoon tour.

Sunday had been a welcome change of pace for Jake and his classmates. The Saturday tour was interesting, although most of the new cadets quickly got bored with the repetitious lectures from Jones about this general or that building. They were allowed to fall out at the table during Sunday breakfast after chapel, but Sunday dinner in the mess hall was a return to the grind of being a new cadet. More yelling, bracing, and even less food than usual. Jake knew he was losing weight; the uniforms that he had been fitted for less than a week ago were already fitting a little looser. He hoped they would soon get to eat more.

THE FOURTH OF JULY

The next day, Monday, was the Fourth of July 1949. As Jake woke up that day he wondered how they would be celebrating. Probably more drill and ceremony, he figured. Would there be a fireworks display? They always had fireworks back in Gary on the Fourth of July. It was his mother's birthday. He wondered whether he would get a chance to call and wish her a happy birthday. He missed home right now.

It turned out to be just like any other day so far at West Point. There was plebe poop to recite for Jones, duties to perform, uniforms to prepare, more meals in the mess hall, more yelling at them, less food. Jake was still losing weight; he felt lighter and weaker than on his first day at the academy. If only those guys would get the table duties right.

Last night's dinner was typical. Flip was the dessert cutter. He had to hold up the dessert, a cherry pie, announce what it was, and ask if anyone did not want a slice: "Sir, the dessert for this meal is deep-dish cherry pie. Would anyone NOT care for dessert, SIR?!" Anyone who did not want a piece would then hold out his fist and forearm, and the dessert cutter had to look briefly around the table and take a count. Then he was required to cut the pie in a geometrically perfect manner no matter how many slices there were to be cut. Eight was the easiest; you could just keep cutting it in half down the center of the round pie dish. But usually everyone wanted dessert, so you had to cut it in ten equal slices.

There was no easy way to do that, and Flip had been trying for three days now. Each time he would cut it, he would send the pie up to Jones for inspection, who would promptly declare it unacceptable and take the whole thing for himself. Jake wondered if they would get to eat it even if Flip got it just right. Jake would have been happy even if he could eat more than a bite or two of his main course, much less dessert. It seemed like he never got more than a couple of bites down before somebody screwed up, and they were all sitting at attention until the offender got it right. He wondered if they would ever get to eat a complete meal. He sure was hungry.

This day turned out to be different by midafternoon. There would be a Fourth of July ceremony today, but they would be in it, not watching it. The entire company formed up at about three that afternoon in the central area. The other three companies formed up as well, just like the big parade they had on their first day when they marched to Trophy Point to their swearing-in ceremony. This time their uniforms were different; they were wearing wide white cross belts across their chests with a brass breastplate and a similar white waist belt and a big brass buckle. They had worked since after lunch to get those belts just right and to shine up those brass pieces. They also wore white gloves.

All these extra uniform items gave the upperclassmen a heyday on their inspections. The slightest scratch on the brass was cause for a tirade. Jones had stood over Jake's shoes and wiggled his fingers to see if he could see their reflection in the shine off his toes. About the third time Jake returned from going back to his room to shine them up again he was successful. But as they marched off there was no relief from the incessant corrections from the upperclassmen.

Jake was marching at the rear of the column since he was a bit shorter than the others. They always formed up with the tallest men in front and the shortest to the rear. It was quite simple how this was accomplished. Once the formation was gathered, the platoon leader gave the command, "If you're taller than the man in front of you, move up!" About half a dozen men then would tap Jake's shoulder to move up ahead of him. Then the commander would shout, "Right face!" After the unit turned he would say, "If you're taller than the man in front of you, move up!" In this manner, when the company was formed on the Plain, the tallest men would be in the right most forward part of the formation, with the shortest at the left rear. Somehow this was supposed to be military.

The problem with being at the left rear, where Jake usually ended up, was that when the company executed a right turn, the whip-saw effect forced the men with the shortest legs to take the longest steps. They could not run and they could not break step with the cadence being beaten out by the West Point band. Jake thought he looked like Groucho Marx doing his comic stage strut. Looked like it was going to be one of those ceremonies, though.

As they marched away from the area toward the Plain, Jake heard a voice from behind him say, "Hey, Jackomis, how about a joke?"

Who in the world was that? Jake wondered to himself.

"Hey, mister, when I call for a joke you better have a joke ready to go and it better be a good one, too. Now let's hear your best joke, Jackomis."

"Sir, I do not understand." Jake gave his fourth authorized answer for the first time in his cadet career, using one of those loud whisper voices.

"Mister Jackomis, you must understand that when you are a runt, you will always have us file closers right behind you. We don't like being back here any more than you do, but no one can see us or hear us as long as the band is playing. So we entertain ourselves at your expense. Now tell us a joke and make us laugh."

This might not be so bad after all, thought Jake. "There was an old lady from Nantucket . . ."

"Oh, no you don't, Jackomis," said the voice behind him. "We've heard that one before. Besides, the way I heard that joke, it ends up with profanity. New cadets are not authorized to use profanity. Try again, ducrot."

Jake didn't know any other jokes, clean or dirty. After a long silence he was relieved to hear the voice behind him say,

"Okay, Jackomis, we'll give you another try next time. Hey, Malavasi, tell us a Polish joke." Before Ray could get out an answer, the band stopped playing and the company came to a halt. "Cease work, Malavasi!" The company was formed on the Plain in line with the others. The ceremony was about to begin. Apparently the fun was over.

There was not much to this ceremony. It wasn't really a parade, it was just a march-on to a formation. Then the announcer said that they would be calling the roll call of states and would the audience please stand. Jake noted that there were several banks of bleachers in front of them with what must have been several thousand people in them looking on at the new cadets. Jake wondered if any of them had a good joke he could borrow.

Then the command "Present arms!" was given, and the entire formation snapped to a hand salute. They held it there while the announcer read off the name of each state followed by a cannon blast. It takes a long time to read off the names of all forty-eight states and let a cannon fire after each one. You couldn't anticipate when it would be over because they read off the states in the order in which they were admitted to the union. After the first dozen or so Jake lost count of how far down the line they were.

His arm ached from holding the salute for so long. So did everyone else's. The heat got to a few guys; Jake saw and heard several fall out. He wondered what happened to them. Did the

upperclassmen just leave them there and march off? Did someone carry them away? He hoped he would never have to find out
directly.

Finally, it was over. "Order arms!" You could see everyone give
their arm a little shake when it got to their side. Hope we don't
have to do that again till next year, thought Jake. After marching
back to the barracks area they hurried up to their rooms to
return their rifles to the racks and remove the belts and brass.
Then it was a march to the mess hall for dinner and back to the
barracks for more of the Beast barracks grind.

Four

Recognition

The only thing different about the second week of beast barracks was on Tuesday. At reveille formation that day, Jones announced, "Men, today after breakfast we are taking a three-mile tactical road march. Get yourselves ready mentally for a tough day. Make sure you have all your field gear ready to go." Now, how were they going to get any field gear ready to go, since they were in formation, Jake wondered. He hoped that they would have time after breakfast. He hoped they would get some breakfast.

THE HIKE

They didn't. It was worse than the usual drill at the table. The hot beverage corporal spilled the coffee as he was pouring it. Jones was livid. He made them all pass their plates up to him at the head of the table, where he stacked them up and turned them back in to the kitchen unsoiled.

When the squad formation arrived back at the barracks, Jones gave them their instructions for preparing for the hike. "You men have five minutes to go get your field gear on and get back down here ready to march. The uniform is fatigue coveralls with combat boots, steel helmet, and rifle. You will also wear your cartridge belt like I showed you yesterday. Now get it all together and be ready to move out. Five minutes, beanheads. Now, double-time!"

Jake and Flip raced up the steps to their fourth-floor room. Jake had put his field gear together in the proper manner yesterday when Jones had demonstrated it to them. Flip had not bothered. Those metal clips that hold the pouches onto the web belt just did not move very quickly; Flip was struggling. Jake quickly had on his coveralls and field gear, then went to help Flip. Somehow Jake managed to get everything on while Flip put on his coveralls. Then they both grabbed their rifles and ran back down the stairs to the area. "Thanks, roommate," whispered Flip to Jake as they stood in their assigned spots.

They were the only ones there, so no one could hear him. Still, Jake couldn't believe that Flip had dared to violate the rules by talking to him in formation. There might have been another upperclassman somewhere who could have heard or seen them. The rest of the members of the squad were still trying to hook pouches onto their belts. Jones was in the division screaming and yelling at them to get a move on it. The last man came straggling out about a minute late.

This time they did not just report and move out. The company commander gave the order to open ranks, and he personally inspected every man's gear. When he came to the squad in front of Jones's, Jake could hear him noting corrections, "Belt too tight, boots not properly laced, helmet not snug." As the company commander spoke, the squad leader was writing on a small pad. Jake wondered how many demerits there would be for each correction. As the commander came down Jones's squad, there seemed to be fewer corrections. "Filipski, your pouches aren't properly closed on your cartridge belt. You don't want to lose your ammo halfway down the road, do you?" The upperclassman's voice sounded almost grandfatherly; there was none of Jones's scorn and disdain. This cadet seemed to be sincerely worried about Flip's well-being. That sure was a change.

"Malavasi, where are you from?" asked the commander as he moved to the man next to Jake.

"California, sir," Ray replied. Malavasi made the military gear he was wearing look almost irrelevant. His broad shoulders caused the rifle butt to dangle in the air at his side about two feet away from his hip. The other men could hold their rifles next to their uniforms. His waist was so narrow that if he were to hold the end of his M1 at his side the muzzle would be pointing outward instead of straight up. He looked like a marching wedge.

"I'll have my eyes on you, Malavasi. Do you know why?" The commander's voice was now almost conversational.

"Sir, you must be from California, too," guessed the plebe, now grinning from ear to ear.

"No, I'm not, but my favorite Army football player was. Who do you think that is?" The commander continued the friendly questioning. It was almost as if this was a way to ask easy questions in a way to compensate for all the plebe poop questions from Jones that Ray had so much trouble with.

"That must be Glenn Davis, sir," affirmed the Long Beach native Malavasi.

"Good work, Mr. Malavasi. Right answer," said the commander, as if Ray had just successfully recited all six verses of the "Alma Mater" from memory. "Now listen, you take care of your feet on this road march. I don't want any foot injuries that can be prevented. Make sure you do just as your squad leader instructed you whenever we take a rest halt. He did give you the foot care class last night, didn't he?"

Malavasi remembered only too well. In between yelling and screaming at him for not knowing the day's plebe poop, he did recall that Jones had discussed what they were to do with their feet whenever the hike stopped.

The commander continued, "Remove your boots, change socks, add foot powder, and get your feet up. I don't want to have any problems with those All-American feet of yours."

"Yes, sir!" shouted Malavasi, his face beaming. No upperclassman had ever taken that kind of interest in Ray before. It gave him a renewed sense of confidence in himself. The commander and Jones moved down to Jackomis.

Jake could finally read the man's name tag as he stood before him. "Shultz," it read. Jake immediately recognized the name as one of the Army team's strong running backs. So that was it. Their company commander was another football player. No wonder he took it easy on Flip and was so positive with Ray. Jake couldn't believe how lucky he was. One football team cocaptain, John Trent, was his cadet in charge of athletics, and another player was his very own company commander. Jake hoped that would make Jones go easier on them.

"Jackomis," said Shultz, "I hear from Mr. Jones that you are fairly well squared away. Is that right?"

Jake pondered his answer for a moment. His humbler instincts told him to say no, because he was not always prepared and Jones had to correct him from time to time. He struggled with the rest of his squad, but he just didn't get called to task as much; probably because Flip and Ray had so much difficulty, they drew most of Jones's ire. But if he gave an answer along those lines, Jones might not appreciate him calling his squad leader a liar. Then again, if he said yes when he knew that he was not always squared away, would he be lying? Maybe he could get away with venturing from his four authorized answers just this once. "Sir, I have my share of difficulty."

"Good answer, Mr. Jackomis, you're a smart man. You help keep your buddies Malavasi and Filipski squared away. We'll need all three of you on the Army team this year. I'll be keeping my eye on you. If you ever need anything, just come around to my room during the academic year and I'll get you squared away. Just keep yourself out of trouble with the Tactical Department. They can really get football players if they want to. Believe me, I know about it firsthand."

Jake couldn't imagine what kind of trouble Shultz might be hinting about. Surely the tactical officers wouldn't harass the star running back of the football team. Anyway, Shultz was a cadet captain. That meant the tacs must have recognized his military leadership abilities as being well above the average. While Jones seemed about average, Shultz was well above the grade. There were only six cadet captains in all of Beast barracks: the four company commanders; the executive officer; and the regimental commander, known as "the king of Beasts." That meant that Shultz was pretty high up in the cadet pecking order to be worried about tactical officers giving him grief like Jones dished out to plebes. Maybe there was more to it.

MOVE OUT

Shultz moved on and completed his inspection. Then he moved to the front of the formation and gave his company a command: "Fourth Company, right . . . face!" He moved to the head of the formation with the company guidon bearer—the man who held the gray and gold flag with a big black "4" centered on both sides—who raised the standard to the high carry. "Column of twos, forwarrrrd . . . MARCII!" The whole company moved out and marched off toward the Plain.

Jones's squad marched on one side of the road, the third squad on the other side. Jones said this was tactical. If they ran into any enemy fire they would take cover on either side of the road until he gave the signal to reform and move out again. He told them that if they heard a loud bang and saw a bright flash, that would be an artillery simulator, and they were to take cover as he instructed. They would also take their breaks by moving off the road in line.

Once they got past the Plain they started downhill toward the north athletic field, where the football squad had practiced last week. Jake wondered when they would have another mass athletics period. He wanted to play football, although this tactical road march made him feel very soldierly.

They were carrying their rifles at "sling arms," which meant they carried them slung over their right shoulders as they marched. Jake then realized there was a reason for putting the canteen on the left hip. The rifle sling began to rub against his right hip, and by the time they got down to the athletic field his skin was beginning to feel a little irritated. If that canteen had been there he would probably have a big bruise by now.

It felt good, though, to have that rifle on his shoulder. Jake had never fired a rifle. This was a heavy, M1 rifle, about the equivalent of a 30.06 high-powered hunting rifle like that Springfield his uncle had at home. Only this M1 was not as heavy nor was it as long and cumbersome as that old Springfield. Jake wondered what it felt like to kill a man with this weapon. He hoped they would soon go to the rifle range.

They had reached the far north end of the athletic field now. The company faced a wooded area where the ground obviously went uphill at a very steep slope. The hill curved around to their left. On their right, past the railroad tracks about a hundred yards away, the Hudson River stretched out about a mile across. There was only one way they could go if they did not head back. That was straight up.

Up they hiked. Up and up the men plodded. At times the hill was so steep Jake could almost touch the ground below him with his nose. About halfway up he broke out in a sweat. This was bad, because the uniform he wore was made of starched cotton. As his sweat beaded up on his skin it dissolved the starch from his coveralls. The mixture was really irritating his skin inside. Then, as it started to drip down the crack of his butt, it started to peel away his skin. Now he had two raw spots from this hike already. This was not fun anymore.

When the column broke over the top of the hill, Shultz ordered the company to take a rest halt for ten minutes. Down they went and off came their boots, as Jones checked each squad member's feet.

"Jake, how you doing?" asked Flip.

"Okay so far, Flip. Hey, your feet stink, did you know that?" Jake held his thumb and index finger to his nose in mock disgust. Flip chuckled, but not too loudly. He didn't want to attract Jones's attention. Flip was glad Jake was his roommate. Jake's sense of humor had been a big help in getting this far in Beast.

Ray Malavasi was just ahead of Jake and Flip and was guzzling water from his canteen. Jones strode up to him and said, "Malavasi, what are you doing, mister?" and the squad leader smacked the canteen with the butt of his rifle, knocking it out of the plebe's hands, spilling and splashing water into the faces of the ducking Jackomis and Filipski. "Don't you know you'll get sick gulping down so much water? Just drink a little at each stop. Plus you're gonna run out too soon. Save it for the whole march. You need some discipline, mister."

Ray Malavasi had never been treated like that before, not even on the first day of Beast. He was boiling mad inside. He stood up and glared at his squad leader. As he picked up his rifle, Jake thought for sure he was about to give the squad leader a powerful butt stroke with that M1. It would probably kill Jones if he did it, Malavasi was much bigger and obviously more powerful physically than Jones was.

"Do you understand me, mister?" yelled Jones without budging or blinking.

"Holy cow!" Flip whispered to his roommate. "Looks like Ray is about to lose it. I don't want to witness this."

"Come on, Flip, we have to hold Ray back. He'll get a court-martial if he hits Jones." Jake only halfway believed that the two of them would be able to restrain the hulking lineman from California.

Malavasi came to the position of attention. "Yes, sir!" He belted out his answer as he glared directly back into his squad leader's eyes. Malavasi was not cool under pressure. Jake could see his eyeballs bouncing in their sockets as Ray's rage seethed inside.

"Well, you'd better, ducrot. We'll deal with this when we get back. Now on your feet, fourth squad, and prepare to move out," ordered Jones as he turned away from Malavasi. Evidently he did not realize how angry Malavasi was inside. Jones had only seen yet another mistake to be corrected and one great opportunity to catch the attention of the rest of his squad in a forceful and dramatic way. He felt a little smug with himself, the way he had seized the opportunity Malavasi had given him. He decided that a clothing formation right after the march would help his new cadets internalize the lesson he had just demonstrated.

The remainder of the march was uneventful by comparison. From the top of the hill north of the Plain they hiked back south to the hills overlooking Michie Stadium. It was a grand sight, but under the circumstances the new cadets were not really in the mood for more sight-seeing. The ordeal was made a little lighter when some other, more entertaining squad leader than their Mr. Jones struck up a marching song. Jones soon had them pick up the refrain, and before long all of Hal Shultz's company was marching in step to cadences and songs being shouted by two hundred hoarse but enthusiastic voices.

When finally they returned to their barracks area, the plebes were tired, sweaty, and hungry, but quite spirited. Before they were dismissed to prepare for dinner, Shultz wanted to speak to all of them at once.

"Men of new cadet Fourth Company, you have just proved how good you are. No one fell out on our first tactical road march and I'm proud of you for that. You have set the example for the rest of your classmates, and I want them to know about it. From now on, whenever I give the preparatory command 'Who are you?' I want every one of you to yell, 'Fourth Company—we lead the way, sir!' Do you understand?"

Jake could feel the adrenaline begin to pump him up, tired as he was. "Yes, sir!" he yelled in unison with the others. It actually was quite a thunderous sound to hear all two hundred of them yelling the same two words at the same time.

"Well, let's try it then," shouted Shultz, "Who are you, men?"

"FOURTH COMPANY—WE LEAD THE WAY, SIR!"

Jake was awestruck by what he had just experienced. He had been at Chicago's Soldier Field when a hundred thousand fans screamed and yelled at the same time on a great play. That was strong. But the effect of two hundred new cadets shouting the same words in cadence was awesome, almost of mythological proportions. He was glad he came to West Point. He was proud to be in 4th Company. He could put up with Jones for a few weeks until football season began.

Shultz dismissed the company for showers, cleaning up their equipment, and changing for dinner. Jake was anxious to rinse off all that dried, salty sweat.

That night, after dinner, Jones introduced his squad to the tradition of the clothing formation. He said it was extra training brought on by their demonstrated lack of discipline during the tactical road march. It was just like the clothing formations of the turn of the century, one of those traditions that just never did die. The squad members knew that it was in reality a form of mass punishment for the incident with Ray Malavasi. Jake and Flip could not figure out why Jones had it in for Ray, but the pressure was relentless the rest of the night.

At the dinner table, Jones had focused his verbal hazing exclusively on Malavasi. No one in the squad got to eat more than two bites of their meal that night. When they marched back to the barracks, Jones had them running up and down the division steps, changing into all eighteen versions of the uniform in the regulation book. Each time, Ray Malavasi had to carry a full canteen and chugalug the entire one-quart contents before Jones gave the order for the next uniform change. Malavasi was a basket case by the time "lights out" came around.

As they finally turned in to their bunks for the night, Bill Jackomis and Gene Filipski could barely manage the strength for a short, whispered conversation before being overcome by sleep.

"Jake, why do you think Jones is coming down so hard on Ray?" Flip's whisper was a bit throaty.

"I don't know. Maybe he has it in for football players and we're next." Jake's voice was more airy and difficult to pick up. "Good night, Flip."

"Good night, Jake. We'll have to help keep an eye on Ray. We're gonna need good linemen to break holes for us running backs." Filipski's voice had dried to a rasp.

Jake answered with a snore.

PRIVILEGES

Except for Thursday at mass athletics, the remainder of the second week of Beast barracks was much like the first. At "mass-ass," as they came to call the mass athletic period, football players again had a welcome relief from the pressure of Beast barracks. This time the plebe football players were led in practice by Bill Yeoman, All-American star of last year's Army team and now a second lieutenant and graduate assistant football coach. Yeoman had been captain of the 1948 squad that had done so well. He seemed to be a lot like Trent and Shultz. All three exuded a positive attitude, were strong physically, and smart mentally. They were the epitome of what Douglas MacArthur had in mind when he elevated the athletic system to equal status with the academic and military training programs at the academy. These men excelled in leadership, studies, and sports, and the academy's administration wanted new cadets to be exposed to them as role models. Jake wanted to be just like them.

That afternoon practice was a bit shorter than it was the first Thursday of Beast barracks. After some light drills they assembled in the football area of the gymnasium for a talk session with Doug Kenna, a graduate assistant who was assigned to help the assistant coach who managed the tutoring program for the football team. Kenna explained to them how the tutoring program would work once the academic year began in September.

Kenna explained that the coaching staff would receive a weekly report from the academic departments, providing the current grade point averages and class standing for all the football players. As members of the C squad, or plebe team, they would be tutored as a group. Members of the B and A squads—the equivalents of junior varsity and varsity, respectively—would be tutored individually. Their tutor would study ahead for upcoming lessons in courses they were experiencing difficulty with. The tutor would then help the players work through the lesson using sample problems similar to those that would appear on examinations, based on the coaching staff's experiences with previous classes over the years. Since the course work rarely varied from year to year, the tutoring would help team members make up for the study time they sacrificed to team meetings, away games, or just being tired from practice. This would help equalize the advantages their non-football classmates would have over them and help them use their time more efficiently.

Kenna explained that this program was just for football players and was in addition to the regular program of additional instruction offered to all cadets. This year for the first time, football players would be given additional tutoring time after dinner, separate from the additional instruction that was offered to all cadets in the late afternoon. For the rest of the Corps of Cadets, additional instruction, or "AI," would involve an hour of an instructor going over the same material that had been covered previously for those who just did not quite get it. For football players they would be covering the next day's material in advance and they would be doing it in the barracks area, down in the basement "sinks" of each division, not in the academic buildings, as with the AI sessions for everyone else.

After taking all this in, Jake wondered why they went so overboard to provide academic help to football players. He guessed it would be helpful to guys like Malavasi who probably needed it.

On the second Saturday of Beast barracks they had a briefing on the privileges they would be allowed to have starting the following Saturday. Jake thought it was a little cruel to tell them a week before they would get to enjoy them, but he figured the knowledge would help them keep their spirits up to endure the coming week's pressure.

As new cadets they would be allowed to go to Grant Hall, an elegantly appointed spacious club room on the first floor of South Barracks building. They would be issued "boodler's checks," which would serve as scrip that could be used to purchase "boodle," or treats and snack foods. They could also smoke in Grant Hall if they wished. In addition they would be allowed to visit with girls in Grant Hall on Saturday "privilege" periods from after lunch until dinnertime during Beast barracks. Longer times would be allowed during the academic year. Whenever they were with girls it was traditional that the girls would buy whatever sodas, ice cream, or other indulgences were available so that the cadets could conserve their scarce boodler's checks. The entire time they would be chaperoned in Grant Hall by cadet hostesses— mature women who were employed by the Army Special Services office for such duty.

This was part of the overall program for allowing and controlling the privileges permitted cadets during their highly regimented life at West Point. They were gradually allowed greater liberty until graduation day, when they were entirely on their own, by then trained by the system not to overindulge. Weekend leaves would begin during their third class (sophomore) year. The previous class had not been allowed weekend leave until their junior (second class) year, and the practice of granting the underclasses weekend leave had begun only in 1947. By 1948 firsties were allowed to drink alcohol as long as it occurred at least twenty five miles away from the academy grounds, and they had been permitted to own a car that same year. Next year, the class of 1953 would be permitted to take spring leave along with the two other upperclasses. Many officers in the tactical department believed that cadet life had been liberalized far too much. A few even believed that it was a secret Communist plot to destroy the academy.

Football players were provided even greater freedom. They were excused from further Saturday tours of the sights of the academy grounds so that they could participate in weekend football practice. In the mess hall they were soon reassigned to tables headed by a first classman who was a football player, rather than sitting at their squad table commanded by their squad leader. When it came time during Beast for the new cadets to select a foreign language, the one academic course they would be allowed to have some choice with (all cadets took the same courses at West Point except for foreign language, where as plebes they chose to take Spanish, German, French, or Russian), football players would be handled separately in coordination with the coaching staff. In reality the coaches made sure that their players who were expected to have trouble learning a foreign language would be placed into the traditionally easier languages, such as Spanish. Jake chose Russian, the most difficult of all the languages to learn.

Starting that Saturday, all new cadets would go to their tactical officer's quarters on post for a social hour to learn about home life as officers. They would be allowed to have ice cream and casual conversation in a structured environment as a way to learn certain social graces that would be expected of them as officers. Football players would go not to their tactical officer's home but to one of the coaches' homes. And on this first Saturday event, the new plebe players would go to Coach Blaik's home.

The uniform for the Saturday social hour was dress gray, the heavy woolen uniform that was one step below the most formal full-dress gray. But Yeoman had put the word out at mass athletic football that football players would be going to Blaik's quarters and would instead wear the more comfortable khaki uniform. As seven hundred plebes set out in dress gray that afternoon for various officers' homes, fifty football players walked off in khaki. They stood out like a sore thumb, but no upperclassman said anything to them, having heard through the football team captain that Coach Blaik had specified khakis for his players.

Lieutenant Colonel Arthur S. Collins was waiting inside his massive red brick quarters for his assigned new cadets to arrive for the Saturday social hour. As one of the most senior tactical officers, he had one of the more impressive sets of quarters on post, in a choice location. As with most other issues of importance, the matter of which quarters an officer's family was assigned was settled first by rank, then by seniority, then on the basis of class standing as cadets. There were several other lieutenant colonels on post from his class, but "Ace" Collins, as the highly decorated war hero was called, was able to get one of the better homes around in spite of his mediocre finish at West Point—number 208 out of 300—because of the importance of his position in the tactical department. It was a large place, only about a block away from his office in the guard tower of central barracks. His war record had won for him one of the two coveted regimental tactical officer slots for the Corps.

Ace Collins was a strict by-the-book disciplinarian, the kind that the commandant, Colonel Harkins, had personally selected for the Tactical Department in the post–World War II period to rebuild the Corps of Cadets after the wartime turmoil. He was concerned, as was Harkins, that in the expansion of the Corps to its wartime size, the quality of the men had been sacrificed. After the war, when the size of entering classes was not reduced back to its prewar limit of about 350, Collins had become even more concerned. Now that the administration was really loosening things up with all these privileges, he was beginning to get concerned that maybe somehow the Democrats under Harry Truman were deliberately trying to undermine the one institution that was trying to maintain America's high moral standards. He would show these plebes how a well-structured life would serve them and their country well.

Collins looked out his window for a moment to catch a glimpse of the view he so enjoyed. His living-room window provided a breathtaking view of the Hudson River, with the highlands towering over both banks. In summertime the shimmering heat waves rising from the river surface seemed to lift the ground up, as if the sacred ground were being brought up into heaven itself. As he gazed into the distance, his reverie was rudely interrupted by a gaggle of new cadets who were flagrantly violating the prescribed uniform of the day. About fifty men were walking boisterously on the sidewalk in front of his house, making the turn up the road to go up the hill, apparently in violation of the instruction that Collins himself had issued.

Colonel Collins blasted out of his front door and yelled, "You men, HALT!"

One hundred shoes came down at once in a massive "clomp!" on the cement sidewalk.

"Just where do you think you are going in this uniform?" Collins directed his question at no one in particular.

Jake had no idea what was up. He knew better than to speak up, but he could think of nothing they were doing that was wrong. A voice from somewhere in the group of plebe football players sounded off, "Sir, we are going to Coach Blaik's quarters."

"Oh, I get it," said Collins with a scowl, "another special privilege for football players. Well, you won't get away with it this time. You men are out of uniform. You are supposed to be in dress gray. Now, I don't know who told you to wear khakis, and I don't very much care. You will do an about-face immediately and report back to your rooms and change into the prescribed uniform. If you still have time before the social hour is over you can march up to your assigned quarters. Now move out."

Jake had no idea who this officer was, but it was clear that he was important. For a moment Jake thought he should explain that they were part of the football team and that they were allowed special privileges. But it did not look like this officer would change his mind. He figured they'd better obey and explain later to the coaches what happened.

They all double-timed back to their rooms to change. Then they ran back down the road and up the hill to the quarters they had been told belonged to Coach Blaik. It was a long run up a hill just about as steep as the mountain they had hiked up on Tuesday. The only easy thing about it was that it was a paved road rather than a wooded trail. Still, Jake was sweating profusely by the time they reached the home.

It was a huge home. Blaik was at the door to greet them with a look of distress on his face. "Come on in, boys. What happened? Where have you been?" As someone explained the incident to the coach, Jake suddenly realized that they were in the presence of one of the greatest football coaches in the country. It was a moment of awe for the speedy running back from Tolleston High in Gary, Indiana. He had never been this close to someone so great. Blaik told them not to worry about it, that he would look into it himself. In the meantime, as he introduced his wife, Merle, he told them to scarf up as much ice cream and cake as they could in the time remaining. As Jake and Flip scooped up their ice cream, they could overhear Blaik in the next room talking, only slightly above the volume he used in conversation with them. "Well, Colonel Harkins, that really was chicken. I'm going to report this to the superintendent. Believe you me, you'll hear about this because West Point needs football a lot more than football needs West Point."

It was a whirlwind of a Saturday, and a little bit odd, the way they were intercepted by Collins. But it was an impressive day to Bill Jackomis, Gene Filipski, and Ray Malavasi. They were eager to enjoy the freedom of privileges next Saturday, but this was an impressive day. They had met the great Red Blaik in person.

TEACHING THE HONOR CODE

After chapel on Sunday they had their first class on the West Point honor system. They were all marched into a large lecture hall in one of the classroom buildings. There a first classman told them about the honor code and its meaning. "A cadet does not lie, cheat, or steal," states the code. "In addition, a cadet who knows about someone who has lied, cheated, or stolen must report him for violating the code. Failure to report a violation is itself an offense against the code," said the firstie. He went on to explain that each company had an honor representative who handled the reporting of violations. Suspected violations would be reported to committees who would investigate and rule on whether the code had been broken. Anyone found by the committee to be in violation of the honor code would be asked to resign from the Corps of Cadets. If he refused he would be brought before a board of officers who would try him for violation of military regulations, or perhaps even face a court-martial. Furthermore, even if the board of officers failed to find enough evidence to convict him of an offense, the Corps of Cadets would impose the "silence" on any cadet found guilty by the Honor Committee and not kicked out by officers. The "silence" involved complete social and professional isolation of the offender; all West Point graduates were not to speak to him for the rest of their lives. The honor code belonged to the cadets, and they had their own ways of dealing with offenders if necessary.

After the session, they broke up into company groups for informal sessions with honor representatives to answer questions they might have. There weren't many in 4th Company. The lecture had made it obvious that the honor code was a very high moral standard. Anyway, it was pretty clear what kind of behavior constituted lying, cheating, or stealing. Most of the men of 4th Company thought they had a good idea of what was honorable behavior and had no intention of violating the honor code anyway.

Beast barracks went by fairly quickly for Jake and Flip. After the second week they had their table duties down cold and got to eat a little bit more than they had during their first couple of weeks. Still, by the time Beast was over Jake had lost twenty pounds; Flip had shed fifteen. They went on four more marches, each one farther than the last. Jake was top man in the outdoor obstacle course, a log and trail affair that was set up in the woods just up the road from Colonel Collins's quarters.

Every Saturday they had a room inspection, then a uniform inspection, and a parade for the public visitors who had gathered to see one of the nation's favorite tourist attractions—a West Point parade. Jake never did learn any new jokes. The Saturday afternoons at Coach Blaik's home were a welcome break and a great opportunity to get to know the man they revered in a more personal way. Once they even got to meet his son, Bob, who was in from the second class training trip and getting ready for the 1949 football season himself. Bob was to be the backup quarterback in 1949 to All-American Arnold Galiffa.

In the first week of September, before Labor Day, all the upperclasses returned to West Point to get ready for the academic year 1949–50. The plebes were assigned to their permanent companies by their size. Jake and Flip were runts and went to the middle companies I, K, L, or M in 1st Regiment; A, B, or C in 2d Regiment. Jake went to I-1 Company; Flip was assigned to B-2. Bigger guys like Malavasi went to "flanker" companies, A 1 through C-1, or K-2 through M-2. Ray was assigned to B-1. He heard that it had several football players and hoped that relief would soon be found with safety in numbers. He also knew that Bob Blaik was a yearling in B-1 and expected that the pressure would be off in that company. Surely no one would harass Red Blaik's son.

Once the new cadets received their assignments they moved their meager belongings to their new barracks rooms. First Regiment was in the old central and south areas while 2d Regiment went to buildings in north area known as new and old north barracks. For a week they were integrated into their new companies. It was called "Reorganization Week," but it might as well have been called "Hell Week" for the plebes. They suddenly found themselves outnumbered by upperclassmen by three to one. With six times more eyes watching them they soon discovered that they could be caught in violations of regulations much more easily and quickly by the ever-vigilant upperclassmen.

The yearlings were the worst. These men had just completed their plebe year and were determined to make sure that the Class of 1953 had it just as hard as they had just had it. They were everywhere, checking out how well the plebes had memorized their plebe poop, staring them in the face as they performed minute caller duties, making sure that the plebes delivered laundry and mail with perfection, and always checking the finest detail of their uniform and appearance. It was a long week, but at the end the entire Corps of Cadets formed up for the parade that Jake and his classmates had been told was a day worth waiting for. The Acceptance Parade was a formal event signifying the fact that the Class of 1953 was certified to move beyond new cadets to become full-fledged members of the Corps of Cadets and would henceforth be known as "plebes." They still had a long year ahead of them—for the next nine months they would still be called "dumbjohn," "ducrot," and various other affectionate nicknames—but at least they had made it this far. About 100 of those who had entered on "R Day" had not made it. Many quit; some had hidden medical problems that were discovered in the course of the rigorous physical activity; and many simply decided that, although they were doing well, West Point was not for them. A few cracked mentally under the stress. But 697 of them made it and were now part of the Long Gray Line.

Forty of them were football players and were accepted into the Brave Old Army Team.

Part Two

Old Cadets

Five

The Pride and Dream of Every Heart in Gray

Bird was an Oriole.

Stephen M. Bird entered the U. S. Military Academy as a new Cadet on 2 November 1918. That made him an oriole.

Orioles occupied a strange place in the Corps of Cadets. They entered at a time when the academy was rapidly expanding to become a factory for lieutenants. World War I was grinding up European junior leaders by the thousands. The U.S. War Department decided that the United States must be prepared to experience those same high casualty rates. By the time Stephen Bird became an oriole, Britain and France had lost an entire generation of young men. Accordingly, the War Department accelerated the West Point program. Cadet Bird was admitted to a Military Academy that had been transformed from a four-year professional institution into a six-month rudimentary small-unit leadership course.

Bird was also an amateur poet. He often spent his precious few spare moments composing couplets of dismal verse. He was not the first poet to attend West Point; Edgar Allan Poe established a legend for such eccentric behavior soon after he came to the academy in 1830. Poe wrote a collection of poems that appealed to Superintendent Sylvanus Thayer, who encouraged him to have them published. But the young bard constantly ran afoul of the Tactical Department; one day he just up and left, never to return.

Bird's sensitivity and creativity made the plebe vulnerable to the obdurate characters typical of the upperclasses of the early twentieth century. They hazed him with ruthless glee.

Hazing was ritualized recreation for West Point cadets in the late nineteenth and early twentieth centuries. It was part of the initiation rite for the freshman class to endure the physical punishment and harassment dished out to plebes to earn acceptance into the Long Gray Line. The upperclassmen's only qualification for higher rank was that they had endured the same torture back when they were plebes. With just about every minute of their day programmed for them by the tactical and academic departments, cadets in 1918 were left with little time of their own and precious few distractions with which to amuse themselves. Over several decades West Pointers elevated the art of pulling pranks on newcomers to a sophisticated, baroque form. When a plebe drew particular attention to himself by being a bit nonconformist, as Bird did with his gloomy poetry, the hazing took on a peculiarly depraved character.

Bird had endured the worst of the hazing through the cold winter that set in at West Point late in 1918. But he could take it no more. On New Year's Day, 1919, he shot himself.

That morning, Cadet Earl Henry Blaik was enjoying one of the few pleasures upperclassmen at the academy could legally enjoy. He had slept in past the normal 6:00 A.M. wake-up time and he rather enjoyed the opportunity to go to reveille formation at seven for the cold, though mercifully brief, march from his barracks on the north side of the campus to the cavernous mess hall a few hundred yards away. He didn't even shave that morning, since there would be no inspection on this holiday. At age twenty-two, Blaik was older than most of his classmates, and he had already completed four years at one college, the Miami University at Ohio. He thought that most of the petty disciplinary rigor was a waste, though tolerable, and he relished this rare opportunity to relax from its grip on his life.

Blaik was on his way down the stairs from his room that morning when a classmate, Harvey Greenlaw, screamed, "Henry, come in here quick! Mr. Bird has passed out!" Blaik's closest friends called him by his middle name, Henry. When he got down the stairs to the room Greenlaw had called him from, and saw Bird's body stretched out on the floor, Blaik remembered the night he and his fraternity brothers at Miami had finally found the body of a woman in the woods outside Oxford, Ohio.

As a youth Blaik had seen more of real life than most other cadets. His family endured the tragedy of being swept out of their home in the great Dayton flood of March 1913.

Red, his popular nickname because of his hair excelled in baseball and football, but he did not do so well in school. Not only were his grades not as distinguished as they could have been—they were barely enough to get by—he was often in trouble with the school administration because of an argumentative spirit. Once, in his senior year of high school, he intercepted a note from a teacher to his father asking for parental help in dealing with the rebellious youth. He never let his parents see it.

Several months later, just a week before his high school graduation, Blaik was discovered in his crime and expelled. Young "Red" was then required to report, escorted by his father, to the Dayton superintendent of schools to appeal for reinstatement. He successfully completed high school and went on to his four years of college at the University of Miami. Once in college, Red continued to excel in football and even managed to improve his grades.

This cold, wintry day at West Point was not to be his first encounter with a seemingly dead body. Blaik and his fraternity brothers had been involved in a search one night for an escaped mental asylum inmate. Red had had the ghastly fortune to stumble onto the body of the poor soul. She had committed suicide. His thoughts raced back to that night as this New Year's morning unfolded.

But Bird was not yet dead. He had propped his service issue weapon—a powerful Springfield 30.06—on the desk in the room he shared with his classmate. A string was tied to the trigger and threaded around the butt of the rifle, revealing Bird's suicide technique. He had apparently inched his chair close enough to the muzzle so that when he sat down he could place his chest right up against the business end of the rifle. When he jerked on the string, the projectile pierced his chest cavity, punctured his lung, and exited out the flesh on his back, miraculously without damaging his heart or a major blood vessel. Bird survived the bullet but later choked on blood and fluid from around his lungs.

As he lay there gurgling, dying, Blaik could barely hear him say with a sigh, "Water . . . water . . ." Two other cadets were in the room vainly sopping Bird's head with cold, wet towels. Blaik went first to the rifle and cleared the action. The spent cartridge ejected, and he noticed that the slug was deeply set in the wall behind the space where Bird's torso had sat erect for a fraction of a second after impact.

Blaik quickly took charge; he could see that Bird was near death and that nothing they could do in the typically cold, dank room would help him. He ordered Greenlaw to stand by while he left to see what he could do. He appropriated a truck that was sitting outside the barracks and drove himself several blocks down the road to the hospital, brought a doctor back, and helped move the young oriole for treatment. No one bothered to put Blaik on report that day for violation of one of the most rigidly enforced rules of the academy at the time—the prohibition against cadets driving any motorized vehicle.

Cadet Bird died just after six o'clock that evening. He had been hazed to death.

HAZING AT WEST POINT
Until the Bird incident, hazing, though outlawed, was in fact tacitly condoned by the leadership administering the academy. The practice had developed out of an evolutionary process peculiar to West Point.

In the late nineteenth century, cadets' lives were regimented to the minute. Every waking hour was governed by a precisely defined schedule of academic instruction, military drill, and mandatory study under the most spartan of conditions. Not long after the end of the Civil War, cadets were even prohibited from smoking, a habit that had proliferated throughout the Corps of Cadets, staff, and faculty. Drinking was against regulations and virtually impossible anyway, since there were no liquor establishments near the academy grounds. The legendary "Benny Havens" tavern had been shut down.

The only diversions cadets had were those they invented themselves. In this environment hazing became a high art form. Despite the opposition of successive superintendents, the upperclassmen at West Point took to entertaining themselves at the expense of the plebes. The hazing took on a remarkable variety and fell into two categories, as reported by a turn-of-the-century investigating board.

Specific acts of hazing included such menial service for upperclassmen as requiring, permitting, or inviting fourth classmen to:

- make down beds;
- clean rifles and equipment;
- carry water;
- sweep out tents.

More physical forms of hazing found by the board included punishments in which plebes were compelled to:

- assume an exaggerated position of attention, commonly called "bracing";
- double-time—a definite number of tours between their tents and the fourth-class sink;
- perform other exaggerated exercises;
- pick up ants in the company street;
- wrestle each other for the amusement of the upperclassmen.

Perhaps the ultimate was "challenging them to fight by offering to give them satisfaction, personal or otherwise, if said fourth classmen are not satisfied with the treatment accorded them by upperclassmen."

During the investigation by the 1909 board of inquiry, several especially heinous practices by one particular upperclassman were uncovered:

> Laying hands on and treating with violence fourth class-men, pushing his hand into the stomachs and chins of said fourth classmen while bracing them as punishment.

> Tyrannizing over fourth classmen; commandant of table, requiring or permitting him to sit for a period of time with feet raised to the bottom of the dining table while at a meal.

Some superintendents issued regulations prohibiting such practices, but upperclassmen were rarely reported for violations. More often than not, even when hazing was prosecuted and punished by dismissal, the perpetrator would appeal to the War Department or Congress for reinstatement, and usually succeeded. Enough West Pointers were in such positions of responsibility that when these kinds of cases came their way, the response, typically, was that hazing was just part of the West Point experience.

Sometimes the upperclassmen would stage a real show for themselves, at the plebes' expense, by holding a "clothing formation." In these extravaganzas, fourth classmen whose performance of duties had been particularly weak or who had committed especially heinous offenses (such as wearing improperly shined shoes) would be ordered to report to a group of upperclassmen waiting for them in the basement area of the barracks. The upperclassmen would then give them a wholly impossible time limit within which to march up the four flights of stairs to their rooms, change into a different uniform, and march back down to the waiting squad leaders for an inspection.

All down the stairway, other upperclassmen were posted to yell and scream at the plebes along the way, adding mental abuse to the physical and psychological stress bearing down on the hapless fourth classmen. No sooner would they report that they had completed their mission than the squad leader would order another uniform change and send them upstairs with yet another impossible time limit as a corrective measure for failure to meet the first time limit. And woe betide the plebe who appeared with some part of his uniform not perfectly displayed on his person in the prescribed manner of wear.

WORLD WAR I AT WEST POINT

By 1918 new cadets had been arriving at West Point for more than a century in early June, spending the summer in an intense training period known as "Beast," then enduring their freshman academic year as "plebes." That first year at West Point was a far cry from freshman year at any other school except perhaps the Naval Academy.

For Stephen Bird and the other "orioles" it was extraordinarily different, even by West Point standards. When Bird and his classmates entered West Point, World War I had been going on in Europe for more than four years. The United States had declared war on Germany in 1917, and by 1918 American troops had been bloodied in combat.

Allied lines stabilized across the Western Front in early 1918 in France, but from March through June 1918 a massive German offensive threatened to break through. The fresh but untested American troops had been thrown into the fight at Château-Thierry, and by August, after the Second Battle of the Marne, the German military machine was halted.

But victory in World War I had come at a terrible price. For this generation of Americans the Civil War was already fifty years old, and their only recent experience with real combat was the Spanish-American War in 1898 (in which a total of 385 Americans died in combat). The more than 320,000 U.S. casualties experienced in little more than a year and a half from April 1917 to November 1918 had a far-reaching impact on the country as a whole and the U.S. military in particular. Nothing like that kind of slaughter had been experienced since the "War Between the States," and the memory of that war was beyond the experience of most Americans. The awful, bloody truth that war is hell had given way in the minds of many in a generation of young American men to visions of glory in battle.

The initial response at West Point to the Great War in Europe was that no change was needed at all in the plodding, tradition-bound crucible of the incipient American officer class. Until 1917 the academy refused to acknowledge the Great War in tactics or academics, adhering rigidly to the curriculum that had been established prior to the American Civil War. In military instruction, the momentous battles of the great captains who had graduated from West Point were the only objects of study, unencumbered by such modernities as the Gatling gun or trench warfare. Academy officials pointed to the success of their graduates as reason to resist change.

There was plenty of validity to their view. In spite of the steadfast refusal to move into the twentieth century, West Point produced another generation of world class military leaders from such classes as that of 1915, out of which came 59 generals from a total of 164 graduates that year, including Omar Bradley and Dwight Eisenhower. The cadets did not want to miss this war, the first chance in fifty years for most of them to have the opportunity to earn their claim to glory in battle.

They began to clamor for early graduation, as had previous classes during the Spanish-American War. The Class of 1917 was permitted to graduate two months early. The Class of 1918 was graduated a year early and shipped off to Europe in late summer 1917 to "earn its spurs" in combat under Gen. John J. Pershing, who was in command of the American Expeditionary Force. They indeed found the greater glory, as 21 out of just over 300 were killed or wounded.

Then in 1917 a policy decision had been made by the Army's leadership to compress the traditional four-year program into three. Graduation for the Class of 1919 was accelerated to get another crop of lieutenants to the war for the 1918 campaigns. As a result, when the academic year began in late summer 1918, there was no longer a senior class ("first class" in formal West Point nomenclature) present on campus.

By late summer 1918 it was not at all clear how this war was going to end. The Allied offensive on the Western Front had been more successful than anticipated, thanks to the spirited fighting of the fresh troops from the United States, but had succeeded only in restoring the butcherous stalemate that had preceded the German successes earlier that year. War Department planners expected the effort to go on for several more years.

West Point, having turned the corner on changing tradition, then accelerated its graduation machine. In early October 1918, the War Department ordered that the second and third classes would be graduated within a month, by 1 November 1918, rather than on their respective three-year dates of 1920 and 1921. The Department also directed that yet another new class be admitted that same month of November, and the academy was to plan to graduate that class the following June, in 1919.

The result at the academy of all this was to thrust several hundred young men, whose judgment was already affected not only by the normal testosterone-driven streaks of inaneness that come with late adolescence, but now also by visions of impending glory in battle, into a heightened state of frenzy. The very night that the November graduations were announced in the mess hall, the upperclassmen compressed the rest of plebe year's customary developmental purgatory into the remaining quarterhour of the dinner meal. Then they shook hands with the plebes in the rite of "recognition" traditionally reserved for the next-to-last full-dress parade on the Plain in June. These men were officially designated as "Fourth Class A."

A few days after the Class of 1918 became instant seniors, the new crop of cadets—"Fourth Class B"—arrived. Because the Army supply system had granted higher priority for gray woolen uniform material to Army recruits, these new cadets were issued standard soldier uniforms in place of the traditional cadet gray. Their wide-brimmed campaign hats sported a bright yellow-colored cloth band just over the brim to distinguish them from real soldiers as new West Point cadets. Hence the sobriquet "orioles."

While this class faced the prospect of bearing the ignominy of having the shortest academy tenure of any class in history— admitted in November 1918, they were programmed to graduate in June 1919—they in fact graduated later. Seventeen of them graduated in June 1921; the others were shuffled into the Class of 1922. None of the seventeen made it to general. Their plebe "year" lasted all of three weeks.

Thus, when hostilities ceased in November 1918, West Point was in turmoil. Blaik's class had been there only a few months, but they were already considered to be "firsties" or seniors. They wore the traditional cadet gray uniforms. Bird's class of orioles had arrived on 1 November and continued to wear the uniform of an Army private with the addition of the yellow hatband. The class that had graduated early in the previous November was returned to the academy to complete their studies, but they had been in the Army as lieutenants and were officially designated as the student-officer class. This class wore their officer uniforms on campus. While the negotiators at Versailles took more than a year in dealing with the mess that Europe had become, reaching the final Armistice agreement on 11 November 1919, the leadership of the Army wrestled with its looming disaster at West Point.

In this milieu, the Bird episode brought about a War Department investigation of the entire operation at the academy and a demand for new leadership. The Army chief of staff, Gen. Peyton March, selected one of the Army's youngest brigadier generals to take over at West Point, not only to sort out the knotty problems that had come with the end of the World War but also to make more far-reaching changes that would bring the U.S. Military Academy out of the mid-nineteenth century and into the twentieth. That man was Douglas A. MacArthur.

Six

Douglas MacArthur at West Point

Douglas MacArthur took over at West Point in the summer of 1919, and in one of his first acts of command he invited several cadets over to talk about conditions at the academy. One of those early visitors was Cadet Earl H. Blaik.

While Red Blaik was ready to provide the general with an earful about all that was wrong at West Point, MacArthur had already formulated his own list of the things that needed drastic change while he was in charge.

For starters, there was the physical hazing that had proved fatal, ultimately, to Cadet Bird. MacArthur was no stranger himself to hazing; he had endured more than his own fair share of it as a plebe twenty years earlier. MacArthur inherited one of the most difficult genetic traits that could befall a plebe, one that resulted in automatic hazing: His father had been a war hero.

In the Civil War at the Battle of Chattanooga in 1863, eighteen-year-old Lt. Arthur MacArthur seized his regiment's flag after two color bearers had been killed during that famous assault up Lookout Mountain and, defying bullets and cannon shot that were slaughtering all those around him, he reached the top and firmly planted the Union's first standard in that pivotal battle. He would later be awarded the Medal of Honor for his heroism.

When Douglas was a cadet, his father, by then a general, was distinguishing himself in battle in the Philippines during the Spanish-American War, making headlines that would draw even greater attention to the local exploits of the new cadet.

For any of the smallest infractions, New Cadet Douglas MacArthur would be told how he could never measure up to his father's level of performance, and then the son would be forced to recite the entire official account of his father's exploits verbatim. This was in fact an easy task for the new cadet; MacArthur revered his father, and he constantly judged his own achievements against those of his father. He would be the first to admit that the smallest of infractions demanded a loud and thunderous rendition of the exploits of Arthur MacArthur at the Battle of Chattanooga.

One summer night during plebe encampment on the Plain in the summer of 1899 was a particularly difficult one for the 133-pound son of a war hero. A group of southern upperclassmen had him braced for hours, reciting his father's exploits in the hot afternoon sun. Then he was made to stand perfectly still and silent for another hour. They next made him do deep knee bends over broken glass again and again and again. The hazing ended well after dark only when he fainted.

He was carried back into his tent to recover, but he soon was overcome by convulsions. His uncontrollable shaking made his feet bang on the wooden pallet that kept the men off the ground while in their tents, and it made such a racket that MacArthur had his classmates put a blanket under his feet so that the noise would not attract any more attention from the upperclassmen. He also made them stuff his mouth so that his screams would not be heard outside the tent. He would accept no medical attention.

Later in that summer of 1899 another plebe died from hazing, and Cadet MacArthur was called to testify before a congressional investigative committee on hazing at West Point. At that hearing he parried and thrusted with the congressmen verbally in a valiant and largely successful effort not to betray the upperclassmen who were, after all, at least to MacArthur's military mind, only cogs in the West Point machine. At times during the questioning by New York's congressman Driggs, MacArthur was outright condescending and arrogant in both tone and demeanor. But he got away with it. Hazing to him, at least at that time, was a necessary part of the process of becoming an officer, in keeping with the vital and glorious traditions of West Point, and Douglas would no sooner reveal the identities of his own tormentors than he would betray his own mother.

In fact, MacArthur's mother accompanied him to the congressional hearings for coaching and encouragement. Indeed, she lived at West Point while he was a cadet, taking up residence in the hotel that in those days was located just off the Plain overlooking the Hudson River. She was his staunchest advocate and principal adviser throughout his cadet days and had instilled in him the personal values and virtues that his emotionally more distant father never had time to develop. As he waited to speak before the committee in Washington, she had passed him a note with a poem and a reminder of her standing orders to him as a boy; orders she had repeated to him his entire young life, "Never lie, never tattle." As he sat waiting to testify, he thought, "Come what may, I will be no tattletale."

With his performance at the hearings, new cadet Douglas MacArthur had won the approval of upperclassmen throughout the Corps of Cadets: his constant striving to live up to his father's reputation, his mother's continual presence at the academy, and frequent interventions on his behalf with the academy's administration and with the Army's leadership, combined with MacArthur's own natural abilities to propel him to the top of his class. In his first class year he was selected as first captain, the highest-ranking cadet in the entire Corps. He also graduated first in academic ranking, with one of the highest grade point averages of all time.

MacArthur later distinguished himself as an officer in an expedition into Mexico in 1914. Outside of Veracruz, a five-thousand-man American force was positioned for possible operations against a Mexican force twice its size. Since war had not been declared, the U.S. force was under strict orders not to come into contact with the Mexican Army, but there was an obvious need for reconnaissance prior to potential hostilities. Under secret orders directly from Washington, young captain Douglas MacArthur was dispatched on a one-man mission into the interior of the country to bring back intelligence on roads, bridges, rail networks, and locomotives that might be available if captured by U.S. forces. In carrying out his mission successfully, MacArthur killed seven men and evaded detection or capture for three days. He was recommended for the Congressional Medal of Honor, although it was never approved.

In World War I MacArthur's battlefield abilities made him a standout as a brigade commander in the 42d Division. As in Mexico earlier, his personal courage under fire became legendary. His acumen in the operational art of war proved to be equally superior as he formed, trained, and maneuvered his brigade in battle after battle during the march toward Germany. General Pershing promoted him to major general and assigned him as commanding general of his division, the famous Rainbow Division. The Armistice came soon after his battlefield promotion, however, and he was reverted to his one-star rank, relinquishing the command before he returned with his brigade to the United States in April 1919.

The chief of staff, Gen. Peyton March, had selected him to be the superintendent at West Point and issued him a directive to revitalize the academy. According to some historians, March had developed a bitter rivalry with the field commander during the war, General Pershing, and had selected MacArthur in part because he was a distinguished wartime commander who was not considered to be a Pershing protégé. March apparently disliked Pershing with a passion.

MacArthur arrived in June 1919 with a game plan of his own for the revitalization mission he had been given. His first goal was to change the plebe system. He believed that the brand of leadership that West Point was instilling in its graduates was wholly wrong for lieutenants in the modern army. It may have sufficed for Prussian martinets of a century before to use extreme physical methods in instilling disciplined obedience to orders, but his World War I experience convinced him that this would not be the case for the American soldier. He felt that "men generally needed only to be told what to do, rather than to be forced by the fear of consequence of failure."

The most important part of his plan to change West Point's methods was to transform the summer camp from a rite of passage to manhood into a genuine training experience. Although the plebe experience at the Fort Clinton camp on the Plain was one of constant hazing and servitude, for the upperclasses it was a grand, summer long picnic. While they would from time to time exercise a few drills in the cool of the morning, afternoons were unstructured, and evenings brought elegant dances with the ladies. There were rousing concerts by the renowned West Point band, and the food was choice, all served by hired laborers to the cadets, who did not need to lift a hand save to raise their utensils to their mouths.

MacArthur wanted cadets to have direct encounters with the actual conditions they would experience in the Army, not the idealized situations artificially created on the Plain. He sent them on excursions to Army bases and brought to West Point Army troops, artillery, balloons, and aircraft. He sent them to Fort Dix, New Jersey, more than a hundred miles away, for much of their summer duty, under the watchful care of regular Army drill sergeants. And at the end of the training period MacArthur's cadets marched back to West Point carrying their own gear.

THE ACADEMIC BOARD

West Point, he knew, would not take to such changes as he had in mind right away. MacArthur introduced his ideas for reform to a select few cadets before he mentioned his intentions to the Academic Board, the staid group of permanent professors who wielded most of the legal authority to run the academy. One of his first official acts as superintendent had been to invite some of the first classmen over to his office for an informal session with their new commander.

In fact, for the cadets, the custom had been well established that the superintendent would hold a formal office call once per year with a few of the firsties to discuss matters of common interest. The cadets were required to wear full dress uniform for the occasion, and the conversation never went beyond the casual and cordial. MacArthur used the occasion to introduce the academy to his radical methods.

He invited some first classmen over for the annual event in the summer of 1919, among them the older man who had taken the initiative in the Bird incident, Earl H. Blaik. When they entered he put them at ease and affected an informal air. He offered them cigarettes—an act of flagrant violation of regulations that had a profound impact on Blaik. Others saw it as an insincere attempt to co-opt the firsties for his coming power struggle with the colonels on the Academic Board.

MacArthur seemed to cultivate an impression of being above the regulations. His uniform was generally unkempt, with his crinkled cap and nonregulation jacket. His hand salute was always more of a wave of his (also forbidden) riding crop than the crisp "one-two" taught to West Pointers from the beginning of day one in Beast. But his war record kept anyone from challenging him on these details. Such violations paled in comparison to the legends that had already grown to surround this giant of a man.

In any case, what he wanted Blaik and the others to do was develop a new fourth class system that would document what could and could not be done to plebes as part of their training as new cadets. The system would become regulatory, and any treatment of plebes outside of those regulations, such as by hazing, would become an offense punishable by the upperclass chain of command as well as by officers. MacArthur hoped that by giving cadets progressive increases in responsibility for governing themselves as a military organization, they would police themselves, much as did the professional officer corps in the Army.

Blaik was the most eager to respond to the general's approach, whether feigned or real. Red came to oppose the "plebe hazing system and the brutalities it could encourage in those with a sadistic streak or those unconditioned by nature to handle authority judiciously when it was thrust upon them." Although he had been at the academy for only a year, under the circumstances of the post–World War I admixture of classes at West Point he was considered to be a firstie, and under MacArthur's new approach he was to be one of those to inherit the mantle of leadership.

MacArthur offered Cadet Blaik the chairmanship of a committee he wanted formed to study the problem of the treatment of fourth classmen. Blaik took the job and tried to get his classmates to agree on how and what to change. But he was no more successful with his classmates than MacArthur would be with the Academic Board.

Blaik was not able to forge a consensus among his classmates to develop a set of regulations; the best he could do for the new supe was to draft, collectively, a pamphlet listing which types of hazing were acceptable and which were not. The booklet did not end the practice, as MacArthur had desired, but Blaik's close association with the general did serve to build an intense loyalty to him on the part of Red Blaik.

The general could impose a new fourth class system on the academy by diktat because it was one of the few areas of life at West Point that was governed exclusively by the superintendent. In almost all other matters the Academic Board ruled supreme. This was the group of academic department heads who, by law, were appointed virtually for life as colonels and permanent professors. The only nontenured voting members were the superintendent and the commandant, and many of those came and went during the career of permanent board members. Under those kinds of conditions, change came very slowly to West Point.

The Academic Board opposed most of the changes MacArthur set out to impose; they believed that what had succeeded in the nation's wars from the Civil War to the present should not be tampered with. At times they were downright rude to the superintendent, and MacArthur was never able to get much movement in his reforms of academic practice. He had warned the Army chief of staff, when informed of his assignment to the academy's superintendency, that he would not be likely to make much change in the place, "I am not an educator," he had told March. "I am a field soldier. I can't do it."

While he could not move them, he did try to wear them down. During the summer of 1919 he had them in meetings daily as he tried to persuade them to adopt his academic reforms. When the professors would not take his suggestion to adopt methods in practice at other institutions of higher learning, he sent them for a month at a time to observe how education had changed across the country. He invited prominent lecturers, such as the controversial Billy Mitchell, from outside the academy to address the cadets. The supe on occasion would even sit in a classroom to observe instructors, often interrupting to offer suggestions.

As if to compete with the Academic Board, he wielded his authority over cadets' military training liberally, bringing modern training methods and treating cadets in a more civil manner than in the "old Corps." He granted them off-post privileges, allowed them to keep money, and awarded more leaves of absence. The disciplinary system was transformed under MacArthur from one that compelled obedience out of fear to one that elicited compliance out of a sense of duty.

HONOR AT WEST POINT

One of MacArthur's most far-reaching and fundamental reforms was the codification of the honor system. Tradition holds that West Point's honor code dates to the early nineteenth century. In fact, the University of Virginia was the first institution of higher learning in America to have a codified system of enforcing integrity among students. In 1842 a University of Virginia professor was murdered by an attacker wearing a hood to avoid identification. In response, the students published a decree stating that an honorable man would come forward and confess. Thus written, the honor system at Virginia has stood the test of time, court challenges, and about a hundred formal cases a year.

West Point's honor code was longer in coming and was not formally recognized until MacArthur's superintendency. In 1806, the very first superintendent, Lt. Col. Jonathan Williams, imposed regulations designed to shape the character of cadets as honorable men. He forbade drinking of alcoholic beverages and dueling. He also required attendance at chapel services every Sunday. He led discussions with cadets and officers about the demand for the highest standards of integrity on their word as officers. West

Point graduates of the day were commissioned in the Corps of Engineers and were entrusted with large sums of public monies used for the construction of the road and waterway infrastructure in the East and for early American expansion westward. Unimpeachable integrity was required because of this special trust and confidence placed in these young graduates of West Point.

Sylvanus Thayer, revered among West Point graduates as the "Father of the Military Academy," is credited with developing the unwritten code of integrity for cadets. He required officers at the academy to accept a cadet's word as truth. Even when providing a written response to an officer's charges of misconduct, the cadet's letter was not to be challenged or checked for accuracy under the Thayer system. Since a gentleman and an officer was always truthful, the cadet's excuse was to be accepted if it adequately explained a valid reason for the offense. Lying and stealing were punished by dismissal, although cheating on academic requirements was in fact condoned and not considered to be under the province of the honor code.

Cadets began to enforce the code themselves sometime around the middle of the nineteenth century. Once, at the end of the Civil War, a cadet suspected of stealing was tarred, feathered, escorted off the post, and warned never to return.

Another thief who was allegedly caught in the act by cadets was drummed out of the Corps before a parade attended only by cadets, with no officers present. The leader of the cadets, knowing that the evidence was circumstantial and not wanting to supervise another tarring and feathering, held the Corps in formation until the escort party had taken the accused to the boat dock to catch the afternoon ferry. But, unknown to them, the commandant had intercepted the escorts and their victim and held the accused thief, who professed his innocence, at his quarters. The incident was reported to the secretary of war, who ordered a full court-martial. The result was that the accused thief was reinstated and the cadets in the chain of command who had handled the matter were found guilty of conduct prejudicial to good order and military discipline, although their sentences were remitted.

Many years later the real thief confessed to his crimes and revealed that he had been stealing to pay off his wife, who was blackmailing him for money and jewelry. Then, as now, cadets were not permitted to be married, and the real culprit had been hiding his stolen goods in the room of the cadet falsely accused to avoid detection himself. This actual criminal could not live with the knowledge that he had done so much harm to an innocent classmate and later killed himself after he had confessed. The incident, however, did little to affect the growing practice of cadet enforcement of their honor system. Cadets took their self-enforcement mission to a new height in an incident that occurred in 1871.

Early in January that year cadets Baird and Barnes departed the academy grounds for a nearby town to retrieve a quantity of liquor for themselves and a roommate. The roommate, Cadet Flinkinger, reported to the sentinel checking rooms that his roommates were on authorized absence. Since he knew them to be illegally off post for an illicit purpose, Flinkinger was in fact lying, and since it was an official report to a guard, it constituted rendering a false official statement. When they were discovered, the forty-six men of the first class were called to meet in secret and determine what should be done.

Six of the firsties refused to take part in the proceedings, but the rest of the class went to the offenders' rooms at midnight, marched them off the post, and told them never to return. The next morning they were reported absent without leave and reported as deserters. When he was informed of what happened, the superintendent sent a detail to the location of the three cadets in hiding and arrested them as deserters. They were urged to resign in lieu of standing before a court-martial. But then the superintendent took the further step of restricting the entire first class, except the six who had refused to participate, to the immediate vicinity of the academic buildings and barracks.

The story made headlines in New York City papers, and Congress launched an investigation at West Point. Cadets told the committee that in recent years whenever they had taken action against violators of their honor code, the accused would appeal to the War Department or to Congress for reinstatement.

Dishonorable men were thus reinstated, in the opinions of the cadets, far too many times. Cadets felt that they had no choice but to take such matters into their own hands to preserve the integrity of the Corps of Cadets.

Later practice tempered the surly attitude of cadets toward their Washington superiors. While MacArthur was a cadet, in 1901, a spontaneous rally began just outside MacArthur's barracks area, probably inspired by spring fever and a recent punishment handed out by the superintendent, Colonel Mills, to first classmen for excessive hazing of plebes. The assembly quickly spread, and soon practically the entire Corps of Cadets was out on the Plain, jeering the Tactical Department for the punishment meted out for hazing. The superintendent's quarters became the target of this cadet mass tantrum, and profanity directed at Colonel Mills himself was loud and boisterous.

Some enterprising group of cadets managed to unbolt the reveille cannon from its mount and rolled it to Colonel Mills's quarters, pointing the muzzle squarely at the front door. The rumor persists that Cadet MacArthur was the mastermind of this cannon episode. Mills was not amused. He took much authority away from cadets in addition to meting out mass punishment. He was, in the process, successful in bringing the practices that had grown to surround the honor code under some control by the authorities.

Mills began to use the informal cadet committees that would arise to deal with individual honor cases as unofficial investigatory bodies that reported to him. His judicious and firm decisions in several honor hearings earned him the grudging acceptance by the Corps of his jurisdiction over such cases. He would use the temporary cadet committees as "vigilance committees," thus, in effect, co-opting the cadets and bringing them under his own thumb.

By the time MacArthur became superintendent in 1919, the vigilance committee had become a permanent but unofficial body, composed of members from each class for the duration of their tenure as cadets. Superintendent MacArthur formalized the arrangement and renamed it the honor committee, with authority to investigate and report violations to the commandant.

He also charged the committee with the responsibility to draw up the code in written form, the result of which was the sentence that forms the essence of the code even to this day: "A cadet will not lie, cheat, or steal, nor tolerate those who do."

ATHLETICS AT WEST POINT

Of all the reforms instituted by Douglas MacArthur during his superintendency, the elevation of athletics to Olympian heights in the academy's program of development was perhaps the most far-reaching and long-lasting. He had been an accomplished athlete himself as a young man and cadet. He grew up on Army outposts with his own pony, on which he and his brother would ride out into the prairie, chasing rabbits and other animals for sport. Before coming to West Point he had attended West Texas Military Academy, where, by his last year there in 1897, he excelled in football and baseball and was the school tennis champ.

At age nineteen, when he entered West Point, his 133-pound body was not particularly overpowering on his five-foot, eleven-inch frame. Having survived his Beast hazing, he drove himself to accomplishment on the academy's baseball team. He never developed the skill of the top players, but his drive earned him a spot on the team with the nickname "Dauntless Doug." In 1901, in the first ever Army–Navy baseball game, he had his one moment of glory on West Point's fields of friendly strife. In the game, played at Annapolis, the midshipmen taunted him mercilessly about his father's exploits whenever he came to bat. He failed to get on base in his first two at-bats, but with the game tied, in his third time up to the plate, he was able to draw a walk. He then scored the winning run on an error by the center fielder. MacArthur dropped baseball in his senior year to concentrate on his studies and his duties as first captain.

His experience in World War I convinced him that good officers become great combat leaders if they have experience in athletic competition. His director of athletics, Capt. Matthew B. Ridgway, West Point Class of 1917, needed no convincing. MacArthur gave to him authority over cadets' time after classes to introduce a program of intramural athletics for all cadets not already a member of a varsity team.

In a surprising contrast to his lack of success with the Academic Board in forcing changes to the educational program, MacArthur was able to persuade the cadets' chaplain to relax the rules about not scheduling cadets' time on Sundays to permit athletic contests to be held on the Sabbath after chapel. The intramural program quickly became popular with cadets; it stressed contact sports and in many ways came to replace hazing as the outlet for pent-up cadet aggressiveness. MacArthur's intent was to capitalize on this to develop essential toughness and attitudes toward the contest of human wills that he believed would serve them well in future combat. Unlike Stephen Bird, MacArthur's poetic bent found acceptance when he composed the stanza that is now carved in stone at West Point:

> Upon the fields of friendly strife
> Are sown the seeds
> That, upon other fields on other days
> Will bear the fruits of victory.

MacArthur found particular pleasure in promoting the varsity sports at West Point. During the war years football was cut back, since most young men were drafted into the war effort. Army's schedule was limited to just one game in 1918, against a pickup team formed from among Army trainees. Upon MacArthur's appointment as superintendent, President Woodrow Wilson told him, "General, I want the football game between West Point and Annapolis renewed. If we could only extend and expand this sport throughout the world, perhaps we would not need a League of Nations." Later, President Harding visited West Point and asked MacArthur, "How goes my favorite group of cadets—the football team?"

MacArthur stretched the rules on behalf of West Point's teams, asking legislators to reserve their appointments for especially talented athletes and extending additional privileges to varsity team members. On occasion he would allow officers assigned to the academy as football coaches a special weekend leave to earn extra money playing football in the semi-professional leagues that had begun to spring up in the early 1920s.

The superintendent took a special interest in his fourth class committee chairman, Earl Blaik, who was one of the academy's most accomplished athletes. Blaik's best sport was football, but he was also a star baseball player in the spring season and an accomplished guard on the basketball team. Blaik could not hit a curveball, and one day while practicing, the superintendent, who would often spend his afternoons observing Army teams in practice, loosened his clothing and stepped up to instruct his protégé.

Blaik was more brawn than brain as an athlete, and the instruction apparently had little impact. Blaik was a physically well-developed outfielder, and his mistakes on the diamond were mental. His basketball play was likewise characterized more by contact than finesse, and he was ejected from one important game, against New York University, before the first half was over. His reputation for physical contact on the fields of friendly strife was of legendary proportions. His aggressiveness carried over from the football field to his relationship with the Tactical Department, where he was often at odds with what he considered to be the trivialities and monotony of the regimentation of life as a cadet.

As with the honor code, Douglas MacArthur did not invent something in his athletic program that had not already been present in some form at West Point for a long time. Cadets managed to get away with a clandestine, unscheduled soccer game as early as 1825. An undocumented factoid persists among graduates of West Point that Cadet Abner Doubleday in 1839 first drew up the field and rules for baseball on the Plain at West Point. In 1890 a cadet baseball team became the first athletic squad to be permitted to play off post, turning in a record of two wins and one tie in a series of games with baseball clubs from Philadelphia, New York, and Governor's Island. That year was also the moment of birth for football at the U.S. Military Academy.

It was another ambitious cadet, Dennis Michie, who brought football to West Point, and he did it by executing a most exquisite deception of the Academic Board in the summer of 1890.

Seven

In the Beginning There Was Football

Dennis Michie knew very well how to get his way with the Academic Board; his father was a very powerful member of it. Lieutenant Peter Michie had been assigned to the faculty of West Point in 1867 shortly after his own graduation. The elder Michie, Class of 1863, had fought in the Army of the Potomac under General McClellan and later in the Union Army, which had taken Gen. Robert E. Lee's surrender at Appomattox. Michie was selected by the entrenched professors at the academy to become one of them, to return for the remainder of his Army career to perpetuate the indoctrination of generations of young officers.

Young Dennis was born into the Michie family at West Point in 1870 and was an endearing personality among officers assigned to the post. By the time he returned to West Point as a cadet from his prep school away from home, he had been exposed to the new game of football. When his father was the senior professor on the Academic Board, Dennis connived during summer leave with some midshipmen to have the U.S. Naval Academy issue a challenge to West Point to a football contest for that fall.

The challenge letter was read aloud to cadets at the noon meal in the mess hall, and all men who weighed 180 pounds or more were ordered to report for tryouts. The administration could hardly turn away from such a challenge, and the elder Michie persuaded the Academic Board to permit the game to be played on the Plain.

Young Dennis was now the proud leader of Army's first football team, which at that point consisted only of himself. Michie found just enough men willing to risk themselves for the glory and honor of the academy to field a full team plus three substitutes. The biggest linemen weighed in at best at 190 pounds, with the running backs in the 140s. One such lineman, John Heavey, when told to tackle the oncoming running back, picked him up and slammed him down on the ground, knocking him out cold. Only Michie, Leonard Prince, and Butler Ames had ever played the game before.

The Army team of 1890 had no plays and no practices other than on Saturday afternoons or when drill and ceremonies were canceled because of bad weather. They had to obtain special permission to change out of their cadet gray for practice sessions. For conditioning, Michie had them fall in for a morning run a half hour before reveille.

In contrast, the Navy team had been playing for some years. When they arrived at West Point for the game, mythology holds that a goat that was wandering loose in a sergeant's yard kicked up its heels as the midshipmen approached. They took it as a sign and adopted the goat as a mascot during the game for luck.

They needed no such luck. Navy's superior experience was evident before the game began. As the midshipmen walked onto the field they formed up on one side and ran through a series of warm-up exercises in cadence. The Navy had also shipped a number of spectators from the academy who were added to the population of the entire West Point garrison, which had turned out on the Plain to watch the contest. As Army's players walked onto the field, the commandant told them, "I shall slug* the first Army player who leaves the field in an upright position."

The couple of thousand fans did not really get to see a contest.

---

*"Slug" refers to a punishment of great magnitude for grievous offenses and might often amount to dozens of hours marching in the area or weeks of confinement to quarters.

Navy took the opening kickoff at twenty yards. In their first set of downs the Army crowd watched in amazement as Navy's quarterback called out such commands as "Clear decks for action," "Helm's a Lee," and "Reef top sails." Each command had a specific meaning to the players and guided them in, around, and through the Army line. Michie caught on quickly and tried to improvise with such plays as "In battery, heave," "Left wheel," and "Forward guide center."

The faculty tried to help by invoking the honor code at one point. When the Navy kicker faked a punt and ran for a touchdown, Army spectators claimed he had broken his word. But it did not help. The mids eventually scored five unanswered touchdowns (for 4 points apiece) and kicked two 2-point field goals. The final score was Navy 24, Army 0. At Army posts around the country the response was to pull together to support the Brave Old Army Team with monetary contributions to buy uniforms and hire a coach to help build a more competitive squad for an anticipated grudge match the next year.

Young Michie recruited a local prep school coach who eventually agreed to take the job but would not accept the pay that had been raised by officers and alumni. Coach Harry L. Williams had played for Yale and toughened up the cadets with regular practices and determined effort two times per week. Williams led the team through a record of 3 wins, 1 loss, and 1 tie on the eve of the Navy game of 1891. The hardened cadets took the game to Navy, winning, 32–16.

It was a bloody, gruesome game. Four players were knocked out in the course of play. Army's Dennis Michie and Navy quarterback Worth Bagley apparently developed some kind of one-on-one feud during the game that carried over into the next two years' contests. But by the time they graduated in 1894 they had developed a close friendship off the field, with each having led his squad to two victories over the rival academy during the first four years of this, by then, nationally popular and highly competitive contest.

THE FULL VIGOR OF YOUTH
Both football players served their country with distinction in their

respective military services. During the Spanish-American War, Bagley was an officer on the U.S.S. *Winslow*. In 1898, while patrolling in the Caribbean near Cuba, the *Winslow* took a cannon shell in her engine room. Bagley valiantly tried to get the ship under control, but was killed when another round hit the ship. He was the only U.S. naval officer killed in that war.

Michie was a captain in the 17th Infantry during the Spanish-American War. His regiment was present at the Battle of Santiago in July 1898. Captain Michie returned from a reconnaissance to report the proximity of Spanish troops. When he returned to lead his men on a patrol along the San Juan River, searching for the enemy, Michie was shot and killed by a Spanish sharpshooter.

The Army–Navy game lived on to become one of the nation's most intense rivalries. After the 1893 game an argument nearly led to a fatal duel, resulting in the cancellation of the game until 1899. By then Army had developed a challenging football schedule and taught its players an especially brutal style of play. Army's coach after Michie was Yale football standout Harmon Graves, whose major accomplishment in his brief two-year stint was to secure one midweek practice session amid an 8–4 record for his teams playing against the likes of Harvard, Yale, and other East Coast powerhouses.

In 1899 the Navy game was renewed after a change in secretaries of war and in West Point's leadership. After Army upset Navy in that game, the rivalry attracted even greater national attention and the game had to be moved to Franklin Field in Philadelphia. By 1901 the game had grown too large even for that twenty-five-thousand-seat arena, and scalpers could get forty dollars per ticket.

In 1903, Navy, stung by consecutive losses, challenged Army's player eligibility practices, claiming that Army's age limit at entrance of twenty-one years old gave the cadets an unfair advantage over the midshipmen, who could be no older than twenty when entering Annapolis. But West Point responded by pointing out that the Naval Academy student body was twice the size of the Corps of Cadets, giving them a larger pool of players to recruit from. The game went on.

But the game got even more brutal as well. Across the nation, in 1905, eighteen men were killed playing college football. The Army–Navy game that year resulted in eleven serious injuries. That was a very large number in the days when players played both defense and offense and teams carried only about a half dozen substitutes for each game. President Theodore Roosevelt, himself an avid football fan and no stranger to the rigors of combat, was appalled. He threatened to abolish football and equated its brutality with cheating at cards.

Some changes were made, but the deaths and injuries continued. In the 1909 Army game with Harvard, Cadet Eugene Byrne was one of thirty college football men to be killed on the fields of friendly strife. The tragedy ended Army's season after Harvard's "flying wedge" ran right over Byrne and left him with a broken neck. After rule changes made the game a bit less murderous, Army continued play in the 1910 season.

The pre–World War I years of collegiate football were dominated by Army teams. Several West Point players were selected on All-America teams, and many cadet football men would later prove their combat mettle, including George S. Patton, Omar Bradley, and Dwight Eisenhower. Army teams would play only the most difficult of opposing teams to maintain their reputation for toughness.

In 1913, that scheduling policy led to a matchup for Army with a team that came to rise above the contest with Navy in inciting emotion and intensity. That was the first time Army played Notre Dame.

Notre Dame's first football game had been three years earlier than West Point's. By the turn of the century, Notre Dame was playing a couple of big regional games each year, along with eight or so local-area college teams. As football became a national preoccupation, colleges such as West Point and Notre Dame began to set their football players apart from the rest of the student body, at least in terms of their age, size, and academic potential.

Elmer Oliphant, one of Army's all-time greats, for example, played for Purdue for three years before he came to West Point, where he played for four more years. Red Blaik, of course, had played for Miami University before becoming a cadet. Notre Dame, too, had begun to recruit players, and by 1909 twelve of its players were from outside Indiana. In trying to elevate its program, Notre Dame tried to schedule a game in 1912 with the infamous Carlisle Indians—including the famous Jim Thorpe—coached by Pop Warner. Warner's approach to football epitomized the sport in the first decade of the twentieth century; he would keep some of the proceeds from his games for himself and bet heavily on the outcome of the Indians' games. Warner would not grant Notre Dame a spot on his schedule in 1912.

At the end of the 1912 season, Notre Dame posted an unblemished 7–0 record but lost money at a time when worse teams were turning a profit for their schools. Notre Dame made a decision to break into the big time and hired a professional athletic administrator and coach, Jesse Harper, to professionalize their entire varsity sports operation. Harper seized an opportunity that was created on the 1913 calendar when Yale would not play Army. Coach Harper wrote to the academy's team manager, and the slate was drawn.

It was at this 1913 game that Notre Dame introduced the forward pass to the big-time eastern schools. Quarterback Gus Dorais connected with Knute Rockne on thirteen passes out of twenty-three attempts as unknown Notre Dame beat the heavily favored Army team. Notre Dame ran away with the game, after scratching out a 14–3 halftime lead, by a final score of 35–13. A new rivalry was born, and for several seasons the Army–Notre Dame contest commanded as much or more national attention as the Army–Navy game. By 1920 the Army–Notre Dame game had grown so big it had to be played in New York City.

Much more than the schools' reputations was at stake in these games. Gambling on college football in America was profligate. Even the coaches and players would bet on the game, with each team betting on themselves. The Army–Notre Dame game became a major wagering event in the country, with players, coaches, and faculty from each side pooling their money and handing it over to a neutral third party during the game. But big money quickly corrupted sports in America; the most infamous result of which was the Black Sox scandal in baseball, in which games had been fixed.

RED BLAIK, END

The 1919 Army squad was a team that rarely passed. It preferred to brutalize its way downfield to score. Line coach "Pot" Graves was a butcherous coach who could be heard telling his players to draw blood in practice. The experience convinced Blaik that football was the closest thing there is in peacetime to war, although he had never experienced combat himself.

Army's head coach then, Charlie Daly, had been in the job since 1913 and had a notoriously explosive personality. His approach was as much mental as physical, and he would write such inspirational decrees on the locker room blackboard as "Carry the fight to the enemy and keep it there all afternoon" and "Break any rule to win the game." That 1919 team went 6–3, losing to Notre Dame, Syracuse, and Navy.

Red Blaik was at his best on defense. In the 1919 game against Syracuse he got in on more tackles than anyone else, throwing Syracuse running backs for a loss each time they came his way. On offense he played right end, but since Army at the time rarely employed the forward pass, he usually blocked for a running back and rarely went out for a pass reception.

Blaik, along with most of the other starters, was to have been given a rest during an early November game at Tufts preceding the Navy contest. Tufts was judged to be a weak team, but it rained that day in Medford, Massachusetts, and the Tufts eleven finished the first half unexpectedly with a commanding two-touchdown lead. Blaik and the others on the first team were sent to dress out and play in the second half, barely pulling the victory out for the Brave Old Army Team. But the rain that day was incessant, and Blaik came down with a serious case of influenza.

He missed the next game, at Villanova, and found himself still in the hospital the Saturday before the Navy game. The supe was concerned for his young charge and would with some frequency provide Blaik with chauffeured drives around the countryside. Doctors prescribed a three-times-a-day dose of sherry to help build his strength more quickly. Blaik played in the Navy game, nearly every minute, and although he was weak from his bout with the flu, he managed to get in on many tackles. Toward the end of the game he took a midshipman's finger in his eye, sending him out of the game and back into the hospital.

MacArthur put Blaik on leave and excused him from semester exams. He was able to finish the year with his class and graduate in 1920, winning the saber for being the outstanding athlete in his graduating class. But even the injury could not keep Blaik off the fields of friendly strife. He played baseball and had a good defensive outing in Army's 10–6 loss to Navy on the diamond. During June Week Blaik competed on the academy's baseball and track teams.

With his father watching proudly and his fiancée, Merle McDowell, looking on worriedly, Red Blaik won the Corps' one-hundred- and two-hundred-yard-dash competitions the very morning the Army baseball team was scheduled to play against an all-Army championship team of soldiers from the 7th Infantry Regiment. Blaik claims he saw double while he was at bat because of the strain of the track meet. He struck out all four times at bat as his father surely wondered how such a son could have won the athletic saber.

Eight

Coach Blaik

Red Blaik marched in his last parade as a cadet on the day before his graduation in June 1920. He was a color bearer for the brigade, marching at exactly the center point in the Long Gray Line, carrying the flag of the U.S. Military Academy. His classmate Milton Shattuck was the other color bearer, carrying Old Glory. Shattuck had the responsibility always to carry the American flag a bit higher than the academy flag and always on Blaik's right, in keeping with the regulations on the precedence of colors.

Blaik's thoughts raced back to a day in March when he and Shattuck marched in a parade in New York City honoring the return of another American Army division, which had come home after the occupation duty that followed World War I. The colors formed a single rank of four men, two color bearers and two color guards, marching between the middle companies, F and G—there were twelve companies in the Corps of Cadets in 1920, companies A through M. The letter J was not used so as not to be confused at a distance with I Company, since the large block letters on the company flag, or guidon, look so much alike. In the parade through Manhattan the Corps had marched in columns of platoons, three platoons per company, making for a magnificently long formation.

That day in March it was so unusually warm that Shattuck had passed out from the heat. As they marched, Blaik had noticed out of the corner of his eye that his classmate had been weaving and wavering, and Red managed to grab the American flag just as "Mit" crashed to the ground. It would have been enough of a disgrace to allow the colors to fall in any ceremony. A parade to honor war heroes was far too important nationally to permit the flag to hit the ground, especially when it was being carried by one who had not seen combat. Another cadet raced up to take the colors from Blaik's free hand. It was a good thing he did; Red was already having severe shoulder cramps from carrying the West Point flag on the long march down Fifth Avenue.

In June, on Graduation Day, the firsties were relieved of their duties to allow the rising seniors to take command for their first official review. Now Blaik could watch as someone else passed in review before him. He wondered if he would ever get a chance to compete again. He knew that in some units of the Army, soldiers were allowed to play on athletic teams formed from among the men, but he doubted that he would ever again see the fields of friendly strife in quite the same way. It had been only two years since he entered the academy as a plebe during the war, and somehow it seemed that he had gotten cheated out of two years of athletic competition by the war-shortened course of instruction.

As the Corps emerged from the sally ports and formed up on the Plain to march off in this last parade of the year, Blaik thought about his Beast barracks. Plebe year; what a year it had been. They had arrived by train up from New York City, just as dozens of entering classes had done before them. But for these men there was a war on, and that made a big difference in their Beast barracks. He remembered that as he had gotten off the train down by the river there had been upperclass cadets assembled there to escort them up the long hill to the barracks for their welcome to West Point. First there was the long line outside of Washington Hall, where he waited to be mustered into the Army and signed into the Corps of Cadets. There they were, hundreds of America's finest young men, dressed in coat and tie, high-collared starched white shirts all soaked through with sweat in the hot June sun.

Every man wore a straw hat in the style of the day and carried the one suitcase they had been authorized to bring with them from home.

Beast barracks in 1918 was much the same as it had been fifty years earlier. For three weeks the upperclasses had the responsibility to strip each new man of the most essential part of his ego and mold him into an indistinguishable brick, mortared into the wall that was the Long Gray Line. It was accomplished with time-tested techniques of drill and ceremony, military instruction, hazing, and lots of yelling and screaming at the new cadets. Many could not take it, and in part that was the purpose of Beast—to identify those who could not withstand stress before they got to the battlefield.

But most endured, surviving the three weeks of Beast to make it to camp. Once they made it into camp the task was not so much to keep up the basics of shining shoes, saluting, and personal hygiene; they had learned those skills in Beast. It was then the basics of military skills and tactics. Camp culminated in a ten-day tactical exercise in which the plebes were split into two armies, "white" and "gray," that marched and maneuvered against each other in the fields and woods surrounding the Plain. It did not matter so much which side won; for the plebes it was at least a few days that they were relatively free from all the harassment.

Blaik remembered it all now as mostly a big blur. He was three years older than most of his classmates and had already put up with a large dose of harassment and hazing when he entered his fraternity at Miami University. He had tolerated the worst of West Point's hazing because for him there was a light at the end of the tunnel. As soon as plebe summer was over there would be tryouts for the football team. That's what he had come to West Point for; he wanted to play for a nationally-recognized football squad, and at West Point he would have his chance. It did not matter that he had already played four years at another school; in those days there were few eligibility rules for college football, and even fewer schools that abided by them.

As he waited for the Corps to pass before him and his classmates formed in a line of company boxes on the Plain, his mind was filled with the tales of combat brought back by veterans of World War I, chief among them their superintendent, Brig. Gen. Douglas MacArthur. If all Army officers were like him, Blaik figured the Army would not be quite so bad. But Red knew better than that. Most of the officers he had come in contact with at West Point were from the "old school," hidebound by tradition. He could not imagine what the peacetime Army would be like, but he was pretty sure he would not like it.

There had already been plenty of war stories to go around once the student officers returned from Europe. These were the men who had been graduated early only to arrive in Europe just after the Armistice was declared. The Army in its wisdom took the class on a tour of wartime sights before deciding what to do with them. They were brought back to West Point to complete their studies and became part of that mess in 1919. They had walked the famous battlefields at Château-Thierry, Belleau Wood, Argonne, and others where thousands of Americans had died in stopping the Hun from his murderous advance through Europe. They toured the city of Rheims, where only thirteen of its seven thousand homes had not been hit by artillery. Though they had not seen a moment of combat, they returned to West Point with a mighty grand sense of their own self-worth in comparison to the cadets around them.

As M Company marched by, his company, Red Blaik hardly recognized the men he had lived with for so many months. Most of Blaik's time had been spent out of the company, either on varsity athletic teams or attending to his duties as vice president of his class and chairman of MacArthur's committee of first classmen selected to make recommendations on a new fourth class system. He wondered what it would have been like to have been a normal cadet, spending his afternoons on the M Company intramural teams rather than on the varsity Corps squads. He had had little free time to spend with his classmates in the barracks, and he never sat at company tables in the mess hall; he sat with his teams when MacArthur instituted the policy of allowing teams to have separate tables in the huge mess hall.

It almost did not matter. During his plebe year he had made the football team, but because of the war they played only one game. West Point beat a team of servicemen from Mitchell Field, 20–0, and that was it for 1918. It was not much of a football program. But the arrival of a new coach in July of that year changed all that.

Charles Daly knew his football. He had played for both Harvard and Army and had been selected an All-American quarterback four times. When he graduated from Harvard he was appointed to the academy from what was even then becoming the home district of the Joseph P. Kennedy family outside of Boston, Massachusetts. Daly was just the kind of coach that Blaik thrived under. Coach Daly was tough, and he was smart. When he left the job in 1922, he had compiled a record of 58–13–3, making him the second most winning football coach of all time at West Point. For Red Blaik, that was the only kind of coach to be like.

But as Cadet Lt. Earl Henry Blaik thought about the games he had played for Army, there was no doubt in his mind that he had fulfilled his purpose in coming to West Point. He had competed and won most of the time. That was what was most important: winning.

LIEUTENANT BLAIK

And now it was finally all over. Once the Corps passed in review he would no longer be a cadet. He would be a lieutenant, an officer in the U.S. Army. After six years of higher education he was not sure what it would be like, but he was sure that he would no longer get to enjoy the thrill of victory in quite the same way. In fact, with the war over and the country anxious to shed itself of the large Army it had built for that purpose, Blaik wondered just what was in store for him out there in the real Army.

Three months later, after an extended furlough, he found out. It was Kansas. He had been ordered to report to the Cavalry School at Fort Leavenworth. It was the real Kansas—hot, dry, and dusty in the summer. Blaik and his fellow lieutenants would sometimes drive in a beat-up old car to Junction City, where they would drink soda pop at Eisenhower's Drugstore. Yes, Eisenhower's; owned and operated by Dwight's brother. Yes, soda pop; not only was liquor prohibited by constitutional amendment, even cigarettes were outlawed at that time in the state of Kansas. Of course, he was resourceful enough to keep plenty of "skags" around, and an even more resourceful comrade built a make-shift distillery to process the apricot mash brought to them by their assigned servant. Blaik was glad to get his orders assigning him to the 8th Cavalry Regiment in the 1st Cavalry Division at Fort Bliss, Texas.

As soon as he reported for duty, in August 1920, the commanding general, himself a West Point graduate, found out that Red Blaik had been an outstanding outfielder on the academy nine. He had Blaik detailed immediately to play on the 1st Cavalry baseball team. No platoon leader time for Red Blaik! When baseball was over he coached and played on the division football team, and then in winter he played on the basketball team. Finally, in 1921, the regimental commander decided that Lieutenant Blaik had better get some troop time into his career, so he made him the commanding officer of E Troop, 8th U.S. Cavalry.

It was not as hard as it could have been on Blaik. While he had no experience in troop leading, he did have a wealth of under-standing and experience in the art of leadership. His style of command was to rely heavily on his noncommissioned officers, and he had some highly accomplished, veteran sergeants who took care of the details of running the troop for him. His top five troopers all had plenty of combat time in France and were highly decorated, tough hombres who could track down their sometimes wayward soldiers to the remotest tequila tents in Ciudad Juárez, just over the border from El Paso. Blaik left most of those kinds of details to them.

The closest Lieutenant Blaik came to seeing shots fired in anger was in 1922, when the cavalry at Fort Bliss was ordered out of the barracks to pursue a Mexican insurrectionist who had holed up near Ciudad Juárez. Blaik's E Troop led the march and conducted the reconnaissance at the site where the next day the entire garrison would cross the Rio Grande. When he returned to the fort to make his report, he found that his prey had surrendered to U.S. forces for protection from his own *compadres*.

A few days later the War Department telegraphed instructions to all Army posts to offer to give to any NCO or soldier a year's pay to leave the service before their enlistment was up. The next day Blaik's troop was reduced to 15 troopers from 135 the day before. From that point on, America had a truly "hollow" Army. Blaik and his fellow cavalrymen at Fort Bliss barely had time to exercise all their horses each day, much less conduct any drill or tactical training. Soon Blaik's E Troop was consolidated with another, and he lost his command.

In February 1922 the War Department extended the early resignation option to commissioned officers. Blaik saw that his chances for promotion were virtually nil. He submitted his letter of resignation on 15 March, and that same morning he was on a train headed back home to Dayton. As the train pulled out of the station, he saw out the window that his first sergeant had lined up the remaining troopers of his unit beside the tracks for a final salute. They had even brought his mount, "Lady," to stand with empty saddle in the customary send-off for departing cavalrymen.

He arrived in Dayton on 17 March. On the eighteenth the mailman delivered a letter that had followed him from Texas. It was from General MacArthur. The general wrote that he was being reassigned from West Point to the Pacific and wanted Blaik to come with him as aide-de-camp. It had apparently arrived at Fort Bliss the day Blaik had left and was forwarded to him in Dayton, Ohio. Although MacArthur's offer might have given his Army career a better chance than Fort Bliss would have, the letter was a day late, and Earl Blaik would never get to know the sting of battle.

ARMY AND THE FOUR HORSEMEN

While Red Blaik was playing outpost Army football in the deserts of West Texas, the Army team was thriving under Daly and his tough assistant coach, Pot Graves. In the fall of 1920 Army continued in its winning ways, including a record-setting score of 90–0 versus Bowdoin College. But it lost that year to Notre Dame and Navy. The 1921 team was 6–4, again losing to Notre Dame and Navy. That was the year Pot Graves quit. The 1922 squad was one of Army's winningest, at 8–0–2, finally defeating Navy, but settling for a scoreless tie in the Notre Dame game that year.

Notre Dame was beginning to be a rivalry of equal importance to that with Navy. This was the beginning of the Rockne era at Notre Dame. His innovative methods made Jesse Harper's deal to get Army to play Notre Dame as a schedule filler in 1913 a real winner. By the 1920s the Army–Notre Dame contest was being turned into an annual profit-maker and odds-beater for both schools. Gambling on the game was lucrative for both sides. For the 1920 game each team raised twenty-one hundred dollars for a winner-take-all pool that was held by a local tradesman.

Betting on your own team was just one of the motivational methods brought to college football by Rockne. Apparently it worked for at least some players. At halftime during the 1920 Army game, Rockne spotted his star, George Gipp, casually taking a smoke break during one of Rockne's trademark halftime speeches. The team was losing to Army, and the coach was trying to spur his players to a greater second-half effort. He yelled at Gipp, "Have you no interest in this game?" Gipp, later to be called the "Gipper," replied that he had four hundred dollars of his own money riding on the outcome. Gipp left the locker room and went into the second half to lead Notre Dame to a remarkable come-from-behind 28–17 win. His performance included a bit of acting on one play when an official caught him in the act of punching an Army player trying to bring him down. The "Gipper" feigned an injury and apparently convinced the referee that Army's player had committed an equally heinous offense, and no penalty was called on the play.

It was this 1920 Army–Notre Dame game that prompted one of Rockne's characteristic halftime motivational talks to his team. He yelled at his players for missing assignments and lackluster play. He would point out an error to a player, and the moment the player tried to explain what had happened, Rockne would cut him off in a burst of rage. His closing words of motivation were simple: "Go after them! Go after them! Knock 'em down. Tear 'em apart. Knock 'em down so they stay down!" It was part of the emotion that helped make the Army–Notre Dame series, in the hearts of many West Pointers, come to surpass the Navy game in importance.

In 1921 the game was so popular with New York City Notre

Dame fans—mostly successful alumni working in Manhattan—
that additional stands had to be constructed on the Plain to seat
them all. Hundreds made the trip to West Point for the day on
special trains chartered for the purpose. Rockne's pregame
thoughts were preoccupied with the memory of his former star,
George Gipp, who was not playing that year. Gipp had gotten
drunk in the winter after the 1920 season and spent the night out
in the cold, wet snow. He contracted pneumonia as a result and
soon died.

With the death of the "Gipper," Notre Dame no longer had the
speed and strength it once enjoyed, but Rockne compensated
with a new formation. The 1921 season was the one during which
football was introduced to the "Notre Dame shift." This was a clas-
sical Rockne innovation in which the running backs all started
moving before the ball was hiked to the quarterback. This gave
them a precious few steps ahead of the defenders and helped
them develop tremendous momentum before the Army team
could react. Army's coaches called the tactic unfair and for a while
would not allow the team to come back out on the field after the
first half. It didn't matter; Army lost the 1921 game to Notre
Dame, 28–0.

By 1923 the Army game had become such a crowd pleaser with
the Notre Dame crowd in New York City that they demanded the
game be played in the city rather than in the isolated Hudson
highlands at West Point. Army, which had just broken ground on
construction of a new stadium in the hills overlooking the campus, relented and agreed to play at the Polo Grounds. This was
the first year of play for the men who would later come to be called
the "Four Horsemen": Don Miller, Elmer Layden, Jim Crowley,
and Henry Stuhldreher.

As it turned out, because of a scheduling problem, the game
was played at Ebbets Field. Army, knowing that they would be playing before a largely hostile crowd, hired Elsie Janis, then a famous
actress, to perform a ceremonial kickoff before the game as a
crowd-pleasing stunt. When newspapers reported the plan a few
days before the game, Rockne handed out St. Christopher medals
to all his players to wear during the game and was quoted by

newspapers as saying, "Joan of Arc will kick for Notre Dame."
Army lost, 13–0.

Then, in 1924, one of the legends of the Brave Old Army Team
was formed out of the game with Notre Dame, this time at the
Polo Grounds. Rockne worked the press hard before the contest, and while the game itself was probably not of historic character, it became one immortalized in the annals of sports. Rockne
had written to a friend that the team was not good, but with all
the hype, reporters needed a story that went beyond the final
score (Notre Dame won, 13–7). Thus *New York Herald Tribune*
sportswriter Grantland Rice wrote of this game one of the most
famous paragraphs in sports history:

> Outlined against a blue, gray October sky, the Four Horse-
> men rode again. In dramatic lore they are known as Famine,
> Pestilence, Destruction, and Death. These are only aliases.
> Their real names are Stuhldreher, Miller, Crowley, and Lay-
> den. They formed the crest of the South Bend cyclone be-
> fore which another fighting Army team was swept over the
> precipice at the Polo Grounds this afternoon as 55,000 spec-
> tators peered down upon the bewildering panorama spread
> out upon the green plain below.

That was the only loss in 1924 for the Army team that went on
to beat Navy by a score of 12–0. In that game all those points were
scored by team captain Ed Garbisch on four dropkick field goals.

The 1925 season was a climax for both Notre Dame and Army.
The Four Horsemen had graduated, and Rockne took his 58–4–2
career record into the season riding on the backs of more than
forty inexperienced players, none of whom had made the starting squad before. His first three games were with easy teams, so
he experimented with his talent in what he called "practice
games." But this squad was no match for the seasoned Army team
of 1925.

West Point had lost the previous nine straight encounters with
Notre Dame and was hungry for a victory. Standout running back
Harry Wilson drew first blood for the cadets on a first-quarter

touchdown run in a pouring rain. Quarterback Harding then threw a forward pass to team captain Henry Baxter for a second unanswered touchdown. In the next sequence Notre Dame fumbled and Army's Bud Spraque picked it up and ran forty-five yards for Army's third TD. Army won, 27–0.

Knute Rockne characterized the contest as one in which "the best Army football team that I have seen since the World War met the greenest and youngest of all Notre Dame teams. . . ." The Notre Dame fans were not so noble, heckling Army's players and coaches throughout the game at Yankee Stadium. Seventy thousand fans, a record for the game of football in New York City, watched Army roll to victory as hundreds of thousands of dollars passed hands.

RED BLAIK, ASSISTANT COACH

In Dayton, Ohio, Mr. Earl Henry Blaik could only read about the Brave Old Army Team. It was a time in sportswriting when reporters could get away with embellishment, bombast, and outright lies. The fans loved it. For $150 or so a coach like Rockne could buy in a major daily newspaper an article that was not much more than a team press release. Red Blaik knew that the stories about Army and Notre Dame were mostly hyperbole, but he loved it. He thought that General MacArthur would love it, too, and he included with his correspondence the general clippings from Dayton papers about Army's football fortunes.

Reading about Army football was just about the most exciting part of Blaik's life after leaving the Army. For now, the thrill of his life was business. Red took up a partnership with his father in the real estate and insurance business in Dayton. He learned quickly how to make money, and his enterprise did well. By the spring of 1923 he accumulated enough cash to take out a building loan and, in partnership with his father, went into the construction business. More than a dozen homes in Dayton were built under contracts handled by the father-son team. Blaik and Son had the potential to become another chapter in the great American success story. But Red was restless.

In the fall of 1923 Red had generated enough income that he

felt he could become a family man himself. He married his high-school, college, and West Point sweetheart, Merle McDowell. For their honeymoon he decided to drive to West Point for the Army–Navy game. It was a three-day trip in his classy convertible Oakland. It was a rainy, miserable game in Baltimore, but Army had defeated the midshipmen in that weird game in which all 12 points were scored on field goals.

In a 1924 letter to General MacArthur (after he responded to the general's request that Blaik be his aide in the Philippines, Red continued to correspond with his former mentor), Blaik had commented that Army's football style had become somewhat staid. MacArthur's response reinforced in Blaik an incipient desire to coach: "I agree personally with what you say that the system of play at West Point is antiquatcd, too involved, and totally lacking in flexibility and adaptiveness," wrote the general. He continued, "Had I stayed at West Point, I intended introducing new blood into our coaching staff. Rockne of Notre Dame was the man I had in mind." Later that year his old coach at Miami University invited Red to help work with his ends.

It was an offer Blaik could not refuse. He coached Miami's ends in 1924 and again in 1925. Then, in 1926, Blaik had to face an even greater temptation. Another of his old coaches had gone on to greater glory to become head coach and athletic director at the University of Wisconsin. George Little spent a winter's night with the Blaiks and asked Red if he would come to Madison for the season and work with the ends on a team that had aspirations to a Big Ten title if not the national championship. Red discussed the proposition with his father, who somehow knew that Red was informing him of his decision, not really consulting.

Wisconsin did not win the Big Ten championship that year, and George Little moved on to concentrate on being the athletic director, allowing a new coach to be brought in. Meanwhile, the fiery redheaded ends coach from Dayton was beginning to attract some attention to himself. He was a tough coach; he drove his players relentlessly in practice, always making them run. One of Army's assistant coaches from Blaik's playing days, Biff Jones, was now the new head coach at West Point and was looking for some coaching help. He invited Blaik to come to Chicago to watch the Navy game at Soldier Field.

In 1926 Army was still a strong team. Coach and former All-American center John McEwan had built a nationally recognized program and left at the end of the 1925 season with a record of 18–5–3. In his first six games as Army's new head coach, Biff Jones had led the cadets to consecutive wins before the Notre Dame game. Notre Dame had more trouble with ticket scalpers than with Army. Notre Dame won, 7–0, on the strength of a sixty-three-yard run behind some of the strongest blocking in the nation. Army recovered the next week to beat Ursinus College before going into the Navy game.

The 1926 Army–Navy classic was again played at Chicago's Soldier Field. Notre Dame's Knute Rockne wanted to scout the game and figured that his own high-flying team would have no trouble with second-class Carnegie Technical Institute. He also stayed in Chicago to promote his team among the assembled sportswriters who would be selecting the national champion. He stayed at the Sherman Hotel, where most of the writers hung out, and so did Blaik. They crossed paths at breakfast on game day, and Blaik wondered to himself why Rockne was not with his own team. Rockne probably wished he had not stayed at Chicago after his team lost, 19–0, and the writers selected Stanford as the national champion for 1926.

In any case, they both were treated to a remarkable football contest. Jones, too, was overconfident that day, and he started Army's second-string players. The midshipmen, undefeated in 1926 and hungry for revenge from the previous year's 10–3 loss to Army, quickly took advantage of Jones's generosity and took a 14–0 first-half lead. Jones put the first team in, and they quickly gained a tie at 14. As the third quarter came to a close, a plebe halfback, a young man by the name of Christian "Red" Cagle, took the ball and ran it for a forty-three-yard touchdown to give Army a 21–14 lead with the point after kick. But Navy marched right back, and the game ended in a 21–21 tie.

After the game, Jones asked Blaik to join the West Point coaching staff for the 1927 season. Red told Biff that he would have to talk it over with his father and that he did not think that their current state of business affairs would allow it. But he really wanted to coach at Army, so he agreed that Jones would come to Dayton later that winter to talk it over. It turned out to be an easy sell; Blaik's father knew that his son's heart was not in the business. He agreed to let Red go for the season, but he realized that it would probably be the last time he would see his son as his business partner.

It was under Biff Jones that Red Blaik learned the fundamentals of coaching football. Jones was well organized, methodical, and thoroughly prepared for every contest. Each practice session had a plan; nothing was left to chance. And he was the man in charge. Although he encouraged discussion among his assistant coaches to argue the merits of trying new approaches, he made all the decisions and allowed no further dissent.

Jones added another new face to his coaching staff in 1927. Cadet Garrison ("Gar") Davidson had graduated from the academy that summer, having played four seasons at end under McEwan and Jones. Davidson had been the paragon of what a cadet should be. He was an outstanding scholar—his yearbook entry noted that many cadets who were having academic trouble could find plenty of help in his room. He was a member of the Honor Committee and was chosen for his outstanding leadership qualities to be "King of Beasts"—the highest-ranking upperclass cadet in charge of training the plebes—for new cadet Beast barracks in 1926.

Davidson was no martinet. As "King of Beasts" he was also responsible for the discipline and training of the upperclass detail assigned to supervise new cadet training. The commandant that year feared another congressional hearing on hazing, so he ordered the first class detail not to yell at all during Beast barracks under any circumstances. Whenever plebes committed some error or offense, company tactical officers would make verbal corrections in hushed tones. Gar Davidson protested to the com that this practice undermined the cadets' authority as leaders. The com not only dismissed his argument, he also took offense at the protest and did not, as was customary, select Davidson to be the cadet first captain for the regular academic year.

As graduate assistant coach, Gar Davidson was not afraid to tell the other coaches what he thought of their leadership styles and techniques. The one he thought most objectionable of all was Red Blaik. He thought that Blaik was a charmer to anyone who was not a threat to his esteem, but an overbearing bully to anyone who might be his rival.

Red Blaik's personality did nothing to defuse the incipient personality clash with Davidson. It was Blaik's first year as a full-time assistant coach, and he made no secret that he held Army football in very low regard compared to his previous teams at Miami University and Wisconsin. As the coach responsible for Army's passing game he drilled his ends and backs hard, and they uniformly resented it. At midseason they mutinied and came to Gar Davidson, asking him to intervene with the head coach, Biff Jones, on their behalf. From that day on, Blaik and Davidson began a feud that was to last for sixty years. Both men took their hatred of each other to the grave.

Starting with the 1927 season, Jones decided that Army football would key on their new running wonder, Red Cagle. Cagle had come to Army before West Point complied with emerging eligibility rules among college teams. He had already played for Southwestern Louisiana State and was the fifth best running back in the country when he entered West Point as a plebe in 1926. He was an unorthodox player; he let his chin strap hang loose so that, when pursued from behind, his 178 pounds could not be dragged down by the helmet. One of his finest games was Army's 1927 encounter with Notre Dame.

WIN ONE FOR THE GIPPER

By 1927, the Army–Notre Dame game was a national event. In the absence of professional football leagues, college ball was the national football league of the day, and Army–Notre Dame was just about the premier rivalry in the country. It was bigger than Army–Navy, since Navy teams were not really competitive nationally at the time.

Navy had chosen to abide by the evolving practice among many schools that players would be eligible for a maximum of three varsity seasons no matter which schools they might play for. The practice had emerged out of response to injuries that had occurred and because of a concern that big-time football was harming the academic focus of the college experience. Against the likes of Army's five- and six-year men, such schools had little hope of remaining peers.

Not so with Notre Dame. Knute Rockne had built a team that commanded a national following that was, by 1927, quite lucrative for the school. With its proximity to New York City, the Army game attracted the attention of tens of thousands of Catholics who had adopted the South Bend school as their home football team. They would get tickets from successful New York Notre Dame alumni, who would get tickets from the school as business favors for customers or clients. They became known as the "subway alumni." For the 1927 game, tickets sold out long in advance of the season, and there were none available to the general public. More than one hundred thousand requests for tickets had to be turned away by Yankee Stadium officials.

The Army head coach, Biff Jones, had concentrated most of his efforts of the season to avenge the 7–0 loss in 1926 to Notre Dame's powerful tackling and blocking game. With Red Cagle added to his All-American backfield, they would have to catch Jones's two stars before they could pound them, and hardly anyone had touched Cagle or Wilson in five previous seasons.

Assistant Coach Red Blaik was responsible for the backs and thus for bringing out the best in both "Light Horse" Harry Wilson and Red Cagle. Cagle was such a natural athlete that he needed little coaching, either in practices, when Cagle would sometimes even help his blockers learn the finer techniques of bringing a man down, or in games themselves. Wilson, too, was a gifted athlete, a little larger and a bit slower than Cagle. Wilson also had a reputation for modesty both on and off the field. Blaik had little problem teaching or motivating his two star running backs behind Army's balanced line attack.

Rockne knew that his "Fighting Irish" (the nickname finally stuck in the 1927 season when a former Notre Dame student, writing for New York's *Daily News,* used the term prolifically) would have their work cut out for them. Most sportswriters picked undefeated Notre Dame to win. But their coach realized that Army was very strong after a good recruiting year. He worked them hard in practice. He changed the uniform color from dark blue to bright green just for this game to help them distinguish themselves among each other on the field in the midst of the black jerseys of the Army team. And as a subterfuge, he assigned new numbers to all his players to confuse the Army players and coaches.

It was all to no avail. Army's running game ran away from Notre Dame. In the first quarter, Cagle took the snap from the center at his deep set back position six yards back. For the next forty-eight yards he cut back, left, and right, ran diagonally ahead and across to completely dazzle the Notre Dame defense, and scored Army's first touchdown. In the third quarter he took a pass from the halfback and scooted across the goal line to score Army's second TD. Spike Nave, Army's quarterback, intercepted a Notre Dame pass in the fourth quarter and ran it back sixty yards to cap an 18–0 win by the Brave Old Army Team.

The 1927 Army–Navy contest was almost anticlimactic. Army had lost only to Yale that year, and would wind up in the top five teams nationally. The Brave Old Army Team had few problems with the midshipmen, although the 14–9 score belied the ease with which Army manhandled the three-year men from Annapolis. Harry Wilson was playing in his last game, and Red Cagle refused to score on several opportunities so that his friend would have the chance to get the glory. After the game, the Naval Academy withdrew from future contests with Army until West Point agreed to comply with the three-year eligibility rule, as Navy had done.

Blaik knew that he wanted to coach again in 1928, and he was pretty sure that Biff Jones would ask him to come back that fall. Cagle would have two more years of eligibility, and Army was sure to be a national contender. Somehow coaching a national championship team more than made up for his lost opportunities to play four years for the Brave Old Army Team when he had been a cadet. After another weekend of persuasion, Jones was able to talk Blaik's father into releasing him from his family business responsibilities for another season.

It was a powerful Army team that took on some of the toughest teams in the nation in 1928. But it was the Notre Dame game that brought the greatest pregame anticipation. The Irish were having an off year. Nine starters from the 1927 team had graduated, and most of those who did start in 1928 were underclassmen. They had barely beaten the outclassed Loyola of New Orleans eleven, then were massacred by Wisconsin, then again barely beat Navy. Next they lost to Georgia Tech in Atlanta, and had a one-week break in play before returning to South Bend to defeat Drake. On the road again they barely won over Penn State before their return to Indiana to prepare for Army.

This was to be the greatest Army–Notre Dame game in the fifteen-year series. Army entered the game unbeaten and favored to win over the team that Rockne was trying to rebuild. Tickets were even more difficult to get than in the 1927 sellout, and sportswriters around the country hyped the game as well. Two sportswriters in particular brought to their pregame articles the memory of Notre Dame's great running back of 1919 and 1920, George Gipp, who had led Notre Dame to that great come-from-behind win in the 1920 game with Army.

Rockne knew he had his work cut out for him; he tried every motivational trick he had in his book before the game and invented some new ones. He was moved by the press coverage to speak of Gipp with writer Grantland Rice the night before the game. As the team walked up to the Yankee Stadium locker room, New York City's finest Irish Catholic cops, lining the road for "security," were yelling "Beat Army!" along the way. He had heavyweight boxing champ Jack Dempsey speak to the team in the locker room just before they ran out onto the field.

In the first half the game was typical Army–Notre Dame combat—head-to-head, bruising play. Both teams went into their locker rooms scoreless. Army was playing Notre Dame in a man-to-man defense, and the Irish were beginning to take advantage of the inherent vulnerability of that strategy by threading a forward pass every now and then to gain considerable yardage. But Army's hard-nosed ends and backs, under Blaik's tough style of play, always stopped them cold and prevented the score.

We don't know what Jones and Blaik said to the Army team at halftime to inspire the cadets to press on in the second half. What Rockne said to his men has become part of American sports mythology after having been immortalized in a movie *(Knute Rockne, All-American)* starring Ronald Reagan as George Gipp. As the legend goes, Rockne did not talk much about the game. Instead he spoke of Gipp and his deathbed wish, known only to Rockne and revealed for the first time since his death eight years earlier:

> He turned to me: "I've got to go, Rock," he said. "It's all right. I'm not afraid." His eyes brightened in a frame of pallor. "Some time, Rock," he said, "when the team's up against it; when things are wrong and the breaks are beating the boys—tell them to go in there with all they've got and win just one for the Gipper. I don't know where I'll be then, Rock. But I'll know about it and I'll be happy."

It probably did not happen that way, but sportswriters of the day and Hollywood producers since then have conspired to leave us with the legend.

Whatever he really said, Rockne's speech did not immediately carry the Irish out to roll over the Brave Old Army Team. Red Cagle scored the first touchdown of the game, going nineteen yards on the ground into Notre Dame's end zone early in the third quarter. Notre Dame tied the game late in the third quarter with a plunge over Army's goal-line stand from the two-yard line. It was 6–6 in the fourth quarter when Rockne sent in a substitute, Johnny O'Brien, who had not yet played in the game.

O'Brien's job was to bring in a play, a post pattern all the way to the goal line. Throwing from Army territory, the Irish passer threw a perfect strike to O'Brien, who had gone deep into Army's zone. O'Brien, who would forever after be known as "One Play" O'Brien, had nearly dropped the ball on his way to immortality, then came back out of the game, having done his job. It was 12–6, with barely enough time left in the game for one more Army offensive drive.

Red Cagle took the Notre Dame kick across the fifty-yard line deep into Notre Dame territory. The "Golden Cutback," as Blaik had nicknamed him, had almost broken through for the score but was brought down by the last Irishman between him and the goal on the Notre Dame thirty-five. There was one minute left in the game. On the first-down play he took the ball from the center and drove around the left end on a sweep to the ten. But on that play, Cagle was hit hard, and the exhaustion and battering took their toll; he had to be led from the field.

On first and goal Army went with a short pass to the Notre Dame four-yard line, then blasted straight ahead on a run to within a foot of the goal line. It was 12–6 with only seconds left to play in the game. The subway alumni were silent, ninety thousand of them holding their breath (the *New York Herald Tribune* reported on 11 November 1928 that the standing-room-only crowd was joined by more than five thousand watching from overlooking roofs and fire escapes) while the cadets chanted in unison. The Army team, believing they had been awarded a first down, did not hurry out of the huddle. They were even more deliberate and confident at the line of scrimmage. Then, just before the ball was snapped, as Army fans rose to see the tying touchdown, referee Walter Eckersall, a writer for the *Chicago Tribune* who had been hired to officiate at the game, blew the whistle signaling time had expired.

Immediately Biff Jones protested, claiming that the Army team had earned a first down and another play by taking the ball past the one-yard line. Newspapers took up Army's cause, but Rockne countered that the referees had erroneously spotted the ball past the one-yard line anyway. For Army the protests were of no avail, and the score stood at 12–6, Notre Dame. For Red Blaik it was an indigestible loss; he had never felt lower.

Nine

The Whip

Army football was successful in the 1928 season, ending with a record of 8–2. Its only other loss was a 26–0 humiliation by Stanford. The success of the Brave Old Army Team was measured not only in its win-loss record; the cadets also turned quite a profit in 1928. There was enough to send the team the following year in a special train equipped with Pullmans to San Francisco on the West Coast for the game at Stanford.

Red Blaik had to have Biff Jones come to Dayton to talk his father into letting Red go to coach Army for the 1929 season. This time the old man did not put up much resistance. Red's mind was not on the business anymore. Blaik was in for his fourth season as an assistant coach at Army. But it was a mediocre season at best. Blaik blamed his players for becoming seized with a complacent attitude because of the 1928 season. Red Cagle suffered from a banged-up shoulder that year and did not play up to his promise.

He did play against Notre Dame that year. Rockne was in the hospital with phlebitis, but the game was again a sellout. This time reports were that more than three hundred thousand ticket seekers had to be turned away at Yankee Stadium. For other big Notre Dame games Rockne would not be held back, and he made the hospital staff roll him out onto the field in a wheelchair. But the Irish were 8–0 going into this one and were practically assured of the national title. Army was still tough, but were a mediocre 5–3. Rockne simply called in to the team before game time and listened on the radio.

In spite of the stock market crash in October, scalpers were selling Army–Notre Dame tickets for three hundred dollars. The temperature was at or below zero during the entire game, and the fans kept warm with bottles of illegal liquor that police had winked at as it came into the stadium. The field was frozen as the Brave Old Army Team played the Irish to a scoreless tie in the first quarter.

Then, just before halftime, Red Cagle dropped back to throw a pass to Carl Carlmark. But the throw was too high for the bitter wind that blew that day, and a man by the name of Jack Elder intercepted it for Notre Dame. Jack Elder was not just another ordinary Notre Dame football player. He held the world's record for the sixty-yard dash. He caught Cagle's toss at his own four-yard line and flashed along the sideline for ninety-six yards to make the only score of the game.

In the Stanford game in 1929 Cagle came out of the game with an injury for the last time in his career. In May 1930, while recovering from a tonsillectomy just before graduation, Cagle announced that he intended to resign his commission soon after graduation. Presumably this was so he could pursue a coaching career. But in the course of the outrage at the academy, word came from Cagle's home state of Louisiana that he was married. In fact, as he then admitted, he had secretly married in the summer of 1928.

This was not only against academy rules, it was also considered to be an offense against the honor code. A cadet was not to be married and upon entering the academy was required to sign a statement certifying that he was not, nor ever had been, married. Cagle had committed the worst of sins: He had lied on an official statement. There was no forgiveness. Even more than a decade later, when he tried to volunteer for service in World War II, the Army would not commission him.*

---

*Apparently Cagle resigned rather than risk court-martial. Garrison Davidson says he was not convicted of an honor violation.

The year of 1929 was the last year of coaching at Army for Col. Lawrence McCeney "Biff" Jones. In keeping with Army and West Point policy, the head coaching job at Army was just another four-year tour of duty for an Army officer, and it was then Jones's turn to move on. He left with a record of 30–8–2 and later went on to coach at LSU, where he once threw Governor Huey P. Long out of his locker room at halftime. The next year he was at Oklahoma and in 1937 went to Nebraska where he remained through 1941. He was replaced at West Point by Maj. Ralph I. Sasse, Class of 1916.

THE NEW COACH

Sasse had distinguished himself in World War I in the newly formed tank corps, then a branch of the horse cavalry. As an assistant coach at Army under Jones he had developed a close friendship with Blaik, a fellow ex-cavalryman. Whereas Biff Jones had been methodical, dispassionate, and highly organized, Sasse was flamboyant, fiery, and emotional. When he spoke to the Corps of Cadets in the mess hall the night his appointment as head coach was announced he proclaimed, "I promise you fireworks!" His next official act was to appoint Red Blaik as his coaching chief of staff.

Blaik was by 1930 a geographic bachelor at West Point. Merle managed to keep their home together back in Dayton, with their two sons, Bill, who had been born in April 1927, and Bob, who was born in May 1929. Many of his fellow assistant coaches were also bachelors, and they kept each other company, giving the Tactical Department fits when it came to the proper deportment and demeanor expected of an officer and a gentleman.

Red Blaik became the teamster of the staff. He was hard, ruthless, and driven. Players called him "the Whip." He relished the reputation for meanness. He was merciless in requiring windsprints from his players, and he was constantly yelling at them—"speed" for the running backs, "heads" to the entire second team to get into their huddle more quickly. Blaik was also the strict enforcer of the team's training rules—no smoking, early lights out, proper diet. He could not, however, control the vices of his boss, and whenever Sasse would go out on one of his occasional binges, Blaik would accompany his friend to bring him back safely.

Gar Davidson managed to extend his stay too, much to Blaik's chagrin. An instructor in the Natural and Experimental Philosophy Department was caught "sparking"* another officer's wife. In those days that was an unpardonable sin among professional officers, and the offender was summarily reassigned to another post. Gar Davidson had been on orders to report to duty in Panama, but when he heard that the faculty position suddenly came open he persuaded the superintendent to get those orders revoked so he could stay on as a coach while teaching. Blaik's nemesis would not go away.

The 1930 season was another good one for the Brave Old Army Team. Sasse broke away from Jones's balanced line attack and moved Army to the double wing. In a key game against national powerhouse Yale, three Army defenders hit Yale's star receiver on a pass interception that knocked Yale's player unconscious and out of the game. Army tied Yale, and sportswriters accused West Point of particularly savage play with the intention of forcing the man out of the game. Army took an undefeated 8–0–1 record into Soldier Field in Chicago for the annual Notre Dame extravaganza.

This was one of Rockne's greatest teams ever. He invented a platoon system under which he actually had three complete teams dressed for a game in addition to numerous substitutes. This allowed him to play an offensive unit with a different set of players from the defensive unit. At the time the practice was unheard of and considered to be unsportsmanlike. But his players were nearly always fresh, and anyway neither Notre Dame nor Army could ever be accused of playing by the rules, much less of conforming to common practice.

This game was played on another miserable weather day. The field was a muddy mess, and the smog of the Chicago air could be sliced at game time. The two great teams played through nearly all of four quarters to a scoreless tie. Late in the game Notre Dame scored and kicked the extra point for a 7–0 lead. Then Army ran

---

*The term of the times referring to the act of consummating an extra-marital affair.

back a blocked punt for a TD in the waning moments of the final quarter. The score was 7–6 Notre Dame.

Once again the decision in an Army–Notre Dame contest went down to the last minute. Sasse was content to kick the point after and preserve Army's undefeated record at 8–0–2 with a tie to the national champions. But Blaik would have none of it. He argued forcefully for a dropkick play to go for a three-point field goal. His hotheaded persistence in seeking the win, not a tie, was overheard by a few sportswriters near the sideline. Blaik won over his friend, but the dropkick by Charlie Broshous went wide.

But Army had to play one more game in 1930. The president of the United States directed that the Army Navy game be rein stituted as an anti-Depression measure. The Cadets won 7–0 in a game at Yankee Stadium that raised three hundred thousand dol lars, which was given away to charitable causes.

A YEAR OF TRAGEDY

The year of 1931 was a tragic one for Army and for football. In March Knute Rockne died in an airplane crash in Kansas. The entire country mourned the loss of one of its most inspirational figures. The loss was especially demoralizing, coming as it did at the depths of the Depression. Sasse had developed a close relationship with his rival and felt the loss deeply.

Then, in the 1931 Army–Yale game, one of Army's reserve ends, Dick Sheridan, went into the game early in the fourth quarter. Sheridan was not a standout, he was a small man to begin with, but he had attracted attention to himself earlier in the '31 season with a touchdown against Harvard on a fumble recovery. The score was tied 6–6 when Sheridan launched a flying tackle from the head of Army's wedge on Yale's kickoff return man.

When the play ended and the players picked themselves up, Sheridan lay motionless on the field. Team doctors, coaches, and officials crowded over him. Sasse accompanied the unconscious Sheridan to the hospital. The team's graduate manager, Maj. Phil Fleming, asked Blaik if he thought the game should be continued. Red saw nothing that could be done for Sheridan at that point and recommended that the game be played on. The cadets' hearts were not in it at that point, no matter what "the Whip" might do to motivate them.

Sheridan died of his injury two days later, while the game ended in a tie. Blaik later attributed Sheridan's injury to an elongated neck shape that should have kept him out of football entirely. The cadets went on to finish the 1931 season with victories over both Notre Dame and Navy. But the death of Sheridan broke Sasse's heart. The next season would be his last as Army's head coach. He asked to be relieved after the 1932 season.

Red Blaik wanted his job. They were the best of friends, and Sasse had recommended that Blaik be his replacement. He had been an assistant coach now for eight consecutive seasons and he knew he could be an effective, winning coach. And he wanted to be Army's coach. He knew the system, he knew the school and the administration, and he knew what winning meant to men who would one day be expected to make the supreme sacrifice for victory.

He also knew that with his friend and mentor Douglas MacArthur serving as Army chief of staff, he could run the Army football program his way. He could get the old grads who ran the academy, the Academic Board, to give in on changing all those rules and regulations of cadet life that made it difficult to run a competitive football program. He believed that he could get MacArthur to order them to give in to his terms. What a team he could build!

Blaik had convinced the academy's adjutant general, Lt. Col. Robert Eichelberger, that the academy should waive its rule requiring the head coach to be an active duty officer. That would clear the way for the Athletic Board to offer the head coaching job to Blaik, who of course had resigned his commission and would not be able to be recalled to active duty since he was no longer on the rolls even as a reserve or retired officer. But neither Eichelberger nor Blaik could convince the Athletic Board to change its rule. Army's head coach for 1933 was to be another of Ralph Sasse's assistants, Lt. Garrison (Gar) H. Davidson.

Gar Davidson wanted the job, too, and he told Sasse that he wanted it. But by this time Davidson had been at West Point for six years as an officer and had never been assigned anywhere else. This was not good for his career development, according to his professional managers in Washington at headquarters, Army Corps of Engineers. He was behind his classmates in assignments and experience, and he needed to get out into the field if he wanted to remain competitive for promotion. He called on Gen. Douglas MacArthur, who was now Army chief of staff, to intervene with the Corps of Engineers on his behalf. MacArthur did so gladly, and Davidson got the job. The only one not happy about this was Red Blaik.

TESTING THE WATERS

After learning of Davidson's selection, Blaik wrote to MacArthur, whom he presumed to favor himself based on their correspondence since cadet days. Blaik's letter implied that he was going to leave the West Point program, but hinted that he might stay if the academy would create, and appoint himself to fill, a position of professor of physical education. He said of Davidson in that letter, "In my judgment he is youthful and lacks worldly experience. He possesses neither the drive and personality of a Sasse nor the football brain of a Jones." No such position was created.

At that point, Red Blaik had nowhere else to go, so he stayed on as an assistant coach. Army's 1933 team ran up a 9–1 record under Davidson behind All-American team captain Harvey Jablonsky. Blaik never warmed up to Davidson. He could not bring himself to accept Gar Davidson as his equal, much less as his superior. Princeton and Ohio State universities had contacted Red later during the year in their search for new head coaches, but Blaik had turned them down, expecting to be offered the position at Army. Now he found himself as an assistant to a head coach who really did not know how to handle the game, in Blaik's own opinion, although behind the superb play of a core of All-Americans, Army's only loss that year was to a mediocre Notre Dame.

Going into the 1933 Notre Dame game, Blaik was again approached, with a more formal offer by Ohio State. His relationship with Davidson was going downhill, and he would have liked to have been closer to home, but he felt that the Buckeyes did not give their head football coach the kind of authority he would need. In December 1933, Yale also tested the waters for Blaik, but opted instead to hire one of its own alums for the job. Red did not want to stay at Army working under a man far junior to himself (Davidson graduated in the Class of 1927, eight years after Blaik). But so far the right alternative had not appeared.

Looking forward to 1934, it looked to Blaik as if he would have to resign himself to another season under the upstart Davidson. And even if Blaik stayed to see Davidson move on in a few years, there was little prospect for the Athletic Board to change its policy. The way Blaik saw it, things just don't change that quickly at West Point. Even his trump card, General MacArthur, could not be played, since the chief of staff was in his fourth year of a four-year tour of duty and was expecting to be forced to retire. Blaik concluded that his time was probably up, since he had reached the conclusion that a coach's future in football is only a year-to-year proposition anyway. He knew there were never any guarantees of lifetime employment.

West Point was not the only school in search of a new head football coach for the 1934 season. So was Dartmouth University. They had considered 126 potential coaches and narrowed their choices to Red Blaik and one other, neither of whom knew that they were under consideration. Their lead candidate was Blaik, and in January 1934, Dartmouth president Ernest Hopkins asked Blaik if he would take the job and give Dartmouth a winner.

Hopkins was offering Blaik all the things he wanted as a head coach. All the things he knew he would have to fight for to get at Army were being offered to him on a platter at Dartmouth. Not only was Hopkins offering him unprecedented control over Dartmouth's football program, but also Blaik would report directly to the university president, and he could have his family with him full-time in a beautiful new home that the university would build for him right on campus. It was an offer Blaik could not refuse.

Blaik hired his own assistant coaches from across the country. He held his first team meeting in February and told his players of the new standard of performance that they would be held accountable to, "We'll be as successful as you men will allow us to be. If there is anybody in this room who is not ready to do some strong sacrificing, I hope we've seen him for the last time tonight."

He saw it as his primary task to replace Dartmouth's "play for fun" approach to the game with a more aggressive, spartan philosophy in which it wasn't how you played the game, it was whether you won or lost that counted. And Red Blaik, now that he was a head coach, was going to instill in his players the attitude that the war had cheated him out of having when he played for Army in only one full season. He would teach his players what MacArthur had taught him, that winning wasn't just anything, it was the only thing. Winning was to be the highest goal his team was to strive for, justifying all the sacrifice required to achieve it.

Blaik also concluded that Dartmouth's players were too soft. Blaik had developed a sense of the severity of the game that he tried to impart to his players. He did it by being harsh with them on the practice field. He also did it by ignoring injuries suffered by his players. He even forced the newspapers to stop reporting on players who were laid up in the hospital. As Blaik put it, "Games are not won on the rubbing table."

He proved his point during a team trip when the trainer took three players out during a game trip and got them drunk. The trainer told them not to worry about what Blaik might do because he would take care of him through his alumni connections. Blaik went straight to Hopkins and got the trainer fired immediately. Then he brought his own man in from Army, Roland Bevan, who had been a high-school team trainer in Blaik's hometown of Dayton. Bevan shared Blaik's approach of ruthlessly refusing to coddle injured players and consciously trying to raise their threshold for pain. Bevan's training room became known as "the torture room." Blaik was proud of his ability to motivate injured players to continue to play despite bleeding wounds and broken bones. And he would not let teammates feel sorry for an injured player nor pause in a game to worry over an injury that happened on the field. The price of victory on Earl Blaik's team was to fight on in spite of the casualties.

Blaik professionalized football at Dartmouth. He introduced

the single-wing offense and developed a complex, shifting formation that kept the opposing defenses off balance. He kept his coaching staff working sixty-hour weeks studying films, scouting opponents, developing new plays, and drilling the team at practice. It paid off immediately for the university. Dartmouth shut out its first five opponents in 1934, outscoring them 125–0. Blaik brought winning back to Dartmouth in his first year as head coach, with a record of 6–3. They gave him a three-year contract.

The next year his team went 8–2 and in 1936 they went 8–1, including a key victory over archrival Yale for the Ivy League title. At that, Hopkins signed Blaik to yet another new contract, this time for five years. In 1937 Dartmouth rolled to an undefeated 7–0–2 season, another Ivy League championship and a seventh-rank finish nationally. This was to be Blaik's peak year at Dartmouth, with the 1938 and 1939 seasons falling shy of this unbeaten mark at 7–2 and 5–1–3.

It was also the year that Blaik began to have run-ins with the Dartmouth faculty. Some professors were concerned with his all-or-nothing approach to football and would not acquiesce to his requests for rescheduling of exams for his players whenever practices or games demanded so much from them mentally, emotionally, and physically. Blaik felt that with all the sacrifice he was demanding of them for football, the professors should be willing to give them some consideration by granting them a chance to get a better grade after more time for study and rest. Most went along with him, but some actively opposed him.

GAR DAVIDSON FOOTBALL

In the meantime, Army football steadied under Gar Davidson. His 1934 team went 7–3 but lost to Notre Dame, then lost to Navy for the first time in thirteen years. They should have won that Notre Dame game. The Irish had fallen on hard times after Rockne's death and by 1934 were in their third post-Rockne head coach in Hunk Anderson. The school was so demoralized they did not even send their cheerleaders to New York for the Army game and asked West Point to provide some to lead the crowd in Notre Dame's fight songs and yells. Army led all the way into the fourth quarter. Then late in the fourth period, with the score 12–7 Army, the cadets tried to punt out of their own end zone. Notre Dame batted down the kick, fell on the ball for a touchdown, and won the game, 13–12. A better-coached team, of course, would have downed the ball in the end zone for a safety rather than attempt such a risky punt so late in the game.

In 1935 Notre Dame tied Army in the last minute of the game on a pass interference call on a "Hail Mary" pass play that was hotly disputed by Davidson during the game and after. After the game the two team captains got into a fistfight over who would get to keep the game ball. Davidson and Notre Dame coach Elmer Layden broke the fight up and made them flip a coin to see who would get the coveted ball. The 6–2–1 Army team did defeat Navy that year, 28–6. In 1936, under Elmer Layden, Notre Dame was the underdog in the New York classic but managed to beat Army again on a last-quarter desperation play, 12–6. Army also lost to Navy in 1936, on yet another late-game pass interference call, and compiled a 6–3 record. Davidson blamed a midseason flu epidemic and another bad call by an official for the loss. In his last year as Army's head coach, Gar Davidson's 1937 team lost again to Notre Dame but managed to beat Navy 6–0 in a respectable 7–2 year.

In 1938 Army football began to deteriorate. Their 8–2 record that year would be the last winning season for a while for West Point. The Army and the academy began to impose severe restrictions on the stature of incoming cadets, to ensure that everyone who graduated from West Point would have what was considered a proper military bearing. That meant being slender and not too tall so that the man would look good in uniform. The rules were that a new cadet had to be 6 feet 4 inches or shorter and had to weigh fewer than 199 pounds. A six-footer had to weigh in at fewer than 177 pounds. This was not exactly conducive to building a good football program, but the Academic Board would grant no waivers for players.

The year 1938 was also the time that West Point finally complied with college football's three-year eligibility rule. It took a presidential decree, but it was done. This immediately made several of Army's outstanding players ineligible, since they had played for other teams before coming to West Point and had used up their three years of permitted varsity play. Notre Dame was ranked fifth in the nation in 1938 and ran over Army, 19–7.

Army's 1939 squad went 3–4–2, profiting only the hundreds of cadets and soldiers who had bet against their team. In those days thousands of dollars changed hands among servicemen, including cadets and midshipmen, in football wagering. New York's Notre Dame "subway alumni" easily won their bets that year as the Irish beat Army again, 14–0, in the twenty-fifth anniversary of the game. The 1940 Army team compiled a discouraging record of 1–8–1, including a 7–0 loss to hand Notre Dame, its twentieth win in the series. America's ambassador to the United Kingdom, Joseph P. Kennedy, was among the rich and famous in the crowd for the spectacle.

The Military Academy was to get a new superintendent that year, Brigadier General Robert L. Eichelberger, who as a Lieutenant Colonel had been Superintendent MacArthur's adjutant in 1919, and was on his way to becoming the thirty-eighth superintendent of the U.S. Military Academy. He was a tough man, hardened in combat. He had won the Distinguished Service Cross, second only to the Medal of Honor for gallantry under fire, as a major in the 1918 U.S. expedition into Siberia.

He was determined to carry out MacArthur's unfinished reformation of West Point, and one place in particular where he believed he could change traditions that had become hindrances was in the football program. After watching the 1940 Army–Navy game, he remarked at his first meeting with the Academic Board, some of whom had been on the board twenty-one years earlier when he had been the adjutant, "I was impressed Saturday by the way the cadets cheered our team right to the end. It looks as if we are developing the finest bunch of losers in the world. By the gods, I believe the cadets deserve a football team that will teach them how to be good winners."

Eichelberger believed that America was about to enter a war for which there would be no substitute for victory. He knew that teaching cadets how to win at football would go a long way to moving America to win this war.

Ten

On the Fields of Friendly Strife

Earl H. Blaik knew before the 1940 season started that this Cornell team might be tougher to beat than his faithful Dartmouth football followers believed. For the first time in three years the Big Green was not nationally ranked. He had watched them lose to archrival Yale, Columbia, and even lowly Franklin and Marshall. Now, facing Cornell in this next-to-last game of the 1940 season, Blaik somehow had to motivate his team to try to hold their own against the number one team in the country. Cornell was picked to beat Dartmouth by four touchdowns.

He had prepared for this game like no other before it. The Cornell offense was very difficult to contain. It was characterized by speed and agility rather than power and strength. Blaik had built his defense around his trademark style of play: Hit them hard, straight ahead, show no mercy. For this game, however, Blaik disciplined his men into waiting to see how the attack would unfold, then moving to the ball to stop the play, rather than the classic Blaik bulldozer approach of trying to blow past the offensive line right away.

The game was scoreless through three quarters. Dartmouth finally scored a field goal in the fourth quarter to take the lead. Then, with less than a minute to play in the game, Cornell had the ball on the Dartmouth one-yard line and it was third down. They tried to drive through the Dartmouth line but gained only inches. After the play was completed, Cornell purposely called a time-out to stop the clock. According to the rules of the day they were charged with a five-yard penalty for delaying the game.

It was fourth and goal from the six for Cornell. Cornell passed to try for the touchdown and the game, but Dartmouth blocked the pass, and possession shifted to the Big Green. The official spotted the ball on Dartmouth's twenty with six seconds showing on the clock. Blaik was jubilant. The players on the bench could not believe that they had beaten number one Cornell after such a disappointing season. But then the incredible happened.

Cornell players argued with the officials that another referee had called offside on both the offensive and defensive lines on the play before the pass was released by the quarterback. This would mean that the play should not have started, and the game would revert to fourth down and goal to go for Cornell from the six. In the confusion, the chief official permitted Cornell to replay from the six. Six seconds still showed on the clock, and Cornell was able to complete a pass into the end zone and make the point after to win the game, 7–3.

But the sportswriters who had attended the game saw no official throw a flag for the offside call on the earlier pass play. They pointed this out to Blaik and told him that possession should have passed to Dartmouth for the last six seconds remaining in the game. They agreed with Blaik's assistant coaches that Cornell's score had come on a fifth-down play. Blaik did appeal to the referee personally after the game, and the officials ruled that they had erred in allowing Cornell to run the play that resulted in the touchdown, but they claimed they were powerless to reverse the victory for Cornell. Only the schools themselves could do that. A few days later, both coaches agreed that the victory belonged to Dartmouth, and the official records were changed to reflect a Dartmouth win, 3–0.

Dartmouth ended the 1940 season with another disappointment, a 20–6 loss to Brown University. It was not a good year for Red Blaik, who had seen his team fall dramatically from 5–1–3 the previous year to 4–5. Blaik blamed the downturn on poor recruiting in the incoming freshmen classes, starting with the Class of '41. He knew that Ivy League schools were not very tolerant of nonalum coaches in the first place, and he could expect them to be even less enamored of such who did not win. From Red Blaik's point of view, this place was not much different from West Point in that way. He could see the end of his minidynasty coming soon.

EICHELBERGER'S WEST POINT

The same Saturday that Dartmouth won the five-down game with Cornell, incoming West Point superintendent Robert Eichelberger had made his speech to the Academic Board declaring his intent to bring winning football back to Army. He also declared to the board, "Our officer head-coaching system has long been outmoded. I propose to ditch it, and, if I can, get Red Blaik back here from Dartmouth."

When he had presented the idea privately to the board in September 1940, just after being named to the post, Eichelberger had not yet officially taken command as superintendent, and the board was cool to the idea. The academy tradition of having a head coach who was a serving officer had an important role, in their view, in setting an example for cadets. Becoming an officer was more important than anything else, and playing football was only one of several activities contributing to that end. The Academic Board did not want football to become an end in itself. One way to ensure that West Point's football program did not become, in effect, the overriding purpose of the institution, as it had at many schools, was to have its head coach responsive to the commands of the Academic Board.

A serving active duty officer had a legal responsibility to follow orders no matter what. A civilian coach, a hired hand, one who perhaps had some experience in the politics of a university, would probably not be so easy to keep under thumb. The board, though disappointed with the 1940 season, was not quite ready to break with tradition. Their choice was Gar Davidson.

Davidson was a proven quantity both as an officer and as a football coach. He had been chosen over Red Blaik to replace Ralph

Sasse in 1933 as head coach. When his four-year tour of duty was up in the spring of 1938, he had been assigned to staff duty in Washington. When he heard that his successor at Army was not working out very well, he asked to be returned to West Point to be head coach again. But it was not to be. Gar Davidson was sent off to train for war instead.

By November, the board members who had been most opposed to the idea of hiring Blaik had retired. On the day of Dartmouth's fifth-down victory, Eichelberger was making his argument to the board again, this time with the deputy heads of the departments sitting at the seats of those who had just retired. Eichelberger thought he could persuade these younger professors, themselves more recent graduates of the academy, when winning football had been a way of life. Those who had retired were members of classes that had graduated well before college football became a national passion and such a tradition unto itself at Army. Still, the board demurred.

But Eichelberger was a man of action. He had already distinguished himself in combat with U.S. forces in Siberia in 1918 as a junior officer; he would go on from West Point to win the Distinguished Service Cross at Buna village in New Guinea as a three-star general. He was now under the gun again as West Point's new superintendent.

Already in November 1940, more than a year before America was to enter World War II, there was pressure to shorten the West Point course of instruction from four to three years in anticipation of wartime needs. In 1931 he had been adjutant at West Point and saw firsthand how the academy was even then still suffering from the drastic World War I shortening of the course of instruction to a year for some classes. From 1936 to 1939 he had served as secretary to MacArthur in the Philippines, and as the Army's leadership began to think about the prospects for a coming war, he came to believe, as did MacArthur, that the West Point system would completely come apart if that were allowed to happen again.

Eichelberger was determined to fix things at West Point before the Army chief of staff, straight-as-an-arrow Gen. George C. Marshall, could intervene and make changes himself. Marshall had pointed out to Eichelberger that he had been a strict disciplinarian as cadet commander at Virginia Military Institute in 1901, when West Point cadets were aiming the reveille cannon at the supe's house at West Point. Eichelberger wanted to show immediately upon taking charge at West Point that he could bring the academy to provide the kind of leaders the nation was about to need on the eve of global war.

Eichelberger gored many sacred cows at West Point. He started with a severe reduction in the required number of hours of horse riding as a mandatory subject of instruction. He convinced the War Department to let cadets get enough flight training to become qualified as pilots before graduation, and he persuaded Congress to begin construction of a massive new air base just outside the academy, near Newburgh, New York. He had cadets shed their summer khaki uniforms and begin to wear special academy fatigue uniforms similar to regular Army fatigues as he shifted their military training away from parade ground drill and ceremony to tactical maneuvers in nearby New Jersey training facilities run by the National Guard. He wanted West Point graduates to be as prepared as possible for the demands of combat, for, as he put it, "in combat there may be no game next week." Not all of these changes lasted beyond his superintendency, but the effect on the academy at the time was dramatic.

He believed, as did MacArthur, that football was the nearest thing on earth to mortal combat between armies. As adjutant it had been Eichelberger's duty to see to it that MacArthur's order was carried out to carve in stone over the portal to the cadet gymnasium that "fields of friendly strife" verse composed by the supe that has now come to be held as nearly sacred by West Point. He knew that if he could restore winning football to the Brave Old Army Team it would go a long way to demonstrating what West Point could do for the nation in war.

But he also knew that some things had to change radically if he was going to keep the heavy hand of Washington off the Hudson highlands institution. Football was not the only thing he wanted to change, but it was the thing he felt could be changed the quickest with the most far-reaching effects. And he knew he would have just the man to make it happen if he could get Red Blaik to coach at Army.

In spite of the lack of Academic Board approval, he wrote to Blaik himself, appealing to his sense of loyalty to the institution and to his patriotism to hold off on signing with any other school before giving Eichelberger a chance. He knew that Blaik was not having a great year at Dartmouth, and he knew that Blaik's job there could be on the line. Eichelberger also knew that Blaik's current contract with the university was up for renegotiation. He believed that it would be difficult to persuade Blaik to leave Dartmouth with the kind of deal he must have from university president Edward Hopkins, but he also knew that this would be his only chance as superintendent to get Blaik back to the Plain. Blaik agreed to meet with Eichelberger at the 1940 Army–Navy game.

It was a tough move for Blaik even to meet with Eichelberger. Blaik still had the support of President Hopkins and could probably hold on for another year, but he would have to turn in a much better record next year if he wanted a chance to build a football dynasty. The victory over Cornell would be enough for Hopkins to keep Blaik around for one more chance to restart Dartmouth's run on dominating the Ivy League. The university had just built the Blaik family a magnificent new home off-campus overlooking Mount Ascutney, which rose just across the Connecticut River, in Vermont. There were many reasons to stay.

But there was a certain appeal to Eichelberger's request. Blaik had been passed over for the head coaching job back in 1934, and it would give him a certain satisfaction to come back as head coach eight years later. There was also an opportunity to convince his many detractors in the Army that he was not a shirker. The men who had resigned back in 1922, when the Army offered them the opportunity to leave the service early, had to bear the disdain of some of their fellow West Pointers who considered those who had resigned to be self-serving and disloyal to their country and to West Point.

If he were appointed as Army's head coach he would have to have his commission reinstated to comply with the tradition of

Army's head coach being on active duty. He would in theory be eligible to be ordered into service in the field, perhaps even into combat when war broke out. Subjecting himself to the similar risk of being sent into combat would give him something to say to his critics who considered him to be a draft dodger and a slackard.

Blaik hoped that, once commissioned, Eichelberger would, of course, ensure that he would not be assigned to a war zone so that he could stay at West Point and build a football program. There was a chance that the Army would deemphasize the game, as they had when he was a cadet, but he felt that with Eichelberger in charge, and with MacArthur still wielding significant influence over the Army, that risk was minimal. He saw Eichelberger's offer as an opportunity he could not pass up.

But he also wanted to avoid all the troubles that had hindered his predecessors as the man in command of the Brave Old Army Team. He decided as he prepared to meet with Eichelberger that he would insist on two conditions. He wanted to be able to bring his own assistant coaches with him from Dartmouth. That would serve two purposes. It would bring him a ready-made staff that could move in quickly, take over the program, and run it the Red Blaik way. He would not have to waste time sizing up or training unfamiliar staff. It would also ensure that there would be no assistants on his staff who would resent his being brought back to active duty and West Point after walking away from it all in 1934. Although it was two years ago that Gar Davidson had left, many of those assistants were Davidson's men. Blaik did not want them anywhere near his football program.

The second policy change he wanted was a waiver on the Army's height and weight restrictions for his football players. He believed that those rules were solely for cosmetic purposes, to make sure that officers looked good in uniform. He thought that was ridiculous. It was devastating for a football program. Under the Army's rules the perfect new cadet would weigh 160 pounds and be six feet tall. The tallest a man was allowed to be was six feet four inches, and at that height he could weigh a maximum of 225 pounds. Most of the linemen in college football in 1940 could not meet those standards. On top of the three-year eligibility rule, the height-weight standards meant that Army simply could not bring in nationally competitive players. Blaik wanted that changed, and he would not settle for a promise from the surgeon general of waivers. He wanted the rule changed in writing before he would sign a contract.

Blaik met again with Eichelberger in December. At that meeting, the supe worked on both Red and his wife, Merle. Eichelberger promised that he would have a new home built for them at one of the most picturesque sites on the academy reservation. It would be a huge home, just a little way from the football stadium. He also told Red that, just as he had reported directly to Dartmouth's president, he would at West Point report straight to the superintendent. Blaik did not know how Eichelberger was going to accomplish that; the power of the Academic Board was not something that could easily be circumvented. But he knew that if anyone could pull it off, Eichelberger would be able to. No doubt the general, from his days as adjutant, was well aware of all kinds of skeletons in closets around West Point and the Academic Board. Blaik figured that Eichelberger would call in a few chips to get his way on that one.

Eichelberger also met Blaik's demand to get a waiver on the Army's height and weight standards for his football players. The supe himself did not believe in those requirements for the Army as a whole. He told Marshall that they were "a hell of a way to run a football team . . . life expectancy in battle for big or little men is just about the same."

COACH BLAIK

That was all that Red Blaik needed to hear. Before the end of December 1940, Blaik and his assistants were signed on as the new coaching staff for the Brave Old Army Team. West Point, and football, would never be the same.

Red Blaik brought back to West Point football the philosophy that victory was everything. He believed that it was a wholly appropriate approach to football, especially for players who soon would find themselves in combat, where to fall short of victory

meant death. He made that point to the team at his very first meeting with them. He was explaining his belief that football games
can be won or lost by any player not performing his best, when
he saw someone staring out a window. "Hey, you over there by the
window!" Blaik snapped. "Where are most football games lost?"
"Right here at West Point, sir," came the reply.

Blaik had gotten the players' attention and made his point that
he was in charge at the same time he had drawn their attention
to a fact they had not realized until then. Blaik set out to change
their attitudes immediately.

He quickly sized up the ills that infected Army football and concluded that the goal of victory had been displaced by ideals that
he believed had no place on the gridiron. Some academy officials
had become self-conscious about Army's domination of the game
in earlier years. They felt that it was all right to lose if it proved
that football was not the main thing at the school. Blaik hated that
attitude more than any other. "The philosophy that there can be
such a thing as too many victories is a bastard one," he wrote. He
began a habit of writing a slogan on the chalkboard in the locker
room, a place where every man would see it every day. It was his
way of instilling a psychological element into his coaching. His
first was aimed at this attitude, which he so hated. "There never
was a champion who to himself was a good loser. There's a vast
difference between a good sport and a good loser."

He also detested the academy's approach to handling injuries.
As he had at Dartmouth, Blaik changed Army's policies on injured
players. He would not coddle them. His rule of thumb was that
80 percent of all injuries should not keep a player off the field.
They just had to be tough enough to play hurt. It would be that
way in combat. His response to players who accused him of being
evil was that if they did not want to play football the Red Blaik way,
they were free to stay away.

He worked them hard during the three hours he had the players for practice each day during the week. The coaches worked
themselves even harder getting ready to get the most out of those
three hours. Blaik had learned the art of preparation for practice

and had honed it to a science. He was relentless in driving his staff to get the most out of practice sessions, scouting visits, and recruiting trips. There was little time left for family or vacation.

It paid off immediately for West Point's football program. Blaik's 1941 Army team was undefeated in four games going into the annual Notre Dame contest at Yankee Stadium. Notre Dame was a heavy favorite in the game.

This was the first year of the Frank Leahy era in Irish football. Leahy moved his team out of the Rockne legacy by discarding the "Notre Dame shift" in favor of the T formation. He was ruthless and would stoop to any subterfuge to win a ball game, including directing a player to fake an injury to stop the clock without being charged a time-out.

Eichelberger was ecstatic with the scoreless tie that Blaik delivered against Notre Dame. It had been a rainy, muddy, bruising contest. The subway alumni were shocked silent. But several Army players were injured in the game, and it was to become the peak performance of Blaik's inaugural season. By the final game of the year, against Navy, West Point just did not have the power to prevail. Blaik's first Army team turned in a 4–3–1 record, certainly gratifying after the solitary victory of 1940, although they lost to Navy, 14–6.

THE WAR

A little more than a week after the season ended, 7 December 1941, the Japanese bombed Pearl Harbor. West Point's program was soon compressed to three years by directive from General Marshall, and General Eichelberger was soon transferred to train one of the Army's newly mobilizing divisions. Blaik was recalled to active duty, as a colonel. He was allowed to put in a preference for where he would serve if required to go to one of the combat zones. He naturally chose the Pacific, where he hoped to be assigned to General MacArthur's command.

Eichelberger had been replaced by Maj. Gen. Francis B. Wilby. Wilby was called to testify before the House Appropriations Committee on the issue of changing West Point's program to help the war effort. Wilby told the committee that sports must go on at the academy because contact sports were good preparation for battle. Eichelberger wrote to Blaik with the same message:

So boy, keep driving ahead on your job, for it's a top-flight project in our war effort, and don't let anyone tell you anything else. And you can tell 'em I said so—and I'm seeing every day fifteen thousand damn good fighting men who'd be a damn sight better if they'd spent their last year in school under you—and never entered a classroom, if that had been necessary.

America's entry into the war brought a new sense of intensity and seriousness to all that went on at West Point. It also brought new talent to the football squad. The freshman rule was suspended so that plebes could play at the varsity level and still get all three years' eligible play permitted under college rules even though Army's academic program had been shortened. Some prospective players came to West Point rather than other schools for patriotic reasons. There are those who believe that some came to Army solely to avoid or postpone military service.

Red Blaik continued his aggressive recruiting campaign. In the spring of 1942 he thought he had grabbed a prize talent in convincing Pennsylvania high-school standout Johnny Lujack to accept an appointment to West Point. But somehow, in June of that year, Lujack reversed himself and instead went to Notre Dame. Blaik was furious. He felt that Notre Dame had cheated. He led the Army Athletic Board to South Bend to protest. They were rejected by Father John Cavanaugh, then head of Notre Dame's Athletic Board, and by the head coach, Frank Leahy.

Blaik felt that this added insult to injury. It was bad enough that Notre Dame completely dominated the series and that Army teams were treated so rudely by the New York City fans. At least Knute Rockne had once come to the Army locker room when Blaik had been an assistant coach to complain about a tackle made on the line. That was unheard of in those days, when the game was so much more physical, but at least he acknowledged that his players, too, were less than pristine. The refusal of the university's leadership to acknowledge that it had cheated in recruiting Lujack away from West Point was, in Blaik's judgment, wholly unprofessional.

Evidently Army's football recruiting got out ahead of Lujack's own preferences. Johnny's congressman, Jay Buell Snyder, had been persuaded by academy officials to give his appointment to Lujack and make the announcement personally at Lujack's high-school graduation. Army's recruiters had apparently pressured Lujack's parents into agreeing to the announcement before Johnny formally accepted it. In fact, he really wanted to go to Notre Dame.

Long before the congressman's announcement, Lujack had visited the Notre Dame campus and visited with Coach Leahy and some assistants. He tried out and won himself a football scholarship as a result. His view of West Point was that the four-year service commitment after graduation was just too much for him. Regardless of what others wanted for him, he wanted to go to Notre Dame, and he did.

Actually, Notre Dame had also benefited from post–Pearl Harbor wartime policies. The school had one of the more aggressive officer candidate programs, started after the 7 December 1941 bombing of U.S. soil. By 1942, officer candidates included more than a half dozen top-rated varsity football players. Military assignment officers had the power to reassign candidates to other schools to fill up the ranks in those battalions of candidates, and Notre Dame's football squad was the lucky beneficiary of more such transfers from schools such as Illinois, Marquette, and Minnesota.

THE RED BLAIK COACHING TECHNIQUE

Nevertheless, Army dominated its opponents early in the 1942 season. By midseason, however, powerhouses Penn and Notre Dame once again showed Red Blaik that he still had some way to go before he could expect to achieve national ranking. His chalkboard slogan during Notre Dame week was, "Physical pressure on the foe is essential. Mental pressure will make him crack."

Blaik used more than just sloganeering to build up his team's cohesion. Special training meals turned out to be highly effective team-building events. His football players ate at a separate set of tables in the mess hall. This not only permitted them to get more protein and carbohydrates, it also allowed them to go over the day's practice session as well as the playbook and game drills for upcoming competition. Occasionally the men would also use the opportunity to trade information about the day's classes. If football players from one regiment took an exam that day, the players from the other regiment expected to be told what kind of problems would appear on the test, since the academic departments used exactly the same test on both days.

In preparation for the game against the Irish, Blaik had the plebe team running Notre Dame's offensive plays using Leahy's T formation as best they could pick it up from game films. It was not exactly the way the Irish ran it, but the T was so very different from any other offensive approach that he did not want his defense surprised.

To Blaik's surprise, his plebes did pretty well against the first unit. It was at that point that he decided to adopt the T formation at Army. He figured that if his plebes could pick it up, surely the varsity squad could, too. It was too late to implement it for this year's game with Notre Dame, however. He decided then to switch to the T as soon as he could get enough drills in with the first squad to make them proficient in all of its complexities.

His slogan for the week was apt. It was indeed a very physical game. The weather at game time at Yankee Stadium for the Notre Dame game was cold, wet, and miserable. The field was a muddy mess. Both teams were affected; it was not a game to be proud of, and Army lost, 13–0.

The Navy game that year was just as tough. The game was held at Annapolis to comply with wartime travel restrictions. Only a few thousand locals could attend, along with Army's football team and a few reporters. The Brigade of Midshipmen had to sing Army fight songs and yell out West Point's cheers on order of the Naval Academy's superintendent. It made for great sportswriter copy. Army never got past the midshipmen's ten-yard line in a 14–0 loss. Army closed out its 1942 season with a record of 6–3.

Red Blaik's approach to coaching was vindicated by his two consecutive successful seasons. His players responded to his motivational techniques and gave him everything they had. For example, at the 1942 Navy game, lineman Robin Olds was hit hard on a punt rush early in the game. He lost four teeth and had his tongue slashed by Navy cleats. He took twenty-three stitches in his tongue and lip; his jaw and cheeks were swollen so that his mouth was shut, and he could not speak. Yet he came back out to the bench after halftime and signaled to Blaik that he wanted to go back into the game. Blaik's slogan that week was, "Games are not won on the rubbing table." The Whip knew he had succeeded in instilling the right attitude, and he played Olds nearly the entire second half of the game. Olds was elected to captain the 1943 squad but graduated early, along with the rest of his class, which was accelerated because of the war.

In 1943 Red Blaik had an opportunity to get even with Frank Leahy for the Johnny Lujack gambit of the previous year. Army and Notre Dame went head-to-head in the recruiting wars that year, with both teams pursuing a Chicago prospect by the name of Bob Kelly. In the fall of 1942 Kelly's father, an Illinois congressman, convinced his son that he should go to West Point. They traveled to the academy in January 1943 to meet Blaik and the coaching staff.

After the meetings young Bob Kelly told his father that he had changed his mind and wanted to go to Notre Dame. Before announcing the changed decision, father and son decided it would be wise to consult with Notre Dame administration officials. They met with Father Cavanaugh, who told them that he was not going to allow Bob Kelly to start classes at Notre Dame because he did not want any more animosity from West Point after the Lujack affair.

Congressman Kelly called Blaik personally about this from Cavanaugh's office, and the highly influential representative told Blaik in no uncertain terms that his son had changed his mind and was going to go to Notre Dame. Apparently Blaik caved in under the implicit threat of adverse reaction in certain powerful committees in Congress. Kelly then had Blaik speak to Cavanaugh to smooth over any potential for hard feelings or retribution from Army. Once again, Red Blaik had been outmaneuvered by Frank Leahy of Notre Dame. Bob Kelly went to Notre Dame.

BLAIK BUILDS A NATIONAL POWERHOUSE

It was in 1943 that Blaik got the break he needed to realize his ambition for Army football. In that year he was able to recruit an outstanding high-school athlete from California, Glenn Davis, a man about whom Blaik said, "there could not have been a greater, more dangerous running halfback in the entire history of the game. . . ." All that Blaik had to do to get Davis to decide on West Point over the dozens of college football programs that recruited him was to get his brother Ralph a chance to take the exams as well. Blaik delivered with ease.

But Glenn Davis also presented a problem for Blaik's ambitions for the Army team. Davis did not have the high-school grades to indicate much probability of success with the rigorous academic program at the Military Academy. He would need special help just to pass the entrance exams, and even more help later to keep his grades up once at West Point. Blaik fixed that problem by assigning one of his officer assistant coaches to help Davis prepare for the entrance exams. Davis and his brother Ralph were brought to the academy grounds late in the spring of 1943 to go through a special tutorial designed to help them pass the entrance exam. He was not taught the test, but he was given sufficient practice in the types of problems that would be on the test that he was able to pass when it came time to take the test for the record. Thus began a football tradition at West Point, the spring cram school for prospective players. It came to be known as "Monster School."

Blaik also set up an extensive academic coaching program for his players. For those plebes who made the cut to the varsity squad, there was special help that began just after plebe year ended. During the summer after plebe year, sophomores, known at West Point as "yearlings," went through two months of advanced military tactical training at a site in the wooded hills outside the academic area. "Camp Buckner," as it was called, was within the military reservation around West Point, but about ten miles away from the Plain. In the midst of a tough Army training program there, the football staff was busy getting some of the players ready for the academic year ahead.

One of the coaches gave them a very thorough course, which included special notebooks that were mimeographed at the football office. These notebooks gave questions and answers to important parts of tough courses they would encounter in the coming academic year. Coaches had prepared the notebooks from the instructors' note cards used to prepare the lessons. Football players kept those notebooks for use throughout the academic year. They proved to be extremely valuable to all football players, even the brighter ones who used the help to get an extra edge to achieve higher class standing among their nonvarsity academic peers who had more time to devote to studies.

Army's 1943 season got off to a powerful start. The Brave Old Army Team won its first four games, shutting out each opponent and accumulating a total of 172 points against Villanova, Colgate, Temple, and Columbia. After a 39–7 blowout over Yale and a 13–13 tie with Penn, Army faced undefeated archrival Notre Dame. The Irish had national title ambitions, but their star quarterback, Angelo Bertelli, a 1942 All-American, was drafted just before the game. Johnny Lujack filled in, and Army lost big, 26–0, with Davis committing several fumbles on Army scoring drives. Lujack and Bob Kelly once again ruined Red Blaik's day.

The cadets also lost to Navy that year. In this game, the Navy team made the trip to West Point, with the cadets doing the cheering for the midshipmen in return for the favor at Annapolis the year before. The cadets who sang "Anchors Aweigh" apparently did so with as much enthusiasm as the midshipmen had sung "On, Brave Old Army Team" the year before.

It was a brutally physical game. But Navy was still just too big and too strong for Blaik. It was not because Army lacked the desire to win that they could not come up with a victory this time. Five fights had to be stopped in the first half. Navy's crushing tackle Don Whitmire rubbed it in by writing the final score on the chalkboard in the gymnasium as the midshipmen departed. It was a hard loss to take, but Blaik's team had showed improvement over the previous year, posting a 7–2–1 record.

Red Blaik had made his mind up that 1944 was going to be the year Army would finally break into national prominence. He wanted more than a winning season, he wanted to beat Notre Dame. He wanted not just to beat Navy, he wanted to humiliate them. Blaik ordered his coaching staff to an 8:00 A.M. New Year's morning meeting to give them a dose of what they had to look forward to in the upcoming season.

Red Blaik was not a partygoer, and he hardly ever drank. That was part of why he was so valuable as an assistant coach at Army a decade earlier; he was more or less a permanent designated driver for the other, more traditional hard-drinking football men around him. His assistants on the 1944 Army team were more traditional in that regard, and it was a hard thing to come to Red Blaik's New Year's Day staff meeting so early in the morning. Andy Gustafson hid his swollen and reddened eyes with a pair of sunglasses. Others did not try at all to hide their misery.

Blaik did not care what they thought or how they felt. This was the year for Army to win it all. He believed that this was the year to bring the Brave Old Army Team back into national contention, and he wanted his staff to give more than 100 percent of their effort to that end. He would drive them harder than they ever had been driven before. He intended for the 1944 team to be the greatest in the history of West Point.

Then in July 1944 Blaik scored his biggest recruiting victory of all when he managed to get Felix "Doc" Blanchard to transfer from the University of North Carolina. Blanchard had been a widely recruited high-school football prospect in 1941. When the war broke out during his first year there, he tried to get into a campus officer program, but was rejected because of his size and weak eyesight. He left school to enlist in the Army and, ironically, got himself into the Army flying program.

Meanwhile, Blanchard's father, an influential South Carolina physician, worked his own network to get his son an invitation to take the West Point qualifying examinations. Felix, Jr., passed those tests and began his West Point days as a plebe in the Class of 1947. In his first college football game for Army, Blanchard helped Army pile up a 46–0 win over his former teammates at North Carolina. In the next game, another blowout, this time against Pittsburgh, Blanchard was again a standout, with one touchdown pass reception and an interception for another six-pointer.

Blaik's boys had honed the T formation to perfection. Red had taken Leahy's innovation and pushed it to the limits of its potential. Blaik intended to turn Notre Dame's own invention back on them in a way they would never forget. He wanted more than anything to be the coach who would break the Irish stranglehold on the Army–Notre Dame series. It had been twelve years since Army had tasted victory over that school.

Blaik came up with an innovation of his own in 1944, the platoon system. It really was not an entirely original innovation; Rockne at one point had suited up three complete teams for some games. The University of Michigan employed separate platoons on offense and defense beginning in 1941.

But it was at Army that modern two-squad football was perfected. Blaik used it mostly to provide ample rest for his players. He did not have them specialize on either offense or defense; most players were expected to play both ways. He also placed most of his younger players on one platoon, with the more experienced on the other. Both teams were quarterbacked by experienced seniors.

In this manner, Army would have a very capable junior squad ready to play whenever Army totally outclassed its opponent. This strategy provided for much more varsity playing time for the younger players, who would, by the time they were in their later years of eligibility, have much more game experience under their belts than their opponents who had been sitting on the bench behind players with greater tenure. It also provided the more experienced squad with the opportunity to rest and recover as a unit before and after the bigger games.

Blaik's strategic innovations and his recruiting successes combined with the cumulative effect of his policy changes on height-weight standards for football players and continued support from the superintendent of the football program (Eichelberger was commanding a corps in the Pacific at this time, and his successor, Francis B. Wilby, was equally supportive of Blaik's efforts) to produce in 1944 a team that was indeed one of the greatest Army football teams of all time.

Blaik also translated his immense success into turning Army's football program around, giving his players and supporters a grand sense of purpose that seemed to transcend his position as football coach. What was good for football at Army was good for the academy, in Blaik's calculations. He convinced Wilby to allow him to expand the privileges for his team. In 1944 Blaik instituted a new special program for the team, a program that was to prove to be his downfall in 1951.

In 1944 Blaik instituted a program of organized academic help for all his players. His intent was noble, but the practice quickly degenerated into an evil that soon consumed Blaik, his team, and nearly extinguished the academy itself. Players such as Glenn Davis were having so much difficulty keeping up with their studies that the coaches formed special tutoring pools to help them remain proficient throughout the academic year. Extra instruction was available to all cadets after class with instructors in the academic departments. But the help they provided was not much more than explaining the day's lesson just completed.

For the majority of the football players who needed more help than that, there was a cadet from the 1st Regiment assigned to provide extra instruction in the early evenings. For Davis, an instructor in the Department of Physics and Chemistry, Lt. Col. Francis I. Pohl, who was feared by all other cadets, provided the tutoring personally.

But even that was not enough. Davis flunked math in his plebe year and was turned back to the next class (1947) to repeat it in 1944. He determined that he would not flunk again; that would jeopardize both his football eligibility and his team's chances for success on the gridiron.

In those days the academy had expanded to double its prewar student population and was graduating cadets in three years rather than four. The Corps was organized into two regiments. In the interest of ensuring equal opportunity for all cadets, exams taken by the two regiments on separate days were identical. Armed with advance notice of what was on the test, a tutored cadet could prepare the answers in advance. Sometimes it worked out that a cadet from one regiment desiring extra help just before an exam would be tutored by a cadet from the other regiment who had taken the test that day. It was not as if they were getting the answers themselves, they were just getting special help in focusing their preparation. In this way, some cadets managed to get just enough help to graduate—Ralph Davis finished number 873 in a class of 875 men in the Class of 1946, Glenn at 305 out of 310 in the Class of 1947.*

---

* In the summer of 1942 the academy admitted twice as many cadets as in the previous year. The class that entered that summer would graduate in 1945, the second three-year class, with 852 members. The Class of 1944 numbered 474. The Class of 1945 had 875 members, but in 1947 (the next-to-last three-year class), only 310 graduated. From 1949, class size was in the 500–600 range and the curriculum returned to the four-year length of the prewar period.

Part Three

Bad Boys

Eleven

Roll the Score Way Up

While Red Blaik was building his storybook team of 1944, Notre Dame was on the slide. Coach Leahy had been drafted to serve in the Navy and was not at the helm of his team for this season. The Irish were not as big nor were they as powerful as they had been in the immediately preceding years, and in at least two of the six games preceding the contest with Army they were entirely unimpressive. They lost to Illinois, 13–7, just before the Notre Dame–Navy game.

Blaik dared to be hopeful as he skipped Army's game with an outclassed Villanova, bringing several of his assistants on a train to go scout Notre Dame at Navy. On the way, one of his men reminded him of the time that Rockne had skipped a game for a scouting trip and returned to find his team had lost. Blaik was confident that Gustafson could handle things. In the end he was glad he had taken the trip; it allowed him to spot several vulnerabilities in the Notre Dame line game as the midshipmen beat Notre Dame, 32–13, while Army crushed Villanova, 83–0.

Red Blaik got his men fired up for the upcoming game. He scrimmaged one platoon against the other at the Wednesday practice, and they both were so highly charged that neither could stop the other from scoring. Spirits were high as cadet rallies during the week were punctuated by unfurled banners outside barracks windows and mock gravemarkers for Notre Dame players were placed on the grounds of the academic buildings.

Notre Dame won the coin toss and elected to receive the kick-off. Doc Blanchard served up the honors and put the Irish back on their eighteen. Three plays later the Irish had to punt. Army marched to a first-possession touchdown and point after to take the lead, 7–0. They never looked back; they showed no mercy. Twelve years of revenge were exacted that day, and Blaik would not let up for a moment.

It was not only Blaik who wanted a rout that day; no one on the team wanted to take it easy on the Irish. Army intercepted eight passes and took three of them into the end zone for touchdowns in the first half. In the second half, even Army's third-string substitutes were beating up on Notre Dame, recovering fumbles and intercepting passes on the way to rolling up the score to a humiliating 59–0. The Notre Dame faithful never forgot the humiliation of that day.

Army's drive in the Notre Dame game typified their approach that year in producing high-scoring games. That approach gave new meaning to a fight song that had been in West Point's *Bugle Notes* for some time. It was titled "The Gridiron Grenadiers," and its purpose was to signify Army's intent to show no quarter on the football field. The most outclassed opponent would be shown no mercy by these "Black Knights" as the Corps sang:

> Eyes right! Watch us fight! Army's going to score.
> We're the boys who make the noise,
> We've licked this gang before.
> We have never known defeat,
> We would rather fight than eat,
> We're the heroes of the Gridiron Grenadiers.

> (Chorus)

> Roll that score—way up!
> Roll that score—way up!
> They will never want to play us any mo-or-or-ore,

Ya-ha-ha-ha-ha! Ya-ha-ha-ha-ha!
We're the heroes of the Gridiron Grenadiers.

The Army team was fiercely physical during this game. Blanchard hit one lineman so hard he dislocated the elbow and sprained the knee of his opposing Notre Dame defensive player on a single broken tackle. On another play the momentum of Army's tackler carried the action right into the official, with the referee suffering a dislocated shoulder and having to leave the game. Blaik and Notre Dame's acting coach, Ed McKeever, agreed to continue to play short one official. McKeever said after the game, "At least we got out of the game alive. We got it and got it good, but I think anyone who knows football knows we got it from a great team." Blaik relished the moment. But in the midst of this game, Blaik showed uncharacteristic nervousness as he paced up and down the sidelines.

The victory over Notre Dame set up the Army–Navy game of 1944 as the national championship contest, with Army ranked number one and Navy number two going into the game. The Brave Old Army Team rolled to victory in that one, too, by a score of 23–7. It was almost anticlimactic for Red Blaik, who basked in the knowledge that it was his team that broke the Notre Dame monopoly on the series. His champion General Eichelberger had listened to the Navy game on a short-wave radio in the battle zone in the Philippines, persisting even through a Japanese air raid.

At the half, Blaik pulled out a telegram from his mentor Eichelberger and read it to the team: ". . . win for all the soldiers scattered throughout the world." It was an inspiration to the team, especially to Hank Foldberg. Foldberg was matched up against Navy's biggest player, All-American Don Whitmire, who had transferred to Annapolis from Alabama. Foldberg's emotion lifted him to a brutally physical game, taking Whitmire out with an injury by the second quarter. Regular left tackle DeWitt (Tex) Coulter was in on the kill with Foldberg.

The emotion came to Blaik after the Navy game when General MacArthur wired to him: "THE GREATEST OF ALL ARMY TEAMS STOP WE HAVE STOPPED THE WAR TO CELEBRATE

YOUR MAGNIFICENT SUCCESS." This was Blaik's finest moment. He told his players in a special pamphlet printed exclusively for them, "Seldom in a lifetime's experience is one permitted the complete satisfaction of being part of a perfect performance. . . . From her sons West Point expects the best— you were the best. In truth you were a storybook team."

Throughout the 1944 and 1945 seasons, Red Blaik was totally consumed by football. He took no breaks during the year. During the day he rarely saw his family. By the early 1940s, however, his sons had begun a phase in their lives when a father's attention was in great demand.

Young Robert aspired to be a musician in his elementary school years. One of his instructors told Merle and Earl that the boy just was not cut out for music. What Bob Blaik really wanted to do was play football. He idolized Glenn Davis and patterned his own style of play after Davis. Bob Blaik excelled at football for his Highland Falls High School team.

Then, in 1946, the Blaiks decided to send their sons away to boarding school. Bob would have nothing of it and came back with his mother the same day she took them to the New Hampshire school. He wanted to finish the season with his team and enter the academy the next fall to play for Army. That fall he broke his collarbone and was sidelined for more than a month, never really achieving the stardom he sought.

A SECOND STORYBOOK YEAR

The 1945 season was another "storybook" one for Army, and the "Black Knights" (a sportswriter had assigned that nickname early in the 1945 season and it stuck) rolled to another undefeated season and a second consecutive national championship. No one could touch Blaik's '44 and '45 teams.

With Doc Blanchard and Glenn Davis spearheading the attack, Army's offense was unstoppable. Blanchard was named Mr. Inside and Davis Mr. Outside by a prominent sportswriter of the day. Davis was the faster man; he set West Point track records in the 100- and 220-yard dashes. Blanchard was also fast but he was noted more for his superior power. The two were the most well known of Army's players that year, but others achieved national prominence as well. Tom (Shorty) McWilliams could erupt for fifty-yard runs from time to time, as could Bob Chabot.

Army again beat up on Notre Dame in 1945. Going into the game Army was ranked number one nationally, while Notre Dame suffered several injuries to key players in its contest with the Naval Academy. Notre Dame was simply outclassed by the Cadets. Even in the kicking game, Doc Blanchard warmed up by booting eighty-yard kicks while the Irish kicker could manage to get the ball barely to the far goal line by taking a ten-yard running start.

Notre Dame was smaller and weaker than Army in 1945; at times the Irish linemen were intimidated by Army. Tex Coulter had been hit repeatedly in the face by William Fischer, who later related the story of how Coulter finally clutched him close and told Fischer, "Listen, fat boy, if you don't behave you're going to get killed." At that point Fischer says he desisted from any further dirty play. Coach Leaky was still away from his team while serving in the Navy. Not surprisingly, Army won again, this time by a score of 48–0.

Army was again undefeated and selected number one in the country by the college polls. West Point was invited to the Rose Bowl, but Blaik turned the bid down. He did not think the team had anything else to prove, and the players preferred not to have their Christmas exam period and leave interrupted.

Just before Christmas, Lt. Gen. Robert Eichelberger paid a visit to the academy, having recently returned from the Pacific Theater. He had had a difficult command, slogging across the ocean from island to island with MacArthur, from Australia to Hollandia to the Philippines. His corps had lost thousands of men in the tough fighting with the Japanese. MacArthur had given him only the toughest missions. With the assignment to take the island of Buna, MacArthur had instructed Eichelberger to secure the island or not come back. Eichelberger credited his West Point character-building with giving him the steadfastness to lead his men to victory. He believed that the football program at the academy had contributed in no small way to instilling in him and his soldiers a spirit of victory, and he was pleased that his decision to fight to get Blaik hired as head coach had turned out so well.

Throughout the campaign one of Eichelberger's divisions, the

24th Infantry, was commanded by the man who had been his commandant of cadets when Eichelberger was superintendent, Frederick Irving. Eichelberger respected Irving's sensibility. In the Hollandia landing, Irving had argued with Eichelberger to land the 24th Division on a beach that was known to be very difficult to travel due to the rocky coral surface just under the water. Smooth, sandy beaches were usually required for amphibious landings so that landing craft would not have their undersides torn up. Eichelberger finally agreed, and it turned out to be the only unopposed site on the entire beachhead.

Irving's attitude had surprised Eichelberger at the time. While Irving was serving as commandant, Superintendent Eichelberger had judged him to be "unassuming, efficient, quiet, almost austere." His opposition to Eichelberger's plan at Buna was uncharacteristic, but it turned out all right. Later, in the long march up the Philippine Islands, Eichelberger ordered Irving to take his division in the lead up a road that was known to be in poor condition and infested with Japanese ambushes. It was the only route the corps could take, and Eichelberger wanted it opened at all costs. Irving opposed the plan, again arguing with his boss that the road would be impassable. He was ordered to launch his offensive anyway. When the enemy artillery tore the road up and when torrential rains literally washed it away, Irving's march bogged down and he was relieved of his command by the Sixth Army commander, General Krueger. Eichelberger was able to salvage Irving's career by fighting to have him moved to the command of another division that was less in the thick of the fighting. A day later, the Japanese surrendered.

None of that mattered to Eichelberger now, at Christmas in 1945. He had lived through the greatest war in history and had fought well. He had returned to the place he loved, West Point, and saw that the legacy he built was intact. West Pointers had served well, and he could take much credit for putting in place the kinds of reforms that had made its lieutenants so effective in battle. Army aviators were led by the cadet pilots graduated out of Stewart Field, which Eichelberger had built. Army football teams made history as they rolled on to victory after victory, setting the tone for the Army in the field. Merle and Red Blaik entertained him in the house he had built for the coach. Eichelberger took justifiable pride in what he had done.

PEACE IN OUR TIME

For the Army and for the country, 1946 brought about a psychological decompression as the reality of the end of the war set in. General Dwight Eisenhower found himself as chief of staff of the Army, following in the footsteps of George Marshall and Douglas MacArthur. One of the dozens of problems he faced in shaping the postwar Army was giving West Point a new direction. He was determined that the institution would not revert completely to the old ways, as it had after World War I.

He assigned his friend Maxwell Taylor, combat hero of the European Theater in World War II, as superintendent with instructions to make sure that the leadership education of cadets was modernized. Eisenhower was particularly impressed with the advances being made in applied psychology, and he directed Taylor to institute a course of instruction for cadets featuring new techniques in leadership and personnel management that would "awaken the majority of cadets to the necessity for handling human problems on a human basis and do much to improve leadership and personnel handling in the Army at large."

Eisenhower was also very much concerned with the health of the honor system at West Point. He believed it to be the most important aspect of the development of an officer, one that grew as the officer matured into his career. For him, honor was something that became an instinctive part of an officer's character, one that controlled his actions without explicit thought. He wrote to Taylor, "The honor system, as a feature of West Point, seems to grow in importance with the graduate as the years recede until finally it occupies a position in his mind akin to the virtue of his mother or sister."

The chief of staff sensed that the honor system was being sacrificed to wartime expediency, and he wanted the slide halted immediately. Eisenhower was deeply affected throughout his Army career by an incident that happened when he was a cadet. Someone had thrown lightbulbs from an upper-story window into the central area. In those days, as it is today, this was a particularly popular practice because when the lightbulb impacted on the ground, it gave off a loud bang similar to that of a loud firecracker. Since fireworks were prohibited, the lightbulb grenade was the next best thing. It was also difficult for the administration to discover who the perpetrator was, since it could have come from any of dozens of windows facing the area.

In Ike's day, however, the tactical officers used a novel method of discovering who did it. Knowing that the cadets themselves enforced the honor code through vigilance committees, the tactical officers held a formation for all cadets and asked each one individually who did it until the guilty ones admitted their sin. Eisenhower was convinced that this was an abuse of the honor system and would serve only to undermine the effectiveness of the code. It meant that cadets who were honest and admitted their guilt would be punished while those who lied or remained silent could sacrifice their integrity for their own hide.

Eisenhower was convinced by his wartime experiences that the leadership at West Point had deteriorated during the war. When the war broke out, the Academy's best officers were reassigned to combat duties. Ike ordered Taylor to have at least the commandant of cadets, if not himself, personally instruct the staff and faculty of the academy never to use the cadets' honor against them in the enforcement of routine regulations. Taylor's response revealed that he did not believe as strongly as Eisenhower that there was any problem brewing at all.

Maxwell Taylor's concern was the football team. He recognized that the academy's national reputation had been built on the accomplishments of the football squad. But he was also aware of the charges that Red Blaik and the academy were harboring slackards and draft dodgers, whose interest in playing football was in escaping the dangers of combat, not in any patriotic sense of calling. Early in his tenure as superintendent, General Taylor reached the conclusion that "big-time college football as it developed after World War II did not fit readily into the West Point pattern of education." He determined to restore football to a less dominant status in the life of cadets.

Taylor was particularly concerned with the increasing level of special consideration being given to football players. He believed that the special tables in the mess hall, the tutoring, the trips away, all had contributed to a deep sense of detachment by the football team. The Corps of Cadets no longer considered the squad really part of them. This, Taylor felt, was a serious problem confronting his ability as superintendent to accomplish the academy's mission of producing effective combat leaders. The idea that maintaining a nationally-ranked football team contributed substantially to that cause simply did not wash with him.

He wanted West Point football to be like it was when he was a cadet, when the Army–Notre Dame game was the biggest event on the campus. Taylor had graduated in the Class of 1922, back in the time when Army played Notre Dame on the Plain at West Point and the whole post turned out for the affair. There was little money in the college game in those days, and Taylor wanted Army football to return to the time when no admission was charged to cheer on the Brave Old Army Team.

But General Taylor did recognize that times had changed and he could not turn back the clock on Army football. He did not want to destroy the football program, he only wanted to restore the sense of ownership of the team that the Corps used to have. He decided that the way to do that was to elevate the status of all other varsity sports at the academy to approach that of the football squad. He instituted a policy of providing cadets in all varsity sports the same privileges as those enjoyed by the football team. All varsity sports, not just football and a few others, would have training tables in the mess hall. The tutoring program would be expanded to any cadet engaged in intercollegiate athletics.

THE COMPETITION RETURNS

The year 1946 was to be a stressful one for Red Blaik and the Army football team. It started with a hair-raising incident for Blaik himself. While on a walk on the academy grounds after dark he was halted by a cadet guard who would not believe that he was Coach Blaik. The guard took him to a telephone and had him speak to the sergeant of the guard. Blaik told him that he was Red Blaik, and the sergeant of the guard replied, "Yeah, sure, you're Red

Blaik and I'm Frank Leahy." He finally got it straightened out, but one thing was correct; Leahy was back to put pressure on Blaik.

It is hard enough to play national-level college football, but to follow two consecutive national championships places tremendous pressure on a team and coaching staff. Army fans and alumni expected a repeat. Opponents and detractors said that Army's moment of glory was gone now that other teams had players back from wartime service. All the big-time schools were gunning for Army.

West Point in fact was not in as good shape in terms of its player personnel for 1946. Shorty McWilliams had been recruited away by Mississippi State. The new superintendent at West Point, Maxwell Taylor, protested—unsuccessfully—to the president of Mississippi State, claiming that the school had illegally offered McWilliams money to transfer. Other key players, including Doc Blanchard, suffered from injuries. Moreover, the three-year eligibility rule was reinstated after the wartime hiatus. Army's varsity squad was grandfathered so key men such as Glenn Davis would be allowed to play a fourth year, but no plebes could play. More ominous was the fact that the largest of Army's linemen had left. It would not matter how fast the backfield was or how well the quarterback could throw if there was no blocking or protection for them on the line.

In spite of the special tutoring Blaik had initiated for his players, grades continued to weigh heavily on the Brave Old Army Team. Tex Coulter, who had beaten up Navy's biggest threat in the 1944 game, was in serious academic trouble. Blaik wrote to General MacArthur in May pleading his case for intervention by the Academic Board and Superintendent Taylor on Coulter's behalf.

It was a tough year for the Brave Old Army Team; no victory was easy. Glenn Davis still suffered from injuries from the 1945 season. Then Doc Blanchard was hurt in the opening game of 1946. He tore several ligaments and a bone fragment in his right knee. He would never be the same; although he played in several games later in the year, he was half the football player he had been. At midseason All-American quarterback Arnold Tucker suffered a shoulder separation and sprained elbow that ended his passing attack, although he continued to play, serving up all running plays. Every game was tough, but none was more difficult than the Notre Dame game of 1946. This was the game Blaik looked to as the ultimate contest for the Brave Old Army Team. In this first postwar football season, colleges around the country were once again able to recruit football players from a pool of young men who did not face the draft into the armed forces. Notre Dame had been able to build a very big team and matched up to Army across the board. The Irish line was bigger and stronger than Army's, and Blaik knew he would not be able to go at them head-on.

Apparently fans were quite vocal and sometimes even physical in their expressions of contempt for West Point's team. New York City policemen were accused of ignoring rock-throwing incidents during the pregame march-on ceremony staged by the cadets. A letter-writing campaign aimed at the academy in 1946 flooded West Point with written accusations of running away from their wartime duties as citizens, since cadets need not worry about serving in battle until after their graduation, no sooner than three years after entrance as a plebe.

Frank Leahy was back in command at South Bend, and he brought his Fighting Irish team to New York early in the week. Leahy boarded them at the Bear Mountain Inn, just down the road from West Point. It was an obvious attempt to taunt academy officials and cadets, since the game was to be played as usual at New York City's Yankee Stadium, fifty miles away. They were looking for revenge after 1945's drubbing at the hands of the cadets, and they paraded their power on the academy grounds that week on tours of the public tourist sites.

During the pregame ceremonies in Yankee Stadium, while the Corps of Cadets was formed up on the field at attention, Leahy had his team doing warm-up drills between the front ranks of cadets and the stands so that all could see his men loosening up while the cadets were on parade.

The injury-ridden Army team could not get its offensive attack going against the spirited Notre Dame line. Neither side made much headway in the first quarter. In the second period, the Irish team fought its way to the Army four-yard line but was stopped cold on the ground. Frank Leahy gave no inspiring halftime speech in this game. His only words were, "All right, boys, Army's out there waiting for you." In the third quarter, Army got well into Irish territory but failed to score.

In the fourth quarter Blanchard ran the ball off a fake and broke downfield in the open. Only Notre Dame's safety was between Doc and a touchdown; from the angle and distance it looked to be a sure Army score. But that safety was none other than Johnny Lujack, who put on a burst of speed no one had ever seen in him before. As he closed in on the mighty Blanchard, he threw a textbook open-field tackle, bringing down his prey and ending Army's final scoring opportunity. That was the only time Mr. Inside had been taken down once he got past the linebackers.

But neither could Notre Dame bully its way past a tough Army defensive line. The game ended in a scoreless tie. Frank Leahy cried after the game. He cried after every loss he coached at Notre Dame, which was not very often. He was devastated by the failure to beat Army. He kept his coaching staff in the locker room well into the night, trying to analyze the reasons for not scoring. Red Blaik had finally encountered an opposing coach who sought after victory with the same passion he had.

Army closed out 1946, wrapping up an unprecedented third consecutive undefeated season, with a dramatic and narrow win over Navy, 21–18. That game was won by three fourth-quarter defensive stands inside the Army four-yard line and proved Blaik's axiom of the day, "Inches make the champion, and the champion makes his own luck." The cadets lost the number one ranking to Notre Dame, but Blaik was chosen as coach of the year. Glenn Davis and Doc Blanchard appeared in a Hollywood movie about Army football, but with neither of them playing the next season, it looked as if Army's fortunes for 1947 were about to decline.

Army faced as tough a schedule as ever in 1947. Powerhouses Illinois, Penn, and Columbia were reaping the benefits of the end of World War II, enjoying the opportunity to play upperclass players who did not face the draft. Men who otherwise might go to West Point to avoid the draft could now go to any college in the country to play football. Athletically ambitious schools recruited vigorously in attempting to rebuild their programs. Army's schedule, which looked easy in the war years, now was ominous.

GENTLEMEN, PLACE YOUR BETS

Then there was Notre Dame. Blaik had to contend not only with Frank Leahy's powerhouse of a team, but also with a very strong Notre Dame following all across the country, especially in New York. Scalpers and gamblers were putting as much pressure on the game as any Army general. The 1946 game, which in effect was for the national football title, had been a huge payday for ticket speculators. Although officials at both West Point and Notre Dame tried to keep tight control over ticket availability, restricting distribution to students, alumni, and friends of the schools, scalpers were able to acquire thousands of tickets. At game day they were going for two hundred dollars apiece. Wagering on the game was outrageous: Five million dollars had been bet on the 1946 game that ended in a scoreless tie. That meant that most bettors lost to those holding the books, since gamblers rarely wager on a tie.

Army–Notre Dame was the premier betting event across the country in 1947 in a business where bookmakers netted more than a hundred million dollars a year. After the 1946 game, bookmakers began the practice of allowing their customers to bet on the point spread as well as which team would win the game. The 1947 game would produce a volume by some estimates of as much as twenty million dollars.

That was the end of the Army–Notre Dame game for a decade. The accumulation of bad blood between the two schools was just too much for Superintendent Taylor, who felt that football had grown immensely beyond the appropriate scale at the Military Academy. West Point, to him, was supposed to be turning out combat leaders, not professional football players. Army's schedule had gotten wholly out of hand in the rush to maintain national recognition. The Army–Notre Dame contest had grown far beyond the attraction of the Army–Navy game, and Taylor thought that was bad.

Moreover, the animosity toward Army had grown as the football program at West Point continued to dominate that of other schools. The accusations of dirty play, shirking wartime duty, and gambling were especially shrill among the subway alumni, numbering in the tens of thousands. Accusations of recruiting violations aimed at Blaik prompted Taylor to reach an agreement early in 1947 with Father Cavanaugh that the game would be suspended after the 1947 contest. Blaik did not particularly like the idea, but he went along with the decision. It would lighten Army's schedule, and it would end all the complaining from New York.

Red Blaik held out hope that he could keep Army's unbeaten streak alive through to the middle of the 1947 season, when the cadets would take on Notre Dame. He knew the Irish would be seeking revenge and that they had grown bigger and stronger since the end of the war. Blaik hoped that by midseason perhaps injuries and bad luck could bring Notre Dame down a notch or two, and his cadets could aspire to at least a tie.

Gambling was not the only vice beginning to affect Army football. Blaik's system of providing extra academic help was beginning to pay off for a number of players who benefited from the extra help in understanding some of the complex math and science requirements of West Point's rigorous engineering program. Others were aided by help in composing the lengthy essays required in the new social sciences courses adopted by the academy after World War II. But by 1948 many football players were getting more than help in understanding concepts from their football tutors. They were, by then, getting answers to exams just prior to taking them.

It became known as "the poop," a term derived from military slang of the day referring to timely information about what was soon to happen. In contrast to the usual rumors, "the poop" was understood to be credible. For the Army football team, "getting the poop" meant to obtain the answers to an upcoming graded event. Sometimes "the poop" came from cadets who had taken the identical exam the day before; sometimes it came from an in-

structor. It always came through a select few football players and
tutors who were sworn to secrecy. It was provided only to a few
players who were in such academic trouble that there was a good
chance they would soon wash out of the academy. It was a way of
preserving the winning tradition that had so painstakingly been
built by Red Blaik in the first half of the decade of the 1940s.

Army approached the 1947 grudge game with Notre Dame with
its unbeaten string intact. They had dominated three lesser teams
and battled their way out of underdog status to tie Illinois, keeping the string intact at thirty-two. But then they looked past their
next opponent in preparation for the Notre Dame game. Blaik
could see on the Friday before the Columbia game that his team
and his coaches were not ready, and he told them so.

As Columbia warmed up on the field, in his pregame talk in
the locker room that Saturday afternoon, Blaik told his team, "You
are not ready for this game. If we don't snap out of it, we're going to get licked. I'm going to give the starting team five minutes
to score. Otherwise they'll be out of there." They responded with
thirty seconds to spare, but Columbia had already taken an early
lead. After trailing at the half by two touchdowns, Army was able
to get a lead in the third quarter. But Columbia rose again in an
inspiring fourth quarter to beat Army by one point. Throughout
the second half, Blaik's boys complained about bad calls from the
officials. Blaik concluded that this team had given up and wanted
to lose. The honor of ending Army's streak would go to lowly
Columbia.

Though they were disappointed that they were not the ones to
end Army's undefeated string, Notre Dame's players thirsted after the chance to drive Army into the ground. The Fighting Irish
finished off Army's hopes for national recognition. They took
Army's opening kickoff all the way back for a touchdown and before the end of the first quarter added another to go into the halftime break with a 13–0 lead. Blaik's young team was hopelessly
outclassed and lost the game, 27–7. They did manage to beat Navy,
ending the year with a record of 5–2–2.

Army's coaching staff was picked apart that year as badly as the
football team when four of Blaik's best assistants went on to be-

come head coaches at other schools. Blaik was devastated at first, but soon came to believe that his own leadership skills in developing his subordinate coaches were very much responsible for other schools' interest in his staff. He was further encouraged by a letter he received from Douglas MacArthur on the matter in April 1948, "It could not have failed to be a great blow to lose simultaneously your line and backfield coaches, both apparently excellent men. However, this again follows the technique of war, for you always lose your best men in the heat of battle."

Blaik was not soothed by his mentor's attempt. He replied, "Though it may seem comparable to conditions created when an Army staff position is vacated, actually it is far more involved as the techniques of football vary so much as to require a complete scrubbing when new men fill key positions on a staff." He praised the cadet players for succeeding beyond their abilities in the 1948 season and gave all the credit to his coaching staff for producing victories from an otherwise mediocre pool of player talent.

Red was able to advance the academic tutoring program for his players considerably. The tutoring program was expanded to be a year-round enterprise for the team. It made no difference to him that tutors from one regiment had begun to provide help to players from another regiment, even when tests were involved. He expected them to live up to the honor code and not use the tutoring sessions as an opportunity for cadets who had taken an exam to share what was being tested with those who were to take the identical exam the next day. He treated them all as honorable men.

The year 1948 was a bad one for recruiting at West Point. The plebe class of 1952 filled only 60 percent of the available openings for new cadets. The United States was entering the postwar period with full-blown enthusiasm for the pent-up demands that had been put on hold during the war years. Army had to compete with many other large schools for football talent and suddenly found itself at a disadvantage to the schools that could offer much that was not available in the spartan surroundings at West Point. But in 1948 the cadets returned to national prominence on the shoulders of All-American quarterback Arnold Galiffa and team captain Bill Yeoman. They were third in the country going into the Navy game and were heavily favored to win that game. Navy came into the game having lost its previous thirteen contests. But the best that Army could manage against the hard-fighting midshipmen was a 21–21 tie. Blaik later blamed rancid Thanksgiving turkey gravy for making his players sick on Friday before the Navy game.

After that tie, Blaik was ready to retire from football. He had been made an offer from Avco Corporation to go into business. One of his childhood friends from Ohio was head of the company in 1948 and tried to persuade Blaik to join him. When Superintendent Maxwell Taylor learned of the offer, he persuaded Blaik to stay by making him chairman of the Athletic Board at West Point. That made Red Blaik the undisputed monarch of athletics, since he held all three athletic decision-making posts the academy had to offer (head football coach, graduate director of athletics, and chairman of the Athletic Board). No one could go around his decision-making authority now unless they went directly to the supe. And even at that, Blaik, who had graduated from the academy two years earlier than Taylor, could almost always get his way. No other football coach in the country had that kind of power over faculty and school administration, and he could not pass that up.

Blaik had high hopes for the 1949 season. His players had matured in the past two years, and he had a hardened core of veterans to begin the spring training session. They positively dominated just about every opponent on the schedule that year, ending with a perfect 9–0 season. For Red Blaik one of the greatest achievements of the 1949 season was that his son Bob would earn his Army "A" as a backup quarterback to Arnold Galiffa. But other events conspired to make 1949 an ominous year for the man who had made the Brave Old Army Team a national football power.

Twelve

1949

Less than half a decade after the end of World War II, American culture exulted in its new dominance of the globe. Arthur Miller's play *Death of a Salesman* won the Pulitzer Prize for drama, while Rodgers and Hammerstein's musical *South Pacific* took Broadway by storm. Popular music featured "Some Enchanted Evening," "Diamonds Are a Girl's Best Friend," and "Rudolph, the Red-Nosed Reindeer." Leonard Bernstein began to startle musical audiences with one of his first discordant symphonic musical compositions, "The Age of Anxiety."

The last chapter of the war was closed with the hanging in December 1948 of Japanese war criminals, including General Tojo. But soon after Harry Truman's inauguration in January 1949, a new era of the Cold War began with the Communist takeover of Czechoslovakia in February 1949 and the formation in April of the North Atlantic Treaty Organization. China fell to Mao Tse-tung's Communists. The State Department's Alger Hiss was indicted for lying about his secret spying for the Soviet Union, and the Soviets tested their first atomic bomb, five years earlier than expected.

Bill Jackomis grew up in Gary, Indiana, the son of an immigrant Greek-born steelworker and a first-generation Russian mother. Bill's father worked as a laborer and tractor driver in the steel mills and could speak only a very little English. As a young man he had been forced to leave his home on the Greek island of Chios when the Turks invaded. Turks were killing all young Greek males, and Bill's grandfather, who was then governor of the island, put his young son on a passing Italian ship, where he made his way to America.

Bill's mother was born in Trauger, Pennsylvania, in 1909 of parents who had emigrated from Russia. Bill's grandparents had fled their native land to escape the Bolshevik slaughter of "White" Russians during the Russian Revolution, and had made their way to America by way of Hungary, Austria, and Czechoslovakia. Bill's maternal grandparents spoke virtually no English at home, and it was from them that Bill, at an early age, learned to communicate with them in their native tongue.

The Jackomis family was broken up early in Bill's life. He was raised by his mother in near poverty and seldom spent time with his father. When his mother's brother returned to Gary in 1945 after the war, all decorated with medals in his Army uniform, Bill made his mind up that he was going to be a soldier. His uncle had served in the Army's famed 2nd Armored Division as a tank destroyer commander, and Bill admired his many war stories.

Jim Pfautz grew up in Chestnut Hill, Pennsylvania, a suburb of Philadelphia. By disposition he favored the arts rather than science or mathematics. In fact, he did not really want to go to West Point; he knew that he would have a difficult time with its rigorous engineering curriculum. But his father put tremendous pressure on him to get an appointment and to go. The elder Pfautz had wanted to go himself as a young man but was never able to do it. He transferred his lost ambition onto his son James.

Jim Pfautz was in school in England the year before he entered West Point. While there he got a letter from a close friend, Joe Santili, who had been a year ahead of him back in Mercersburg, Pennsylvania. Santili had just finished his plebe summer for the Class of 1952. In his letter to Pfautz he described the honor code and how it made things go so much more efficiently at West Point than at any other school. You could really trust your schoolmates, Santili wrote to his friend. That was enough to convince Jim Pfautz to give West Point a try.

Jim Pfautz was also an accomplished athlete in high school. A slender but strong man, he was an outstanding swimmer and caught the attention of West Point athletic recruiters. Pfautz was able to get an athletic appointment not needed by the football coaches.

Football brought both men into the academy. Jackomis was recruited by Blaik's scouts for his overall athletic ability and his potential as a running back. Bill played football in Gary and was a standout athlete in several sports. His greatest claim to fame was in track. He set new records at his high school for the shorter distances and as an eighth grader became Gary's city track champion. He was also an outstanding leader in high-school ROTC and was a recognized top leader at Indiana Boys' State. Since Bill's family could not afford to send him to college, he sought an appointment to the academy by joining the Army National Guard's 113th Engineer Battalion. Bill became an expert marksman and a highly qualified technician on the unit's classified cryptographic equipment. The battalion commander pegged Jackomis as a West Point prospect and arranged for him to take the National Guard competitive examination as a means of getting an appointment. He also brought Jackomis to the attention of the football recruiters, who assisted with his appointment.

Bryant E. Moore, West Point Class of 1917, took over as superintendent of the U.S. Military Academy on 28 January 1949. He was a rather unlikely candidate for the post; as a cadet he never made rank and was not particularly outstanding in any field. He played on no athletic squads and laid claim only to one passion: literature. He spent much of his free time in the cadet library reading the classics. His initial assignment after graduation was with the 50th Infantry, a regiment that never made it out of the Stateside training camps before the Armistice was declared. He served nearly five years in the interwar period as an instructor in French at West Point.

EVERY SOLDIER GETS HIS WAR

But it is said that every soldier gets his war, and Bryant Moore's war was World War II. He was assigned to the Pacific right after the attack on Pearl Harbor, and in October 1942 the infantry regiment he commanded went in just behind the Marines at Guadalcanal. In 1943 he was promoted to brigadier general and reassigned to the European Theater, rising in a few weeks to two-star rank when he took command of the 8th Infantry Division for the final ferocious battles in Germany.

He returned to the States to train a new division for the anticipated invasion of Japan when war's end came. He was again transferred to Europe, where he took command of troops occupying a piece of disputed territory between Italy and Yugoslavia. While most occupation forces in Europe formed police-style constabulary units, working out of garrison barracks, Moore resisted pressure to stand down his division and instead kept them organized and trained in combat units. This proved to be the key to keeping the Italian and Yugoslav factions from fighting each other because they respected the ability of Moore's fighting troops to prevent either side from forcing ill-gotten territorial gains in the tense aftermath of World War II.

Glory had evaded him for twenty-five years, but in World War II and its subsequent geopolitical denouement his combat proficiency earned him a total of three Distinguished Service Medals and two Silver Stars. After a brief stint in 1948 as the Army's chief of public information he was selected to be superintendent of the Military Academy. But he knew that in going to West Point he would have a hard act to follow.

Moore was taking over an academy that was about to enter one of the most difficult periods of its entire history. Maxwell Taylor left it in good shape, but probably no superintendent could have been sufficiently prepared for the events that were about to unfold.

When he was notified by Washington that he was to be Maxwell Taylor's replacement, Moore called Red Blaik down to the Pentagon to talk about his transition into the superintendency. He told Blaik, "You are the athletic director and football coach. I don't know anything about football. Tell me something about it." But not long after Blaik began to speak, Moore told him that he didn't want to talk about football anymore. After a minute-long silence accented by Moore's whistling of a song, he sent Blaik on his way. Blaik figured that he had a really odd character on his hands compared to Maxwell Taylor.

Red Blaik faced several challenges early in 1949. Not only did he have to break in a new superintendent, he also had to break in yet another new assistant coach. It was the fifth time in three years that Blaik had lost a key assistant to the lure of a head coaching position somewhere else. This one was brought on by the departure of his offensive line coach, Sid Gillman. Gillman was enticed away from Army by the offer of the head coaching job at the University of Cincinnati. Gillman had been at Army for only two seasons but had introduced the practices of "rule blocking" and grading each player on each play of every game.

Given Army's record under Red Blaik, it was not difficult to find plenty of job seekers looking to fill Gillman's position. Blaik had expected 1948 to be a "rebuilding" year but had managed to assemble his fourth undefeated season in five years. Under his determined coaching, West Point won the Lambert Trophy as the best team in the East and ended the year ranked sixth in the nation. Twenty-five applicants submitted their résumés for the job, but Blaik turned to his longtime sportswriter friend Tim Cohane for a recommendation. Cohane suggested that he consider a highly successful freshman coach at Fordham by the name of Vince Lombardi.

VINCE

Blaik interviewed Lombardi three times and finally asked Cohane why Fordham would let him go if he was so good. Fordham had a reputation for poor coaching staffs in those days, so Blaik wanted to be sure that Lombardi had the drive for excellence he demanded of his assistant coaches. Cohane assured his friend that Lombardi, who had previously coached a high-school team to a string of undefeated seasons, would have what it takes to succeed at Army.

Blaik said that he saw that Lombardi had the sparkle in his eye that showed he could do the job, but he had his chief assistant, Murray Warmath, interview Lombardi as well. When Vince passed that test he concluded that Lombardi could learn the art of big-time coaching under Blaik's mentorship. Blaik offered Lombardi a salary of seven thousand dollars—average among assistant coaches of the day—and threw in some extras, such as housing on post for his family, access to the Army's medical care at West Point, and shopping privileges at the Post Exchange and Commissary. As an extra, he told Lombardi of the standing reservation the entire Army football coaching staff had at Gene Leone's famous Manhattan Italian restaurant, Mama Leone's. Lombardi took the job.

Vince Lombardi would learn much about coaching from Red Blaik. With Army he had to learn to teach "rule blocking" to his offensive linemen. For years linemen simply lined up man-for man, shifting assigned defensive linemen on each offensive play depending on the formation used by the defense. To execute well, offensive linemen had to memorize several different types of defenses for each offensive play they might run in any game. Blaik had perfected a technique for teaching his linemen to remember a few rules that would guide them to the direction in which they would block. Did the defense line up with a man over the center? If they did, the interior linemen would block while the tackles would cut. If there was no one over the center, the defense was set back and the offensive linemen were to cut off the defenders' pursuit of the ball. It greatly simplified things and was especially useful for Army, since they had so little practice time with players. Lombardi learned quickly and aggressively applied Blaik's techniques in a nearly servile manner.

While he was satisfied that he had made the best selection in taking Lombardi to replace Gillman, Blaik worried about the 1949 season. He had lost some talented players after the 1947 season, but he had lost big numbers of good men after 1948. Nineteen lettermen graduated or were ineligible for play in 1949. Nearly the entire defensive unit did not have the experience to earn a varsity letter. The plebe team from 1948 was unimpressive, losing four games. Three of the most promising freshmen players were at risk of becoming ineligible because of their academic performance. Blaik even complained to General MacArthur that his own son Robert ". . . has that serious disposition which sometimes forces one to try too hard. This was in evidence during his play last fall."

Red Blaik's 1949 thus got off to a worrisome start. Bryant Moore's tour of duty began with high drama when one of the Class of 1948's highest-ranked cadets, Richard D. Cudahy, publicly renounced his academic awards and returned them to the academy on 5 January 1949. He said to newspapers who reported the incident that he had won them through cheating on examinations.

Moore did not involve himself much in such isolated incidents. As the Army's former public information chief, perhaps he knew that some bad news does indeed go away if you just ignore it. It would turn out that he could not ignore what was happening to the academy's honor system.

Bryant Moore practiced a style of leadership in which most of the responsibility for academy policy and operation was left up to his subordinates. He led a personal style of management in which he basically set the example he expected those under his command generally to follow. His hands-off approach gave Coach Blaik a welcome relief from what he considered to be undue interference from Maxwell Taylor. Blaik now had a free hand to run the football program as he wished.

Red Blaik was hard on his players, but he was ruthless with his coaches. Everyone on the coaching staff was required to be at their desks by 8:00 A.M. Blaik held meetings with them through midafternoon in which they went over plays, scouting reports, and game films, and planned the upcoming daily practices. Practice was from 4:00 through 5:30 P.M., and Blaik would not let his coaches use notes; they had to have all plays and the day's practice routine completely memorized. After supper Blaik had the coaching staff back in the offices going over game films.

Lombardi thrived on the hard work and the relentless daily schedule. He spent January through March 1949 totally immersed in game books, practice plans, and films. He thought of Blaik as a perfectionist who considered superior performance to be the normal course of affairs. Blaik brought out Lombardi's fierce temper, a character trait that apparently had not shown itself at Fordham. Blaik told him he needed to get his temper under control, but Red also saw it as a strength when it got a player's attention and instilled a sense of fear of the coaches in the cadets.

On his first day on the practice field in the spring of 1949, Lombardi was working with the offensive line when Blaik called him over to talk. While they were talking, Lombardi noticed something he did not like among his players, so he broke away from Blaik, ran back to his men, and yelled at the offender loud enough for all to hear. When he returned, Blaik informed him that the Army manner of coaching did not allow that kind of behavior.

On another day at spring practice in 1949, Blaik had given Lombardi fifteen minutes to teach the offensive line five plays. When the time was up, Blaik told him to run play number 10. Lombardi sheepishly responded, "I'm sorry, Colonel, but I didn't have time to put it in." Blaik glared at his new assistant, then told him to run number 11 instead. Despite the demands, Lombardi considered Blaik to be the greatest coach he ever knew of.

By 1949 Red Blaik was involved in things outside of Army football. His admiration of Douglas MacArthur had led him into politics. From his proconsulate in Japan, MacArthur superintended the attempt to bring democracy to the Far East. In August 1948 he installed Syngman Rhee as president of South Korea. By June the last American soldiers were off the Korean peninsula entirely. Throughout the summer of 1948 some Republicans were urging MacArthur to run for the presidency.

Thomas Dewey and Robert Taft were the leading candidates going into the convention, and to break out of a deadlock, a group of Republican Party leaders convinced Blaik to urge MacArthur to return to the United States from Japan to make a last-minute run for the party's heart. Led by a prominent senator from Blaik's formerly adopted state of New Hampshire, party leaders convinced Blaik that MacArthur could unify the party. Perhaps they also argued that his own fortunes would rise if he could persuade the general to return and accept the nomination by acclamation at the convention.

Blaik wrote a lengthy letter to his mentor, laying out the political terrain in some detail. He told MacArthur that the nomination was his for the taking, he would not even have to campaign for it, but he would have to return to the States and attend the convention. MacArthur was not moved. He stayed in Japan, and Dewey managed to win the nomination and lose the election.

Red Blaik faced pressure from yet another unusual circumstance in 1949. His son Bob was a yearling in the Class of 1952. During all their time at West Point, Red Blaik hardly had time to get involved in his younger son's life. Bob developed into an above-average athlete and was a standout at the local high school in football, hockey, and baseball. After graduating from Highland Falls High School he spent a year in prep school at Phillips Exeter Academy to prepare for West Point's entrance exams and was a football star there as well, setting school records in the grudge match with archrival Phillips Academy of Andover, Massachusetts.

But throughout his high-school years Bob saw little of his famous father. He would not even let the elder Blaik observe his games at Highland Falls High School, just outside the gate at West Point. In 1949 Bob Blaik hit it off well with Vince Lombardi. He learned to loosen up after hours under Vince's fatherly care, even though he never let up in intensity on the football field. Lombardi said of Bob Blaik, "Bob doesn't make the same mistake twice . . . [and is] . . . an exceptionally intelligent football player. . . ." Bob Blaik's father said that his son was not a natural athlete. Red Blaik had no idea at that time just how seriously estranged from his son he would soon become.

BY THE BOOK

Bryant Moore had no idea how troubled his Tactical Department would soon be. The head of the TD was Col. Paul D. Harkins. Harkins was commandant of cadets from 1948 to 1951. By early 1949 he had reaffirmed at West Point the rigid style of discipline he had built his reputation on as George S. Patton's operations officer and deputy chief of staff throughout World War II. *Newsday* magazine had called him a ". . . ramrod [whom] pistol-packin' Patton picked to get orders carried out in a hurry."

In some contrast to George Patton, however, Paul Harkins was a quiet man. He did not like any of his own subordinates to draw attention to themselves, and he detested those he called "prima donnas." He followed the rules "by the book" and he expected all those under his command to do so. His doctrinaire approach to life nearly got him killed once as commandant. He imposed the regulatory punishment on a cadet who had misappropriated a truck. The cadet's father stormed into Harkins's office one day later, called the general a Commie, and pulled out a gun. He apparently never got to do the deed he intended on the commandant.

Harkins' Tactical Department had a few characters even more dogmatic than he was. Lieutenant Colonel Arthur S. Collins was a company tactical officer and later commander of the 1st Regiment of the Corps of Cadets. Collins had seen his share of combat duty in World War II on the line in infantry regiments throughout the entire conflict. He believed that many young men had gone to West Point during the war years to evade the draft and avoid fighting. In 1949 he was concerned that Academy graduates were causing disciplinary problems in the Army's basic schools, and he resolved to instill the proper motivation in the cadets who passed through four years in his regiment. He particularly loathed the large number of football players admitted to the academy in 1949 whom he believed lacked the necessary educational qualifications to be cadets. He called them "recalcitrants who would do anything to break regulations."

Lieutenant Colonel Tracy B. Harrington would become Colonel Collins's regimental executive officer. He shared Collins's contempt for football players. One summer two football players, cadets Charlie Kuyk and Donald Mackey, misappropriated a truck so they could drive back to the main post from Camp Buckner. They were caught in the act, and Mackey was apprehended while Kuyk was in the cadet store buying the goods they had conspired to take back out to Buckner. Harrington was Mackey's tactical officer at the time and had him brought up before a Commandant's Board. This was one of the most serious disciplinary panels at the academy, empowered to impose the most severe levels of punishment short of dismissal. A "Com's Board" consisted of several officers chaired by the commandant himself and could put a cadet on the area enough hours to keep him out of circulation for nearly an entire academic year.

Under questioning, Mackey refused to identify his coconspirator to the members of the board. Harrington was furious. He recommended that the board impose the maximum punishment on Mackey, and Harkins gave him six months on the area. Later, Coach Blaik called Colonel Harkins and revealed Kuyk's name. While both cadets were marching off their punishment tours, Blaik appealed their case to the superintendent, asking for special dispensation for these two key players whose absence from the football field would hurt Army's chances of winning. Moore gave in and commuted their punishments after they had served fewer than two-thirds of their walking hours.

By 1949 there was a rising degree of animus between the Tactical Department and the football coaches. Tacs believed that all the special privileges for football players hindered their ability to maintain proper discipline among cadets. Even the football team trainer had the authority to excuse players from military duties, and many tacs believed that this power and others at the disposal of the coaches were wielded far too often. Blaik and his staff would frequently intervene in matters that were supposed to be the domain of the tactical officers or the cadet chain of command, such as room assignments and table seating in the mess hall.

It is the superintendent's job at West Point to keep his staff working together as a team. This is not an easy task when dealing with great egos and powerful personalities such as those of Harkins and Blaik. The clash between the commandant and the coach became a struggle for power that each man determined to win at the expense of the other. The superintendent, Bryant Moore, simply was not up to the task of forcing these men to work with each other in spite of their differences. He probably did not even realize that he had such a problem. He certainly had no clue that there was a far more serious problem brewing in the honor system.

Early in the second semester of the 1949 academic year, a clumsy attempt at cheating was discovered in the Mechanics Department. An instructor for the solids course, Maj. L. B. Fisher, noticed that an examination paper was missing from the classroom he had set up just prior to the cadets' entry to take the test. The customary practice for tests was for the instructor to place the "writ" papers face down on each desk just prior to the beginning of the class period. As cadets entered they would stand behind their seats until the section marcher reported to the instructor at the appointed minute marking the beginning of the period that all cadets were present. Once the instructor gave the command "Begin work," each cadet was authorized to turn over the examination paper and begin work.

It was easy for Fisher to see not only that a test paper was missing, but since he knew who was assigned to each seat, he also knew whose test was gone. The man, a football player, was confronted and admitted to removing the papers before the class and revealed his scheme. He had arranged with a classmate, another football player who was in the fluids course on the same day, that they would share intelligence on tests. Since both men took both courses the same year, he knew that his classmate would have the same solids test the next day. Whenever a fluids test came up the favor would be reciprocated. These two were caught and forced to resign for cheating.

Later in the semester, Lt. Col. W. L. Winegar, the history of military arts professor who had many of the lower-ranking cadets, the "goats," suspected something was up in his classes. Normally all his sections carried about the same grade average, barely passing. About halfway through the semester he noticed that the cadets who had his class second hour in the morning were averaging considerably better than those who took the class first thing in the morning. He suspected that the first-hour cadets might be sharing test answers with the second-hour cadets, but never obtained any hard evidence to prove his suspicion. Football players dominated these lower-ranking sections, and Winegar later thought that the cheating probably centered on the football team.

The academic coaching system for football players contributed to the appearance of unfair advantage. In 1949 Lt. Edgar Kenna was assigned the duty of organizing the academic tutoring for football players. Kenna had been an outstanding football player himself and was an accomplished student as a cadet. After a short tour of duty in Germany he was assigned to West Point in 1946 as an assistant coach.

His responsibilities as organizer of the football team tutoring program brought him into contact with cadet life in the barracks, since that was where the tutoring took place. He learned much about the internal workings of cadet society. In particular, by 1949 he discovered that resentment was building within the Corps between football players and the rest of the Corps. Cadet companies compete fiercely for a coveted award known as the Banker's Trophy, which is awarded annually to the company with the best intramural record across all sports for the entire year. Flanker companies usually had a difficult time competing for the Banker's Trophy because so many of the bigger cadets played on varsity teams, especially football, and therefore were unable to play on intramural teams. Kenna believed that some companies deliberately tried to make bigger men ineligible to play on the varsity squad so they would be able to play for their intramural team. Perhaps fed up with such pettiness, Kenna resigned his commission in 1949 and left the Army to go into business.

The cheating that had begun on such a small scale in the early 1940s had grown to larger proportions by 1949.

THE POOP

At the 1949 spring "Monster School" two candidates had advance copies of the entrance examination with the answers marked. Of course, it must have taken a fairly advanced intellectual effort to memorize the answers; nevertheless, those two football players probably would not have passed the examination on their own. These two later had trouble in English. They used their access to the cheating ring to get advance word on answers to tests to maintain a passing grade and to be eligible to play football.

Word about the cheating even spread outside the academy. One football player was recruited by being told not to worry about the possibility of having academic trouble. The football recruiter told him that all he had to do was "get the poop" and he would do just fine. This particular player did indeed learn how to "get the poop," and by the spring of 1949 he was right in the middle of the conspiracy to keep varsity athletes out of academic trouble by providing answers to upcoming test questions. Ironically, after this cadet settled into the West Point routine, he was able to keep his own grades proficient without the need to cheat. But by his yearling year in 1949 his primary social group was the cheating ring, and he could not break out of it.

Another football player had so much academic trouble he had to repeat both his plebe and yearling years. In 1948 the upperclassmen running the cheating ring told him about the illicit enterprise at the football training table in the mess hall. They brought him into their confidence and provided him with answers to upcoming tests. For the younger player, the cheating became an addiction. He had to keep coming back to the upperclassmen to maintain a passing grade; he became so dependent on them he could not turn them in. He became known and liked among others by his association with these popular varsity players. They became the focus of his social life as well. He figured that someday he might get caught, but he believed that he would graduate before the administration could catch on.

There was even an inside man. In the spring of 1949, when each class held its elections for the next year's Honor Committee, a member of the cheating ring was elected from one of the flanker companies dominated by football and hockey players. This gave the ringleaders enormous power to protect themselves. Without ever revealing his identity, the mole could influence investigations before they ever came to a committee hearing. He could also warn ring members whenever suspicions were aroused.

Honor Committee members were the first points of contact for reporting suspected violations of the honor code. Whenever a cadet reports a suspected violation, the Honor Committee representative first makes a judgment as to whether there is reasonable suspicion that a violation has taken place. If he thinks it has, he then reports it to the committee, which then decides whether to mount an investigation. But if the initial honor representative arbitrarily decides that no violation has been committed, the issue never goes any further. Hence, having a member of the cheating ring on the Honor Committee meant that whenever a violation was reported to him, it was sure not to be investigated or even reported further.

All during the spring of 1949 the membership in the ring expanded rapidly. Soon "the poop" was being passed in the mess hall and the varsity locker room. One football player who observed English poop being passed at first thought it should be reported but did nothing. Later he availed himself of the opportunity provided by the cheating ring when he needed "the poop" to pass a social sciences examination. In fact, he did not even seek it out, he simply sat in on "poop" sessions for others and used the illicit information to improve his own already high grades.

Despite such undercurrents in the Corps of Cadets, Bryant Moore had no clue that something was seriously wrong at West Point. He put in place grandiose plans for celebrating West Point's sesquicentennial three years hence, in 1952. It was to be a grand commemoration of the academy's first 150 years and a symbol of the steadfastness of the institution so imbedded in America's culture that it would continue to grow for at least another 150 years. He wanted it to highlight all the virtues that had served the country so well, duty, honor, country. He was so convinced that nothing was amiss that in his annual address to the Association of Graduates in June 1949 he said, "The honor system was never in better hands, or, I think, in better shape, than the present first class is leaving it." He was so wrong.

Royalty at West Point: The Prince of Wales and Brig. Gen. Douglas MacArthur, Superintendent, at the Academy in 1922.

Founder of Army football, Dennis Michie, class of 1894. Michie went on to become a fallen hero at the Battle of Santiago during the Spanish-American War in 1898.

The more experienced Navy team shows Army's rookies how the game is played in the first Army-Navy contest in 1890 on the Plain at West Point. Navy won 24-0.

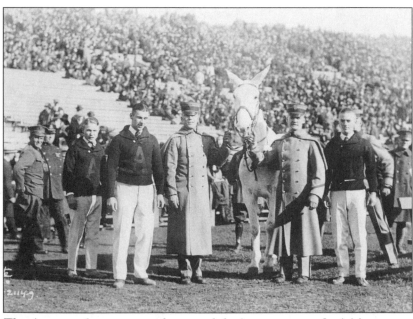

The Army mule warms up the crowd during pre-game festivities.

The 1891 Brave Old Army Team was more experienced by the time of the second Army–Navy game, which they won 32-16.

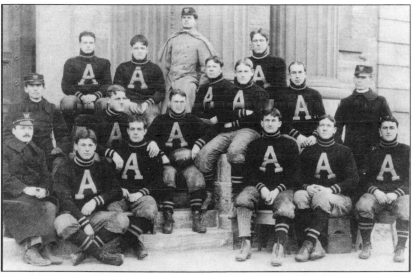

The 1899 Squad upset Navy in the first Army-Navy game since the 1893 game led to a near fatal duel, an outcome that led the Secretary of War to cancel the contest for the next five years.

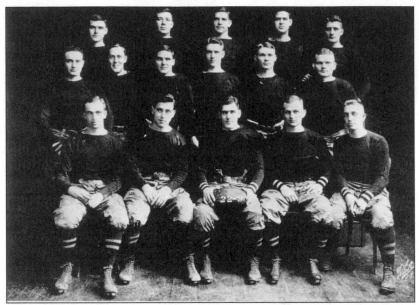

This Army team played Notre Dame for the first time in 1913, losing 35–13, due to the Irish's new secret weapon, the forward pass. By the time of this photo at the Army-Navy game, the Army team was tougher, bigger and stronger than most of its East Coast opponents.

Harvard was a football powerhouse in this 1904 photo of their game with Army on the Plain.

Cadet enthusiasm on campus the week before the Army-Navy game leads some to sacrifice even bed sheets in support of the Brave Old Army Team.

Early tackling dummy, circa 1900–1925, shows sack tied up to hoist with a player pulling on rope to get dummy in air while other players tackle sack.

By 1925 Army football reaches national prominence; the Notre Dame game is moved to New York City and the notables are eager to be seen. Gen. John "Black Jack" Pershing, left, looks on.

Red Blaik was a lean, tough football player in 1919.

Young head coach Gar Davidson offers advice to the team at a practice in 1937. Red Blaik was stung that someone so junior to himself (Davidson graduated in 1927) was selected as Army's head coach that year.

Parade of Cadets before Army-Notre Dame in 1939. New York fans were so partisan toward Notre Dame that even the police were accused of not providing protection to the marching West Pointers.

"The Whip," as he had been known when he was an assistant coach, had a commanding presence. Here Coach Blaik has the undivided attention of his players at the first practice of the season in 1942.

Superintendent Robert Eichelberger worked behind the scenes to get Blaik appointed to the head coaching job. Usually the staid Academic Board, whose policy had been to appoint only a serving officer to the post, makes the decision. Here Eichelberger reviews the 1941 team with Coach Blaik.

Glenn Davis and others discuss the next day's Notre Dame game with Coach Blaik in 1944.

Red Blaik told his 1945 squad at their first practice that he expected them to be the greatest team in the history of West Point football. Bob Chabot, Arnold Tucker, Doc Blanchard, and Glenn Davis were a large part of the reason for Blaik's confidence.

One former Notre Dame player later wrote that he once watched Doc Blanchard kick a ball 80 yards for a field goal during pre-game warmups. Here Doc shows his skill before the watchful eye of Coach Blaik in 1945.

Part of Blaik's deal with Eichelberger was that he could bring on his own assistants, including Andy Gustafson, Averell Daniel, Spec Moore and Harry Ellinger, shown in this 1941 photo of Army's coaching staff.

Red Blaik with his team in Yankee Stadium before the 1944 humiliation of Notre Dame 59–0.

Glenn Davis and Doc Blanchard seen here running together.

Red Blaik called his son Bob a "manufactured" athlete, shown here throwing a pass in 1950.

Under publicity manager Joe Cahill, who would later become an Army head coach in the 1960s, Army developed a powerful sports information machine, capitalizing on such posed shots as this 1950 glossy titled "Backfield In Motion."

A recent photo of Red Blaik's prominent grave marker at the West Point National Cemetery. (Courtesy Jeffrey Blackwell)

Michie Stadium as it looks today. Several influential Blaik supporters have tried to get the stadium renamed for their hero, going so far as to appeal—as yet unsuccessfully—to the president of the United States to get him to issue an order to that effect.

On Brave Old Army Team

The Army team's the pride and dream
    Of every heart in gray,
The Army line you'll ever find
    A terror in the fray;
And when the team is fighting
    For the Black and Gray and Gold,
We're always near with song and cheer
    And this is the tale we're told:

The Army team. (whistle)

Rah Rah Rah BOOM!

Chorus:

On, brave old Army team,
On to the fray;
Fight on to victory,
For that's the fearless Army way.

—*Bugle Notes,* 1950. p. 137

Thirteen

Plebes

Bill Jackomis ran down the gray granite steps out of the mess hall and onto the concrete that stretched out across the area to the stoops of the barracks. All plebes had to move at a "double-time" pace whenever they were outside; that meant they had to run everywhere they went. Jake had become accustomed to this, but this morning he had more reason to run than he had during Beast barracks or Reorgy Week. Today was the first day of class.

He had twenty minutes from the time the plebes were dismissed from the breakfast table to get back to his room, put the final touches on his prebreakfast cleanup job, grab his books, and run back outside to stand in formation to be marched off to the classroom building for his first instructional period. Those precious minutes went by quickly, and the faster he ran now the more seconds he would have to get it all done.

He ran up the stoops of his division, making sure he hit each step with one of his feet. He had learned that I-1 yearlings were especially on the lookout for plebes who skipped steps. Then, as he rushed into the doorway, he hugged the right side of the stairwell as he double-timed up the stairs to his fourth-floor room. Blasting past the open door, he went straight to the washbasin to brush his teeth. As he reached into his wall locker for his toothpaste, his roommate, (a roommate was also known as a "wife" in cadet parlance) J. F. "Johnny" Bleecker from Wisconsin, came in and joined him at the washbasin to brush his teeth as well.

They said nothing at that point. They got along all right, although not nearly as well as Jake and Flip had during Beast, but there just was no time for casual conversation at this moment. They cleaned and dried their basins when they finished with their teeth. Both men finished their chore, then moved over to their desks; 647 other plebes were doing almost exactly the same thing at that moment. Jake picked up his mathematics books and his slide rule text. Those were the classes his schedule told him he would go to this morning. He had studied last night until "lights out" at 11:00 P.M. and felt pretty confident that he was ready for his first math class. Jake was pretty good with mathematics; he practically coasted through algebra and geometry back at Tolleston High in Gary, Indiana. He did well enough that he took a semester of introduction to calculus, figuring it would help him get ready for West Point.

Last night's math assignment for today's class was not too difficult. There was about a five-page reading assignment, just basics really, then there were about fifteen practice problems in the textbook; the assignment sheet they were issued said to be prepared to work all of them in class. Jake had taken the time to work through each one and was satisfied that he knew this lesson cold. Bleecker had more trouble with his problems, but Jake explained some of them and Johnny felt he knew enough to get by.

They also had a half-hour class down in the company sinks the previous night from their honor representative, a second classman—in cadet slang, a "cow"—named Duane Tague. Tague explained the "all right" system to them. It was a way of using the honor code to make the enforcement of regulations more effective and easier on cadets. A cadet on duty, such as a guard or charge of quarters (CQ), could ask you, "All right?" You are expected to respond with the statement, "All right!" which means that you are making an official statement that you are going on an authorized visit and nowhere else, and that you had observed and would continue to observe regulations with respect to gambling, hazing, limits, liquor, and narcotics. At taps every night the CQ would check each room, asking for an "All right." When that response is given it means that, to the knowledge of the cadet responding, all occupants of the room are undressed and in bed.

Bleecker had stacked his class materials on his desk so he could pick them up quickly. The stack was pretty tall, actually. There were two math books, one giant-size volume with a black hard cover that the yearlings told them was called the "Black Death." Sooner or later, the old hands said, the Black Death would get you. The book was oddly shaped, longer and wider than most textbooks. That made it hard enough to carry under his arm. Then the math problem book was smaller than ordinary and had a paper cover. His second-period class was to be military topography and graphics, and that required him to haul a map book, a slide rule textbook, and a workbook. The whole pile was quite awkward and the smaller paperback books tended to slip out. Bleecker turned to his roommate and said, "Man, Jake, I hope I don't drop one of these on the way to math. I just know some yearling will be watching and write me up if I do."

"Don't worry about that, Bleek," said Jake. "Even if that happens, Mr. Beck will be okay on us." Don Beck was the yearling in their squad assigned to take care of Johnny Bleecker and Bill Jackomis. Beck was responsible for inspecting his plebes before formation and checking them off for their memorization of plebe poop. He was not a particularly tough yearling, at least compared to other third classmen in I-1 Company. Beck was on the varsity football team, and, as with most football players, his inclination was to go easy on most military details. His mind was mostly on football. Since Bill Jackomis was on the plebe team, Beck kept his eye on him, too. And because Bleecker was Jackomis's roommate, Johnny had it a little easier as well.

THE CLASSROOM
But nothing could make it easier to carry those clumsy books. Jake and his roommate clutched them tightly and double-timed down the stairs to the class formation now shaping up in the central area. Plebe math students filed out from the barracks and formed

up by section. About three hundred men would be taking plebe math today, starting promptly at 7:55 A.M. The West Point way of getting every man to the right seat on time was to form them up ten minutes early in the exact order in which they would be seated, then march them into their classrooms. Jackomis and Bleecker found their assigned sections and fell in line. The plebe at the head of each twenty-man section was designated as the "section marcher." He would check the roll to make sure everyone assigned was there, then march the section off into the classroom.

Jake's section marcher got the job by being the alphabetically-ranking man out of the twenty. They marched out of the area, across the street, and into the East Academic Building. At least while they were in formation they were not required to double-time. They filed into the room and lined up behind their chairs, standing "at ease" until the instructor entered the room. They had a few minutes to kill, and Jake let his thoughts wander to the events of the past two months. It was quite a trip so far. He hoped football practice this afternoon would be worth all this.

Without warning, the section marcher yelled, "Section atten-shun!"

Jake snapped to attention and rudely brought his mind back to the present. From his angle he could clearly see the instructor as he entered the room. He was an officer, wearing a stiffly pressed army uniform. Jake could read his name tag. "HALL" it said in white block letters on a hard black fabric plate. He wore captain's bars on his shoulders and had only two rows of ribbons on his chest. Most of the tactical officers he had seen during Beast were majors or lieutenant colonels, and they had row upon row of ribbons reaching up from their pocket nearly to their shoulder, indicating much combat experience and perhaps a number of instances of bravery under fire. This math instructor must not have had as much combat time in World War II, thought Jake.

He had one redeeming quality, though. Jake noticed that his lapel sported the brass insignia of the armored corps. That meant that Captain Hall was trained in tanks. Whatever time he had spent with troops before coming to West Point instructor duty he spent in the tank corps. That's where Jake's uncle had spent his

time, and Jake knew from the war stories the old man had come
home with back in 1945 that this captain must have had his own
set of tough times. Jake hoped the instructor would take some
class time to tell war stories.

Captain Hall marched stiffly into the classroom and went to his
desk at the head of the class. The seats for the plebes were arranged in a squared "U" so that all desks faced the instructor and
he could easily see every man while they were standing at attention. The students of course could not always see him since, while
standing at the position of attention, they were required to keep
their heads and eyes rigidly to the front. Captain Hall moved from
his desk and stood directly in front of the section marcher. What
was supposed to happen at this point did not. Captain Hall departed from the script that the plebes had been told would be followed at the start of each class.

Instead of taking the attendance report verbally from the section marcher and ordering the class to "take seats," Captain Hall
said nothing. Absolutely nothing. Jake would not dare to turn his
eyes to the side to see what he was doing. Hall made no noise, so
it was impossible to figure out what was going on.

Captain Hall then clicked his heels as he moved from the section marcher to the next man down. Then the officer spoke: "Harris, improperly shined shoes, two demerits."

So that's what was up. This captain was inspecting them. Jake's
heart plunged. He was not ready for this. He knew his belt buckle
had not been shined correctly. In fact, it had not been shined at
all. Mr. Beck had told him that he could just leave the lacquer finish on his class belt buckle rather than rubbing it off, as all the
other plebes were required to do. Removing lacquer was a tedious
process and took about an hour of solid rubbing with Brasso. With
all the lacquer off, Brasso would bring a brass belt buckle to a brilliant shine as long as there were no scratches on it. The problem
was, you had to keep shining it during the day or smudges and
prints would show up as dark spots and streaks. Beck thought it
was a waste of time, since the lacquer held up a shine just fine.
He told Jake to wear a highly shined buckle anytime they were in
a company formation, but when he was just going to class he

would let him wear another buckle that had the lacquer still on it. In that way he could save a lot of time, and from a distance no one could really tell whether the lacquer coating was on or off.

Captain Hall could tell. "Mister Jackomis, you get ten demerits today, unshined buckle. If you had at least attempted to shine that brass you would only get three demerits for improperly shined buckle. But you get the prize for trying to get away with the most. Next time I see you in my class that belt buckle better shine."

Hall checked every man and found something wrong with about half of them. Then he went back to the section marcher and took the report. "Sir, fifth section is all present for class," said the plebe at the head of the section as he rendered a stiff hand salute. Captain Hall returned the salute and said, "Fine, take boards!"

That was a command they were not expecting. They were told that the instructor would take the report, order them to "take seats," then go over the material they studied the night before. This instructor did not do that. He seemed to assume that they all understood everything. Hall continued, "Write your name and company in the upper right-hand corner of your board, as you see on my demonstration board up front, then stand at ease facing inward for further instructions."

Around the room each wall was covered with chalkboard from end to end. The board sections were separated by a heavy white line and numbered in the upper left corner. Each seat had an assigned chalkboard. Jake was at seat number five, and his board was just about directly behind him. He went up to it, looked at the board at the front of the room, and copied it precisely on his own board. He drew a small rectangle in the upper-right corner in which he wrote his name and company. Then he drew a straight vertical line from top to bottom precisely down the center of his board, using the yardstick hanging from a nail to the right of his board.

When each man had completed this task, Captain Hall then spoke up again. "Take your problem books to your boards. Even-numbered boards work even-numbered problems, odd-numbered boards work odd-numbered problems. Begin work. When you are finished put your chalk down and face your own board until the command 'Cease work' is given."

So that's how education was going to happen at West Point. Jake opened his problem book and began to work problem number one. He wrote out each step in the solution, then drew a line under his work as he moved on to problem number three. It wasn't too hard, he had tried each one last night. The only thing that was difficult was concentrating on his work with all the noise of twenty guys simultaneously banging chalk on a board. He also had to try hard not to look to his left and right as he worked.

It was not that he wanted or needed to look at his classmates' work to get through the problems himself. But they were so close to each other it was too easy to glance to the side and catch a glimpse of the work of the guy next to him. Of course, it would not have done him any good to try to copy, since he was working on odd-numbered problems out of the problem book and the men on his left and right were working even-numbered problems. He got to number nine in seemingly no time at all when he suddenly heard Captain Hall bellow, "CEASE WORK! Place your chalk in the tray and take your seat."

Jake put his chalk down, what was left of it. He saw that he had just about used up an entire stick of the white stuff. What was not on the board was on his hands, he noticed, as he brushed his palms together to try to remove the powder from his skin. He sat down in a seat for the first time since breakfast in the mess hall and he noted on the clock on the wall that it was now eight forty-five, meaning he had been on his feet for an hour and forty-five minutes. Suddenly Jake was sleepy. He was not particularly tired, but his eyes just wanted to close at that instant. They had been open for some time and had taken in quite a lot of things already this morning into a brain that seemed suddenly to be trying to shut down and conserve energy.

"Mr. Smith, go up to your board and explain how you arrived at your solution to problem number one," said the young captain. Smith was the last man in the section, and he struggled with the explanation. It was obvious from his words as well as from his work on the board that he had no idea how to solve that problem. Hall let him go on until he reached a conclusion.

"Smith, that is entirely wrong. You'll be written up for being unprepared for class. It will be up to your tactical officer to decide what your punishment will be." Apparently Captain Hall believed in the negative leadership approach to teaching, Jake thought. It reminded him of his Beast squad leader. Six other men in that math section had the opportunity to explain a problem that morning before a bell rang in the hall signaling the end of the period. Hall released them, and they exited in a hurry. As he was leaving, Jake saw Captain Hall putting a grade on each board and writing it down in his grade book. It was going to be a long semester if this was how each class was going to go. They had math class every day for an hour and twenty minutes, six days a week, including Saturdays. Jake wondered if his old friends from Tolleston were doing the same things in their math classes.

Every class was run just about the same way. "Topo" was especially difficult because it required mastery of a number of skills, from the slide rule to the compass and protractor. Even in English and foreign language class the instructors made the students go to the boards and work their homework problems in chalk so they could check and grade the work easily, although in those "words" courses they did not go to the boards as often as every day. Sometimes they would write on paper at their desks the entire period. Only rarely would the instructor lecture on the day's lesson. Cadets were expected to study and grasp the concepts on their own. The classroom was for reinforcing the teaching points through repetition.

Jake actually liked his Russian class. He did quite well in the verbal exercises. His family was part Russian, and many of the old folks spoke the language at home. He found it easy to mimic the instructor's guttural accent, much easier especially than his classmates from the Deep South. Jake was fascinated by his instructor, Mr. Maltzoff. Maltzoff wore no rank, and his lapel bore the insignia of a USMA professor, meaning he was really a civilian serving in the Army for a career at West Point. He had a very heavy accent, and after a few lessons began to share his story with the class. Maltzoff was a refugee from the Soviet Army who had escaped from the Soviets at the end of the war and came over to the American side. Every now and then Mr. Maltzoff would relate some bone-chilling tale of his intelligence work on behalf of the Americans. Jake didn't know how far he could be believed, but it sure broke up the monotony of daily academics.

Only physical education class offered a regular break from the academic routine. Every other day, for forty-five minutes, they would learn a skill, then practice. Every now and then they would demonstrate their skills for a grade before a PE instructor. Every plebe had to pass every PE skill, including wrestling, gymnastics, swimming, and boxing. Jake liked boxing, there was a tough young instructor named Mr. Kroeten who taught them along with a coach for the soccer team by the name of Pallone. They seemed to enjoy teaching how to bloody someone in a fight. They were very good at it.

PLEBE FOOTBALL

Academics and PE were secondary to Bill Jackomis. He did not dislike them and he performed well, a little above average most of the time. But his first love was sports, and he really looked forward each day to the end of classes so he could rush over to the gym and suit up for football practice. The first week of class they basically continued the light drills and workout they had begun during Beast in mass athletics. But soon Coach Vince Lombardi had them running and learning the Army way of football.

Lombardi was a flamboyant coach, always moving around among groups of players working on different skills. He practically worshiped Red Blaik. At one meeting, Lombardi suggested a new technique for the offensive unit. Blaik came over to observe.

"Men, I want you to pay attention here," barked the former line coach, who now was offensive backfield coordinator, "I have a new way for the quarterback to take the ball from center." Lombardi had worked with centers for years at Fordham, but now that he was at Army he could visualize innovative ways to do things. "I want the quarterback to get up real close like this, see," and Lombardi got himself snugged up against the center's haunches, placing his hands right in his crotch. "Instead of hurling the ball way behind you to the quarterback three yards away, I want the center to jam it securely into his open hands."

"Wait a minute, Coach Lombardi," Red Blaik's officious baritone voice brought a sudden silence to the entire plebe team practice field. "You can't do that. The quarterback will get hit too soon and the play will get broken up before it even gets off." Blaik's tone was corrective and condescending.

"Look, Colonel, I can do it." Lombardi moved as if to grab the ball from the center when Blaik broke off his intended demonstration.

"Yes, Vince, I'm sure you can do it, but not everyone is built like an ape like you are." The head coach was not about to let his subordinate embarrass him in front of the other assistant coaches. Vince was jolted into silence. He halted his attempt and told the players to go back to their accustomed manner of taking the snap and drill it. He was passive and moot for the rest of the meeting.

Jake did not pay much attention to the posturing among the coaches. What he cared about was making the team. To do that you had to work hard at practice and keep your grades above passing. That was not easy, but when it came time for final cuts, Bill Jackomis made it. He was a fullback on the plebe football team at West Point. He could not wait to play in their first game.

Freshmen teams did not have as many scheduled games as the varsity teams did. Jake's first encounter with live Army football would be the first varsity game, Saturday, 23 September, 1949. It would be played at Michie Stadium after class at midafternoon. Every cadet was required to attend. The administration did not have to pass a regulation to make Bill Jackomis go to the game; he would not have missed it for anything in the world.

The week before the game there was an attempt to get the Corps to work up some team spirit. At lunch formation on Friday the twenty-third, the Cadets' cheerleaders, a group of about a dozen men called "Rabble rousers" (the football team was known as the Big Rabble) stood on the steps of the mess hall during formation and led the Corps of Cadets in one of those cheers that the plebes had known until then only as memorized verse from their plebe poop.

The head Rabble rouser had a bull horn and was yelling in a quite animated way, as if he were intoxicated, "All right men, let's do 'The Rocket!'" Jake had wondered how that one might go; it seemed silly when spoken to a yearling checking him off. The hard part was the first syllable, which was actually a whistle:

> Whhhhhhhhhht . . . Boom! Ah!
> USMA rah-rah
> USMA rah-rah
> Hoorah, hoorah, Armay rah.
> Team! Team! Team!

When paced to the rhythm set by the Rabble rousers, it made quite an impression. The weird part of it, though, was that only the plebes actually did any yelling. None of the upperclassmen bothered to do likewise. Maybe it was just for plebes to do, figured Jake.

When game time came the next day, Jake could not believe what good seats they had. There they were, Jackomis and Bleecker, sitting not more than ten rows up from the field on about the thirty-five yard line. You could not buy better seats. Still, the cadets seemed a bit subdued as the game began. It soon became clear that Army's opponent on this day, Davidson College, was wholly outclassed by the Brave Old Army Team.

Davidson took Army's kick to start the game and drove down to midfield. Then Davidson attempted a pass, but Army had put in a substitute linebacker, Don Beck, who grabbed it for an interception on his own forty-five yard line. Jake, beaming, said to Bleecker, "Did you see that, Bleek? Beck picked it off, he picked it off! That's our yearling, that was Mr. Beck!"

At halftime the Military Academy marching band, all soldiers assigned to the academy, demonstrated its skills at precision marching. But the highlight of the twenty-minute break was a message received at West Point during the halftime festivities. As soon as the band was finished, the public address announcer pronounced in ominous tone, "Ladies and gentlemen, we have just received a special message from the supreme commander, Allied Powers Pacific. It reads as follows, 'Men of the Brave Old Army

Team . . . there is no substitute for victory. End of message'." For half a second not a sound broke the silence that had settled in over the twenty-six thousand gathered at Michie Stadium. Then all at once in a mighty roar, the highly partisan fans voiced their approval of the message, the philosophy it reflected, and the man who had sent it.

It was a great moment for the two plebes; they felt as if they had something to do with their yearling's success on the field. They felt the pride that comes from watching your friend do well. They felt like they were part of a single great body that transcended time and space. They knew at that moment that they were part of the Long Gray Line.

Army went on in the second half as well to dominate its opponent. Jake again felt that sense of pride when he saw his Beast company commander, Hal Shultz, carry the ball several times up the middle. John Trent, who had coached the plebes during mass athletics during Beast, recovered a blocked punt and went in for an Army touchdown. By the end of the day the Brave Old Army Team had outclassed Davidson, 47–7.

It felt good to win, but it was tiring. Later that night, back in the barracks, while Bleecker was at the plebe hop, Jackomis returned from dinner to his room to read and relax. At the stoops, Don Beck passed by and told Jake to meet him down in the sinks, and they could talk about the how the game went down on the field. They were in the basement sinks just shooting the bull about the game. Beck said, "Yeh, it was really pretty easy to pick that quarterback off, he telegraphed his throw. I just waited until I saw in his eyes which receiver he was going for and that time it was going into my zone, so I took a chance and went for the ball."

"Ah, come on, Mr. Beck, it's never that easy," Jake tried to get the yearling to take some credit for what he thought was an outstanding performance on that interception.

"Look, let's get something straight, Jake, when we're in the sinks it's just like football practice with you and me. Call me Don. In fact, I want you to call me by my nickname. I just got my nickname today as a matter of fact. You wanna know what it is?"

"Sure, Don," Jake still had to strain to call an upperclassman by his first name.

"You see, no one really expected me to pull down the interception, especially on our own team," explained the speedy sophomore. "Coach Lombardi told us that whenever someone made an interception it was important to let the rest of the team know so they could all go the other way and anyone close to the ball could throw a block. We set up a code word to use. If someone intercepts he's supposed to yell 'Boom-Boom.' Well, I got so excited when I caught the ball in my first varsity game that I must have lost track of what was going on. Lombardi told me later that I yelled 'Boom-Boom' ten times. From then on during the game everyone started calling me 'Boom-Boom' Beck. Looks like it's gonna stick, too."

"Yeah, sounds like a natural, Boom-Boom." Jake was somehow more comfortable with the code name than the surname. "That Lombardi sure is a good coach."

"He sure is. He's tough, but at least he has a heart. He almost seems out of place at Army, at least the way Coach Blaik runs things. I hope he sticks around and moves up to work with the varsity team some more. Well, you better head on up before someone sees you falling out, Jake," Beck said, signaling the end of the session.

"Okay, Boom-Boom. And thanks for helping me through plebe year so far." Jackomis stood up, braced, and double-timed up the stairs out of the sinks and back up to his room. Bleecker was not back from the hop yet, but Jake didn't wait up for him. Jake just turned in early, losing himself in dreams of playing on the varsity team next year.

Fourteen

"We Don't Play Notre Dame . . ."

Ray Malavasi did not have the luck that Bill Jackomis did when he got to his regular company. Ray went to B-1 company, where there were several football players. Among them was backup quarterback Bob Blaik. One of the B-1 yearlings for this academic year was Hal Loehlein, star defensive end for the Army team and rising star in military aptitude. But the atmosphere in B-1 was very different from that in I-1. As much as he wanted to, Bob Blaik could not befriend any of the plebes from the football team. The tactical officer made sure of that.

Lieutenant Colonel Raymond Marlin took command of B-1 that June, and he quickly determined that too many of the football players in the company had gotten special treatment from his predecessor, who had been an Air Force officer on duty at West Point. Football team captain Bill Yeoman was in B-1 and rose up through the cadet ranks to become cadet battalion commander of the 1st Regiment's 1st Battalion for the academic year 1949–50. But since he was always out with the football team, Yeoman never marched in front of the formation on parade. Marlin did not like that at all, and he decided he was going to bring B-1 back into the Corps of Cadets. He intensified his daily inspections, letting the football players, especially the juniors and seniors, know he was in charge. The demerits added up quickly.

Bob Blaik had his hands full just keeping himself out of trouble, much less giving Malavasi a hand as Beck was doing with Jackomis. Bob Blaik had always worked hard to get where he wanted to be. His father had described him as a "manufactured" athlete, meaning he did not have as much natural ability as other players but that he made up for it with hard work. Bob Blaik always worked hard. Though he was about average in intellectual ability, he studied hard and applied himself, making it into the top third in class standing by the end of his plebe year.

He worked hard on the gridiron, too. It was hard enough being the head coach's son, but Bob also bore the burden of playing backup to All-American quarterback Arnold Galiffa. Blaik's touchdown pass in the fourth quarter against Davidson was gratifying. He proved his potential all by himself. It was almost therapeutic for Bob, who was under stress from all corners, it seemed, although it was largely self-inflicted.

Vince Lombardi worried about Bob Blaik. Vince sensed almost from his first day at Army that the younger Blaik was under constant pressure to perform. He took a personal interest in Bob, and the two hit it off well. Although Blaik would have to play behind Galiffa, Lombardi knew that he would soon graduate, and he wanted Bob Blaik to be part of the varsity team in a year or two. Lombardi found ways to help Bob work through his stress. He found a release for the young cadet in the game of golf. Bob took well to the game's more individual character and often joined Lombardi for a round.

Bob Blaik had a good game that day against Davidson. When it was apparent that Army was going to win, and Arnold Galiffa had enough offensive statistics, Red Blaik put his son in at quarterback in the fourth quarter. And Blaik did well, delivering that touchdown pass to his classmate and fellow substitute Al Pollock.

But there was no fellowship among football players in the B-1 area as there was in I-1. The tac and the cadet chain of command made sure of that. As much as he wanted to, Bob Blaik could not help Ray Malavasi get through the tough plebe courses. Ray struggled with all his academic courses, barely keeping a passing grade in any of them. He was in the special tutoring sessions for football players every evening over in the projection room of the gymnasium. Each night from right after dinner until just after 8:00 P.M., a tutor would help plebe football players work through the next day's math problems.

Of course, there was the opportunity for Malavasi, in the 1st Regiment, to find out what was going to be on a test when he went for tutoring the night after 2d Regiment took an exam that he was going to have the next day. The honor code, of course, strictly held that if he were to get answers to a test from a cadet in the other regiment who had already taken the exam, it would be cheating and thus a violation of the code. But they found ways to work around that. The tutors who provided the instruction were led by another cadet, Ed Courant, who made sure that the practice problems worked the night before an exam were similar but not the same.

Only at the football training table in the mess hall could Malavasi talk to the other players in B-1 about what was actually going to be on a test. He was able to get what he needed, although mostly they talked about how screwed up things were in the company ever since their old tac left and Yeoman, with his promotion to the battalion staff, no longer lived in the company area.

The next game was going to be against Penn State. The academy turned on its public information machine to promote the prospects for another Army win. The cadets were favored to win, but it was going to be a tough season later, and with a team made up of so many sophomore starters, Army sports public information officer Joe Cahill figured he had best maximize the support they could get early in the year. The campus monthly magazine came out that week, and it featured a cover photo of John Trent and Hal Loehlein, defensive ends.

In the game itself, the cadets began with an overconfidence that could have cost them the game. Penn State's quarterback quickly established their passing game in the first series of downs, but the Army secondary was able to keep them out of the end zone. Then, in the second quarter, with Penn State quarterback Bill Luther back to punt on fourth down, Loehlein broke through and brought down the kicker with an impact even the fans could sense. Watching from the stands, Jake figured he would draw a flag from the official, since he had gotten the kick off several seconds before Loehlein made contact. The penalty gave the ball back to the Lions, and ten plays later they scored on a Luther pass. Penn State led at the half 7–0.

In the second half, Army's running backs bulldozed their way to a Penn State goal-line stand. The Nittany Lions intercepted a Galiffa pass but had to punt their way out. Galiffa finally scored for Army in the third quarter on a keeper, tieing the score at 7–7. That seemed to break the curse on Army's offense, and Galiffa led the cadets to three more touchdowns. In the fourth quarter Bob Blaik came on to drive for two touchdowns in his continuing development as a varsity player as Army won, 42 7.

WINNING IS THE ONLY THING

By mid-October academics were beginning to take a toll on the football team. Math especially was keeping several of Red Blaik's recruited players off the team until they could bring their grade averages up. Ray Bara, a sophomore in the fall of 1949, had been brought to the "Monster School" so he could pass the entrance exam, and he needed more help as the academic year wore on. At the football table one night, he asked one of his classmates in the other regiment if he could tell him what problems would be on the quiz the 1st Regiment students would have the next day. Bara got the answers he needed and aced his problem set the next day.

The game for the next Saturday, 8 October, would be an away game, so Jake and his classmates would have to listen to it on the radio. Each Army game was broadcast by the Mutual Broadcasting System around the world so that servicemen could tune in each week and hear how the Brave Old Army Team was doing. The Army's leadership believed this formed a vital part of keeping up the troops' morale. For Jake it was just the same that he was not going. Michigan had a twenty-five-game winning streak going into this game and was favored by the oddsmakers to win against Army's younger team.

This was the kind of game that brought out the best in Red Blaik. He believed that there was a way to beat the odds and give Army a chance to win. He had his coaching staff study Michigan game films over and over, and they discussed the Wolverines' strengths and weaknesses. Finally Blaik concluded that Michigan's greatest weakness was in the very thing that gave them so many advantages: their size. Blaik saw in the films that Michigan's players were almost man-for-man taller and heavier than all their opponents, and that would be the case against Army as well. That meant that they had a high center of gravity, and if the cadets could hit Michigan low, then the laws of physics would take over and equalize the power of the players. The bigger men would simply fall harder and faster if they were hit while in motion and below the belt.

Blaik provided the brains behind the strategy, but Vince Lombardi provided the brawn. His rock-solid build became just the asset that Blaik needed to drill the cadets in the low block. Lombardi drilled the offensive linemen over and over until they could make the block in their sleep. With big lineman Fred Jones it took a while to add to the rule-blocking technique that had taken so long to imprint on his mind. On the first day of practice that week, Lombardi stood over Jones at the blocking dummy as the big cadet hit it nearly a dozen times. Lombardi yelled at him the whole time as the other linemen watched intently, hoping that by the time they got to it with Lombardi they would figure out how to do it much quicker. Jones finally crouched low and blew right from his three-point stance straight ahead into the canvas bag, barely coming up off the ground. Lombardi suddenly stopped his yelling, grinned from ear to ear for the first time that day, ran out from behind the tackling dummy and, slapping Jones on the shoulder pads, said, "Great block!" That was about as close as Lombardi ever came to passing out a compliment. He turned to the starters and told them that if they wanted to play Saturday they had better hit like that.

Blaik worked up a play sequence he intended to use in the first possession. It would be an unusual series of plays for Army, which normally ran the ball until the secondary closed in. Army would run the "belly series" off the basic T formation with the sweep, fullback off tackle and inside the end forming the principal tactics. Michigan would be expecting Army to run an average of twice as often as they passed and hardly ever twice in a row. Blaik had Galiffa work up a straight set of passes that they would execute in rapid order once the running game was well established during the first quarter.

The only problem with the plan was that Army's star fullback, Gil Stephenson, sustained a leg injury in the second play of the game that would keep him off the field for the rest of the day. Stephenson, Army's strongest runner, was key to Blaik's strategy of establishing Army's running game early.

Blaik did not worry about injuries to his own players during the game. He knew they would eventually heal and in his style of coaching they would work hard to get back into the game quickly, usually faster than the doctors wanted, but that was what Blaik expected of his players in developing a winning attitude. In combat the enemy would not let up on anyone carried on an injured reserve list. He had a bigger problem right now, and that was how to adjust the team and the strategy. He had very little time before resuming play to make a decision. He did not usually seek the advice of his assistants in times like these.

But Vince Lombardi came up to him and recommended he move Galiffa to fullback. Galiffa was a powerful running quarterback and was probably second to Stephenson as Army's strongest running back. Vince figured with Arnold running the ball he could put Bob Blaik in at quarterback to execute mostly hand offs. But Red did not share Lombardi's confidence in the Army backup quarterback. In fact, Blaik's judgment was that Bob was still too tense in the game and could not perform as smoothly as needed to win against the likes of Michigan. He also thought that Bob did not pull off the fake hand-off very well, and this would seriously hamper the running game so important to beating Michigan without Stephenson in the lineup. He kept Galiffa as quarterback and put senior Bob Abelman in at fullback.

It worked. Even with a substitute, Blaik ran the series he had developed just for this game. They ran a fake sweep right off the belly series. Everyone ran the sweep as before, except Galiffa, who faked the hand-off to the left halfback and kept the ball, running right up against Michigan's right tackle. Then Jones threw a special block, firing at his man's feet, then locking up his left elbow toward his ankle and rolling him to the right. This made a momentary hole for Galiffa to punch through the middle, where he ran smack into Michigan's All-American defensive back Charley Ortmann. Ortmann was injured on the play and had to leave the game. After seven straight runs in Army's first possession, Galiffa had Michigan's defense lulled into waiting for yet another hand-off. Then he threw to right end Bill Kellum for twenty and then to left end Dan Foldberg, who broke three tackles to gain eighteen yards. Two plays later Frank Fischl plowed right through the middle of Michigan's line behind Lombardi's bowling ball tactics of Army's offensive line, drawing the first score of the game. Army never trailed in going on to win, 21–7.

It was a hard-fought battle and a well-deserved victory. But in a postgame interview a Michigan professor claimed that on the play in which Gil Stephenson was injured, the Army fullback kicked his tackler right between his eyes and gave him a concussion. The scholar accused Army of deliberately trying to cripple its opponents. A Harvard faculty member, reflecting on the 20–7 drubbing the Crimson had received from Army in 1948, agreed, and wrote a paper that argued that Army had fielded the dirtiest team in nearly a quarter century of intercollegiate football.

Between Vince Lombardi's tough-minded line coaching and Red Blaik's brand of offensive attack, Army did play a very tough brand of football. But it was all legal by the rules of the day. Game films later showed that Stephenson had nothing to do with Ortmann's injury. Red Blaik later pointed out that Ortmann had been hit by one of his own players on an offensive drive. Army defensive end John Trent was covering Ortmann when Michigan attempted a reverse. When Ortmann surged forward to trap Trent away from the direction of the play, a reverse, Trent stepped back, allowing Ortmann's momentum to bring him crashing to the ground all by himself. As Ortmann tried to get up, the Michigan guard, who was pulling and shifting to block for the reverse, crashed into Ortmann, with his knee thrusting into the back of Ortmann's head.

John Trent was that kind of football player. He could do just about anything he was asked to do. He worked his way up through the ranks of M-2 Company over his cadet career and was the battalion supply officer for 3d Battalion, 2d Regiment. He was not particularly suited to West Point's academic rigor and had been admitted as a qualified alternate to play football. He was one of the few players in Army's two-platoon system to go both ways. His primary position was defensive end, but in the 1948 season, when offensive end Dan Foldberg was lost to an injury, Blaik played Trent both ways. It was an inspired move as Trent caught a game-winning Galiffa touchdown pass in the Penn game that year. Trent was named co-captain of the 1949 squad.

The next game was at Harvard. Army came out hitting hard again, and created several scoring opportunities for themselves by causing several fumbles. Behind the hard blocking of Lombardi's linemen, Army's running game overwhelmed the Ivy League's finest in the first half, creating a 41–0 advantage. But just before the second quarter ended, Army drew two big penalties during a Harvard possession, allowing Harvard to move deep into Army territory. The attempt failed when left linebacker Elmer Stout intercepted a Harvard pass attempt and ran it back seventy-five yards for another Army touchdown.

Rather than roll the score beyond decency, Red Blaik put his younger players in for the third quarter, including Bob at quarterback. Harvard managed to score twice on long drives that again were aided by penalties called on Army, but the outcome of the game was never really in doubt as Army won, 41–14.

The following week, back at Michie Stadium, Army engaged another Ivy League rival, Columbia. Again Red Blaik was able to give his sophomores plenty of game time as Army rolled the score up to 63–6. Bob Blaik provided a standout performance, playing the entire second half, including a fine broken pass play scramble of eleven yards around the left end for a touchdown.

West Point hosted Virginia Military Institute on the last weekend in October. Again, the Army team outmatched VMI, which in fact had a quite nationally respectable team in 1949. In the first quarter, the Lombardi style of blocking off the line on offense produced a fumble recovery by J. D. Jackson, who took the ball in for his first college touchdown. The cadets ran the score up, and Blaik was again able to put in the second string early in the second half on the way to another lopsided win, 40–14. One of those VMI touchdowns was scored on an intercepted Blaik pass that was run back fifty yards for the score.

BOOM-BOOM BECK

Bill Jackomis's first two months of academics at West Point were a breeze, made quite enjoyable by Army's football success and the positive atmosphere produced by his friendship with Don Beck. Boom-Boom had a second opportunity to demonstrate how he earned his nickname with an interception in the VMI game. He also sported a missing front tooth that had been knocked out during the tough Michigan game. For two weeks he often flashed the open space in his smile as a badge of honor. The West Point Dental Department fashioned a temporary replacement that he could remove whenever he needed to—for example, when he played football or when he ate a particular food such as corn on the cob or an apple.

Wednesday nights were steak nights at the Academy's mess hall. All the football players enjoyed partaking of this special meal, none more than Don Boom-Boom Beck. He relished the chance to indulge himself, and the Wednesday night after his VMI interception Beck got so involved in his enjoyment that he forgot he had removed his false tooth and placed it on the side of his plate while eating. He was all the way back to the D-1 Company area and about to enter his room when he realized he had left his tooth on the plate in the mess hall. He ran back across the area, up the steps, and into the still-opened doors. He dashed through the maze of tables, dodging waiters cleaning up and setting tables for the next morning's breakfast. When he arrived at the far side of the room he saw to his chagrin that his table had already been cleared, tooth and all. He ran into the kitchen, which was situated in the spaces between the wings of the huge facility, and sought after the waiter who was assigned to his table. The waiter told him he had not seen any false tooth and that he had already tossed all the leftovers and trash into the trash cans outside. Beck ran out the back door of the kitchen and dug through each and every trash can until he found his tooth. Almost before he got back to his room, the story of Beck's dash had begun to make it around the barracks. Beck turned into a legend in his own time and was featured in November's *Pointer*, the cadet magazine. Now Jake's yearling was a real star.

But all was not fun and games that week at West Point. It was also time for midterm examinations, which at the academy were known as written general reviews, or WGRs. Beck was pretty good in math, at least compared to most other football players. He stood about in the middle of his class in that subject and well above average in overall academic standing. He was assigned to the football tutoring team to help his classmates who struggled in the subject. In advance of the math WGR for yearlings, Beck was given several problems by the tutoring staff to help his classmates work through for practice. The next day, when he took the exam himself, Beck discovered that the very problem he had helped the others learn was in fact on the test.

He was horrified, because he realized that he had participated unknowingly in helping another cadet cheat. He went to the cadet in charge of football tutoring, Charles Mitchell, and confronted him with the fact that someone must have known that the problem he was explaining was going to be on the test. Mitchell explained that the whole football squad had unauthorized information and that was just the way the "football poop" worked. He told Beck that if he ever tried to turn anyone in for passing out "the poop" they would certainly get to him before he could do anything about it. Beck figured that it would do no good to go to his company honor representative because he reasoned that the honor rep must be in on it, or it never would have happened in the first place.

Somehow, all of Blaik's boys made it through WGRs with proficient grades and were allowed to play for the rest of the season. Even Al Pollard managed to pull it off. That was no small feat because Pollard was miserably poor in mathematics. He was let in to a very special part of the tutoring team handling the football poop. Pollard was beyond help in understanding how to work math problems. He had to know the problems in advance and simply memorize the answers. He met with his tutor between exam periods to get the list of answers to the WGRs, memorized them on the spot, and passed each math test.

So the Brave Old Army Team had all of its key players available for the final stretch of games for the 1949 season. It was a good thing because, after they got by Fordham, which they expected to be an easy affair, they faced two of the best teams in the country in their final two games, Penn and Navy.

Fordham was not expected to do well against powerful Army, but they were undefeated and they were playing fairly close to home. They filled their side of the stands at Michie Stadium with hundreds of raucous, rowdy fans reminiscent of Notre Dame's subway alumni. This was to be a grudge match for the Fordham faithful; after all, they were playing against the team that had stolen their assistant coach, Vince Lombardi.

In the first quarter Army threatened to score three times, only to trip themselves up with fumbles. In the second quarter, Fordham was forced to punt after their first possession, and Army's charging guard Lynn Galloway blocked the punt. In the process he got in a fistfight with two Fordham players and was ejected from the game. Army failed to convert on the opportunity that they created for themselves on the blocked punt and suffered two more penalties in giving the ball back over to Fordham only twenty yards from a touchdown. Army finally broke through and scored three touchdowns before the end of the half. But in the point-after attempt following the third score, officials called Army four times in succession for illegal use of hands: Then Fordham was called twice for the same violation. Army went on to win, 35–0, but it was not very pretty. In all, 23 penalties were assessed in the game, 12 against Army for 147 yards, and 11 against Fordham for 131 yards.

Pollard was now very close to failing in mathematics. He was in the last section, and it was his daily work that was keeping him down. As he approached his next written general exam he needed help to make sure he passed it with a very high grade to pull his average up. He could not afford to let a grade keep him off the playing roster now. After the game he got the trainer to have him admitted to the hospital for a problem with his eyes. That got him out of taking the exam when the rest of his class did. He then took the test later, while he was still in the hospital, and he got a perfect score on it.

For the game against the University of Pennsylvania on 12 November in Philadelphia, Army was favored to win by twenty-one points. Everyone, even the coaches, looked past Penn to the game against Navy that would be held two weeks later, also in Philadelphia. Everyone thought that this would be nothing more than a transportation rehearsal for the Navy game. Everyone, that is, except Penn.

Army could not score in the first period. Penn drew first blood with a touchdown in the second quarter but could not get the point after. Army caught up, then went ahead with a touchdown and a point after. Late in the first half, Penn drove to the Army six-yard line and called a time-out with only three seconds on the clock. But the referee overruled the linesman keeping time because it was Penn's fourth time-out in the half. The rules permitted only three. The ref called the halftime and Army went into the locker room with a 7–6 lead.

In the second half, with Penn mounting a drive at midfield, Boom-Boom once again displayed the instincts that earned him his nickname, with an interception that set up another Army score and put Army ahead, 14–6. Late in the third quarter Penn came back with a seventy-eight-yard drive that produced their second touchdown. This time they made the kick after, and the score going into the fourth quarter was 14–13 Army.

In the last period, Bob Cain fumbled on an Army run and Penn picked up the ball on their own forty-seven-yard line. They drove straight ahead to the five. The Army defense mounted a spirited goal-line stand and forced Penn to attempt a field goal. On the snap, Hal Loehlein drove like he never had before and reached the ball as it ascended, blocking the field-goal attempt and saving the game for West Point.

ARMY–NAVY 1949

In the run-up to the contest with Navy, Red Blaik was more concerned than ever that his team was beset with overconfidence. The Penn and Fordham games had proven that to him. What was ironic was that he had not picked this 1949 team to be undefeated going into the annual Navy game. He had only a few returning letterman from his number six nationally-ranked team of 1948, and although he had a number of prospects, he had figured that this would be a rebuilding year. Yet here he was going into the Navy game with his unbeaten string still intact at nineteen. Army had not lost a game since the last of the Notre Dame series in 1947. This was not going to be like his heyday of 1944–46, but it was a pleasant surprise to have done so well in 1949.

Navy was not doing very well in 1949. Coming into Philadelphia for the 1949 game with Army, the midshipmen had only three wins to four losses and a tie. But Blaik knew that Navy's record was deceiving. In many ways Navy was the victim of their scheduling, which was far too ambitious. Navy's problem was not a lack of talent and ability; they was simply worn out from an all-major schedule.

But to lose to Navy due to overconfidence would be humiliating. Blaik drove his staff and the players to fear him more than they feared the Navy team. He had his assistants scout Navy's game plans no less than seven times late in the season. Blaik wanted to have advance intelligence about every nuance of every play. He worked his coaches late every night going over game films to identify each Navy man's strong and weak points. By game week he believed he had a complete book on his opponent and that his players were peaking at just the right time.

Then once again, the Army team's psychological sharpness was attacked. The first attack came from another allegation in the media that Army was playing dirty. Two days before the game a New York sports columnist, appearing on one of the first television sports broadcasts and a national radio program, alleged that Blaik was telling his players to hurt his opponent's key players to make it easier for Army to win. Blaik would not dignify the charge with a reply, but it hurt his own confidence to have his integrity attacked this way.

The second attempt to affect Army's mental sharpness was from the Navy Brigade of Midshipmen. As the thirty-five hundred Navy students took their seats after their march-on ceremony, and as Army began their march-on into Municipal Stadium, Navy struck up a new fight song. It actually was a parody of Army's fight song, one that attempted to embarrass Army fans by reminding them of how comparatively easy the Brave Old Army Team had had it in 1949. Sung to the tune of "On, Brave Old Army Team," it consisted of just one chorus:

> We don't play Notre Dame,
> We don't play Tulane,
> We just play Davidson,
> For that's the fearless Army way.

Navy had lost, 40–0, to Frank Leahy's national champions from Notre Dame. The hoopla was to no avail as Navy went down to Army nearly as badly, losing to the cadets 38–0.

The Navy game ended the football season at West Point. For some of the players it might as well have been the end of the world. Professional football in 1949 was not yet the career option it is today. In many ways intercollegiate football at the national level provided the best in the game. Seniors who had used up their eligibility faced an uncertain future even if they did go on to play pro ball. For players at the academies there really was no option to go into the professional ranks because they were required to serve in the armed forces for four years after graduation. That drained the competitiveness out of all but a very few who could maintain their skills and strength through almost half a decade of soldiering. Army's firstie football players suddenly faced the stark reality of life without football. They also had to face the prospect of earning grades high enough to graduate successfully. Anyone determined by academy officials to be failing would likely be forced to leave without a diploma and could be ordered to serve his obligatory time as an enlisted man.

For the underclass players, of course, there was the prospect of moving up to replace the departing seniors. For the majority of the Corps of Cadets, players and nonplayers alike, the one thing they really looked forward to after the Navy game was Christmas leave. Only plebes were required to remain at West Point during the Christmas holiday, and even they looked forward to having the run of the place with the upperclassmen gone for nearly two weeks. A win over Navy would keep spirits high and make the time pass quickly. The only major obstacle was the series of term-end examinations that had to be passed. Every cadet had to take a final in every course.

THE CHEATING SEASON

All this pressure bearing down on cadets to perform well in academics increased the temptation to some to cheat in order to keep pace. The intensity of the pressure to keep the team together led some to aid and abet those who needed to cheat to stay up. Richard Hunt was a promising quarterback prospect in the Class of 1953 who was doing quite well in academics. He was well into the upper half of his class in mathematics and had no need to cheat to maintain his academic eligibility to play football. But his roommate was Al Pollard, who was horribly deficient in math.

Hunt watched the night before the math exam as another classmate brought into the room a copy of a math test that had the next day's problems on it. Pollard copied the problems and answers, then memorized them before going to bed. Hunt knew that he had witnessed a violation of the honor code but did not turn in his classmates to the D-1 Company honor representative. That failure to act on a known honor violation made him guilty of breaking the honor code's "nontoleration" clause. The incident was not an isolated one, and it was not unique to 1st Regiment.

Over at the other end of the corps, in M-2, another cheating incident was covered up. Michael Kelly discovered that cheating going on in his company during that winter exam period as well. Kelly was not on the football team, but his roommate, James Jackson, was. Jackson had a difficult time with English, although he was not deficient in other subjects. Kelly was doing quite well in English.

One night during the December 1949 exam period, Jackson came into their room with a handful of examination papers with the answers marked on them, all soon to appear on the yearling English final exam. Jackson had had a great football season and, as one of Blaik's promising yearlings, looked forward to greater exploits on the field next year. But he had to get his grades up to stay proficient and participate in next spring's drills. The football office provided him with copies of examinations containing the questions known to be on the English final, with the answers written in by tutors.

Kelly recognized Jackson's haul and its illicit content and decided to turn a blind eye. He hoped not to gain any advantage himself so he avoided direct eye contact with the answers. But he also was afraid for himself, knowing that his failure to turn in his roommate implicated him for toleration. He asked Jackson what he was doing, and his roommate explained that he needed to get "the football poop" so he could pass English. He also revealed that he was serving as a courier for other football players in M-2 as part of a syndicate designed to keep key football players proficient in their academics. Michael Kelly could not keep this to himself, although Jackson warned him that the cheating ring was very small and had the power of Red Blaik behind it. If he knew what was good for him, warned the big defensive tackle, he had best keep quiet about it. Kelly decided he had to talk to someone about it anyway.

Michael left his room and sought out his friend and football team captain John Trent. Trent had been in M-2 Company, but now was detailed to the battalion staff as the supply officer. Away from the M-2 Company area, he would be able to talk freely to Trent without risk of being overheard by his classmates. Trent was alone, and invited Kelly to enter his room when he saw the concern on the yearling's face. Kelly related what had just happened in his room and told Trent of his concern that so many football players were involved.

John Trent told Michael Kelly that the football office did indeed authorize the help for players because Colonel Blaik had always told the football team that they were the rock on which the corps was built and that the help was necessary to keep the team competitive. Trent told Kelly that he had to keep a lid on it and not do anything about it. He assured the yearling that it was okay and he would have a word with his company commander about the affair. Later that night, Kelly's cadet commander, A. J. Dielens, came to him and told him the same thing.

Kelly returned to his room. John Trent represented everything he believed was honorable and befitting a cadet. Somehow, he figured, the honor code would surely accommodate the way the football office was bending it.

Bill Jackomis, over in I-1, struggled through his exams like just about every other cadet in the corps—long hours of studying the night before each exam, and agonizing minutes during the tests writing out his answers as best he could. English was his best subject, but he was pretty well average across the board in his other academic subjects. He excelled in physical education and did better than average in military tactics. By the last day of exams, 22 December, he could finally relax and think about enjoying the upcoming plebe Christmas.

For Red Blaik the end of the semester brought welcome relief. The season was over, and his young team came out of it much better than he had expected. With so many key players on the 1949 squad being sophomores, Blaik was surprised to come out of the season undefeated. He knew that if he could just keep his players proficient in academics and healthy, Army's prospects for 1950 were great, and by the 1951 season he might recapture the glory of the war years. That would prove to his critics that his program was consistent. Even his players' academic performance was encouraging. He wrote to General MacArthur, "Although we had eleven plebes turned out as well as four upperclassmen (*sic*), through a determined effort by all of these men, probably combined with a little mellowness on the part of the Academic Board, we have not lost a player. Several of them were placed on a condition basis, which the men themselves will soon rectify."

Part Four

Good Men

Fifteen

Gloom Period

They call it gloom period for good reason. It is nearly always gloomy and gray at West Point after Christmas. The overcast sky alloys with the stones of the gray walls of the campus, and the bleached concrete of the roads is smeared dim by the refraction of all the surrounding grayness. The frequent snow, in the 1950s, turned gray quickly from all the belching from the academy's furnaces, fireplaces, and steam plant, and the roads were kept clear with gray sand and gravel spread to keep traffic flowing. Mountains of crystalline compounds of ash and ice formed where plows pushed the snow and sludge out of the way.

The cadets, all dressed in gray, were well camouflaged with their surroundings. Even if the temperature were to let up and they could shed their gray overcoats, the next alternative outer garment prescribed by the uniform regulation was a gray jacket. Even their faces were pallid, stuck as they were for more than three months between Christmas leave and traditional spring break with few opportunities to leave the campus and its pressures.

In 1950 West Point did not get a true spring break. Instead there was a short respite in the routine from 15 through 18 March, officially called "suspension of duties." That was a rare opportunity to get away in the midst of academics and blow off steam. For some, it was just enough time to go home. For others, it allowed for a wild weekend in New York City. Either way, on return to West Point's grayness, the mood returned to sullen.

For Jim Pfautz, gloom period was swimming season. He was a superb swimmer, and he made the varsity team as a plebe. That was unusual because plebes usually did not have the stamina to keep up with the training regimen required of a nationally competitive team. Beast barracks and the other assorted activities associated with plebe year wear the body down considerably, and most young men lose ten pounds or more during the first half of plebe year. But Pfautz was no ordinary man. He lost weight, but managed to maintain his stamina through Christmas break, when he could recover. When swimming season opened in January he was not yet back in his top form, but he was much farther along than most of the rest of his classmates.

West Point's swimming team sorely needed Jim Pfautz in 1950. Most of the varsity swimmers were seniors, competing in their last year of eligibility for the Brave Old Army Team. Coach Gordon Chalmers eyed Pfautz as a key building block for future West Point swimming squads. He entered Pfautz in just about every meet to give him plenty of competitive experience. Pfautz did well. It helped carry him through gloom period.

Gloom period was a most depressing time. But on the varsity track and field team, Bill Jackomis could soar above the gloom for three precious hours each weekday. When released from classes, at 3:15 P.M. daily, members of the varsity athletic squads, in Corps of Cadets jargon known as "corps squad athletes," were excused from the weekly parades and preparatory drill that everyone else was required to attend.

Some of the more military-minded cadets, known as "makes," actually looked forward to those parades as a chance to show off their skill at drill and ceremony, and their higher rank among cadets, in the especially challenging winter environment. For Jackomis and most of the rest of the corps, though, it was just another opportunity to get nailed for more demerits because of a smudge on a brass breastplate or some other such minor offense, compounded by the occasion to freeze their tails off in the often bitter cold northerly winds whipping down the Hudson River Valley from the Arctic.

On this cold day in March of that year, it was an especially fine day to leave class early and work out with the track team. Since the beginning of the semester back in January, the track team had been working out inside the warm confines of the field house, a giant structure down below the Plain and about five hundred yards up from the river. Today the temperature was above freezing for the third day in a row, and all the ice and snow had melted so that the team was going to work its first day outdoors.

Track practice was held outdoors at River Field, a flat, open area just north of the field house and stretching out along the very banks of the Hudson River. From the starting blocks on the field, Jake could see, a few hundred yards away, the boat landing used a hundred years earlier to row over for Sunday school to Constitution Island on the far side of the river.

There, below the level of the Plain, West Point's parade ground, the rules were relaxed for team members. Indeed, the field rests a hundred feet lower than the main campus, and corps squad athletes lucky enough to be on the track team were "out of sight and out of mind" for 180 glorious minutes. Jake relished his time there. The competition in track and field was Bill Jackomis's self-esteem builder in his school years. Jake's athletic ability, on top of his better-than-average grades, had won him his coveted appointment to West Point.

In football, while Army had several accomplished running backs, Jake could only hold out hope that he could make it into one of Blaik's platoons and get in on the field once or twice in a game, if he could make the "A" squad, or first team. In the fall he had played on the "C," or freshman, squad. They lost all four of their games, but developed a camaraderie that provided cohesion and motivation to play against the odds. Now, in the second semester of his plebe year, Jake could look forward to being on the "B" squad, or junior varsity. The "B" squad played an important part in Blaik's system. They had to learn the opponent's offense each week prior to the varsity game on Saturday and run the enemy's plays against the first-string defensive unit. Jake realized that with his size he would get hit a lot by Army's power-ful defensive backfield, but he also knew that it was good for his development as a running back.

But that was football, which was not to come until later in the spring. For now, Jake reveled in his sprinting on the varsity unit of the track and field team. It was especially nice to leave class early each day and go to the field house for the workout on the indoor track. On this cool day in March it was finally warm enough to go out onto the field where home meets were held.

In the quarter-mile event no one could catch Bill Jackomis. He liked the notoriety his speed brought him. It made him something special to the upperclassmen on the track team. He especially liked the fellowship with yearling Dick Shea, who was in G-1 Company, located just a few divisions down from his own I-1 Company. Shea was a lot like Jake in that in his event, the mile run, no one could catch him. Shea was also a lot like Boom-Boom Beck over in D-1 in that he did not take the fourth class system too se-riously. Shea was far more concerned with physical performance of the more important combat-related skills, such as keeping your rifle clean and free of dust, than he was with the more "chicken" requirements such as plebe poop. Shea, like Beck, would talk to Jake with a measure of familiarity that few other plebes enjoyed with yearlings.

Of course, in March 1950, combat was a distant prospect for the Corps of Cadets. While most of their tactical officers were ma-jors or young lieutenant colonels who had risen rapidly during the war years, with the country demobilizing rapidly there was not much prospect for Jake and his classmates, who were to graduate in 1953, to see any real action. After all, World War II had elimi-nated the last remnants of totalitarianism from both of America's flanks, Europe and the Pacific. While the Communist Chinese were winning their war with the Nationalists and the Soviets were bringing down an "Iron Curtain" over their occupied territories in Europe, no one believed that war would come to affect the United States.

No one, that is, except a few in foreign policy circles in the United States and Great Britain. A secret Central Intelligence

Agency report on 10 March 1950 carried an assessment of a massive troop buildup in North Korea and predicted that North Korea would attack South Korea in June 1950. Not many in the Truman administration in Washington nor in MacArthur's headquarters in Japan took the report seriously. In May 1950 Secretary of State Dean Acheson, in a speech before the National Press Club in Washington, D.C., implied that if Formosa (Taiwan) and South Korea were to be attacked, the first response would have to be from their own armed forces. He would for decades later deny that he meant to signal the North Koreans that the United States would not defend South Korea. In fact the United States had just concluded the new but then highly-classified national security policy of containment, in which President Truman declared that the United States would resist Communist aggression anywhere. Acheson's special assistant John Foster Dulles tried obliquely to signal the new policy in a speech to the South Korean National Assembly on 17 June, but was ambiguous and in effect implicitly reinforced the signal to the Communists that, if the North were to move on the South, the United States would not have a vital interest at stake and would not oppose the move. For the moment, though, the focus at West Point was not on the prospect of war; it was on the usual routine cadet concerns, including academics, duties, athletics, and what to do with the precious remaining free time.

ACADEMICS TAKE THEIR TOLL
For James Davidson, academics were beginning to take their toll. He had done all right in first semester of plebe year, but now he was starting to have some difficulty in English. He was near the bottom of his class in mathematics and did not do well in military topography and graphics. He even had low grades in military tactics. But he really struggled in English.

Davidson had gotten by in his first semester in K-1 Company. He never drew much attention to himself, but in the second semester that all changed when roommates were rearranged and Davidson drew William West. West quickly developed a reputation as a troublemaker. Although he was a football player and had a propensity to get into arguments, Davidson and West managed to get along well at first. Perhaps it was because they were both struggling with academics. By March, with spring football drills about to begin, West decided that they could make it only if they helped each other in more direct ways.

They sat at their desks one night with their English texts open to the next day's lesson on literature. There was going to be a test soon on "John Brown's Body," a long, dry narrative that neither of them had the time or the interest to read. West, the hulking football player, turned to his slender but strong roommate and said, "Hey, James, you know I might be able to get us some special help from the football academic coaches. You know we can get the poop for players who are in trouble."

Davidson had never considered looking for help outside of normal academic channels. In fact, he did not have time even to avail himself of the help from the instructors available in the afternoons. He had not considered looking for help anywhere else. "How can you do that, Will?" With that question James Davidson opened a door to temptation that he would regret for the rest of his life.

"It's not too hard. The deal with the football poop is that anyone who wants it can get it if you help put it all together. In other words," he explained, "if you want to take something from the system you have to give it something."

"Well, what can I do?" asked the unsuspecting Davidson.

"Easy. You have English in first hour. After you take the writ, go to the solution room like everyone else and check the answers. Only make sure you get there early and memorize the answers to the really hard questions that you know the rest of us will have trouble with. Then when you come back to our room, write the question and its answer down and I'll take it to the football office, where they pass out the poop. That way the others who take the test after you will do okay on those questions. Later, when the other regiment takes a test before you do, the favor will be returned. It's that easy. Over the rest of the semester you ought to be able to raise your grade and help other athletes do the same for themselves, too."

Davidson knew that this would be cheating and it would violate the honor code. But it seemed like it would work, with not much risk that they would get caught. Anyway, if the football office was in on it there could not be too much danger of anything being done about it even if they were caught.

"Okay, Will, I'll do it."

Several times that semester, Davidson brought English answers back to his roommate. It turned out all right for Davidson in English after all; he finished up plebe year with a passing mark. West ended up almost the last man in the class, but he passed English, also. Davidson never did get the benefit of receiving the football poop in English; they kept telling him it was because he was in the first-hour class and no one took an English writ before he did.

Al Pollard continued to struggle with his academics, too, especially with math. The football coaching staff knew that they would have to continue to give Pollard an extra measure of help if they were going to have him available next year for football. Blaik rated him as an excellent open-field runner, but the head coach knew that he lacked the kind of competitive spirit he demanded of Army players. Pollard was so overwhelmed by the academic requirements that he could never keep his mind on the football field.

For the second semester of his plebe year the coaching staff at least managed to keep Pollard on corps squad tables in the mess hall. The football team would not get separate tables until April, when spring practice began. In the meantime, Blaik had Pollard listed on the varsity lacrosse team. That way he could sit at lacrosse tables, and since there were several football players who also played lacrosse, Pollard could get the football poop when he needed to. Blaik did have to weigh in with the cadet first captain, though.

The first captain by regulation controlled seating assignments in the mess hall, and the rules held that each athlete had to spend at least one season sitting at his company tables. This rule was in place to make sure that team members held some loyalty to the cadet chain of command they were assigned to and maintained some contact with the cadet company they lived in. Most of the nonvarsity athletes developed that sense of belonging during intramural athletics. The commandant kept this seating rule in place so that varsity athletes would not become disassociated from the kind of life led by the majority of the rest of the Corps of Cadets. In Pollard's case, sitting at lacrosse tables meant that he would end up going through the entire year without sitting at a table in the mess hall with his classmates and leaders from his home company, D-1. Blaik, in his capacity as director of athletics, sent a memorandum to the first captain telling him that Pollard would constitute an exception to the rule because of his need to be on both the football and lacrosse teams. Of course there were others, upperclassmen, who also were on both teams, but it was the first time that a plebe would not sit at his company tables at all during the academic year. For Red Blaik the needs of Army football clearly transcended such a minor regulation.

Thus, by the spring of 1950, the cheating ring had expanded beyond its original purpose from the 1940s. Designed initially to provide only a few selected football players help once or twice at strategic times in the course of an academic year, it was now a full-time conspiracy aimed at keeping every football player proficient in all his classes throughout the entire year. It was available at any time to any player who needed the extra help and who did not, or could not, work his way through the intellectual process of learning either on his own or with the tutoring assistance available from the academic departments after class. All the instructors offered was to spend additional time reviewing the day's work. The football poop was much more than help; it was providing answers to tests so that the recipient could pass even without understanding the material. Not all football players availed themselves of the help all the time, but with more than twenty tutors specifically assigned to help football players, and with organized collection and selected clandestine distribution of test questions and answers to selected players, it was now a full-fledged cheating ring.

With the enticement of James Davidson to help, the ring became a syndicate. It was now an organized crime operation designed to do business in illicit intellectual property by unethical means. What had been a closely guarded secret among a limited number of participants began to grow to far greater proportions. The growth of the ring forced its members to change methods in order to preserve the ability to operate without detection. Since cheating was first and foremost a violation of the cadet honor code, the ringleaders had to compromise the honor system itself and defy the traditions of integrity embodied in the code. To do that, they would have to co-opt members of the Honor Committee.

AN ODD SPRING

Just before the spring break, the Class of 1953 was scheduled to elect its members to the Honor Committee. There was already on the committee one member from each company out of the two upper classes. In the fall semester the yearling class (1953) elected their representatives to the committee, with each company in the cadet military organization electing one yearling who would serve an apprenticeship period, then serve as a member of the committee. There were thus several dozen cadets on the Honor Committee for the entire corps. For any alleged violation of the code, a subcommittee of three would be formed to hear evidence and vote on whether to open a full honor board. If two of the three agreed, then a full honor board of twelve members would be appointed to review the evidence, take testimony, and judge whether a violation had indeed occurred. A unanimous vote of the twelve was required to find a cadet guilty of an honor violation. The votes were cast by secret ballot, and whenever the committee so voted the cadet was asked by the board to resign or face prosecution by the Tactical Department under the Articles of War, a provision that, in the rare event that it occurred, would result in a court-martial.

It was an important strategy, therefore, to attempt to place a few members of the cheating ring in positions where they could ensure the ring's continued safe operation. First, if a member of the ring were to be elected to the committee, whenever an investigation was opened any members of the ring implicated could be warned and coached as to how to respond to the investigating group. If enough ring members were elected to the committee, they could even be assured that one of their members would probably be selected to serve on full honor boards. In that way the ring could guarantee that they would always be in a position to cast a dissenting vote to prevent a guilty verdict for members of the ring. Several yearlings in the Class of 1953 got together before their election and campaigned to get ring members elected to the Honor Committee. They succeeded.

Other odd things happened that spring. Cadet Richard C. Cox disappeared without a trace. He was a flanker from M-2 Company. Cox was an oddball who generally kept to himself and who earned a reputation in his plebe year as a nervous eccentric. He did well in physical education, but he had an emotional streak that kept his classmates largely at a distance. He had served in the Army before coming to West Point, but he did not do well in his military subjects, nor did his performance evaluations by his classmates and cadet chain of command bode well for his future as a soldier.

When he disappeared, a few of his classmates figured he was part of the cheating ring and had been discovered. There was some speculation among the Class of 1952 that Cox had been given a "blanket party" as in the old days of the Vigilance Committee, when cadets took honor punishment into their own hands, and that he had committed suicide rather than face the ignominy of being branded a cheater. He was last reported seen going down Flirtation Walk, alone, one chilly spring day, and he never returned. A few days after his disappearance, when repeated calls home turned up no sign of him, the academy administration, fearing the worst, launched a massive search along the Hudson River shoreline, drained Delafield Pond, and dragged Lusk Reservoir, expecting to find his body. It was never found. The only unusual thing his roomates knew was that he had recently been seeing an old Army buddy in his spare time. On 14 March 1950, in accordance with Army regulations, R. C. Cox was dropped from all rolls. The story that some cadets came to believe was that he had been murdered.

The superintendent, Maj. Gen. Bryant Moore, had no clue of the widespread disaster he was sitting on. He spoke to a gathering of academy graduates in April and proclaimed, "The honor system, under the direct control and supervision of the first class, is in most excellent hands." In fact, it was permanently penetrated by a syndicate of organized cheating aimed at perpetuating Army's football superiority at all costs. In some ways, the cadets' attitude toward integrity was not much worse than that of academic instructors. It became common practice among many professors to teach class in such a way as to let cadets in on what they were to be tested on. A few instructors adopted a pattern of simply teaching the tests from class to class. Some officers teaching economics and law developed reputations as instructors who could often be expected to begin class, not with the command "Take boards!" but instead with the opening line "I'll give you the straight poop today."

In many ways the entire country was caught up in a pernicious psychosis of integrity. The United States was just about evenly divided along conservative and liberal lines in a nationally split personality reflected in a Congress controlled by Republicans while Democratic president Harry Truman was in the White House. Though Truman labored to convince the public that he was a staunch anti-Communist, his Republican critics hit him again and again with accusations of filling important government jobs with Red sympathizers. When it was discovered that Alger Hiss, a highly placed State Department official, was feeding the Soviets regular reports of some of the country's most vital secrets, the president's detractors began to question directly Truman's own integrity and loyalty.

Red Blaik was among those critics. He wrote to Douglas MacArthur in May 1950, "At large the country as a whole is completely fed up with the present administration, but there is constant anxiety that the labor union combined with the millions of government workers are too strong to be voted out. The president enjoys his position and desires more, and unless the Republicans generate more wallop to win, the present administration is merely setting the stage for the next generation of the ever-ambitious Roosevelts." Blaik never gave up hope that his mentor would enter the political fray and perhaps take him along on his coattails.

CHEATING IN FOREIGN LANGUAGES

In the meantime, he had a festering problem to deal with in the cheating that had sprung up around his football team. By early spring it spread beyond the more difficult subjects, math, English, physics, and chemistry, to the easier, "soft" courses. It even spread to courses that were difficult to cheat in, the foreign languages. West Point offered five foreign languages to cadets. Everyone had to take at least two years of a foreign language and develop some proficiency in speaking, reading, and writing the foreign tongue. Tests consisted mostly of translations and comprehension drills where you either knew it and could demonstrate it, or you did not and it showed equally obviously.

For football players who were not particularly proficient at learning a foreign language, about the only assistance the football office could render was to influence which language a player would take. Since Spanish was generally considered to be the easiest, Blaik's staff tried to get any of their players known to have such difficulty into Spanish courses. Since the academic departments controlled the assignment of foreign language classes, this was a difficult proposition. Nevertheless, with especially important players recruited for their football prowess and known to have problems with language, the football staff leaned on the Spanish Department. But for some players, even that was not enough. They soon developed cheating techniques even for Spanish exams. They used the technique perfected in English, where several cadets would take the exam, go to the solution room and memorize a portion of the answers, then assemble their illicit "poop" for quick ingestion overnight by the favored player.

West Point was not the only school where cheating to maintain academic eligibility developed into an organized ring. At Harvard a young prelaw student was having his own difficulties with Spanish and turned to cheating to keep playing ball. He had no expectation he would get caught, nor did he have any reason to suspect that his cheating would soon be connected with that going on at West Point. Ted Kennedy, too, was a football player struggling to maintain his Spanish grade.

Edward M. Kennedy was the youngest son of the most ambitious man in America, Joseph Kennedy, who at age fifteen had owned a baseball team, by twenty-five was the youngest bank president in the United States, and who made a fortune during the Depression. By 1950 Joe Kennedy was one of the wealthiest men in America, worth about $400 million. Young Ted did not share his father's burning desire to win at all costs, especially on the gridiron. He played the game for the fun of it. At 200 pounds and six feet, two inches he was not very fast but he was a smart blocker and a tough tackler. He played right end for the Harvard University freshman team that beat up on Army in the fall of 1950.

But in the spring semester, Ted Kennedy struggled with Spanish, just as he had at Milton Academy for four years before entering Harvard. As the final exam neared, Kennedy needed to pass the test to maintain his grade at a passing level. Maintaining a passing grade in all courses was a requirement for the Harvard football squad. While he did not share his father's passion for victory at all costs, he did have an unstoppable desire to prove himself to his father through athletic achievement. Ted wanted to do something that neither his father nor any of his older brothers had done—earn a football letter at Harvard. To do that he had to pass the Spanish exam, but he was miserably weak in Spanish. Ted Kennedy did not think that he could pass that test.

His classmates in Winthrop House, a dormitory for jocks at Harvard, convinced him he could get away with a minor deception if he would pay cash for it. The idea was that he could hire someone to take his Spanish exam for him. No one ever checked names on the examination paper, they told him, so he could just pay someone to take the test for him and put Kennedy's name on it. He bought the scheme, but his hired hand got caught in the act by an alert test proctor, who immediately hauled them both up before the dean. Kennedy was expelled and told he could reapply the following year. Instead he enlisted in the Army and soon found himself in Germany serving as a legal clerk. He would not get back to his own formal education for two years. When he came back, he not only successfully completed his undergraduate degree at Harvard, he also earned that football letter. Ironically, Kennedy would be rejected by Harvard Law School and would instead earn his Juris Doctor at the University of Virginia, the school where a formal honor code had been institutionalized more than half a century before West Point's. Bill Jackomis's life was soon to be affected by Ted Kennedy's experiences, but that was still a few months away.

Sixteen

The 38th Parallel

Spring football practice at West Point in 1950 went for six weeks, from the end of March through the first week of May, under Red Blaik's care and attention. The weather was unusually cold and wet, forcing the squad indoors at the field house for all but six days. Blaik was largely satisfied with the progress made by his young team. In two scrimmage games the Brave Old Army Team trounced its opponents, Villanova and Boston University, allowing them to score only one touchdown apiece. Several plebes earned themselves spots on the varsity squad, and a few won starting jobs. But Bill Jackomis was content to advance to the B squad. He knew he would be fodder for the varsity defense at practice each day, but at least he would be on the team and might make it to the varsity unit next year.

His Beast roommate, Gene Filipski, made it as a substitute defensive back, while another classmate he knew well, James Jackson, made it as a starter on the defensive line. On offense, Michael Kelly made the squad as a substitute on the line, while Al Pollard would back up Gil Stephenson at fullback and Richard Hunt would work behind starting quarterback Bob Blaik. Hal Loehlein was the starting defensive left end, and team captain Dan Foldberg was the starting offensive left end. Jake was glad to have several friends among the upperclass starters and several of his classmates on the A squad. He would work hard this spring and next fall on the B squad and hope for another shot at the varsity next year. Maybe someone would get hurt or would get into academic difficulty, creating an open slot for him. Maybe when Stephenson graduated there would be a chance for Jake to move in to play halfback in the same backfield with Al Pollard at fullback.

Army had another successful "Monster School" in May 1950. Twenty-four prospective players attended under the care and attention of two officers and two hired civilians who helped them pass the entrance exam. Red Blaik was concerned most with his offensive line for the upcoming season. His assessment after the spring work was that if they could develop during the first few games, Army's potent runners would be able to handle all but three of their more difficult opponents. Of course, all of these ambitions depended on the cadets passing their academic courses in order to maintain their eligibility to play the following fall. Many of them helped themselves as semester's end neared by availing themselves of the assistance provided by the cheating ring.

In May, the cadet company commander of B-1 Company, Jere Sharp, received a report from a yearling section marcher that three yearlings had absented themselves from a class lecture. The next day, Sharp reported them to the company tactical officer, Lt. Col. Ray Marlin. Marlin imposed the maximum punishment for this offense, a couple dozen hours on the area and confinement to their rooms during their free time. He suspected that they had absented themselves to pass out the football poop for an upcoming examination, since two of the cadets were football players and the third was their football-assigned academic tutor. He could not prove that they were cheating, but he did speak to several other third classmen in the company about the incident, explaining his suspicions and counseling them not to tolerate such behavior among their classmates. He was surprised when several of his yearlings told him that they thought the section marcher should not have turned in the three offenders in the first place.

Marlin was shocked. He did not expect cadets to openly express such contempt for the disciplinary system. He feared that they were covering their own toleration of the cheating he suspected was going on. Colonel Marlin spoke to Hal Loehlein one day in passing. Marlin hoped that he could persuade the well-respected football player from B-1 Company to speak to the yearlings in the company and preach better adherence to the standards of discipline and integrity required of cadets. Marlin was once again surprised when Loehlein told the tac that he, too, thought the section marcher went out of his way to report his classmates. The idea held by Loehlein and many other cadets was that the section marcher's duty ended once he reported that everyone was seated in the auditorium at the start of the lecture. If cadets later left the room it was up to the academic department instructors or the tactical officers themselves to catch the cadets in the act. Loehlein went on to express the prevailing view among cadets that the section marcher had in fact violated the confidence of his classmates by reporting them when he did not have to do so.

Bill Jackomis did well on all his final exams. English and Russian were his best courses, and with his high marks in physical education he managed to finish at number 376 in overall class standing out of 626 in his class. Exams ended on 1 June, and soon the Corps was into the annual graduation week ceremonies. Jake and his roommate Bleecker donned their dress gray-over-white uniforms on Tuesday morning, 6 June 1950, for their recognition parade.

RECOGNITION

"Well, Jake, this is it, our last official act as plebes. Once this parade is over we can fall out and be real human beings for once. No more bracing, squaring corners, or double-timing up the stairs," Bleecker said to his roommate.

"Yeah, I sure am glad we got into I-1. Those guys over in B-1 really had a hard time."

They were a mostly average bunch, those I-1 plebes. They never did much to attract attention to themselves nor did they do much of anything particularly outstanding. Lieutenant Colonel Jim Milner, I-1's tac, preferred it that way, what with several other tacs drawing so much attention from the football staff. Jake liked it that way, too. He wanted to be left alone by the chain of command so he could run track and play football. He found I-1 to be a company mostly hospitable to his ambition. Recognition would be important but almost anticlimactic.

As they formed up for parade the upperclassmen got in a few last licks. "Hey, Jackomis, let's hear a joke." Jake recognized the voice of his squad leader.

He thought he would try a little humor on him. "There was an old lady from Nantucket," he started the old dirty limerick.

"Cease work, Jackomis, bang your simple little chin in, that one still doesn't work," said his squad leader, with a chuckle; he obviously remembered that day back in September when Jackomis had attempted the same response during the Reorganization Week parade. "Ah, what the heck, it's Recognition Day, you might as well be allowed to indulge yourself a little. Go ahead and finish the story." It had been so long, he could not remember the rest of the rhyme. Fortunately for Jackomis, the company commander, Bill Slade, called the company to attention for the march-on.

As I-1 marched in company block through the sally port out of the central area and onto the Plain, Jake felt an exhilaration he had not often felt before. It was a mixture of relief that plebe year was finally over and pride in what he had accomplished. He believed that having completed plebe year, there was nothing to stop him now from finishing three more years at West Point and graduating to become part of the Long Gray Line. His entire family would be proud of him now. Jake imagined himself as a yearling next fall and decided he would be just like Boom-Boom Beck. Jake would follow the rules himself and not let anything blatant get by him from next year's plebes, but basically he would leave them alone. And he would make sure he helped football players get over the difficulties they might have with the fourth class system, just as Beck had done for him.

They were formed on line by companies on the Plain now, facing the first captain and the brigade staff. Jake listened carefully to the commands being shouted as he never had before. You could get by just following the guys in front of you once you knew the basic procedure of a parade at West Point. Most of the time he followed the routine by rote, disengaging his brain from the doldrums of the parade's sequence. This time, though, the parade was for him and his 625 classmates, so Jake listened carefully to every word.

"Sir, the Corps of Cadets is formed for recognition of the Class of 1953!" shouted the first captain, John Murphy, to the reviewing officer, the superintendent, Maj. Gen. Bryant Moore. After a few ceremonies, including salutes and the national anthem, Moore passed on the order to the commandant, Col. Paul Harkins, who in turn gave the command to Murphy, "Pass in review!"

Murphy rendered a saber salute, executed a crisp about-face, and repeated the order, "Pass in review!" Jake thought about the joke they told each other every time that order was heard. The first captain had to shout it out loud and had to hold each syllable for an elongated time in order to be heard. Cadets were sure they taught the higher "makes" to say "Piss in your shoe!" and it came out sounding like "Pass in review!" Jake thought he would like to know, but figured he would have to wait to find out until he became a first classman. He wondered if he was likely to be selected by the tacs for high rank.

It was now up to the commander of A Company, 1st Regiment, to get the next part just right. A-1 would be the first to begin marching and the commander had to give the command of execution in just the right cadence so that his company would step off at precisely the same moment that the band struck the first note of the marching song. It was a tricky bit of timing and usually did not go exactly right. This time, though, it was perfect. Charley Kuyk, despite the stolen truck incident, was the cadet captain in charge of A-1 Company. Red Blaik considered him, along with John Trent, to be the epitome of what an Army football player should be, tough on the field, tops in military prowess, and well above average in academic achievement. The Class of 1950 had done well as cadets and so far had served their country well in bringing along Bill Jackomis and the Class of 1953. These plebes were ready to be recognized as upperclassmen.

When the parade was completed, the I-1 plebes formed up in the company area and stacked their rifles in tepee-like stands so they would have their hands free for the official rite of recognition, a handshake from each upperclassman in their company. Jake and his classmates stood in four ranks with their full-dress hats cradled in their left arms while each upperclassman passed by taking their right hands in the age-old act of mutual recognition among men, the handshake. Along with the handshake, the upperclassman was also required to address each plebe by his first name. It was a somewhat ironic turnabout in which the upperclassmen had to memorize some "poop" of their own in remembering the first names of each of the thirtysome plebes in each company.

But the year was not quite over. There was one more parade to go, graduation for the Class of 1950. That would occur in the afternoon, and then on Wednesday, 7 June, the class would receive their diplomas to officially become second lieutenants in the U.S. Army. The graduation parade was different in that the firsties marched away from their company and the remaining three classes conducted the parade before them. A new chain of command was chosen by the tacs, with second classmen taking over for the firsties and yearlings moving up to the squad leader jobs held all year by the second classmen.

It was all over by sundown on Wednesday. For Bill Jackomis and the Class of 1953 it marked the start of a month's summer leave. By dark he was on a bus headed back to Gary, Indiana, by way of New York and Chicago. He would have to be back by 7 July for summer military training at Camp Buckner, but for now his mind was on spending a month at home.

THE COLD WAR GETS HOT

The Class of 1950 went home, too. They would get about a month's leave before they would report to their first duty station as Army officers. For some football players, such as John Trent, their first duty assignment would be at West Point, to serve as graduate assistant coaches for a short time before heading off to their posts. Everything seemed to be going in routine fashion, much as had their entire cadet experience, until the end of June.

On Saturday, 24 June, at 3:00 P.M. Eastern Daylight Time,

North Korea invaded South Korea in a massive infantry and armored assault. The North Korean troops quickly pushed their way well into South Korea and overran the capital of Seoul as the South Korean Army collapsed before the superior strength and well-equipped armor of the North. On 28 June Gen. Douglas MacArthur left his headquarters in Japan by airplane and conducted a personal tour of the battle lines, landing for a short time in Tacjon against the protests of his staff, who were concerned for his safety. Based on his visit, MacArthur was convinced that the United States would have to intervene with its own troops to prevent a quick Communist takeover of the entire peninsula. On 29 June he reached the Army chief of staff, Gen. J. Lawton Collins, with his call for troops, and Collins informed thirty-four-year-old Secretary of the Army Frank Pace, who in turn notified President Truman. Truman wasted no time agreeing to provide MacArthur with the troops he wanted, and soon the first elements of the Army's 24th Infantry Division were on their way to South Korea.

All of this action threw West Point's summer military training completely off track for the Class of 1952. These men who had just completed their yearling year were to have undergone an extensive orientation on the U.S. Air Force. In the summer of 1950 the U.S. Air Force Academy was yet to be created; academy graduates who so desired and were qualified would have the opportunity to compete for commissions in the Air Force upon graduation, and the competition was keen. Rising juniors each summer were sent on a trip to several Air Force bases to provide them with an orientation on the Air Force and on the application of airpower in modern warfare.

This trip was a transportation nightmare, and for purposes of controlling it the class was split into two groups. Group I, consisting of about half the class, 289 cadets, would depart on 13 June, a few days after graduation ceremonies. They were to fly on Air Force transports to Mitchell Air Force Base in New York, Langley Air Force Base in Virginia, Fort Bragg in North Carolina, and Eglin and MacDill Air Force bases in Florida. At each site they would be introduced to a different aspect of the Air Force. While the official purpose was to educate cadets, each subbranch of the

Air Force viewed the visit as its opportunity to prove to cadets how it was better than the others and thus deserving of the cadets' choice for service after graduation.

Bill Johnson and Fred Jones were paired as roommates for the trip, and they liked that. Jones made the varsity football squad that spring and was going to be the starting offensive center. Bill Johnson was on the B squad. The two were in L-2 Company during the regular academic year and knew each other well. Fred Jones had struggled to get admitted to the academy, eventually making it into the Class of 1952 through a preparatory school in Cornwall-on-Hudson, New York. Jones had already experienced the fierce academic competition that led many to cheat. While at school—New York Military Academy—a man who would eventually become a member of the Class of 1953 stole several pages of Fred's algebra test papers from Jones's desk during a test. Jones caught him and recovered his test papers in time to complete his exam. Fred Jones struggled through every class, yet endured to arrive at his second class year solidly on the road to graduation.

Bill Johnson, Jr., came from a distinguished West Point family. His father graduated from West Point in the Class of 1926, and Bill was born at Fort Benning, Georgia. The elder Bill Johnson was an All-American basketball player who was later inducted into the Basketball Hall of Fame. Bill, Jr., also had younger twin brothers, who graduated from West Point in 1958. For the Johnson family, West Point was everything. In 1931, when his father was assigned to the academy, Bill, Jr., was the adopted mascot of the varsity soccer team. In the summer of his cow year, 1950, he held forth great promise to carry forward the Johnson pedigree: He played a strong lineman's position and achieved his highest marks in military instructor training, although he often struggled in the more academic courses.

Jones and Johnson found themselves together temporarily for the air indoctrination trip. At Mitchell Field they were taught by the Air Force the basics of the air defense of the continental United States against the only potential foe that might dare to strike, the Soviet Union. At Langley Field they saw flying demonstrations of America's latest jets, the F-86 fighter and the B-47 bomber. Then, at Fort Bragg, the cadets were put through the paces of airborne training, completing just about all the steps a trooper goes through except the actual jump from an aircraft. At Eglin they were treated to a spectacular air show that culminated in a bombing exercise that shook everyone to the bone. Eglin also hosted the wildest party on the trip, including not only a dance but also day trips to beaches along the coast of the Gulf of Mexico.

The next-to-last stop on the trip was MacDill Air Force Base, just outside Tampa, Florida. It was also the longest stop, from 25 June to 3 July. The flight orientation was for the big bombers, the B-29 of World War II fame and the B-58 nuclear bomb-carrying "Hustler." Whether it was the additional time or the attraction of the local area, for some reason the MacDill leg of the air indoctrination trip provided the greatest temptation for cadets to get in trouble. Hal Loehlein was with the group, and he slipped away one evening to Indian Rocks for some late-night escapade. He was reported absent after taps when the nightly bed check revealed he was missing.

The commandant's punishment guide called for four months' confinement to be imposed for such an offense. But Loehlein was given only one month. Colonel Harkins was furious with the lenience of his tactical officer's punishment award, especially for a football player. Harkins thought it was an ideal opportunity to make an example of a prominent player to show the football office that their special favor had worn itself thin. Red Blaik poured oil on that fire when he later sent a memo to the superintendent, through Colonel Harkins, requesting that Loehlein be permitted to serve his punishment by walking extra hours on the area at the end of August rather than sit confined to his room. This would free the Army team's star defensive end for early fall practices and scrimmages. Harkins wrote a scathing reply to the supe arguing that granting Blaik's request would be seriously prejudicial to good order and discipline in the Corps of Cadets. Moore overruled the commandant and granted Red Blaik's request.

After the first half of the Class of 1952 had completed the air indoctrination trip, on 5 July, they were granted a month's summer leave. The second half of the class had already been on leave and was supposed to go on the air indoctrination trip starting in July, stopping at the same bases the other half of the class had hit. The Korean War intervened, however, and the Air Force had to divert all its transport aircraft to meet the crisis. In July 1950, while the U.S. Air Force mounted a massive airlift into the Pusan Perimeter, where U.S. forces had finally stabilized a defensive line on the far southeastern corner of the peninsula, the other half of the Class of 1952 pulled administrative duties, helping the firsties at Beast barracks. The commandant granted them two weekend leaves to get away and blow off steam as small consolation for missing out on the trip.

The Class of 1952 did get one climactic military exercise to cap their summer of 1950. In August the entire class came back together at West Point for one more month of military training. This time it was to participate in the annual cadet-midshipman exercise, a yearly training mission conducted jointly by West Point and the U.S. Naval Academy at Annapolis to give both schools' prospective officers training in putting together a large joint amphibious exercise. The culmination of the training was an actual amphibious landing conducted by the Atlantic Fleet, with cadets and midshipmen participating in a live-fire exercise and assault landing.

One difference between the two academies, however, was that Navy's football players did not participate in the "Camid" exercise. It seems that their new coaching staff, hired from out of the professional ranks after Navy's humiliating loss to Army the previous year, did not want its players to risk injury during the training period. Red Blaik got wind of the idea and cried foul but later tried to convince Moore to excuse Army's football players as well.

CAMP BUCKNER

Bill Jackomis was oblivious to all the goings-on of summer training between the football staff and the tactical department. On 7 July, after nearly a month of relaxing back home at Gary, he came back to West Point for third class summer training at Camp Buckner. All the upperclassmen and even some of the tactical officers told the new yearlings that this would be the best summer of their lives. It was.

The class was divided into four companies and trucked out to tin barracks at a military camp about ten miles away from the main campus. Some of the land had been donated to the academy during the war years by Gene Leone, owner of the famous Mama Leone's restaurant in Manhattan. Leone gave the land as part of his contribution to America's effort to liberate his homeland, Italy, from the Fascists. The camp was set up to provide yearlings with basic individual and small-unit tactical training in the military skills they would need as junior officers in the Army. Jake looked forward to the training; he hoped to get away from the dull garrison routines that he put up with in Beast barracks.

He was not disappointed. In the very first week at Camp Buckner his company went to the firing ranges and learned how to shoot their M1 rifles. It was not easy shooting at barely visible targets two hundred and three hundred yards away. Somehow every man came out of marksmanship week qualified at least at the marksman level. Jake wondered if some of those target "hits" he had been awarded by his spotter were actually misses, but he did not score himself. That was done by the first classmen who were detailed to train the new yearlings during the Buckner month. Those firsties were the ones who did not quite make the grade to be selected for the Beast barracks detail and were relegated to the less glamorous details of supervising Camp Buckner training for yearlings. For the firsties the duty was dull and repetitive, but as one firstie put it, it was just like what they could expect out there in the real Army.

After qualifying with their rifles, Jake and his classmates were allowed to fire all kinds of small arms for familiarization training, including machine guns, pistols, and automatic rifles. They also got to carry those heavy weapons in day and night tactical exercises. The second week was armor week for Jake's company. A tank battalion was deployed from Fort Hood, and its mission was to allow the cadets to learn as much as they could about tanks by letting them do as much as they could. Jake got to drive and shoot the Army's new M24 light tank, but concluded that it was for his uncle, not for him. Jake still wanted to be a paratrooper, and he could not wait until his second class summer when he could go to Fort Bragg like his B squad football buddy Bill Johnson. The days rolled on, and the Class of 1953 was introduced to the artillery, signal, antiaircraft artillery, transportation, and quartermaster branches of the Army.

The final event in summer training at Camp Buckner was "Buckner Stakes." This was a competitive exercise in which each of the eight companies selected its best two squads to compete for the honor of being named the best company at Camp Buckner. The stakes were made up of a series of twenty-four stations. At each site the cadets were to be tested on an aspect of the tactical training they received at Buckner. The course was laid out on a run of about three thousand yards, taking the contestants over the familiar ground of Camp Buckner—steep hills, rocky slopes, densely wooded forests and lots of poison ivy. At each station they were required to demonstrate their proficiency in completing a task they learned during the summer, or they were given a written quiz concerning some military doctrine or practice they should know. Each station had to be completed quickly and accurately, and both time and score were recorded. In the morning the stakes involved completing tasks together as squads in calling for artillery fire, building an expedient stream crossing apparatus, putting a field artillery cannon into action, and conducting a reconnaissance patrol. For the afternoon events they competed as individuals, demonstrating their skills in a variety of weapons and other pieces of equipment. The top cadet was to receive a symbolic set of field glasses from Mrs. Simon Bolivar Buckner, widow of Lieutenant General Buckner, killed on Okinawa in 1945, and the top team won a picnic for the entire company. Of course, what was really at stake were bragging rights for the rest of yearling year.

Jake was on his company's team. He was strong and fast, and he was well above average in the assembly and disassembly of most of the weapons they had been trained on at Buckner. It was bright and early on the morning of 28 August 1950 when the sixteen squads turned out for the starting formation in the Buckner Stakes competition. The first class detail was nearly totally committed to manning the testing stations, so for once the formation was led mostly by Jake's own classmates. Gene Filipski, his old roommate from Beast barracks, was his acting platoon leader for the day, and after he took the morning report, he came over to encourage his old friend. "Best of luck to you, Jake. I hope you win it for us. I'd love to chow down at that picnic."

"Thanks, Flip," said would-be fullback Bill Jackomis to his classmate, who had made the varsity squad ahead of him. "Maybe I can win a spot on the A squad with a win here today."

"I don't know, Jake," replied Flip with a note of concern. "I hear that some other company teams have managed to get the poop on some of the stations. I hope that's not true. It would be a shame if they treated these military subjects just like any old academic course. You know there's a war on now, and we can't afford to cheat our way through these things. Our lives will depend on really knowing this stuff if we all end up in Korea."

Jake had not thought of it that way. Flip was right. He never even thought about trying to get the poop at Buckner; most of these military skills seemed to come naturally to him. He guessed that some guys probably never did catch on and would need to get the Buckner poop, if there was such a thing. Maybe there was if Flip had heard about it.

About half an hour after he had finished, they posted the final scores in the individual competition. Jake finished about in the middle of the pack, just about where he always was in everything else. Oh, well, he thought, he had given it his best shot. He came out on top in the shooting and the low crawl. At least those were the ones that would stand him in good stead when he got into the airborne. And they probably would be the ones he would need the most if he wound up in Korea. The war was taking its toll of American troops, and Jake was now more concerned than ever before with developing important individual combat skills.

GO TO THE AIR

In fact, the Korean War had cast a pall over most of America by late August. The unprepared American troops who had been thrown in from garrison duty in Japan had gotten badly mauled at Suwon, south of Seoul, and were pushed back down into the Pusan Perimeter badly beaten, though they had fought as bravely as any Americans ever had. Despite heavy losses, their courage in facing up to the onslaught of the North Korean Army provided the motivation for the South Korean Army to conduct a disciplined, fighting withdrawal rather than suffer a complete rout.

Arnold Galiffa was a brand-new second lieutenant sent into battle that summer after an abbreviated officer training program. In August he was sent into battle with the 24th Infantry Division as a replacement soon after the early August disaster at Suwon. His men had tried to stop North Korean tanks with bazooka rockets that just bounced off the enemy's thick armor plate on the Chinese-made, Soviet-designed T35 tanks. Later, in a defensive position near Taegu, Galiffa's platoon was ordered to attack to silence an enemy machine gun nest that was cutting down the rest of the company with flanking fire. Galiffa's platoon was positioned about fifty yards from the North Korean machine gun, and he led his men in a classic Fort Benning "follow me" frontal assault covered by fire from his own best marksmen. The assault was beaten back in a bloody repulse.

Galiffa took stock of the fifty yards of no-man's-land between his remaining men and the enemy machine gun nest and realized it would serve no purpose to try to assault once again. He would just lose the rest of his men, and the machine gun would still be there. There was no artillery fire to call in, and all the big gun ammunition was being carefully saved for emergency, final protective fire (FPF) situations should the enemy suddenly try to overrun American positions. But Galiffa not only knew how to run, he also could throw. After all, he had been Army's greatest quarterback, and was an All-American passer. But could he toss that nonaerodynamic, two-pound, turtle-shaped hunk of steel across fifty yards of terrain and into the narrow slit of the machine gun position? He had to try, but he would have to stand straight up to do it. That would be sure to draw enemy fire right at him, and they already knew where the Americans were from the assault of a few moments before.

Galiffa pulled the pins in two grenades, stood straight up, took aim, and tossed them one at a time toward their goal. Just as he released the second grenade, a dozen North Korean .52-caliber lead bullets went off, whizzing by Galiffa's head. He dropped down into his radioman's lap as the grenades blew up right on target. He said to his RTO with a gasp, "Colonel Blaik always told me when we were held in the line to go through the air." The machine gun nest was silent. Galiffa was unhurt.

Seventeen

Things Begin to Crack

After the B-1 fiasco, Lieutenant Colonel Marlin was no longer effective as commander of the hundred-plus cadets assigned to the company. He was eased out of his command by the end of the year. Ordinarily, if a commanding officer lost control over his people to the extent Marlin had with the football players in B-1, it would be more than enough reason for him to be officially relieved "for cause." That was fatal to an Army career. It required a senior commander to take the action to relieve a subordinate officer. It was not done often nor lightly.

Regulations required the senior officer to carefully document and spell out the reasons for the relief in great detail and to complete an evaluation report, which remained in the relieved officer's personnel file permanently. Relief for cause was approved only when a commander was grossly negligent to the detriment of the safety, discipline, or good order of his command.

Marlin's immediate superior was the commander of 1st Regiment, Lt. Col. Arthur S. Collins. Collins disliked football players. He thought most of them were below the minimum intellectual and character standards of West Point and were at the academy only because of their prowess on the gridiron. He was convinced that the academy had made a gross mistake by making exceptions to admission standards for football players. Collins wanted officer material, not football material, and he believed the two were mutually exclusive.

Colonel Collins did not believe that Colonel Marlin had been responsible for his own demise. Collins was convinced that there was a great conspiracy afoot at West Point, one designed to undermine the traditional values and practices that had made the academy great in the history of the nation. He believed that the football team, led by Red Blaik, was at the core of the conspiracy. In Collins's judgment it was not Marlin who had lost control of B-1, it was Blaik who had wrested it from him.

Ace Collins was not about to let Blaik get away with it. Collins's calculation was that if he were to relieve Marlin for cause it would only encourage others to try more bold and insidious stratagems in the near future. Blaik would view Marlin's relief as a win in the football program's war with the Tactical Department. He did not relieve Marlin, but he could not leave him in command, either. B-1 was indeed out of control and needed a stronger man to come in and take over. Collins made room for new blood by promoting Marlin up to the regimental staff, to be the operations officer, or S-3. This position was normally reserved as a prize assignment for the most accomplished subordinate commander in a regiment. Marlin got it far ahead of his contemporaries as part of the larger struggle between the football staff and the Tactical Department.

Football players had plenty of encouragement if they were indeed involved in a conspiracy to co-opt the authority of their tacs. By 1950, Army team members had accumulated a wide array of special privileges never before enjoyed by previous Brave Old Army teams. During the season, for example, they no longer had to pull their share of barracks guard or "charge of quarters" duty. For yearlings such as Bill Jackomis and Gene Filipski, that afforded them a considerable advantage over their classmates, who could otherwise expect to pull a twenty-four-hour CQ tour once a month. Cadets on guard duty were not excused from completing academic work due on the date of their tour of duty, and they had to find time to make up all the work missed from classes they did not attend. Football players had to make up missed work from games, but did not have the added burden of making up work missed from guard or CQ. On Sunday mornings the chaplains held a special early and abbreviated worship service for football players, who were then excused from normal chapel service to attend football meetings or watch game films.

In fact football was not the only program besieging the academy's Tactical Department in the fall of 1950. To rank-order cadets more precisely in terms of their aptitude for future military leadership, Colonel Harkins had instituted a new aspect to the system of peer ratings. Under this system, each cadet rated his classmates in his company on a series of qualities deemed to be important for a career as an Army officer. The ratings were numerical scores from one to one hundred, averaged across all the qualities to come up with a single score for each man on the hundred-point scale. The tactical officer also rated each cadet on the same qualities, and his score was averaged in with the average of all the peer ratings on each individual. All cadets in each class were then rank-ordered by their peer rating score as a way of evaluating their aptitude for military service as officers. This score was also averaged into the cadet's overall order of merit, which was otherwise composed of a weighted average of his grades.

These peer ratings had been started in 1943 as subjective ratings and were conducted twice each year, once each academic semester. Under Harkins's reforms they were integrated into class standings and made more quantitative. At the end of the year the records of the men in the bottom seven percent of each class were reviewed. Many were turned back to the next rising class to give them another year of leadership development and maturity. Some were passed on probation, and a few were dismissed as a result of consistently low peer ratings, which usually were symptomatic of larger problems anyway. Most football players continually had difficulties with the peer rating system.

A few football players were outstanding in their military leadership ratings. Frederick Denman was number thirty-four in his Class of 1951 in military leadership, and Hal Shultz ranked number fifty-six. Bob Blaik apparently was rated highly by his classmates; he ended his second class year ranked number ninety out of a class of 579 men. But these few were the exceptions to the rule. Most players individually were below average in military leadership aptitude, and the football players' average ranking as a group in military leadership was well below the average for their class as a whole. Most football players were in the lower half of their class in these peer ratings.

THE ROOT OF EVIL

Other movements were at work to reinforce Collins's and Harkins's notions that someone was out to undermine the traditions of West Point. Starting in 1950, yearlings were granted spring leave. That was a serious break with tradition, which had for decades kept cadets on post except for summer leaves until they were second classmen. Already these senior leaders in the Tactical Department were convinced that wholesale violations of "sign out" privileges were being ignored by cadet leaders. It was commonly accepted among tacs that many of the senior cadets in charge of running the Corps of Cadets looked the other way when an underclassman signed out stating he was going to an authorized place to participate in an authorized activity, when in fact it was known that he intended to do otherwise. This was not only a violation of regulations, it also was a breach of the honor code. In fact, the intent of the "sign out" regulation was to use the honor code to enforce regulations that were otherwise virtually unenforceable when violated wholesale by most cadets. Collins knew this was going on and was convinced that it was mostly being done by football players and that many cadets covered for them by not reporting known or suspected violations.

Collins's fears were reinforced by Harkins's experiences with the football team. Together they convinced themselves that they had to root out the evil that had grown up within the academy by purging the football program of its leader. The struggle between the football program and the Tactical Department was not easily solved, since the director of athletics and the commandant of cadets were of equal status legally in the hierarchy of the academy administration. The infighting reached a peak in the early fall of 1950 over seating arrangements in the mess hall.

The cadet first captain controlled seating assignments in the mess hall. Every man was placed by the senior ranking cadet either at tables assigned to his company or at tables with an athletic team. Regulations dictated that players had to be listed on an official team roster maintained by the coaches and could only sit at team tables during the specified season for that sport. Coaching staffs were to send the rosters to the first captain, who would then take those cadets off company tables and place them at seats reserved for those teams. It was a complex task for the first captain, who had to make sure that every cadet had a seat, and only one seat, and that the mess hall staff were kept informed of how many tables needed to be set in the designated separate areas set aside for regiments and teams. The mess hall was on a very tight budget governed strictly by Army regulations and got only enough money to buy food for precisely the number of cadets on the rolls of the academy. There was no margin for error; the only money available to the mess hall to buy food was provided by the Department of the Army, and it was only a few cents per man per meal. Any over- or underassignment of seats would upset that precise accounting and would result in the mess hall being over or under budget. If it was under budget in a particular month the excess would be applied to the next month's rations and the academy's next month's food allotment would be decreased accordingly. If it was over budget, cadets went hungry.

The first captain normally was personally involved in making sure that the seating assignments were meticulously managed by his cadet S-4 logistics officer. But the football coaching staff did not believe that it needed to go through such bureaucratic hurdles to get its team members their seats. In the summer of 1950 Blaik had his staff prepare a seating chart for tables in the mess hall that he wanted for the team and issued assignments directly to his players. But since the assignments had not gone through the first captain, those cadets were also assigned to company tables by the cadet S-4. In the confusion, some players sat at their company seats, others went to the football tables assigned by Blaik. But the first captain also had assigned those tables to other companies. On the first day of academics, the mess hall was chaos. Twice more Blaik drew up seating assignments and issued them directly to players, but the first captain had assigned those tables to other organizations.

Blaik tried to insert his table assignments into the first captain's roster. Since he had never sent his roster to the first captain, William J. Ryan, the football team still did not have tables assigned officially. Rather than comply with the Tactical Department's bureaucratic rules, Blaik sent two of his players, Harry James and John McDonald, to make their way into the S-4's office and steal the official seating charts to bring them back to the football office. There, Blaik intended to forge his table assignments in place of those made by the first captain. James and McDonald were not able to finger the charts, and eventually the football staff returned a roster to Ryan's room. Only then did Ryan assign tables to the team and take the football players off his company table's assignments.

The special seating in the mess hall was a privilege given to the football team to provide them a time to build camaraderie and to continue to work on team building before game time. It also made it easier on the mess hall staff, since the football team came in late and left late because of the practice schedule. Once the table seating issue was resolved things settled into something more like a routine for the Army football team of 1950.

One of the first things to get organized during the academic year was the tutoring program. Red Blaik was proud of the fact that his players were supposed to be held to the same high academic standards all cadets were held to. There were no "basket weaving" courses for football players at West Point, and instructors graded varsity squad members against the same standards they used for everyone else. Most other nationally competitive football schools made academic life much easier for players, but Blaik had been a player himself as a cadet as well as an assistant coach, and he knew that the Academic Board would never explicitly ease up on the Brave Old Army Team.

But Red Blaik also knew that many of the players he recruited would have trouble with the rigorous course of academics at the academy. The special tutoring program he developed over the years, beginning in the early 1940s for just a few players, grew rapidly until, for the 1950 season, twenty-eight players were tutored by sixteen specially selected, academically above-average cadets.

The cadet tutors were organized by one of their own, cadet Charles Mitchell, from E-2 Company, who matched tutors to players and scheduled their tutoring sessions. Five second class football players were in the tutoring program for 1950: Conway, Jones, Johnson, Pollock, and Roberts. The Class of 1953 yearlings had the greatest number of players being tutored, including Filipski, West, Pollard, Malavasi, and nineteen others. Mitchell was supposed to make sure that each player was matched to a tutor from the same regiment but from the next higher class. With this arrangement, each player would get help from a cadet who had already successfully completed the entire course. But Mitchell had a difficult task matching classes and regiments so that the tutor would not be put in a position where he had advance information—either from having taken the same course the year before, or from a cadet in the opposite regiment who had taken an examination the day prior—that could be passed on inadvertently to his player-pupil. In 1950 there were so many players in need of tutoring that Mitchell could not maintain the integrity of the system. Inevitably some tutors were from the opposite regiment as their pupils and would be exposed to cadets from their company who would have information on what problems were posed or which questions were asked on tests that his pupil would see the next day. It made for temptations that proved to be too powerful to resist.

A NEW YEAR BEGINS

On 5 September, West Point's academic year 1950–51 began much as any previous academic year had. The superintendent, Maj. Gen. Bryant Moore, had not changed much since he had taken over for Maxwell Taylor. The academic courses were much the same as they had been since Taylor revamped the entire West Point program after the end of World War II. Moore's basic approach to the administration of the academy was that enough change had been made by his predecessor. Moore's objective was to bring about a greater sense of stability to the academy, to allow it to absorb the changes already made.

Under Taylor, new courses in behavioral and social sciences had been added to the classes required of cadets, and entire new academic departments had been created to provide the instructors needed to administer and teach these new courses. A typical day in a cadet's life during the academic year was considerably busier than it had been before the war. Firsties took a total of eight courses in the year, with morning classes alternating among military history, military engineering, economics, military hygiene, and ordnance. In the afternoons they took tactics and leadership, English, and law. Second classmen in the Class of 1952 took only five courses, with long class and laboratory sessions each day in mechanics of solids or fluids, military instructor training, and electricity in the mornings. Afternoons were occupied with social science courses. Yearlings had the more traditional courses in mathematics, physics, chemistry, foreign languages, English, military hygiene, and military topography and graphics. They were also introduced to the new postwar discipline of basic psychology. Plebes took courses that their grandfathers would have recognized in mathematics, English, foreign language, physical education, and military topography and graphics. At the end of the class periods, all cadets participated in intramural athletics and parade, except, of course, for the corps squad athletes. For all it had become a very busy day.

But it was not so busy that they had no time for a social life during the academic year. The upper classes enjoyed increasing access to recreational facilities during their occasional free time. Much of this was supervised by a small group of women volunteers who served as cadet hostesses. These were mature ladies who provided instruction in the social graces and even ballroom dancing for cadets who otherwise led a comparatively monastic life. The hostesses were led by Mrs. Barth, who worked out of an office in Grant Hall, the main social meeting place for cadets to see their guests in public.

Mrs. Barth was a widow whose husband had been killed in combat. She developed a special closeness with many cadets who frequented Grant Hall. For some she was a big sister who could warn them when a girl might be cheating on them. For others she was a mother who could help them understand a girl's feelings and motivations. Upperclassmen who had the privilege of inviting guests into the mess hall sometimes had Mrs. Barth as their official dinner guest.

One night in September she was at dinner with one of her protégés when she overheard a cadet tell her host that he was not going straight back to the company area after dinner because he had to go to someone else's room to get the poop for a test tomorrow. Her host told his classmate that he had better be kidding because if he was not he would have to turn him in for violating the honor code. His classmate said of course he was kidding, but two days later he was somehow moved to another table. Mrs. Barth later had to testify as to the interchange.

The fact of the matter was that the cheating ring that had begun among a few football players had expanded so widely that it was difficult for any cadet to avoid learning about it in the 1950–51 school year. In the previous year, his plebe year, James Davidson had helped someone in the ring get answers to some test questions from a solution room and pass them on to a contact in the other regiment who was to take the same test the next day. He was frustrated in his desire to get help in his English exams when his contact told him the ring did not have anyone who was taking the class the day before he did.

Soon after classes began in 1950 his contacts reached him and asked him to get some test answers as he had the previous year. They assured him that his confidentiality would be protected because the members of the ring all had to cooperate in order to pull it off and graduate. They told him to leave his exam early, go to the solution room, and memorize the answers (no writing materials were allowed in the solution room; cadets were allowed only to look at approved solutions briefly after they took an exam as part of the learning process for themselves). Then he was to meet his K-1 Company cheating ring leader, who would write down the answers and pass them on to other company cheating reps, who would pass the answers on to others who were to take the test later that day or the next day. Often Davidson's roommate William West would be there to get the poop directly, since he had English after Davidson did on the same day.

James Davidson was beginning to get concerned about his involvement in the cheating ring. Last year he had thought he would do it just that one time, when he needed help on one test. Although he did not get the help he needed, he was trapped by his own honor violation in providing help to the others. He could not refuse to help them because they threatened to turn him in. This year they assured him that he would not get caught because the ring had expanded to so many cadets that there were enough ring members in K-1 to elect one of their own to the Honor Committee. In fact, they told him, there already were some cheating ring members on the Honor Committee, and with the addition of several more from the Class of 1953 the cheating ring would be virtually guaranteed always to have enough votes to prevent an investigation from proceeding against one of its members.

In September 1950 James Davidson was enmeshed in the cheating ring. The more he tried to escape, the tighter the noose gripped on his life. West Point, his dream, was about to turn into a living hell.

NEW HOPE

Korea was already hell for American soldiers hastily deployed to combat. After disastrous defensive battles at Suwon and Taegu, Douglas MacArthur's U.N. forces fell back into perimeters around Taegu and the eastern port city of Pusan. Pusan was to be defended at all costs while reinforcements were formed in the United States, trained, and shipped into battle. In the summer of 1950 it looked like it would take as long as a year to put together the size force needed to break out of Pusan and send the estimated eleven to fourteen attacking North Korean divisions back across the 38th parallel.

MacArthur knew that the American people were not likely to withstand a year or more of defensive operations and mounting casualties in an Asian war. They had just demobilized after winning the greatest victory in history and were not interested in another prolonged conflict. But MacArthur's forces, in some areas outnumbered ten to one, could not get enough troops to do anything more than form a defensive perimeter around the southeastern cities of Taegu and Pusan. He had to find a way to avoid a year of staying hunkered down.

His solution was a daring maneuver around and behind the invading North Korean forces. MacArthur calculated that if he could cut the North's supply lines the invaders would be forced to withdraw or face the prospect of dying a slow death from lack of food, medicine, and ammunition.

He had his staff prepare an ambitious plan for an amphibious assault on the western coast of the Korean peninsula that would come ashore at the port of Inchon and move rapidly to retake the South Korean capital city of Seoul. Back in the United States the joint chiefs demurred, arguing it was too risky, but MacArthur prevailed and pulled off one of the most spectacular military stratagems in history.

The news of the Inchon landing hit West Point in mid-September like a breath of fresh air. It gave the old Army traditionalists in the Tactical Department renewed pride in the accomplishments of their recent graduates. It gave Red Blaik and his football staff new reason to celebrate the strategic brilliance of their idol MacArthur. It seemed to have spurred on the Brave Old Army Team to accomplishments beyond what was expected of them going into the 1950 football season.

The 1950 team was a good one. It was not one of Red Blaik's "storybook teams," like the 1944 and 1945 national championship teams, but it looked like it was going to be very good, probably competitive nationally among the top ten college squads.

Blaik's son Bob, a junior, had won for himself the starting quarterback position, but the position was hotly contested by yearling phenom Richard Hunt. Two other yearlings also made the squad as backup offensive players, including fullback Al Pollard and Gene Filipski at halfback. Army's first game that year was at home against Colgate, and after running up the score early, Blaik pulled his more experienced men and let the yearlings have a go at it.

They relished their varsity baptism by fire; Al Pollard kicked four field goals, scoring nearly half of Army's twenty-eight points that day. He scored a touchdown on a long run around the end. Gene Filipski scored a touchdown after a headlong run up the middle of the line. Bob Blaik had a solid start.

A week later, Army ran up the score on Penn State, 41–7. Again Bob Blaik quarterbacked with great confidence, and Richard Hunt saw playing time as well, passing for a touchdown. Team captain John D. "Danny" Foldberg continued to turn in strong performances at end in these tune-up games, aiming for a repeat of his junior year first team All-American selection, and it looked like Army might be headed for a better season than expected.

Red Blaik was confident that his football program had resulted in the creation of a real powerhouse in spite of the lack of the kind of talent he had back in the forties. He criticized professional football for lacking the qualities his program had at the intercollegiate level, and in an interview for *Collier's* magazine he openly slammed pro football. He said that pro football was more like show than sport. He stated that pro linemen never rushed the passer to the full extent of their ability. He said that no pro team could stand the test of the schedule kept by top college teams. That started a nasty dialogue in that magazine, with pro football players and coaches criticizing Blaik and his methods in return.

The academic program began to take a toll on Blaik's cherished football program. It happened first to the B squad.

Bill Jackomis kept up his pursuit of a spot on the football team. He did not enjoy the punishment he took each week as the B squad played Army's varsity opponent offense against the Army varsity defense, but he looked forward to a time when he could gain the experience and be recognized for the skills he had developed. He knew he was a smarter player than his competition. Jake had better basic mental aptitude than the typical football player, and he hoped to use his acumen to his advantage.

But Jackomis struggled with one course in particular, which he did not like nor have much of an inclination for: English Literature. The sixty-three lessons of third class English were devoted entirely to literature. Jake just did not have enough time in the day to do all that reading, which included the requirement to read two complete novels and write a formal, critical book review of each. Selected readings during the course exposed the cadets to the classics, romanticists, and realists. This was a lot more difficult, especially for football players, than plebe English had been. Last year's course had been broken down into smaller segments of grammar, composition, and speech, and, like math, grades were given every day. In plebe English if you had a bad day, a few more days of higher grades would average out. But with literature you had to pace yourself to do well on the few graded exercises there were. If you got the equivalent of an *F* on one book review, even getting an *A* on the other would result in no better than a *C* average.

Ironically, Jake's best class was his foreign language, Russian. Russian language was a recent addition to the curriculum at the academy, having been added only in 1945 as a result of the Cold War that fell upon the nation immediately after World War II. For Bill Jackomis it was a language spoken frequently at home, although there was no love lost among the Jackomis family for his mother's former homeland now that it was in the hands of the Communists. For Jake, his familiarity with the script, pronunciation, and construction made it seem almost easy for him to master the language. It was his best class and he would, much later in his career, turn his aptitude to his advantage.

MORE HELP
But Jake's classmate in K-1 Company, James Davidson, did not get Russian so easily. At Camp Buckner the previous summer, a football player had asked Davidson how his roommate, Will West, was doing. Davidson replied that West always had trouble and that James, too, was beginning to have some difficulty, especially in Russian. The player offered to get Davidson help in Russian if Davidson would help West in his academics. The team needed West as a starter, the argument went, and James would be helping the team to a winning season if he would help Will stay proficient in his academics so he could continue to play throughout the season.

Soon after academics started in the fall of 1950, Will needed help in math, and James was falling behind in Russian. James went to his football player contact, who provided him with the name of a cadet in the cheating ring who would give him answers to the next Russian test if James would help West right away. By a quirk in the scheduling system, Davidson had math first hour in the morning and West had the same class in the second half of the morning. Davidson's assignment was to come back from his early math class, meet West back in their room, and quickly pass the poop as to what was on the day's quiz and what the answers were.

Later Davidson helped another cadet in physics, who in turn provided James with the help he needed to get by in Russian. And "get by" was all that Davidson was able to do; he still nearly failed the course, finishing only fourteenth man up from the bottom of his class in Russian.

West stayed proficient and continued to play throughout the fall. His classmate Al Pollard was in worse shape academically, but he, too, exploited the cheating ring to stay proficient for football. In the 14 October game against Michigan, Pollard had his inter-collegiate debut as a star running back. Michigan would go on that season to win in the Rose Bowl, but they lost this day to an inspired Army team playing at Yankee Stadium. Just before the first half came to a close, with Army down by six and with the ball on their own two-yard line, Bob Blaik kicked a tremendous sev-enty-four-yard punt to put the Big Blue out of scoring range. In the next series of downs the cadets managed to score a touch-down, although Pollard's point-after attempt was blocked. The half ended with the score tied at 6–6.

In the third quarter, after Foldberg fumbled on an end-around, Pollard, scooting around the left end, scored the next touchdown on a lateral from Blaik. Pollard kicked his own point after, and Army was ahead to stay. James Jackson had a personal best game, too. In the third quarter, with Michigan attempting a naked re-verse play, Jackson penetrated the line, then blocked Michigan's star quarterback in his pass attempt. In the fourth quarter Jack-son became one of only a handful of linemen who would pene-trate Michigan's offensive line to sack Chuck Ortmann.

Pollard's mighty foot was to score again on two more conversions, and he made another touchdown in the best game of his career thus far. The next weekend, against Harvard, Pollard would best himself again by scoring seven field goals in a 49–0 rout of the Crimson.

On the Monday after the Harvard game, the corps took its midterm exams. This was critical for Al Pollard because a low grade on these exams would immediately pull his average down below proficiency and instantly bench him from the football team. He had been getting by so far by getting the poop before each math class from James Davidson, but there was no way Pollard could even cheat his way through the midterm written general review (WGR). This test was an hour and a half long and covered all the material they had done thus far in the semester. He had to find another way to get a good grade; he was having too good a season to cut it short now.

The football staff provided him with his escape. Army's football team trainer was Red Blaik's old friend Roland Bevan. Bevan knew how important Pollard was to the team and was aware that Al would flunk the exams miserably if left to his own mental capacities. Bevan had been associated with the Army team ever since Blaik brought him over from Dartmouth in 1940, and he knew how to beat the system. The football team trainer was authorized by regulations to excuse cadets from class because of injuries, just as the post's Army doctors were. Bevan simply wrote out a sick slip for Pollard that stated that the cadet had been injured during the game and had to be admitted to the hospital for observation of his injuries. Bevan knew that the doctors would examine Pollard and find nothing wrong with him, but it was not unusual for the trainer to be overly cautious with a star player right after a game. The regulations further allowed a cadet who was in the hospital during exam periods to take his exams in the hospital. The instructor was to send the test papers to the cadet via one of his classmates, and Pollard was on his honor to take it in the same time allotted to his classmates, then turn it in to the hospital staff, to be delivered to the Math Department for grading. Bevan also arranged for a member of the cheating ring to bring Pollard the questions and answers for the test from the solution room in the morning so that by the time Pollard received his test paper, he had all the answers written down near his bed. More than a few eyebrows were raised when Pollard's math WGR came out with a perfect score!

Eighteen

Merry Christmas

The cheating ring never seemed to get to Pollard's conscience, nor to that of the dozens of players and fellow travelers who accepted it as the way business was done. But by this time, the iniquity of it all was beginning to wear on some of the others. Bill Johnson was one who was about ready to break from the strain brought on by the burden of guilt.

Johnson and his L-2 Company roommate, Ralph Martin, were both in on the cheating ring. Johnson was a B squad football player who needed help mostly in the hard sciences of mechanics and electricity, where his grades kept him close to the bottom of his class. In social sciences, military tactics, and, of course, physical education, he did well enough on his own. His roommate, Martin, was an oddity in the ring because he did not need to cheat to stay proficient. He was right about at the middle of his class and was not even on the football team. Martin cheated in an attempt to push his class standing higher.

In the fall of 1950 Bill Johnson began to seriously doubt himself and his involvement with the cheating ring. He talked it over with Martin, who convinced him to stick with it because so many others would be brought down if Johnson were to squeal on them in a moment of self-pity. But Johnson had West Point in his blood. His father had been an outstanding cadet and his brothers were soon to follow him into the Class of 1958. Johnson had been born at West Point and at one time was the soccer team's mascot. He knew that what he was doing was wrong, and it was eating away at him.

Johnson in a way could understand how those who wanted badly to be in the Army, like himself, would cheat to stay in West Point so that they could graduate and become officers. But those he had come to detest were the football players who were just too dumb or too lazy to make the grade as cadets. They should not be officers in any case, thought Johnson. Johnson made his mind up to quietly drop out of the ring at the end of this semester.

Army football continued its winning ways, beating Columbia, 34–0, and Penn. In the Columbia game Don Beck had another of his patented Boom-Boom interceptions, and at Penn, Gene Filipski stole the show. Beck's interception broke a string of seventy-four previous passes without an interception by the quarterback. Filipski scored three touchdowns in Army's 28–13 victory, but Al Pollard fumbled, although he did score on four conversions.

In the Penn game Fred Jones suffered a compound fracture in his right hand. He taped himself up so the coaches could not see the bone pushing through his skin. After the game he underwent seven hours of surgery. The hand later got infected, Jones believes, because trainer Roland Bevan cut the cast off four days later and inadvertently thrust it into a dirty whirlpool. Whatever the cause, Jones underwent surgery again at West Point during exam period and, while still under the influence of anesthesia the next morning, took his exams verbally from an instructor. He passed all his exams that term. Later, while he was recovering, Jones had his arm, still in a full cast, under his rain cape one rainy day as he passed by Lieutenant Colonel Collins. As prescribed by regulations, Jones did not raise his arm in a salute; he simply greeted Collins with "Good afternoon, sir." Collins was angry, even after Jones showed him the cast, and told Jones he would still be written up for the offense.

James Jackson was a big man from Texas. He was the stalwart

of Army's defensive line at the tackle position. He was probably the toughest man on the 1950 Brave Old Army Team, and opposing teams rarely tried to drive through his right side of the Army line. Against Penn State he had blocked a punt, and against Harvard he recovered a fumble. He was pretty bright, too, but he was also part of the cheating ring.

Jackson's roommate in M-2 Company was big Michael Kelly. Kelly was also a football player, and he was about average as a student at West Point. But the two of them just sort of fell into the habit of using the information made available to them in the cheating ring to help in passing their exams. Now Kelly decided he was through with the cheating and wanted to get out of the ring.

Michael told his roommate, Jackson, that they had to get out of the ring, because it was wearing on his conscience and because he saw that it was getting to be so large that it was bound to be discovered soon. Jackson would have nothing to do with leaving the ring; he needed the grades and was having a great year on the varsity team. Besides, argued Jackson, it was too late; they had already committed enough honor violations to be thrown out of the academy several times. Anyway, if they were to quit, the ring now involved so many people that there was no way the academy would throw them all out.

STORMY WEATHER

That Saturday Army was to play the University of New Mexico at Michie Stadium. The Boy Scouts of America were having a national jamboree at West Point that weekend, and more than sixteen thousand scouts were to watch the game. The weather turned sour that week. The scouts were just about washed away, and the Army team had only been able to hold one outdoor practice before playing New Mexico. That was all right for this game, because Blaik had deliberately scheduled an easy game prior to going to San Francisco the next week to take on a tough Stanford team. Jackson pounded away at New Mexico's offense, holding them scoreless. Al Pollard scored a touchdown and kicked seven field goals as Army won, 51–0.

But the weather did not clear up for practice in anticipation of taking on Stanford. In fact, it rained every day, and Blaik had to bring his men indoors. It was not conducive to practicing for such a major contender.

Half a world away, in Korea, Lt. John Trent found himself on a rain-soaked battlefield. His 15th Infantry Regiment was sent ashore at Wonsan with the 3d Infantry Division in October. Trent was a platoon leader in E Company. The night before the landings he wrote home, "We are landing on Wonsan tomorrow. The port is not as yet secure and we may have to fight." In fact, the amphibious assault on Wonsan was unopposed.

The Wonsan landings occurred as MacArthur and the U.N. forces expected the war soon to end. The Inchon landings had sent North Korean forces into a general retreat, U.N. forces had surrounded the North's capital city of Pyongyang, and U.N. troops were pushing north quickly to reach the Yalu River and prevent the entry of China into the war. The North Koreans did not offer resistance at Wonsan, and Trent's regiment quickly settled into defensive positions.

The 3d Infantry Division consisted of three American regiments and one South Korean regiment. The 65th Infantry, the division's best-trained, was assigned to the forwardmost defensive position, responsible for clearing out pockets of enemy resistance left over from the linkup operation with the rest of Eighth Army, moving up from Pusan, that had already occurred. The 15th Infantry was given the defensive sector considered least threatened by enemy resistance.

At first there was no resistance until early November, when patrols reported back isolated sightings of North Korean soldiers. By the second week of November, the 15th Regiment's supply convoys were intercepted frequently by snipers and ambushers. Lieutenant Trent was assigned to take his platoon along one of the convoy routes and establish a blocking position so that enemy infiltrators would no longer disrupt the division's line of communications.

On the night of 15 November, Lieutenant Trent's platoon had established its position and began to receive enemy fire. Trent himself was positioned at the end of his line when his platoon sergeant started out on his regular perimeter check. Trent told him that he wanted to make the rounds himself this time. It was then that the North Korean attack came and Trent saw the enemy attempting to get around his flank. The platoon fought fiercely, stopping the North Korean movement, but in the fight, Trent was mortally wounded. In his dying words he is reported to have said that the North Koreans were "stupid thinking they could turn my end." But Colonel Harkins's replacement as commandant, Colonel Waters, later said that the circumstances of Trent's death were not so clear, and testified that he heard that Trent had been shot by his own troops. Trent was buried at a Marine Corps cemetery in Wonsan.

The news of the death of one of the legendary heroes of the Brave Old Army Team cast a pall over the already gloomy academy. It was still raining in New York on Saturday, 18 November, when Army played Stanford. Blaik had not been able to run a full outdoor practice for nearly two weeks at either West Point or at Stanford. The team traveled by train to San Francisco, and when they arrived it was raining there, too.

They were in the Bay Area for only two days and it rained incessantly while they were there. At game time the rain was pouring down. Cadets in the stands scrounged up pots and pans to cover their heads from the downpour. Army was picked by the sportswriters as a twenty-point favorite going into the game, but the rain became a great equalizer. The field was a pool of mud, and neither team could get its running or passing attack going. Late in the third quarter, with both teams' players thoroughly blackened with the caked-on mud, Army failed to convert a third-down play, and Bob Blaik went back on fourth down to punt. He kicked a boomer that went out of bounds on the Stanford four-yard line. Stanford failed to convert and had to punt. Army took the ball on the ground and finally made a first down at Stanford's seventeen. On third and eleven, after a holding penalty, Bob Blaik risked passing in the rain and mud. Dan Foldberg caught it on the five and jumped over for the score, and Al Pollard kicked the point after. Neither team could score again, and Army squeaked by, 7–0.

NAVY WEEK

Back at West Point, it was now Navy Week. But it was also getting close to the end of the academic semester. The pressure was on, especially for those cadets who were close to failing in any particular course. To play, your overall average had to be passing, and if you had failed several exams and quizzes already, then a single day's grade could affect a tenth of a point in your overall average and make the difference between passing and failing. You could always make up for a low average on the final exam, which sometimes counted for as much as a third or a half of the entire semester's grade. But right now it was the daily graded exercises that made the difference between being on the team or being dropped from the roster. The pressure was on nearly every day.

And the pressure to cheat mounted as well. In one company one yearling caught another in the act of cheating, but when he confronted his errant classmate, they got into a fistfight. Incredibly, the incident was never reported. The cheater pointed out to his accuser that there were so many others involved in similar behavior that there was no way he would be convicted alone, and if the Honor Committee were to take on all those involved in the ring, it would paralyze the academy. The accuser saw the point, gave up his accusation, and joined the ring himself. The exchange of graded material in the mess hall became so open that members of the basketball team several rows away from the football team were able to observe it happening. They, too, chose not to report it.

It was peer rating time in the Corps of Cadets. Lieutenant Colonel Herman Smith was the brigade aptitude officer. Smith was not a West Point graduate. He was an Air Force officer on the staff of the newly formed Department of Military Psychology and Leadership. This department was created by Maxwell Taylor in response to Dwight Eisenhower's letter in 1946 urging the supe to modernize the academy's approach to leadership by adopting the methods and techniques of modern psychology to the traditions of the academy. In the academy's jargon the department became known as "MP&L."

MP&L was unusual among the academic departments at West Point because it had direct impact on both the academic instruction and the military development of cadets. The department's instructors taught courses in psychology and leadership. There also were two special staff officers to perform functions in the leadership development program for cadets. The staff psychologist, Dr. Douglas Spencer, provided counseling to troubled cadets and faculty and provided official opinions on the fitness for service of cadets and faculty in cases where behavior or attitude revealed particular problems.

Colonel Smith was responsible for administering the cadet aptitude evaluation system. This was an elaborate method of reducing a wide variety of behavior and attitude measurements into a single numerical score that would permit the rank-ordering of all cadets in terms of their "aptness" for service as Army officers. The system took into account the number of demerits a cadet received for various minor offenses, greater punishments that were imposed by senior officers or boards for the more serious violations, and subjective evaluations of a cadet's potential for service by the company tactical officer. These factors had been under consideration since 1943 by a study committee formed during the war. The committee had been established to consider changes to the academy's traditional system of relying solely on the tactical officer's evaluation of a cadet's potential for leadership. It took Eisenhower's 1946 letter to Taylor to stimulate a more fundamental change in the aptitude rating system.

Ike had no idea how his letter was affecting the Army football program in 1950. He was finishing his second year as president of Columbia University and was named to be the first supreme Allied commander, Europe under the new North Atlantic treaty creating NATO. Back at West Point, the academy was now using IBM punched cards to record each cadet's scores on the various elements of the rating formula. Machine card readers then did all the math and printed out everyone's score, producing the rank order list within a few minutes, a chore that until 1948 had been done manually, requiring MP&L hundreds of man-hours to complete, then check, correct, double-check, and recheck.

The ratings proved to be a powerful tool in the hands of the academy's administrators. Those cadets who consistently showed up at the bottom of the rankings became the focus of attention of tactical officers and the commandant's staff, who provided help for cadets who were going through a temporary period of stress or who needed personal development to improve themselves. They also provided evidence in the determination of whether a cadet's behavior or attitude were indicative of deeper, more permanent problems that were not likely to be solved before graduation. The academy's approach to such cadets was to dismiss them from West Point before they became officers and so prevent someone incapable of performing a leadership role in combat from ever getting into a position of authority over soldiers.

In 1948 a major addition was made to the aptitude rating system, in which the ratings of a cadet's peers were added to the numerical scoring scheme. In a way, the addition of cadet peer ratings was a technique to deflect criticism away from the Tactical Department. Until 1948 the only input into the system was from the Tactical Department, so if a cadet was rated low it was clearly by consensus of a number of officers. Often the cadets themselves would disagree with their superiors' opinions of a particular cadet. After all, it was the cadets themselves who lived with these men minute-by-minute every day. Cadets sometimes felt they had a better perspective on an individual's fitness for service and that the tactical officer's views were not only skewed, but occasionally unfair. There was a peer rating system at the time, but it was not factored into the tactical officer's ratings in the determination of aptitude for service.

Modern psychology reinforced this view with research in the workforce showing that peer ratings were sometimes more accurate than supervisors' ratings of job performance. The research also showed that peer ratings could enhance the motivation of a labor force by giving the workers themselves a sense of empowerment over their future. Colonel Smith thus added the peer rating element to the aptitude system in 1948.

Just before the Navy game the results of the fall aptitude ratings were released by MP&L. Yearling defensive lineman Bob Volonnino came out very low in the ratings and was up for review by his tactical officer. Volonnino was in B-1 Company along with

Bob Blaik. After a counseling session, the new B-1 tactical officer wrote a letter to Volonnino's father reporting that Bob was rated low and needed to improve his aptitude in order to continue at the academy. Volonnino's father was angered, and he called Red Blaik about the letter.

Blaik never did like the aptitude system. He felt that it was unnecessary and would not be needed if the Corps of Cadets had the kind of leadership it used to have. Blaik called Colonel Smith and told him so. In fact, said Blaik to the non–West Pointer in charge of the aptitude system, the corps was just not led like it used to be, and that was the real problem with the academy. Smith was stung by the insulting manner in which Blaik spoke to him about Volonnino. He reported the call to his boss, the department head, Col. Samuel Gee. Gee spoke to Blaik about it, but it had no impact on Blaik's anger toward Smith nor on his attitude toward the aptitude rating system.

AND THE RAINS CAME

And it kept on raining at West Point. The rains went on so long that Red Blaik never held an outdoor practice for his men since before the New Mexico game. Blaik figured that it would be all right in the run-up to Navy; the cadets were heavily favored to win, and the coach did not want to work out the team in the weather and risk some of them getting sick. Blaik also closed the practices to anyone outside the football team. He was very nervous about the Navy team's new coaching staff spying on Army's practices, and he did not want knowledge of any of his plays to leak out. He knew that Navy's coaches had been recruited from the ranks of professional football after last year's humiliating loss to Army, and he figured they would try some of the scouting tricks used in the pros. Blaik did not want to risk even the chance that Navy's scouts might hang around outside the field house and pick up bits and pieces from cadets after the practice was over. No one other than football program personnel cleared by Blaik himself were allowed to observe Army's pre-Navy practices.

On 24 November a powerful storm, packing gale-force winds,

struck the Hudson River Valley from New York City to the Adirondacks. Twenty-three people were killed, hundreds injured, and electrical power was out for several hundred thousand buildings. The weather had already been quite strange that fall; a cold spell hit in September, dropping temperatures to seventy-five-year record lows. Then in October a record-setting heat wave lingered, keeping the mercury near ninety. The November storm caused more than $300,000 in damage at West Point, cutting communications cables and felling trees everywhere.

This had a depressing effect on the corps' attitude toward the game. Navy week at West Point is typically a time of high-spirited demonstrations of support for the Army team. Rallies are held after dinner, all kinds of high jinks are pulled in the attempt to show how committed the cadets are to their team, and emotions in favor of the team generally run high. But in 1950 all this was depressed by the growing division between the team and the Corps of Cadets, a condition that was further dampened by the stormy weather. Blaik's barring practice from observation by the corps did not help in that regard. At one rally, team captain Dan Foldberg, who was expected to give a rousing speech on the determination of the team to fight on to victory for the glory of the academy, instead complained that the corps was not behind the team that year. That only reinforced the feeling, by then widespread among cadets, that the team had taken on an air of separateness from, and even superiority to, the rest of the Corps.

In spite of the rain and the sour relations between the team and the rest of the academy, Bill Jackomis was enjoying his first trip to the Navy game as an upperclassman. It had been a good yearling year so far; the B squad team had won all five of its games. It was nice just not being a plebe anymore and not getting yelled at by three out of every four other cadets around you. They had to get up very early that morning to board the special train out of the West Point station, but he didn't mind at all getting up that morning. He could sleep again once inside the car assigned to I-1 Company. Maybe next year, he thought, he would be on the A squad and make the trip earlier in the week, with the team. He knew he could be a good running back, but of course he was glad that at least his friend from Beast barracks, Gene Filipski, had made the team. Maybe with graduations there would be room for Jake next year.

Meanwhile, he was enjoying the first Saturday in a long time with no early morning classes. He could sleep on the train, eat his box lunch at noon, then enjoy one of the greatest games of all as Army would inevitably beat Navy that afternoon. It would cap a perfect season and make it twenty-nine straight wins for Red Blaik and the Brave Old Army Team. After the game there would be parties all over Philadelphia, especially in the cadets' headquarters hotel, the Benjamin Franklin. Jake was really looking forward to that.

At midafternoon the trains unloaded their gray living cargo and two thousand cadets formed up to march into Philadelphia's Municipal Stadium. Typically, the Naval Academy's midshipmen would march in somewhat more haphazard and ragged array, with weaving lines and many marchers obviously out of step. West Point prided itself on being the better marching unit as a whole, and it showed in the march-on with the cadets' much more disciplined parade drill.

As Jake stood there in close order formation in his company, he felt a certain pride in being a cadet. He knew that they were good at what they were preparing to do and that soon they would be off to war in Korea. At this moment in time he knew that the newsreel films would capture the confidence that the Army team and the corps showed on this field, and he held his head high with his stiff salute as the band played the national anthem. Then the cadet cheerleaders led the corps in a rousing version of the corps yell, and just as he expected the commanders to order the march into the stand, there was a loud bang down on the field as a dozen artillery simulators went off, signaling the arrival of Army's mascot, its mule. Typically, both schools tried to steal each other's mascot during the previous week's run-up to the game, and to protect their mule Army had taken him away to a secret hiding place at a local New York farm. With the boom from the pyrotechnics, a large plywood mock-up of a tank fell apart to reveal Army's mule inside and the return of the mascot to the ranks of the corps. It looked like Army was about to win another one from archrival Navy.

But it was not to be so. In the first quarter, Bob Blaik pitched out on a roll to his right, aiming for running back Al Pollard. But the ball went high, way over Pollard's head and out of reach. Pollard got to the loose ball first, but he stumbled as he bent over to pick it up and by then Navy players slid in and fell on the ball for the recovery. The midshipmen drew first blood on the error and went on to score first. In the second half, Navy pulled a surprise play, a naked reverse, catching Army completely off guard, and went in to score. At the half Navy led, 14–0.

The only score Army was able to get that day was on a Navy mistake. Bob Volonnino blocked a Navy punt in the third quarter, and the ball bounced back into Army's end zone. Army fell on the ball, resulting in Army's only points of the game, a two-point safety. The Army stands were dismally quiet for the entire fourth quarter. While the partying in Philadelphia after the game was as rowdy as ever, it was not as enjoyable a ride back to West Point as Bill Jackomis had anticipated.

On Sunday the team arrived back at the campus on their special train. Ordinarily the entire corps turns out at the train station to welcome back their heroes, win or lose. This year no one was there to greet the team as they came off the train. The officer in charge of the football trip was incredulous. He called the cadet senior officer of the day (SOD) in the guardroom and asked why the corps was not there. The SOD reported that Coach Blaik had called him to say that the corps was not behind the team before and during the game so he did not want them there at the station for the arrival. The cadet took that as an order from the graduate manager of athletics, an official title that gave Blaik a standing as high as that of the commandant of cadets.

Gloom period is bad enough in early winter. It was made worse by a loss to Navy. For three weeks afterward, until the upperclasses departed for Christmas leave, everyone was just plain miserable. The most depressing part of the time between the Navy game and

Christmas leave, however, was the prospect of facing semester final exams in the last days before departing from West Point.

For football players these exams determined their eligibility for next spring's varsity trials. If they were proficient after these exams and kept a passing average at the time of the actual tryouts, they would be able to eat at football tables and get all the special considerations the football team got during the regular season in the fall. If they did not pass an exam they would be "conditioned" in that course, and even if they maintained a passing grade next semester they could not participate in the varsity sport until the conditioned status was removed, which would not even be considered until the end of the second semester. That would pretty much end any hope of making next year's team. For the yearlings and cows, the Classes of 1953 and 1952, this exam period was crucial to their collegiate football career.

At this point in time the cheating ring went into high gear. The lapse in integrity was not limited to helping in the academic areas. It even came back to haunt the football program itself. The team was issued special long overcoats to stay warm during the game. Each player was handed a coat to use for the entire season. There was no accountability for the coats, but each man was expected to return it at the end of the season so it could be cleaned and repaired if necessary, then reissued the next year. They were very expensive wool coats made exclusively for the Brave Old Army Team. The team managers simply collected the coats at a turn-in point in the locker room, then asked each player for an "all right" on overcoats. This was in effect using the honor system for property accountability in that by giving a report of "all right," the player was indicating that he had turned in the overcoat he had been issued at the beginning of the season. Most other property issued to cadets was accounted for using the standard Army supply receipt procedure of signing a document and keeping it on file until the item was returned. Using the honor system made such property accountability much more efficient. But it depends on the integrity of the persons involved. Even after receiving an "all right" from every football player, the team was missing one of those expensive coats and much other equipment. The team's property manager lost confidence in using the honor system for property accountability.

Al Pollard exploited his membership in the cheating ring. Going into exams after the Navy game, he was sorely deficient in military topography and graphics. His assigned cadet tutor, Charles Russell, from L-2 Company, was the number one man in the class in that course and by a quirk in scheduling had the class on the same day as Pollard in the earlier hour. Pollard got a perfect score on that exam and squeaked by for the semester.

Jake and Flip heard all about the cheating from football tables. In December 1950 it was a matter of open discussion for team members, who would ask each other if they had or needed "the poop" for a particular course. There was an open exchange of who had access to what answers to which tests, on a daily basis. Ironically, neither Jake nor Flip needed the help that semester. By the end of the term their grades were adequate and their own knowledge of the subjects was enough for them to pass their exams. But they knew all about what was going on.

James Davidson heard that Jim Pfautz was having big trouble in math again, although at the time Pfautz was holding his own with "The Black Death," as the math text was called. Davidson invited Pfautz to join the cheating ring. Jim said no, but it really bothered him that his good friend, a man who had spent time with Pfautz's family in his home the previous summer, would even think about asking him to do such a thing.

Red Blaik was discouraged. With all his other concerns for the academy and even for the country, he was nearly depressed. The night before the Navy game, from his post as president of Columbia University, Dwight Eisenhower had sent a telegram to Blaik. It was intended to inspire Blaik and the team on to victory the next day:

Dear Red,
Tonight, I send to you and to Captain Foldberg and the team my fervent hopes for victory tomorrow. In these times of tension and conflict it is especially important that West Point's Corps of Cadets continue to give to all of us a flaw-

less example of perfection in teamwork, courage, skill, and loyalty. These qualities will not only best the Navy, but their demonstration by our future leaders will bring renewed confidence to everyone who is concerned about the welfare of America. Good luck, and may blocking be sharp, tackling clean, and ball handling perfect.

Eisenhower

It failed to get to Blaik before game time. In his letter responding to Ike's telegram, Blaik said that its late arrival made him even more sick than the loss alone, since he would have liked to have read it to the team at halftime. He went on to blame the Corps of Cadets, the officers on post, the weather, the Korean War, and the general bewilderment of America's youth at the time for piling on to cause the Brave Old Army Team to lose to a Navy team they should have defeated. Others laid the blame at the hands of professional football scouts who somehow managed to find out about Army's strategy and weaknesses and fed this intelligence, along with recommendations on how to exploit it, to their colleague Eddie Erdelatz, the new Navy head coach and former pro coach.

Exams ended and Christmas leave began for the upperclasses of the Corps of Cadets on 22 December. Jake went home to Gary confident that he would make the grade in academics and eager to get his chance to make the A squad football team in the spring.

Part Five

The Easier Wrong

Nineteen

The Investigation

The more things changed at West Point the more they stayed the same. The rooms occupied by cadets in 1951 were just about the same as those that MacArthur had built after World War I. Red Blaik could return to the same division and stoop where he had witnessed the death of Steven Bird more than thirty years earlier. But this year the supply officer changed one thing: He had every cadet bunk painted white. It was at least an attempt to lighten up the gloom.

The Mechanics Department did get a new jet engine for its laboratory work. That was big news. The Allison Engine Company provided a working ground-mounted version of its immensely successful J-33 turbine along with a cutaway version to allow cadets to see the principles of jet engine operation up close. The Math Department showed up in its section rooms with yet another device to dazzle and teach cadets. Math was the first department to get the overhead projector for instructors to work out problems for all to see without taking up extra board space.

The second term began the day after the New Year began. After the usual celebrations all cadets had to embark on the return journey for what always seemed to be the longer semester. This year, 1951, war clouds from the Korean conflict cast an even darker shadow over West Point. The Department of the Army was reacting to increasing casualties as U.N. forces continued to move deep into North Korea. Military planners anticipating the possible entry of Communist China into the war began looking seriously at mobilization plans that lay dormant since before World War II.

One of the measures implemented right away was the recall to active duty of thousands of retired, reserve, or limited service personnel. The Pentagon ordered all Stateside military organizations to draw their active duty strength down to less than seventy-five percent and to make the remaining one-fourth of their assigned soldiers available for duty in combat units. One of those soldiers called to duty was the academy's superintendent, Maj. Gen. Bryant Moore.

Moore was working with his graduate manager of athletics and friend Red Blaik one afternoon in mid-January. In the midst of their meeting, Moore took a phone call: "Yes, I can be ready. . . . You mean five today? . . . No, five A.M. at LaGuardia. . . ." then hung up. They returned to their work, but Moore called Blaik at home about an hour later.

"Red, you know where I'm going, don't you?"

"I can make a pretty good guess," answered Blaik.

"Come over to my quarters and sit around with me."

Blaik entered the supe's quarters to see his boss rolling a cigarette in his living room. "Red, I've been given a corps in Korea, and I leave LaGuardia at five tomorrow morning." Moore's bags were packed and ready to go, so eager was he to get back to a combat unit.

But life went on at West Point. This was not the first war to distract the cadets, staff, and faculty from the routine. Athletics provided the antidote to gloom period's infection with fatigue. Dick Shea was the star of the corps, with dramatic performances already in the fall on the track team. He would go on to set new records in the mile and two-mile events.

Bill Jackomis had come to admire Shea's competitive spirit and to appreciate his friendship. He spent a lot of time with Shea learning about what made him tick. He learned that Shea had enlisted in the Army in 1944, and had found himself in Berlin just as the war ended. He was appointed to the academy from the USMA preparatory school and as a plebe had set an academy record for the mile run with a time of four minutes, twenty-six seconds. That was all the more remarkable because plebe year was a cadet's lowest stage in terms of physical stamina. Shea told Jake he just never let up. During competitive events Jake and Shea would shout encouraging words to each other. As a yearling Shea continued to double-time, even up and down stairs. It was great training, according to Shea. Apparently it paid off for him.

Even company tactical officers found themselves swept up in the enthusiasm of the competition. Their focus was on the intramural season which, in winter, involved hard-nosed individual contact sports such as boxing and wrestling. Some tacs formed a betting pool on which company would take the Banker's Trophy, the coveted intramural championship award. A few were even ruthless in keeping some of their better athletes off varsity teams so they would be available to compete on company intramural teams.

Jim Pfautz was off to a great yearling year. Physics and chemistry hit him hard, but he worked diligently and stayed proficient. He raised his grades in German and English and managed to keep his overall average almost exactly the same as it had been in plebe year. That was all he needed to remain on the corps squad swimming team roster. He was a standout for Coach Gordon Chalmers and drew nationwide attention that year when he set a new academy record in the individual medley.

The commandant now began to act on his fears that there was a conspiracy to undermine West Point's key role in the nation's security. He became convinced that something was wrong with the honor system. He developed a feeling that a sinister influence was at work causing some cadets to use the honor system as a shield to get away with frequent and serious violations of regulations. He directed his attention at the football team, despite reports from Korea on Blaik's boys who had acquitted themselves well in battle; men such as Arnold Galiffa. Galiffa's longest forward pass killed twenty-four North Korean Communists and saved his platoon. But Harkins would not be moved; in his mind football players were the problem that had to be rooted out of the academy.

Perhaps it was because America had plunged into the abyss of McCarthyism—Communists appeared to be everywhere and seemed to be undermining our nation's very survival. Senator Joseph R. McCarthy had his list of Communists in high places, and others were soon to follow. Harkins was determined to root out this little conspiracy going on inside his little piece of America. The departure of Blaik's close friend Bryant Moore gave Harkins the chance he had been waiting for.

There was plenty of evidence to support Harkins's theory. Someone told him that Ed Stahura, one of the yearlings who earned a varsity letter in the 1950 season, was giving an "all right" when chapel call came around but was not in fact going to the football team's early chapel service. Social sciences instructors told him they thought that some cadets were getting answers to quizzes by arriving outside the classroom minutes before their class was to begin and were stealing answers to the day's quiz by looking at the reflections, on the transom glass over the classroom door, of the papers of cadets still taking the test.

CHEATERS GET CAUGHT

Early in January a football player was caught stealing and attempting to destroy deficiency reports—"quill"—from his tactical officer's administrative "in" box. He was brought before the Honor Committee but acquitted on a 9–3 vote. Harkins was furious. He removed the chairman of the Honor Committee and declared the cadet first captain to be the chairman of the Honor Committee for the rest of the year. As the highest-ranking cadet the first captain usually developed a close professional relationship with the commandant, who in fact made the selection of the cadet who was to be first captain. Harkins knew he had picked a man after his own heart to be the top cadet for 1950–51 in William J. Ryan. Ryan was no academic standout; his grade average placed him in about the middle of his class. But he proved his antifootball mettle to Harkins in September over the table seating affair with Blaik in the mess hall. Harkins was now able to exploit his choice.

One of the first things Ryan was to report to Harkins was an incident in which an honor representative approached a cadet to inform on others suspected of cheating. The intended informant, yearling John C. Calhoun, refused to tell on his classmates. Harkins told Ryan to wait just a little while longer, Blaik's boys would give them the opportunity they sought. They did not have to wait long.

Later in January, a mechanics instructor, Lt. Col. Charles Register, had his second classmen in the last section of the solids course at the boards working through the day's assigned problems. As was usual with this group of men with the very lowest grades in the course, one cadet was having a particularly difficult time at the boards. Register moved over to him to help. The procedure for getting help from the professor during a graded board exercise was very simple and well understood by all, especially by the time a cadet was in his third year at the academy. If a student needed a hint or even a big clue, the professor would write it on the cadet's board in green chalk. This would remind the instructor later as to what part he had provided help on so that the cadet's grade could be adjusted downward after class when the professor walked around grading each man's work. Under no circumstances was the cadet to even touch, much less erase, anything on his board written in green.

This time, when Colonel Register moved to this cadet's board, all the green markings had been completely removed and the cadet had produced a perfect solution to the problem in record time. Not bad for a man who had never quite gotten the gist of solids problems all that year, either before or after that day.

In February the new superintendent arrived. He was Maj. Gen. Frederick Irving, a former commandant who had been relieved of his division command in World War II. Now Harkins had his chance to go for Red Blaik's professional jugular. With the mounting evidence of incidents running against the football team and with a new supe taking over, Colonel Harkins was convinced he could once and for all restore the proper balance of authority to the academy's senior leadership. He was sure he could make Irving see things his way. Harkins was also sure that the conspiracy among football players to undermine West Point's system would give itself away; the violations had become so brazen. He allowed himself to feel a sense of anticipatory triumph as the supply officer had a new carpet delivered and installed in the commandant's office.

Harkins nearly got his chance right away. A Spanish instructor, Major Kosiorek, suspected football players of cheating. Kosiorek was in charge of all yearling Spanish instruction and had oversight into all cadet graded papers. He noticed in early February that two of his yearling football players consistently did much better on their written tests than they did on their daily quizzes in the classroom. He figured that they might be getting the answers from someone in an earlier hour. Every day his Spanish students would be given a passage from the assigned readings to translate from English back into Spanish. One day about midmonth Kosiorek changed sentences on his quiz between the first and second hour of the day. His two football-playing suspects failed the quiz miserably, confirming the instructor's suspicion, although not with sufficient proof for the commandant to launch a formal investigation.

West Point was stunned in late February when the academy received word that Major General Moore had been killed in Korea. Moore's IX Corps was working along the western side of the Korean peninsula around Seoul. Rising waters had cut two ford sites vital to the movement of supplies north across the Han River, and Moore's engineers were working feverishly to restore the flow of matériel through the crucial line of communication. Moore was on an inspection trip when his helicopter suffered mechanical failure and went down into the river itself. Apparently all right except for a minor injury to his leg, Moore went right back to work. But a blood clot had formed in his leg and soon loosed itself in his circulatory system, cutting off his circulation and causing his heart to fail. All West Point was saddened to hear of the untimely death of General Moore.

As gloom period began to end in March, the widespread cheating going on among ring members was a widely shared secret among many cadets and some instructors. But no one seemed to have enough evidence to come forward and break it open. Lieutenant Colonel Collins shared Harkins's concern for the honor system as well as his contempt for the football team. In early March Collins wrote a long memo to Harkins expressing his own concern for the state of affairs with the honor system. Collins then spoke to the first captain about his concern. Having now heard from the two senior colonels in the Tactical Department, the commandant, and the tactical officer for 1st Regiment, Bill Ryan, the highest-ranking cadet in the Corps exercised his authority as first captain and called a rare assembly of the entire corps. With no officers invited Ryan spoke to them of their obligations under the honor system and of the growing concern of the Tactical Department for their compliance with the letter and spirit of the cadet honor code.

Adding to the somber atmosphere, another high-ranking academy official died. Early in March the head of the Ordnance Department was killed in a plane crash in Germany. He was posthumously promoted to brigadier general and buried at the West Point cemetery on 16 March. On 3 April Bryant Moore was buried there, with dozens of very senior Army officers in attendance. The increasing numbers of casualties from the Korean War were stressing the interment capacity of the West Point cemetery and the frequent sight of a military funeral was a major factor in the extended gloom period of 1951.

So was the more frequent requirement to attend lectures in the late winter. The month of March was loaded with several really boring lectures that had to be endured by all four classes. Bill Jackomis could hardly believe it when his English class had to attend a lecture on his most hated topic in English, the novel.

LIKE OIL AND WATER

Perhaps it was the extended gloom period on top of the bad weather of the previous fall on top of a terrible Navy game that caused tempers to flare between the Tactical Department and the football program in March. Two incidents that should have been dealt with on a more professional level became opening skirmishes in what was soon to become open warfare between these two giant and indispensable parts of the West Point system.

Offensive line coach Murray Warmath was having dinner with

some of his favorite linemen at Mama Leone's restaurant in Manhattan one night in March when Colonel Harkins happened to enter the dining room for dinner himself. When he saw Warmath eating with several of Army's big players who happened also to be Italian Americans, Colonel Harkins came up to Warmath and began to castigate the cadets for lacking proper social graces and military etiquette in public. Warmath stood to defend his charges and got into a heated argument with the commandant. Only the fact that they were in a very public place kept the men from blows.

Red Blaik soon got a chance to lose his temper with the Tactical Department. One of his most promising plebe football players was again being harassed by the Tactical Department's officers, according to Blaik, and he wanted to know why.

Cadet Frederic D. Meyers had been recruited by Blaik and apparently came into his Beast barracks with an overblown sense of self-importance, at least by West Point standards. Early in Beast barracks the previous July, Meyers's company commander called his tactical officer to report that Meyers had been recalcitrant and belligerent. He had refused orders to brace, and the cadet chain of command could not handle him. The tac, Lieutenant Colonel Garrett, who during the regular academic year was the tac for E-2 Company and had experience in dealing with football players such as, among others, Elmer Stout, called Meyers into his office and dressed him down thoroughly. A couple of days later Garrett got a visit from a plebe football coach, Maj. Joel Stevens, who came to tell Garrett that he had been too harsh with Meyers. Garrett blew up at him, too, saying that this was his new cadet company and no football coach was going to tell him how to run it.

Now Meyers was to begin spring football drills, but Blaik learned that he was too far behind in his academic work and had too many discipline problems in his regular company to be permitted to come out for the spring trials. Meyers was deficient in math, and when he faced the midterm written general review, Blaik arranged for him to get a "stayback"—an authorization to be excused from a graded exercise—from the head of the Math Department. Only a department head or the dean himself could grant a stayback, and they almost never did for major tests such as a WGR. Colonel William Bessell wanted to give Meyers a chance to talk about his difficulties personally. It did not help him recover his math grades.

Meyers's disciplinary problems did not go away after Beast barracks. He was placed in K-2 Company to give him a chance to start anew under a different set of leaders. The tactical officer, Maj. Frank Clay, had little patience for this man who was, to him, so obviously out of place at the military academy. Clay was one of the Army's finest young officers. He graduated from the academy in 1942 and was a tank company commander in Italy during World War II, winning the Silver Star and two Bronze Star medals for valor. He would later make it to major general and retire from the Army having filled a position as an assistant secretary of defense. But he almost did not make it past major after this run in with Red Blaik. Meyers had built up so many demerits in Clay's company that he was on two months' restriction. Blaik wanted to know why.

The young war veteran did not hesitate to tell the revered football coach that Meyers had too much involvement in football to perform his duties or to pass his classes. Blaik was furious. He asked Clay the names of the other football players in K-2 Company. Meyers was worried that Blaik was going to call them all that night, so he immediately called his cadet company commander, Lloyd Johnson, to warn him of any suspicious sudden flurry of calls. Clay was too late. The first class football players in the company had already come to Johnson seeking permission, as required by regulations, to recognize Meyers, meaning he would not have to comply with the fourth class system around them. It would have in effect ended Meyers's plebe year and permitted him to act as if he were already a yearling. Johnson would have none of it and had turned down the firsties' request.

Clay was distressed. Here he was taking on the most powerful man at the academy, Red Blaik. But he believed he was right in subjecting Meyers to the discipline he was undergoing. Meyers just did not have what it takes to make it as an officer in combat, so Clay kept up the pressure on him. But the football staff could mete out discipline of its own, and Clay was so harried that he sought counseling from the staff psychologist, Dr. Douglas

Spencer. This was a risky move for Clay. Although such counseling was to be strictly confidential, if word got out that he was being treated by the "shrink," his reputation would be ruined. While it turned out all right for Clay, Meyers never did turn around his performance. At the end of plebe year, although he was a top-notch athlete, finishing seventh in his class in physical education, he was dismissed for being so deficient in math.

SUSPENSION OF DUTIES

With the rest of the Corps of Cadets, gloom period droned on. The monotony was finally broken by the arrival of "suspension of duties," the annual three-day extended weekend that served as West Point's spring break. It was punctuated by a decree issued by New York's governor Dewey that 16 March would be West Point Day all across the state, in recognition of the academy's 149th anniversary and as a signal for the start of preparations for the big sesquicentennial planned for the following year, which also happened to be an election year.

Douglas MacArthur provided his own pyrotechnics to liven up gloom period in late March. MacArthur's ideas on what to do about the war were at odds with the policy of his government. MacArthur thought that a conflict with China was inevitable and that the Korean War provided an excellent opportunity to take war to China on terms favorable to the United States. He wanted to destroy China's war-making potential to keep them at bay for a long time. He had proposed to allow the exiled Nationalist Chinese, operating from the island of Formosa (Taiwan), to conduct naval raids on Communist Chinese shipping, and he wanted to provide military assistance to Chiang Kai-shek's forces for later operations to restore the Nationalists to power on the mainland after Mao Tse-tung had defeated them in the long civil war that had ended in 1949. In his drive north into Korea in 1950, MacArthur frequently requested permission to strike targets in China that he argued were used to support Chinese operations against U.N. forces.

The Truman administration had concluded that the reality of the situation was that the Communists were going to be in control of China for the foreseeable future and had to be dealt with. Truman did not want a war with Red China; he was convinced that the United States could not win against the vastly more populous mainland Chinese. Through a series of messages he made it clear to MacArthur that he was not to take any military action that might provoke the Communist Chinese into action against the United States, even though there was increasing evidence that the Communists were providing support to North Korea. MacArthur acknowledged his superiors and indicated he would comply with his instructions.

But he did not like it. And he let them know of his disagreement publicly. On 20 March, the Truman administration sent a draft proposal for truce talks with the Chinese Communists to the Allies for review and coordination. MacArthur told the administration it was a good idea since he could not launch an offensive anyway. But he then issued a proclamation to the Chinese that in effect told them to surrender to him on military terms, since they did not have the wherewithal to take on the might of the United Nations. The Chinese called him a fanatic and swore they would not negotiate their survival. Truman's diplomatic strategy was completely demolished, and the president decided to relieve his Supreme Commander of Allies in the Pacific (SCAP). More inflammatory pronouncements followed, and a member of Congress sent MacArthur a draft speech, for MacArthur's comment, in which the congressman condemn Truman for committing so many soldiers to war without seeking victory. MacArthur replied to the congressman that there was no substitute for victory.

The congressman gave his speech and read MacArthur's endorsement into the *Congressional Record* on 8 April. Meanwhile, rumors had reached MacArthur that he was about to be relieved. He let out a counterrumor that he was about to resign. When Truman learned of this he accelerated his plan to relieve General MacArthur and in the process made the move a humiliation that took on political overtones, with MacArthur by now widely mentioned as a possible Republican presidential candidate. MacArthur found out about his relief by cable from the joint chiefs chairman, General Bradley, only minutes before the word was beamed around the world by radio over network news broadcasts on 11 April. Secretary of the Army Frank Pace, at thirty-four years old Truman's youngest cabinet officer, had been visiting troops in Korea and was sent by the president to MacArthur's head-quarters in Japan to deliver the order later in the day.

Red Blaik was devastated that his mentor had been humili-ated. He immediately cabled MacArthur, "AMERICAN PUBLIC STUNNED. TIME IS OF THE ESSENCE TO OFFSET ADMIN-ISTRATION HATCHETMEN." Blaik was still active in Republican Party circles and harbored hopes that MacArthur would run for president in spite of MacArthur's halting steps in the run-up to convention season back in 1948. Blaik saw in MacArthur's relief a political motive on Truman's part to ruin any chance that MacArthur might run against him in 1952.

MacArthur was invited to address a joint session of Congress on 19 April. It was to be one of the greatest presentations of all time, the one in which he delivered his famous line "Old soldiers never die, they just fade away." But he also repeated his dictum on war, "There is no substitute for victory." Blaik was inspired to encourage the general to preach his message around the coun-try to prepare the way for a presidential campaign. President Tru-man was unimpressed. His response to his closest aides was not to worry about the response MacArthur was getting on the speech because it was ". . . nothing but a bunch of bullshit."

While Red Blaik was occupied with political ambition, his foot-ball players were about to give the commandant the break the com needed to sever Blaik's hold on power at the academy.

Jim Pfautz was still having trouble in some classes. His class-mates James Davidson and Will West had nearly as much trouble in academics, though West seemed to be getting by despite all the time he devoted to football. Pfautz figured that being a football star helped. Jim was on the swimming team and was just ending his season. Swimmers had in many ways a more difficult season than football players. Swimmers worked out early in the morning before breakfast as well as in the designated afternoon athletic pe-riod. Jim knew that James and Will were getting help from the cheating ring, but he had managed to keep his grades just barely proficient and had avoided the temptation so far. His best subject was English, and he actually enjoyed the yearling year with the study of the novel. His high grade in English brought his overall average high enough to avoid worry about being dropped from the swimming squad for academic deficiency. At least the swim team beat Navy that year.

Twenty

Harkins Strikes

On 2 April, James Davidson asked Jim Pfautz if he wanted to join the cheating ring. Davidson was having a difficult time with English but could not get help from the cheating ring on that subject because he could not find someone with English first hour in the morning willing to meet him clandestinely to give him answers to the quizzes on those novels. He surely did not have the time or the inclination to read them all himself. He proposed to Pfautz that if Jim would help him in English, Davidson would pass on to him the physics and math answers he was getting from the ring.

Pfautz told Davidson that he was stupid and crazy for trying to get away with cheating like that. Sooner or later, Pfautz warned his classmate, he was bound to get caught. Davidson replied that just about everyone at West Point was in on the ring, and even Pfautz was technically guilty by not reporting his own knowledge of it. Besides, he told Pfautz, the authorities must know about it and approve of it so that the academy could field a good football team.

Pfautz resented the implication that the football team was so important that it was worth cheating to keep good players at West Point. It was the honor code that had held so much attraction to

Jim Pfautz in the first place. Besides, he thought, the swimming team was at least as important as any other team. And no team was worth compromising the academy's integrity. He decided he could no longer look the other way while he knew of the cheating going on all around him.

But how could he go about reporting what was going on? He had heard all the talk that at least some Honor Committee representatives were in on the ring, and he feared that the first class rep in K-1 would not act on any reports Pfautz might give now, so close to graduation for the Class of 1951. If he wanted to, the first class honor representative could simply stall the process long enough to escape the problem altogether. At worst he might find ways to make life difficult for Pfautz until he gave in or gave up. He went instead to the honor representative from the Class of 1952.

After receiving Pfautz's report that Davidson had just tried to recruit him into the cheating ring, the second class honor representative told Pfautz to return to his room and say nothing of the matter until he had a chance to take it up with the committee. He went to the K-1 first class honor representative, Daniel Myers, with Pfautz's revelation. Perhaps because of the recent talks by the regimental tactical officer, or perhaps because he feared the Honor Committee was compromised, Myers took it straight to Lieutenant Colonel Collins rather than bringing it up, in normal Honor Committee procedure, to the cadet Honor Committee's investigating subcommittee for 1st Regiment.

Collins told Myers to go straight to Colonel Harkins with his report and immediately called the commandant to tell him that they might have the break they had been looking for. After Myers told Colonel Harkins what Pfautz had reported, Harkins told Myers that he wanted to talk it over with the first captain and with the deputy commandant before doing anything about it. Harkins felt that there was insufficient evidence to accuse anyone of an outright honor violation but that this might be an opportunity to collect enough information finally to do something about it.

Harkins sent for the deputy commandant, Col. John K. Waters, who was to be Harkins's replacement in June when the senior colonel was to be transferred to his coveted general staff job in

Washington. First Captain Ryan soon came into the commandant's office and became visibly upset when told that they would not be able to get a conviction out of the evidence Pfautz had presented so far. It would have been plenty for the Honor Committee to use under its procedures. But the problem was that the Honor Committee was probably compromised and could not be trusted to get a conviction. The commandant then figured he had to plan on presenting the case to a board of officers that would have the administrative power to discharge Davidson and any others they might be able to nab out of the ring. The difficulty with that approach, however, was that under the regulations a board of officers was bound by more strict rules of evidence and protections for the rights of the accused than an honor board. The advantage of the procedure, on the other hand, was that it was not a full-blown court-martial, which would have been even more stringent and, worse, would eventually be opened to public scrutiny, as with any other court case. Army administrative boards were not subject to public disclosure, and this procedure would permit the commandant to move swiftly without review except by the superintendent and a perfunctory overview by the Army staff.

The three discussed ways of getting more information, including placing hidden microphones in the three yearlings' rooms. Eventually they decided that the only way to get a solid conviction even in a commandant's board was to get Pfautz himself to provide more evidence. To do that they had to convince him to go back to Davidson and get him to commit an act of violation of the honor code that could be witnessed by others in addition to Pfautz. The only way they could see of doing that was to somehow persuade Jim Pfautz to become an informant, join the ring, and report back to the commandant with more solid evidence.

The three also feared that Pfautz might not cooperate, so they decided to seek the cooperation of another yearling whose roommate they believed to be in the cheating ring. The design was to get this second informant to collect incriminating evidence on another cadet, William West, as well. Harkins called in the honor representative from neighboring I-1 Company, Duane Tague, and told him what had just happened at K-1. Harkins told Tague to get someone in the cheating ring from I-1 to turn informant and focus on catching West in the act. Tague recruited Jeffrey Rich, who also happened to be on the swim team with Jim Pfautz. The next day First Captain Ryan bragged confidentially to his law instructor, Lt. Col. Edward O'Connell, that he would be greatly shocked by what was soon to be revealed concerning a cheating ring that was about to be exposed.

Meanwhile, Myers told Pfautz that he had done the right thing by informing him of the existence of the ring and that he wanted the names of as many ring members as Pfautz could provide. He assured Pfautz that he would be protected from retribution whenever they started to take action against ring members that he had named. Pfautz was worried. He knew he was doing the right thing, but he also knew that the cheating ring was powerful—after all, it had the backing of the football program. There was no backing out of his role as the informant now that he had gone to his honor representative, who, in turn, had gone to the commandant of cadets. Myers told him that there was another informant from a different company who would also be providing names, so Pfautz realized he had to be accurate and complete in his information. If the information he provided did not closely match that provided by the other informant, one of them might be accused of holding back to protect a few of his own friends.

WHAT TO DO

For two weeks Jim Pfautz contemplated his dilemma. If he were to agree to the commandant's proposition he would become in effect a "stool pigeon," likely to draw the wrath of fellow cadets for breaking open the cheating that had been accepted by so many cadets, officers, and coaches as perfectly permissible. Would they threaten him when they found out his identity? What could they do to him? How far was the commandant prepared to go to protect him? But if he were to back down now, his honor representative and the commandant himself could accuse him of knowing about the cheating and failing to follow through in his duty to report the honor violations. According to the honor code a cadet who tolerates a violation is just as guilty as the violator.

Jim turned to his family to help him think this through. One weekend in April he spent his free time with an uncle from New York City who was an attorney. They walked around Michie Stadium and Lusk Reservoir talking and thinking out loud about the situation Jim Pfautz found himself in. Jim told his uncle that the only way out of the dilemma was to resign from West Point. He saw no other course of action, and anyway he was more inclined toward the arts rather than the academy's heavy emphasis on math and science.

His uncle told him that he had done no wrong himself; after all, Pfautz had not cheated. And he had not lied about nor covered up for the cheaters. In fact, Pfautz had done his duty, and that was the very best defense there was should anyone try to turn the tables on him and accuse him of somehow acting improperly. No, his uncle said, he should not leave now, while he was under fire; that would only make things worse. With that strong case made while looking out over the springtime turbulence in the waters in and around the reservoir, Pfautz was persuaded to go on with his mission of exposing the truth about the cheating ring. He told Myers he was ready to see the commandant and cooperate.

Jim Pfautz and Jeff Rich were called in to see Colonel Harkins on 2 May. The K-1 second class honor representative was at the meeting as well. Pfautz told the commandant that he had names he was ready to turn over to him, including the names of honor representatives whom he knew to be involved in the cheating ring. But before he gave him specific names he wanted to be assured that the Tactical Department would back him up through the process of revealing the names and dealing with the offenders. Harkins assured him that he would be protected.*

Jim Pfautz told Harkins about the cheating he knew of, such

---

*In Collins's report, Harkins claims that Pfautz was willing to turn in hundreds of names. Pfautz denies this and says he provided only the names of the few men he saw commit an honor violation.

as that of Davidson, as well as of those he had seen passing "the poop" at team tables in the mess hall. He even produced a copy of test answers brought to him by James Davidson from a chemistry exam for which James had been provided those answers by one of the ring members. Pfautz explained that the ring had designated "messengers"—brighter cadets—who were to rush from the first hour of a test with the correct answers to provide to second-hour, less academically inclined ring members who would memorize those answers on the way to taking the test themselves. Harkins examined the cheat sheet carefully and had the Chemistry Department head called over to bring Davidson's actual test paper in for his examination. He found that the answers on Davidson's test sheet matched exactly the cheat sheet he had given to Pfautz, even the wrong answer to one question. Davidson's test sheet and the cheat sheet had "condensation" as the answer to the question whose correct answer was "concentration." The commandant was convinced that he could now begin to collect enough evidence to bring formal proceedings against ring members, but the cheat sheet was plausibly deniable before a board of officers. He still needed more direct evidence of West's, or someone else's, cheating before he could begin to break the entire ring wide open. He told Pfautz he would need his further cooperation.

That night Jim Pfautz reported that he had again been exposed to the cheating ring. This time Davidson had bragged to Jim Pfautz about the ring and the names of the cadets who were in it. He also showed Jim another cheat sheet he had gotten from his "messenger," this time for a math test. Jim Pfautz gave Myers a copy of the cheat sheet and a list of the names he had gotten from Davidson. Myers took it to Colonel Harkins the next morning.

Harkins again confirmed the test answers with the department head, in this case Colonel Bessell. Then Myers expressed his concern about the prospects for further investigation. He said it was going to be very difficult to get any additional evidence on West; already Davidson was getting suspicious of Pfautz. Moreover, Myers told the commandant that he believed many of the names on the list Colonel Harkins was building were purely speculation and that even Pfautz doubted the full involvement of many of those listed. Colonel Harkins told Myers to continue to draw Pfautz out and that meanwhile he would take up his concerns with First Captain Ryan.

It was nearly three weeks before Pfautz came forward with more evidence. On 23 May he told Myers that Davidson had given him a solution sheet to a test in electricity. Meanwhile, Jeffrey Rich had finally obtained a cheat sheet from West. It was a solution sheet from a written general review in physics. Later that same day Rich remarked to West that he wished he could get help for tomorrow's English writ. Will said he could help and left to go see his "messenger." West returned later with the test answers for the next day's English exam, which, of course, were identical to those on the English exam taken by the other regiment that day. But when Will returned, Rich's room was in the midst of an inspection, so West had to hold on to the notes until he saw Rich again the next morning. Rich ended up taking the exam without the benefit of West's cheat sheet but turned it in to Tague anyway. Tague told the commandant that he was beginning to get worried that West and Davidson were on to Pfautz and had already shunned him.

On Monday, 28 May, Colonel Harkins received one more set of test answers passed on from cheating ring members. It was again a physics test. He brought in the head of the Physics Department to confirm that the cheat sheet answers were in fact from the physics test. Colonel Counts and the instructor for the course involved, Lieutenant Colonel Arnold, said that the answers on the cheat sheet were in fact identical to the solution to that day's physics test. With that Colonel Harkins finally decided, after two months of investigation and barely a week before graduation, that it was now time to move in. Conveniently, the Class of 1951 was in the midst of taking the Graduate Record Examinations, the two-day standardized test taken by college seniors across the nation, and were about to depart on a trip the next day, Wednesday, 30 May, for their class in ordnance at Aberdeen Proving Ground, Maryland. They would not be at West Point as the board began to call accused cadets. Harkins would focus the hearing on the yearlings in the Class of 1953.

After nearly two months of conducting this undercover operation himself, Colonel Harkins finally notified the superintendent of what he was doing. He told Major General Irving that he now had sufficient evidence to begin a formal inquiry by a board of officers and that he intended to start the proceedings right away under his authority as commandant of cadets. While Harkins had the authority to conduct the inquiry he knew that the supe could order it suppressed if he believed that Harkins was trying to railroad the football team. He could have directed that it be placed in the hands of the Honor Committee, or he could have appointed a superintendent's board to conduct the procedure, thereby involving a more widely representative board of officers than the commandant could convene. Colonel Harkins did not want the academic departments involved in this proceeding; too many of them were too soft and part of the problem themselves. He could compose a board only of tactical officers, which, of course, was his design. In fact, a rumor reached the superintendent that if Harkins was not permitted to convene his board many tactical officers would ask to be relieved in protest. The supe told Harkins to proceed with the utmost vigor. If necessary he was prepared to hold up graduation for the Class of 1951 if any first classmen were involved. The commandant was ready. Harkins had already picked his man to preside over the board, his most trusted tactical officer: Ace Collins.

ACE COLLINS'S MISSION
Colonel Arthur Collins had noticed all during the spring parade season in April and May that the commandant had been carrying a brown envelope under his arm as he stopped to observe the afternoon drill and ceremony on his way home from his office. It was curiously out of character for Harkins to have anything in his hands in the presence of so many cadets and subordinate officers. For one thing, it made it awkward for the commandant to return the salutes of just about anyone else on post who passed him by; military courtesy demanded that the salute hand be kept free for this purpose. Furthermore, in the Army of the 1950s, officers by custom simply did not take work home. They stayed at the office until the day's work was complete and did not leave until it was done. When an officer went home he did not bring the office with him. Harkins, having written several books on military customs

and courtesies, and a stickler himself to the finest detail of proper service tradition, would violate one of his own precepts only for the most extenuating of circumstances. On Monday, 28 May, Collins was to find out what had so captivated his commander's attention.

Harkins handed Collins the brown envelope that afternoon. The commandant told the 1st Regiment tactical officer that there was something inside that would shock him. Collins was to open it at home and keep it in his sole personal possession. He was to execute the order contained in the envelope and clear up the entire affair before Harkins was scheduled to depart for Washington in three weeks. Collins was to conduct his own, formal investigation of the matters and to let the chips fall where they may.

The order was succinct:

MACC   28 May 1951
SUBJECT: Letter Orders
To: Officers Concerned

    1. A Board of Officers consisting of
        Lt Col Arthur S Collins, Inf
        Lt Col Jefferson J Irvin, Inf
        Lt Col Tracy B Harrington, Armor
and the following alternate members
        Lt Col Cornelius DeW W Lang, Arty
        Lt Col Joseph A McChristian, Armor
        Lt Col Birdsey L Learman, Inf
        Lt Col Robert W Garrett, Inf
is appointed to investigate the alleged honor violations of Cadets Ford, RW and Davidson, JG, 3rd Class.

    2. Report of the Board in quadruplicate will be submitted to the Commandant of Cadets at the earliest practicable date.

BY ORDER OF COLONEL HARKINS

In the meantime, Colonel Harkins had been busy selecting the slate of cadets to be next year's highest-ranking cadet officers. The soon-to-graduate first captain for the Class of 1951, Bill Ryan, offered some advice to his successor from the Class of 1952. He told him that he would have problems with table assignments in the mess hall, just as Ryan had last year, with the football office. "Don't let them get their foot wedged in the door and get you under their thumb like they have so many others around here. You run the dining hall." Harkins's message had gotten through. His wrath was about to be unleashed.

Ace Collins convened the board that evening. The first cadet to be called before the three lieutenant colonels was James Davidson.

Davidson spilled his guts before the board. He told them that he had first heard of the cheating ring in his plebe year but did nothing about it. After Christmas, James began to have trouble in English. They had just rearranged room assignments, and one of James's new roommates, William West, told James that if he wanted to he could get James help. All he had to do was bring Will the writ questions after a test and he could bring answers to his next test before he took it. James did this plebe year, but after he got the questions from James, Will told him that he could not get answers for James because he had English first hour in the morning, and it was just impossible to do it for him. At the start of yearling year West pressed Davidson to help out again; this time he was more forthcoming in providing Davidson with help in return.

Davidson went on to describe what he had heard from various cheating ring members about how the whole thing got started and that they had several members of the Honor Committee in the ring to provide themselves with protection should anyone be reported. Collins gave Davidson a roster of his classmates and told him to indicate which ones were involved in the ring. James did so and was dismissed from the proceeding.

THAT'S MY STORY
The next cadet called before the board was Randy Ford. Ford had been identified as one of the academic coaches who was receiv-

ing the copies of tests taken by a ring member, filling them in with the correct answers, and sending them back out with one of the "messengers" to the ring member who needed to memorize the answers on his way to take the test. He was a "star man," who stood in the top ten percent of his class academically.

Ford said he knew of no group of cadets passing unauthorized information and he denied ever having worked writ problems for someone he was coaching academically. Colonel Collins reminded Ford that he was under oath, but Ford said that he would make no change to what he had just told the board.

Collins dismissed Ford and adjourned the board for the evening. He reconvened it on the morning of 29 May.

The first to appear that morning was William West. At first West thought he was appearing before yet another disciplinary board, and he told Colonel Collins that before he said anything he wanted to talk to another cadet who was also involved in the incident West thought he was being brought up on. Collins informed West that this was a board to investigate alleged honor violations, not a conduct board. Then he advised West of his rights and swore him in.

West denied any involvement in or knowledge of the cheating ring. He also pointed out that he was not going to say anything at all about the football team if that was what the board was after. Collins told West that the board had nothing to do with football players, it was about honor violations. Collins said that the only reason anyone was brought in was that they had positive proof that he had been cheating. West again, this time nervously, denied any involvement in cheating and said that many people at the academy—for example, his own tactical officer, Major Shedd— just did not like football players.

A third time Collins asked West if he knew anything about the honor violations. This time Will said that he had heard of the ring but that he himself was not involved in it in any way. He said that he sometimes had gotten indications of what to study the night before a test and that his roommate often had upward of fourteen people in the room coaching them.

Bob Volonnino was called in that day. At first he denied knowing about any group passing information on test questions and answers. Collins asked him to recall what he did the previous Thursday, 24 May. Volonnino's defenses broke, and he admitted that he had written down the questions to a test and had intended to bring them back to his room and work out the answers with his roommate, who was to take the same test the next day. He said that he did not actually give his roommate the test questions but carelessly left them lying out on his desk.

Al Pollard was called before the board and denied ever receiving unauthorized help, even when he was in the hospital. When reminded he was under oath, he stuck to his story.

One first classman testified:

> Once when I was deficient, Cadet Doe and Cadet Smith* gave me the idea that it was okay "to get the poop." However, I do not wish to incriminate myself. Just about all the football team is involved. Anyone in the football area knows about the exchange of unauthorized information. . . . I didn't take it to the honor representative because I just didn't have the moral courage. After all there were so many upperclassmen doing it, and I was just a fourth classman.

This firstie, as was the case with all twenty-five accused first classmen, was acquitted. Others in the lower three classes were dismissed from the academy on far less incriminating testimony.

All told, nineteen cadets appeared before the Collins Board on 29 May, including three firsties, three cows, a plebe, and twelve yearlings. Only four actually admitted to participating in the cheating ring, but from their testimony it was apparent to the board that the ring was far larger than even they had anticipated.

"WHAT'S WRONG?"

Red Blaik was walking from his office in the gymnasium building across the Plain over to the baseball field on the 29th when some-

*Cadets from the Class of 1950 whose identities are not disclosed.

one told him that there was an honor investigation under way but that it was probably not very serious. Returning to the gymnasium, Red Blaik went to a previously scheduled late afternoon meeting in the projection room with several key players from the rising senior class (1952), going over game plans for the fall season. A short while after they started, fullback Bob Volonnino burst into the room. He was in tears, having just come from the inquisition before the Collins Board. Fred Jones was there, and when he saw Volonnino he said, "What's wrong, Bob?" He could not imagine what would bring this giant of a man to tears.

"What's wrong? I'll tell you what's wrong," bawled Volonnino. "I'll tell you what's wrong. I'm gonna be thrown out of West Point for passing the poop, and other guys are, too." He told of his ordeal to the astonished group. Blaik then turned to the others and asked if they had ever heard of such practices. All three men there said that they had indeed and that it was widespread in the corps. Blaik told them, "You men, as leaders of the academy, need to help straighten out this situation by going to the commandant's staff and telling them what you know. If you and your fellow ballplayers set the example, the corps will follow."*

Later that night, when Blaik was back at home, a yearling called him to ask him to come to the projection room to meet with a group of his classmates from the football team. When Blaik arrived there were a dozen men in the room, few of whom had yet appeared before the board, but all were intensely worried that they would be found guilty of an honor violation.

The coach told them all to go before the board and tell the truth without hesitation. The players left and Blaik went over to Superintendent Irving's house, throwing pebbles at his bedroom window to get his attention in the night. Irving listened as Blaik told the story that he had heard from the twelve. Blaik then begged the supe to take the investigation out of the hands of the

---

*This afternoon encounter in the projection room is presented as related to the author by Fred Jones (pseud.). Jackomis's recollection is that Volonnino's outburst occurred in the evening session.

Collins Board and place the responsibility with the Academic Board where, in Blaik's opinion, more mature judgment would prevail. General Irving could not change the course that had been set by the commandant. At this point in the Collins Board proceedings, unless there was some evidence that the board itself was violating regulations, he had to let it run its course. To interrupt it now would leave the superintendent open to charges of tampering. His own son was in the graduating class, and he could afford no appearance of interfering with the official investigation he had already authorized Harkins to undertake. Rebuffed, Blaik departed.

After getting briefed by Collins on the day's proceedings, Colonel Harkins called Myers and Pfautz in to talk. The commandant told Pfautz that West and Davidson would be called in again to be given another chance to change or add to their testimony. West would be given another chance to change his story and admit to being in the ring. Davidson would be asked to tell more of what he knew. For both men, Harkins told Pfautz, if they would make the list of cadets involved in the cheating ring as large as possible, then they all would probably not be dismissed. The academy was just not prepared to deal with so many cheaters as it looked like were involved in this business, the commandant implied.

Jim Pfautz returned to his classmates and told them what the commandant had said. They were overjoyed at the prospect that they would get off the hook. Pfautz allowed himself a moment of satisfaction in having done the right thing all along.

Bill Jackomis heard about Blaik's message to the football players, that they were honorable men and should tell the truth and all they knew about the matter. He was aware of what was going on, but doubted that he would be called before the board because he did not believe he had done anything wrong. He did remember the time at corps squad tables when someone who had just taken an exam commented to another cadet who had also already taken it, "How did you do on the map exam?" The other cadet responded that he had not had time to finish it all. Jake immediately knew that the exam for his own section in the same course, which would be given the next day, would focus on the map portion of the test, not the text. That evening when he studied, he concentrated on the maps, only briefly reading through the text portion. He did very well on the exam the next day.

On 30 May the Collins Board reconvened its investigation by recalling ten cadets who had appeared the day before. Again the first one up was Will West, who retracted his statement from the day before. He admitted getting the answers to a physics test on 24 May and using them to help him pass the same test. Collins told West that he had not gone far enough in his revelation of his own and others' cheating. Will then went all the way back to his plebe year and explained how he got started and what the procedure was to obtain help now.

Meanwhile, Bob Blaik had been notified that he was to appear before the Collins Board. He went to his father's office to tell him that he was involved in the passing of information at the tables and that he saw nothing wrong with that. He told his father he was prepared to testify to that effect when called before the board and that he did not view that as less than honorable. He also said that he did not intend to say anything about other football players if asked; he would only admit to his own role in the affair. The elder Blaik could not believe what he heard and, exasperated, simply said to his son, "How could you?"

Like West, all nine of the others who had been recalled also retracted their statements of the previous day. Some filled out class rosters providing the board with additional names of those they said they knew to be cheating. The three second classmen called for the first time that day also admitted to being members of the cheating ring.

Boom-Boom Beck was one who admitted that he had known about the cheating ring all along but had failed to report it. His testimony about the reach of the ring caught the board by surprise:

> I am guilty of honor violations, and I know of about a hundred fifty more people who are. I believe that if you found them all, there might be four or five hundred. I was surprised when I first found out about it at the end of my plebe year. I used to discuss discontinuing it with others in the company,

but we kept on doing it. The group isn't just football players; it is throughout the corps. It runs back six or seven years.

Beck then filled out a drill roll of those he thought were in the ring, including Jackson, Pollard, and Hunt from his company, D-1.

At this point the board members conferred among themselves. They were overwhelmed with the reported size of the cheating ring. In fact, they openly wondered if the size of the ring was deliberately being exaggerated in an attempt to threaten the ability of the Collins Board to sort through all the accusations. They spent the night going over the lists of alleged ring members as provided in the cadet testimony thus far. They compiled a single list of probable ring members based on how many times a name recurred among the lists. The board members convinced themselves that they had a "remarkably valid" list and decided to call in suspected ring members by class beginning the next day.

Twenty-One

Mister, Do You Know Why You Are Here?

It was early Wednesday evening, 30 May 1951. This was the next-to-last day before term-end exams were set to begin on Friday, 1 June. Jim Pfautz had spent the afternoon studying for his Thursday morning classes, then went in formation to the mess hall for dinner. He came back to his room a little after 7:00 P.M. and was thinking about what he would do the rest of the evening when Will West came into the room.

"Pfautz, I can't believe what you did," the large enraged football player said. He was livid. "I don't think we're getting off the hook like you said. They didn't say a word to me about it; they just kept coming at me with more questions about what I've done. You dumb son of a bitch, don't you know what happened to Cox?" With that West left the room, slamming the door on his way out.

Jim Pfautz grew concerned. West was tough on the football field and had a mean-looking exterior. Will generally acted the part of a comedian around his classmates and other cadets off the field, but the mention of Cox was cause for concern. R. C. Cox had disappeared in the spring of 1950. Word was that the academy's investigation turned up no clue as to what happened to him. Whatever really happened, it was not good,* and Pfautz believed that West might take matters into his own hands.

It was clear to Jim Pfautz what West meant. Now how was Jim going to react? Hardly anyone was around the barracks, it was Wednesday night, and just about everyone was in their rooms, studying. Only the cadet in charge of quarters was in the company orderly room, and he had to stay there except to make his hourly checks. There were no cadets on guard duty in the barracks; anyone who wanted to slip in and get Pfautz could easily evade detection. He could not contact the cadet chain of command because so far his identity as the informant had been kept secret. If word got out that Jim Pfautz was the one telling the com who was in the cheating ring, he would have a lot more than Will West to worry about, and that was already enough of a concern.

Pfautz decided to call Dick Miller, the Class of 1952 honor representative for K-1. Miller, in turn, called Colonel Collins at his quarters. He told the colonel about the threat and that he thought it was serious. Collins told Myers to post a guard outside West's door to make sure he could do no harm to anyone. Collins also ordered Pfautz confined to his room. That night Jim called home and told his parents about the situation. His mother told him that she was disappointed because she had taught him not to tattle. Jim Pfautz did not sleep very well that night. He was mostly angry that Collins had confined him to his room during the excitement of June Week.

On Thursday, 31 May, the first class returned from their trip to Aberdeen. Collins realized that the three firsties who had been before the board on 29 May had gone on the trip and probably put out the word about what questions were being asked even though they denied being in the cheating ring themselves. As soon as they returned, the twenty-two other members of the Class

---

*One source, considered to be quite reliable, told the author that Cox left on his own and later was recruited by an East European intelligence operation in the United States.

of 1951 on the board's list were called in for questioning. Before the board began its proceedings, Collins called Harkins about the threats reported by Jim Pfautz the night before. Harkins told Collins he would get the military police involved. When he notified the provost marshal, Harkins was told that it would be appropriate to get the Federal Bureau of Investigation involved because it involved an alleged felony on a federal installation, an offense that fell into the jurisdiction of the FBI. Soon after notifying the FBI, Harkins was told by both the FBI and the MPs to cease his looking into the allegations and that they would take care of it from that point forward. Harkins thought that was curious, but at least it was one less thing for him to worry about.

The first four men to testify before the Collins Board that Sunday denied any knowledge of the affair. The fifth man said he had heard rumors about it and thought it might be happening at football tables but did not report it, because he did not have information about any specific violation. He also told the board that as an academic coach for his company he had worked out types of problems for those he was helping but that his answers did not contain unauthorized information.

After another cadet gave a perfunctory denial, the next firstie reported that the only unauthorized help he had ever gotten was one day in economics class when an instructor said to him personally, "I'll give you the straight poop today." The cadet told the board that he knew that meant that the answers to that day's writ would be given out in class that day. Another firstie identified instructors by name who gave out answers in class.

One senior said only, "I know nothing about this affair. My conscience is clear." Another said, "I am no goody-goody boy, and I may have been involved in some petty honor violations. I have discussed the matter at the table, talking about how somebody can get a five point nine on a writ when you know he just can't do it. . . . I am aware that unauthorized information has been passed around the corps squad area. . . . I could not report anything to [my company honor representative] because I did not want to tell on the fellows in the corps squad."

The next first classman told of the notebooks that had been

handed out to the football team at Camp Buckner in his second summer at West Point and how he went from the sixth section to the first using those notes that had answers to test questions in them. The final first classman to appear before the board again denied any knowledge of the cheating ring, then told Colonel Collins that he thought the Tactical Department was moving into the field of the Honor Committee too much.

The board recalled four firsties, and three of them said they believed for sure that the fourth had committed honor violations but that they would not be willing to testify to that effect in any further formal proceeding. Colonel Collins and the other board members spent the rest of the night discussing the twenty-five firsties they had heard from at the board. They decided that the firstics apparently had had the opportunity to get their stories consistent during the Aberdeen trip. They concluded that there was insufficient evidence to convict any of them, although they believed that at least sixteen were in fact guilty. Although at least three of the firsties they heard from gave testimony that was similar to that given later by underclassmen who were convicted, the board decided not to proceed to demand resignation from any member of the Class of 1951. They would begin on Friday with the Class of 1952.

THE HEARINGS PROCEED

Over the next three days, the Collins Board took testimony from fifty-four cadets, ten of whom were repeats and one who appeared a third time. It was grueling, but the board was tenacious. They had to schedule the appearances of cadets around their examinations, which were going on at the same time. The board sessions went well into the night.

The first cow to be heard had testified on 29 May. He was asked if he had anything else to add. He told the board only that there was one man whom he knew to have cheated. That cadet was called next, and he denied cheating himself but named three firsties whom he knew to be cheating. He also told the board that the football team was suddenly being very friendly to him and in fact several players had told him that when he testified he should name as many men as he could think of so that the total number of cadets implicated in the cheating ring would be so high that the administration would not be able to dismiss more than half the entire Corps of Cadets who would be named.

The next man tried to be a little more subtle, "Any man on the football, basketball, or baseball squad who tells you he didn't know unauthorized information was being passed is either lying or is too dumb to be in West Point. There were so many people in on it that it seemed almost to have official sanction. The first time I knew positively what was going on was two weeks ago. I had suspected it since plebe year." With that the board members concluded that he was giving them the story line that too many cadets were involved to be handled by the Collins Board. Collins demanded that he name names. The cadet said that he wanted assurance that they would not be thrown out. Collins told him that no such assurance could be given.

Some cows were evasive, "Cadet Doe saw me sometime on the Armed Forces Day trip (19 May). He said something to me to the effect that there was something going on that I didn't quite understand. He discussed only generalities and asked no advice. We certainly made no promise to each other not to discuss that which we had talked about. What he told me was so vague that it meant nothing to me." Others were more blunt in their denial: "I do not participate in the exchange of unauthorized information and I know of no other cadets who have done so." Some came back before the board to change their previous admission of guilt, claiming they did not want to incriminate themselves. To Collins it was clear that not only were some cadets getting their stories consistent before appearing, but also now they were getting legal advice.

Some provided an almost humorous break: "Perhaps I haven't been suspicious because I can't see four feet in front of me." Another cow said that he even deliberately missed some answers just so his grades would not get too high. A few retracted their previous denial of knowing about the ring; while still claiming not to be involved themselves, they did name others who were involved. On 3 June, the board wrapped up its testimony from the Class of

1952. Again there were some denials, some retractions of previous admissions, and some who came forward to admit their guilt. One man said he had inadvertently become part of the ring when he was performing his duties as academic coach, working out problems for his assigned cadet to solve, and it turned out that the problems he worked were on the test. When he realized he was in fact unknowingly part of a cheating ring, he wrote an anonymous letter to the commandant, but tore it up when he realized it could eventually be traced back to him. He continued to work the answers to tests sent to him by the cheating ring's messengers.

Some reported that they had been threatened: "I first found out about the exchange of unauthorized information at Christmas this year in Doe's room. My classmates were working on a problem in electricity. I just happened to remember the answer. The next day in a written general review, I noted that the answer was the same. I went back and asked Doe what it was all about and he said it was football poop. I realized that even if the football office was supreme around here they wouldn't go that far. I am not a corps squad member. They then told me I was involved, too. There were so many in it and it was so big that I was afraid and did not report it to anyone. Doe told me that if I told I would find myself in the Hudson River. They talked freely in front of me, saying, 'If we go, you go, too'. Besides, they said they had a vote in the Honor Committee. . . ."

Michael Kelly was the last man from the Class of 1952 to come before the board. Kelly admitted getting and giving unauthorized information and also told of how he had attempted to report it through John Trent and Bruce Wilson in 1950. He concluded with a commentary on why it happened, "Colonel Blaik has always told the football team that they were the rock on which the corps was built. This and other similar things had a tendency to set the football team apart from the corps."

All told, the Collins Board concluded that thirty-six men from the Class of 1952 were guilty, although they asked the judge advocate to review the record of testimony on two of them before they felt they could forward a recommendation for dismissal to the commandant. Only three were judged to be not guilty. On

Monday, 4 June, the Board was to begin taking testimony from the yearlings.

In the meantime, the normal June Week activities proceeded at West Point. As usual, even as term-end exams were given during class time, there was a parade every day. On Friday, 1 June, it was a retreat ceremony at which drill streamers were awarded to the companies judged the best in marching, drill, and ceremony during the year. On Saturday, 2 June, there was a parade in honor of athletic awards being presented to winning teams, companies, and cadets, then an afternoon of games and entertainment. On Sunday baccalaureate services were held for all three faiths, and General Irving held a reception at his quarters for all members of the graduating class and guests. On Sunday night there was yet another review and presentation of awards for academic and military achievement to firsties. On Monday, 4 June, was the big alumni parade in the morning and graduation parade in the afternoon.

Starting on 4 June the board was to hear from fifty-two men in the Class of 1953. Six were to return to change their testimony, retracting a prior denial. Only six stuck to their denial of involvement in or knowledge of the cheating ring. Ace Collins was already convinced that the Class of 1953 was infected worst of all with this honor scandal, and he found plenty to confirm his belief on 4 and 5 June. As one yearling testified, "I did know and did participate in passing and receiving unauthorized papers. I entered into this during the spring of 1951. I heard talk about this cheating from the cadets on football. I was on B squad during the fall and made A squad this spring. I did not need academic help at all. It seemed like a drug; once I took the aid I couldn't stop. . . . I knew it was wrong and knew we would be caught, but out of loyalty to the group I did not turn them in." Another yearling provided confirmation of the attempts to place cheating ring members on the Honor Committee: "[we] . . . tried to elect [Doe] to the Class of 1953 Honor Committee so that he could give us protection in the event we were found out."

On the morning of 5 June, Graduation Day, Collins still had two dozen yearlings to hear from. But Major General Irving wanted to know right then whether any first classmen were going to be recommended for dismissal. The supe had committed himself to holding up graduation for any first classman implicated in the cheating. His own son was in the graduating class. That morning two men from the Class of 1952, George Williams and John McDonald, came to Collins and told him they would testify that two first classmen were in the cheating ring. Collins interrupted the board's proceedings to bring those firsties in before the graduation parade got started.

Before they reported to the board for a second time, one of the two firsties cornered McDonald and pleaded with him to reconsider what he had done. The firstie was getting married right after the graduation ceremony and had a large family group arriving at West Point later that week. He promised that if McDonald would back off before the board he would send word back after graduation that he was indeed guilty. McDonald agreed.

The two firsties appeared before the board with Williams and McDonald present. The firsties again denied involvement in the ring. Both Williams and McDonald then withdrew their statements as to their guilt, and the board took no further action against those first classmen or any others.

Later that morning the superintendent asked Collins about the firsties under investigation. Collins told him that they were not going to recommend that any firsties be dismissed. The graduation ceremony proceeded for the Class of 1951 with the secretary of defense, General of the Army George C. Marshall, as the commencement speaker. The yearlings had to march in the parade but, both before and after, the Collins Board pressed on with its deliberations.

JAKE'S MOMENT

Bill Jackomis's name had shown up on one of the drill rolls that the board drew up on 29 May. He finally had his turn on 5 June after the graduation parade. He had gone the extra mile to prepare for his day in court. By this time he knew that these things were far from congenial, fact-finding sessions. This was a formal board of inquiry by some of the most respected—and feared—

Army officers assigned to duty at the academy. All three were straight-by-the-book tactical officers who shared the commandant's distaste for the special privileges and considerations afforded to the football team. Jake knew that half of his battle with these hardened combat veterans and stalwarts of the Army's spit-and-polish tradition would be his own appearance and demeanor.

The graduation parade had rendered one complete set of belts and brass unfit for this occasion. Rain had threatened that day, and the ceremony had been held in the field house. Jake had perspired profusely in all the humidity, and the salty sweat left smears all over his brass and dissolved all the starch from his white cotton belts. He would have to put on a new set of whites, spit-shine his shoes again, and polish up all his brass.

He spent hours that afternoon getting ready, not by thinking about his involvement in the cheating or rehearsing what he would say, but by polishing his brass and shining his shoes. There was not a scratch on the brand-new belt buckle he had bought for this moment, and he had buffed it to a high luster with Brasso liquid polish. His shoes were so clear and black that he could see his reflection off their toes. His hair had been trimmed to its precise length requirement by regulation; then he made the barber take another quarter of an inch off. He had, of course, shaved in the morning, but he shaved again to get it extra close and to eliminate his "five-o'clock shadow."

He walked briskly and stiffly from his room to the hearing room in the guard tower of central barracks. Outside the board of inquiry's hearing room, Jake stood at a position of attention that would have gotten him into President Truman's honor guard that day—his feet together at the heels, and toes separated at an exact forty-five-degree angle. There was not the slightest break in the crease of his trousers, his arms were straight as boards with his fingers cupped and thumbs resting just behind the leg stripe along the side of his heavy woolen trousers. His head was erect with his stomach in, his chest out, and his chin forcibly held back toward his neck so that a wrinkle or two would show in the skin folds around his Adam's apple. It felt a bit uncomfortable, and he did not really want to look like a new cadet in Beast barracks, but Jake knew it was just what these officers expected of lowly cadets, especially those accused of violating the honor code.

In strict accord with the procedure for such boards (the formalities are scripted in detail in Army regulations), Jake rapped sharply on the door of the hearing room three times.

"Sir, Cadet Jackomis requests permission to enter!"

"Enter!" bellowed Colonel Collins.

"Sir, Cadet Jackomis reports to the president of the board as ordered!" proclaimed Jake with his sharpest hand salute. This, too, was a precisely executed maneuver that Jake had practiced over and over again before reporting. The hand was to become a part of the plane of the forearm, with fingers perfectly parallel, extended, and joined. The upper arm was raised to form a ninety-degree angle with the torso, then the forearm hand assembly brought swiftly up toward the head in a rapid movement until the tip of the index finger touched the forehead just above the right eyebrow.

Collins returned Jake's salute. Somehow it always seemed that those old guys had a crisper salute than cadets. Maybe it was the starch in the khaki brown uniform worn by the tacs that simply exaggerated the movement. Perhaps it was the more mature hair on the arms that made them seem more military. Once Collins's arm had safely completed its salute and returned to its position, with the right hand folded together with the left hand while he was seated at the table in front of him, Jake completed his own salute by then bringing his hand even more expeditiously back to his own side.

Jake then began to sweat. He was a profuse sweater. His forehead beaded up, his palms got moist, and drops of the salty stuff began to cascade down his back off his tailbone and down the crack of his butt. This had not happened since plebe year. At that moment he wished he could break loose in a hundred-yard dash. He knew he could set a new personal record and the wind would dry up the sweat.

"Mr. Jackomis, do you know why you are here?"

"Yes, sir, I do."

"Then what do you have to say for yourself?"

All three board members stared at him. He wondered if they ever blinked. He knew that several others before him had lied and told the board that they had no earthly idea what was going on and that they had not been involved in cheating of any kind nor did they know of anyone else who was. Jake remembered what Blaik had told them Thursday night in the football projection room.

"Sir, I am aware that cadets have exchanged unauthorized information, but I am not involved. I first heard about it this last fall. I was sitting at a football table, and I heard them talking about unauthorized matters. It was just that one incident; and I didn't realize at the time exactly what it was. I didn't know what to do about it, so I didn't do anything."*

"That's all we need, Mr. Jackomis, you are dismissed," barked Colonel Collins. "We will inform you of our findings."

That was it. The entire session lasted fewer than three minutes.

---

*The Collins Board did not keep a verbatim transcript of its proceedings. A recorder apparently reconstructed each cadet's testimony afterward. Jackomis and several others believe that the record is not entirely accurate and that what Jackomis said was to the effect that everyone knew that cheating was going on, but he denied admitting to knowledge of a specific act of cheating. His account of his testimony: "Sir, I am aware of what is going on. I am aware that, on occasion, unauthorized information has been discussed at the corps squad training tables. However, sir, I have never used unauthorized information, nor have I ever taken advantage of any of my classmates."

Twenty-Two

Jake and Joe[*]

Jake went back to his room, not knowing what the board's verdict would be, although rumors were running wildly through the Corps of Cadets that perhaps a thousand—half the entire corps—were about to be drummed out for cheating. Surely the academy would not take such a drastic measure. It would be devastatingly embarrassing for the institution. He felt somewhat secure in the hope that he was part of such a large enterprise that whatever he had done it was not really cheating, it was just the way things were done.

Yet the proceeding was troubling. It was not an honor board; those were convened by cadets. It was a board of officers, a procedure usually invoked for serious disciplinary violations. It was not a court-martial, with all the legal trappings that accompanied a formal trial proceeding. It was instead an administrative hearing. Such panels could not throw you in jail, nor could they dismiss you for cheating, they could only make findings of fact and

---

[*]This chapter is reconstructed from the Collins Report, except where noted. In some cases the official report is supplemented with the recollections of the cadets as related to the author.

recommendations to the commandant or superintendent. The supe, in turn, was empowered to convene a court-martial, to dismiss a cadet for misbehavior, or to drop all the charges entirely. No one knew what Major General Irving would do with this one. It was very big, reaching perhaps even to his own son.

Outside the clouds eventually broke and the sun set over Fort Putnam late that evening. From his room in south barracks, Bill Jackomis watched the night sky settle over the academy grounds, and he wondered what would happen next. Tomorrow he was scheduled to move out with the rest of his class to Camp Buckner to prepare for summer training camp. He was to be assigned as a squad leader for the next yearling class rising out of the Class of 1954, who would undergo eight weeks of advanced military training, having completed their plebe year. Jake and several hundred other new cows were to form the cadre of leaders who would provide the day-to-day training, discipline, and accountability for the new yearling class. Previous classes had spent cow summer on a trip around the country getting familiarized with Air Force facilities, but with the Korean War keeping most air bases preoccupied, that was canceled last year. Anyway, Jake was looking forward to an enjoyable summer at Camp Buckner lakeside beach, where he would train cadets in the rigors of Army life.

But would he go to Buckner, or would they put him in "boarder's ward"? Known officially as "transient cadet quarters," this was a series of rooms set aside to isolate cadets awaiting the outcome of academic, disciplinary, or honor boards whenever it looked like the outcome might be dismissal. Such cadets were kept away from the rest of the corps of cadets for their own protection as much as to prevent them from exerting any further negative influence over their fellows. Jake did not expect to go to boarder's ward because he knew there would be no room for the hundreds who had done deeds exactly like his. Besides, Coach Blaik would probably intervene with the supe, he figured, and would get them all off with some sort of reprimand.

Collins, Harrington, and Irving conferred for several more hours, going back over every man's testimony. On some they asked the judge advocate for an opinion as to how the evidence might stand up in a legal review. In the end they recommended dismissal for just about everyone who had appeared before them, except, of course, the first classmen, who were all let go. The list included thirty-seven football players, just about the entire 1951 team, including Bob Blaik, Ray Malavasi, and Boom-Boom Beck. In the end, they agreed that twenty cows and thirty-seven yearlings admitted cheating, five cows and fifteen yearlings admitted cheating and false swearing, two cows and one plebe admitted false swearing, two cows and two yearlings admitted guilty knowledge of cheating, and ten cows did not admit cheating but that there was enough evidence to support such a charge.

All three board members agreed to recommend that all ninety-three individuals be offered the opportunity to resign and be discharged. Any who chose not to resign should be investigated in further detail and considered for trial by court-martial. The board also recommended that another board be appointed to study the problem to determine what had contributed to its occurrence in the first place.

In a separate personal annex, a minority report, Collins also recommended that Michael Kelly be granted special consideration because he had tried to report the cheating ring earlier to his company commander. He also recommended that despite the aspect of the honor code that requires a cadet who knows of a violation to report it or be considered guilty of the same offense, three cadets (Beck, Martin, and Lawrence) were judged to be guilty of such toleration only by their own admission before the board. With no other evidence to corroborate their testimony, had these cadets chosen to avoid testimony by invoking their rights under the Articles of War, then there would be no admissible evidence to convict them. Collins therefore recommended that those men not be dismissed. Finally, Collins recommended that the man who had been asked, but declined, to become an informant be dismissed in spite of his denial of any guilt. The other two board members did not agree with Collins on these matters. Ralph Martin ('52) and Eugene Lawrence ('53) went on to graduate with their classes. Two of the four on Collins's minority report were football players who resigned, Kelly in August and Beck in December.

Collins had a seventy-three-page report prepared for signature by the board members and delivered it to Colonel Harkins at his quarters on 5 June. The movers were there packing and loading the Harkins family household goods for shipment to Washington. D.C. Harkins signed the report on a footlocker that was about to be taken out and told Collins he was from that point on to deal with Colonel Waters on this issue.

Meanwhile, none of the cows and yearlings who had appeared before the Collins Board were told anything about what was going to happen to them. For a while it appeared as if they would not be prosecuted. After all, the firsties had been allowed to graduate without any of them being held up for honor charges. The rumors ran rampant.

Half of the Class of 1952 departed on the annual combined arms trip by mid-June. The other half stayed to prepare for the new crop of plebes at Beast barracks. Some of the Class of 1953, including Jackomis, were trucked to Camp Buckner for summer cadre duty with the new yearlings from the Class of 1954. It soon became apparent that something was amiss. The class of '54 did not arrive, and the cadre was given only "make work" tasks— police call, weed cutting, rock painting, etc. Accusations went back and forth among the new cows as to who had turned in whom. The barracks at Camp Buckner several times were the scene of heated arguments and sometimes even fistfights. On 25 June one man was sent to the hospital for injuries he received when a group of his classmates beat him up after accusing him of lying to get himself off the hook from the cheating scandal.

When the rising firsties returned from their trip in late July, those who had been recommended for discharge by the Collins Board were moved into the psychiatric ward of the cadet hospital. Discipline there deteriorated rapidly, but Colonel Waters saw that he had nowhere else to put them. The com sent them away on a specially authorized leave while their classmates went about their normal summertime details.

THE COLLINS REPORT
Meanwhile, the superintendent traveled back and forth to Washington several times, providing the Army chief of staff and the

secretary of the Army with information on what was happening with the cheating incident. They all recognized that something had to be done soon or word would inevitably leak to the press. On one trip Irving allowed Red Blaik to accompany him to plead his case for leniency to the army chief of staff Gen. J. Lawton Collins. General Collins would not overturn Irving's decision to accept the Collins Board recommendations. But he did go along with Blaik's request to seek a decision by Secretary of the Army Frank Pace to appoint an external review board to examine the dismissal decisions.

In late June, General Irving had two senior officers review the Collins Board report, Brig. Gen. Harris Jones, dean of the Academic Board, and Col. Charles J. Barrett, head of the Foreign Languages Department. Each reviewed the Collins Board report and its judgment on each cadet. As they proceeded, Col. James W. Green, professor in the Department of Electricity, coordinated between them whenever there was a difference of opinion. These senior officers were appointed under official Army Regulation 15–20 as investigating officers. Under this regulation each cadet was to have had an officer appointed as counsel to represent him, and the proceedings were to follow a written procedure designed to ensure that the legal rights of each cadet were preserved. Each cadet was to be given the opportunity to expand or alter his previous testimony to the Collins Board. None of the cadets were in fact given theses rights. The reviews did result in some of the accused cadets adding an admission of cheating to their previous admission only of guilty knowledge, and a few admitting cheating after having denied it before the Collins Board. In total, eighty-three cadets admitted their guilt. Forty-four others from the Classes of 1952, 1953, and 1954 were retained because of lack of evidence. Superintendent Irving signed a letter to the secretary of the Army on 2 July recommending that all eighty-three be offered the opportunity to resign or face administrative dismissal under academy regulations.

Shortly after the review boards completed their findings, Secretary of the Army Frank Pace went along with Irving's request to appoint an outside panel to review the academy's handling of the affair and signed a confidential order convening his own review board to examine the report of the Collins Board and Major General Irving's actions taken afterward. Pace appointed one of America's most distinguished jurists to head the board, Judge Learned Hand. Hand, though decidedly liberal in his outlook on the Constitution, had been considered for appointment to the U.S. Supreme Court by both Republican president Herbert Hoover and Democratic president Franklin D. Roosevelt. Pace also appointed two retired Army generals to the board: Lt. Gen. Troy Middleton, who was then president of Louisiana State University, and Maj. Gen. Robert W. Danford. Danford had been commandant of cadets from 1919 to 1923, under superintendent Douglas MacArthur, when Red Blaik was a cadet. The Hand Board was charged with recommending to the secretary of the Army what he should do about the matter.

Judge Hand had his board study the Collins report and the subsequent review board reports. They visited West Point on 23 and 24 July. While there they interviewed the three members of the Collins Board and seven members of the cadet Honor Committee. They also saw seven faculty members, including Irving, Waters, Blaik, and others. In addition, the Hand Board interviewed four of the cadets named in the Collins report as guilty, including two football players and two nonathletes, all from the Class of 1952. In the course of his interview with the Hand Board, Red Blaik came to believe that he had persuaded them not to go along with the dismissal of those found guilty by the Collins Board.

In their deliberations the Hand Board considered two alternative courses of action to the one recommended by the supe. They could recommend that the guilty cadets be suspended for one year, or they could consider a course they termed, "intramural cleanup," by which they meant to allow the guilty cadets to stay while the academy developed a method of rehabilitating them.

In debating the solution to the problem the board determined that the overriding consideration should be the preservation of the honor system at West Point. That made their decision fairly simple; anything less than dismissal would in effect be an admission that the honor system had broken down. Whatever they might have meant to say to Blaik, in their written report they simply stated as their recommendation that, "The course of action as contained in the letter of the superintendent to the secretary of the Army, dated 2 July 1951, be followed." The board did go one step further and also recommended that the academic departments start giving different tests to classes taking an exam on different days so that cadets would not be tempted to cheat. The board's report went to Secretary Pace on 25 July.

BAD NEWS COMES OUT ON SATURDAYS

Major General Irving took charge of the process of publicly releasing his final decision on actions to be taken. No one was in charge of informing the cadets involved. A press release was prepared and provided to the news media on the afternoon of 3 August. This was a typical press strategy designed to make sure that bad news hits the papers on Saturday mornings, when few people bother to read and those who do are not at their offices.

The news did hit the radio waves, and the cadets who were involved heard of their expulsion for the first time by that means. The next day they were brought back from Camp Buckner and placed in a separate section of the barracks from the area where Beast was going on. The members of Class of 1952, who were still on leave, received an urgent telegram from the superintendent, "BALANCE OF YOUR LEAVE CANCELED. YOU ARE DIRECTED TO RETURN TO WEST POINT IMMEDIATELY." And *The New York Times* of Saturday, 4 August, ran a banner headline, "WEST POINT OUSTS 90 CADETS FOR CHEATING IN CLASSROOM; FOOTBALL PLAYERS INVOLVED."

Judge Hand had accurately predicted what would happen when the dismissals were announced:

. . . when it breaks in the newspapers, it will bring an instant storm of criticism and abuse upon the academy. . . . there will be outraged public sentiment, criticism and political clamor that will not subside for months. . . . in effect wipes out the varsity football squad . . . the sports pages will comment and enlarge on the enormity of the disaster for a very long time to come. . . . would cut the very heart out of this [sesquicentennial] celebration. One hundred and fifty great and history making years capped by the greatest group of delinquents in its history!

The reaction was all that and more. Some would even claim that it was all a Communist conspiracy.

On Saturday, 4 August, Red Blaik had gone to see MacArthur, intending to explain to him why he was indeed going to resign. On the way Blaik's car broke down and he left his wife, Merle, with it while he hitchhiked a ride into New York City to meet with the general at the Waldorf-Astoria Hotel. After several hours MacArthur told Blaik, "Earl, you must stay on. Don't leave under fire."

General Collins sent word to Blaik that he was not to make a statement to the press about the incident. But Blaik was not about to be muzzled. He invited forty sports journalists to meet him at Mama Leone's on Thursday, 9 August. While some of those at Leone's expected Blaik to announce his resignation, he instead launched a spirited defense of the honor of the men who were to be dismissed. He then released the names of thirty-one football players who were to be dismissed.

Several cadets found themselves quoted in the papers over the following days after the academy's announcement. Senators and congressmen called for investigations and hearings. Young Massachusetts congressman John F. Kennedy used the opportunity to get a long article written about himself in *The New York Times Magazine* in which he outlined his own procedure for appointing cadets to the military academies. He was the first to institute a system of standardized testing across his district and having the top scorers interviewed by a special committee he appointed for this purpose. The committee was composed of a clergyman who had been a combat chaplain, a psychologist from Harvard Medical School, and a retired Army doctor. This committee rank-ordered the candidates and the congressman appointed the top selectees regardless of political connections or athletic recruiting pressure.

On 13 August the special review board appointed by Irving in keeping with the recommendation of the Collins Board report began to hear witnesses. This board was chaired by the head of the Department of Electricity, Col. B. W. Bartlett. Other members were Col. F. M. Greene from the Physical Education Department, and Col. C. H. Miles, the Academy's fiscal officer. Bartlett and Greene had lettered in football when they were cadets. Bartlett had been one of the student officers at West Point during Blaik's days as a cadet and graduated early to go to World War I in November 1918, then graduated again in 1919. Greene was in the Class of 1922. They would hear more than eighty different people provide information on the cheating scandal, the Collins investigation, and previous incidents related to the present affair. They would not hear from Red Blaik until the day after most of the accused cadets were to resign.

JAKE SIGNS OUT

Bill Jackomis shuffled around his footlocker in his dingy floor space at the Camp Buckner hut. He had been trucked out to Buckner with the rest of his accused classmates assigned to summer detail for the new yearlings, even though their cases were pending. Living accommodations at Buckner were spartan, even by academy standards, more like troop billets than the dormitory-like rooms they were used to at the academy proper. The buildings were fairly new, but they were tin-roofed Quonsets with plywood and two-by-four walls standing on concrete slab floors. Forty bunks were arrayed in two rows against each side of the building with a footlocker at the foot of each bed. It was intended to give cadets an experience similar to that of their troops when they got out into the "real" Army. Bill Jackomis did not expect to see the real Army or any other Army now that he was up for dismissal by the superintendent.

Jake could not believe what had happened in the past two months. One day he was getting ready to be a squad leader at Camp Buckner, then after a few nonchalant answers to the Collins Board weeks afterward, he finds out that he was to be convicted of an honor violation. What other evidence could they have collected on him? Who told them what? Jake had no enemies at all; in fact, he was pretty well liked by just about everyone. Most of all, he wondered who turned him in. Whoever it was had it all wrong. Jake did not cheat; he was just there when others did. Even if that was technically toleration, there sure were a lot of other men who were guilty of the same thing, many more than the few who were brought up before the Collins Board.

It did not matter anyway. There was nothing anyone could do about it now. Coach Blaik had fought for them all the way to Washington, but it looked like the Army's mind was made up. They had to go for the good of the Army and the academy's honor code. Jake supposed that was just the way it had to be, and he would try to make the best of it. He was to go along with the others at Buckner back to the West Point main post and get "processed out." He wondered what "process" there was to go through. How hard could it be? Spam was "processed" meat. What did they do to cadets?

On 17 August Jake found out. That day he was ordered to get into full-dress uniform to see the superintendent about his case. Jake did not bother to prepare his uniform for this visit. What could they do to him if his brass was not shined or if his shoes were scuffed—throw him out of West Point? The Buckner detail trucked them in and a firstie marched him over in a squad of five others to the supe's office. They went into the square area in the center of the Administration Building, a place where Jake had not been since his first day at West Point, "R Day," back in 1949. They went through one of the corner entryways and walked up a long flight of stairs to a hallway leading to a small room. All five of them went in at the same time. They stood before a group of five officers while one of them told the cadets they could sign their resignations right there or they could refuse to sign and face dismissal proceedings.

Jake had already thought this one through, too. He knew that the academy's administration would not have gone through all the trouble they were now facing unless they were sure they could get them all out through normal procedures. The resignation was just an easy way for them to get out. If he could have pleaded his case to an honor board, he could have defended himself before fellow cadets. Even if it had been a court-martial he would be allowed to have a lawyer present to advise him and to present his defense. But none of that was available to him now. It was either resign or be thrown out by the supe. There was no real choice. For Jake this was the quickest way to get on with his life. He signed. So did all but three of the cadets recommended for dismissal. And even those three were out on the street before the end of September.

When he got back to his room he was told to pack everything into his suitcase and footlocker. He would be allowed to ship the footlocker home. He would be given the money left in his cadet treasury account after deductions had been made for uniforms, books, and supplies issued but not turned in. For Bill Jackomis there was little more than bus fare back to Gary, Indiana.

Even that was not an option for Jake. When he called home to tell his family about what had happened to him they had already read about it and saw his name in the Gary newspaper. He found no sympathy or understanding at all. His war hero uncle said he had disgraced the family and was probably a Communist. Jake's mother told him not to come back home; he was no longer welcome. Jake had nowhere else to go. He bought a bus ticket to downtown Manhattan and figured he would shack up at the YMCA for a few days and think about what he would do.

He could wallow in his sorrow just as easily in New York City as in Gary, Indiana. In fact, he could think of a lot of things he could do in Manhattan that would salve his emotional wounds better than anything Gary had to offer. Jake boarded the bus at Grant Hall and stared out the window as it left the West Point gate. This was a very different kind of a trip than the bus ride into the academy had been two years ago. The bus was packed tighter and it stopped more often. One thing was the same. Just about everyone smoked, and it did not take long for the bus to fill with white clouds of swirling exhaled smoke. It was hot that day, and Jake broke out in a sweat. He hated it when that happened. There was nothing he could do for two hours while the bus made its way down the Hudson highlands into Manhattan.

JAKE IN MANHATTAN

The bus arrived at New York's downtown bus terminal. Jake got off and walked a dozen blocks to the YMCA, where he had heard you could get a room for fifty cents a night. It was true, fifty cents a night was all it cost, but it was hardly a room. It was more like the platoon bay he had left at Camp Buckner, with rows of bunks stacked two high in a large open area that probably used to be a gymnasium. Jake went to his bunk, tossed his suitcase on the floor, and climbed up on the mattress. He would take a nap, shower, and then worry about what to do next.

The next morning Jake had a big breakfast at a coffee shop, then set out for the docks. He remembered that an old high school buddy had gone into the merchant marine and worked on a steamer home-ported in New York. He had no idea which ship it was but he figured he had nothing better to do than check each one. By late afternoon he located his old high school classmate working in the boiler room of a ship as part of the skeleton crew manning it while it was tied up in port. After cruising through a few bars and reliving old times, Jake told his friend that he had no money, nowhere to go, and needed some help. They cooked up a scheme in which Jake took the name of another crew member and walked up the plank with his friend when the crew reported for work the next morning. That would get him onboard for the next few days while the rest of the crew was still off duty. But in three days he would have to leave because the full crew was to return to take the ship back out to sea.

The deception worked, and it was Jake's room and board for the next three days. He was never caught, and when he left, he returned to the YMCA. There he ran into a few other former cadets who told him that they had heard there might be some help available at St. Patrick's Cathedral. Jake went to find out about it, and when he inquired he learned of a remarkable opportunity.

An anonymous benefactor had promised to pay full tuition, room, and board at the University of Notre Dame for any among the dismissed ninety cadets as long as the cadet could qualify for admission, was in financial need, and would promise not to play intercollegiate sports while there. A priest told him that all he had to do was talk to Father Cavanaugh, president of Notre Dame, and see if he could qualify.

Jake's response was immediate. He had nothing else to do,

nowhere else to go. He would certainly give up football and even running for the chance to get into Notre Dame. He went to the nearest pay phone and spoke to a Father Norton, setting in motion his plans for a trip to Notre Dame. He could not believe his luck had taken such a turn. And he could not believe there was someone out there so generous.

In fact, that generosity came from a most unlikely source. The anonymous gift was announced publicly on 21 August as provided by a "wealthy man" who said that he felt, ". . . with millions that in the American tradition a man who makes a mistake should have a reasonable chance to rehabilitate himself." It would be a decade and a half before Jake would learn that his anonymous benefactor was Joseph P. Kennedy.

Perhaps it was motivation from the experience he had come through the year before with his own son Ted that led Joe Kennedy to make the offer to his longtime friend Father John J. Cavanaugh. Cavanaugh was relaxing with Kennedy on the family yacht *Marlin* on Saturday, 4 August, eating a leisurely lunch and reading different sections of *The New York Times*. Kennedy had the front page with the headline about the West Point cheating story and suddenly fired a question at Cavanaugh: "What would it cost to send all of these young fellows through Notre Dame?" Cavanaugh quickly estimated that for all of them to go it would probably cost upward of half a million dollars. Kennedy said, "I want every one of them to have an opportunity to go through Notre Dame, all expenses paid. Let us agree upon two conditions. My name will not be made known, and none of these young men should participate in intercollegiate athletics at Notre Dame. Otherwise, people will think that Notre Dame's benefactor is trying to buy athletes for the university."

For Bill Jackomis and the twelve other former cadets who eventually went to Notre Dame on the Kennedy grant, it was a gift from heaven. Father Cavanaugh told St. Patrick's to put him on a bus to Chicago. The next day, Jake was in a big Greyhound bus motoring westward to the Windy City. He did not even mind all that cigarette smoke in the bus. He was on his way to Notre Dame!

Back at West Point, Red Blaik soon turned his attention away from the cheating scandal. General Irving had released a public letter to the alumni association that really stung: "The cheating was concentrated in and associated with the football players. The remainder were their roommates and other close associates. . . . The crisis has passed, but the lesson will be remembered." Blaik wrote to his mentor Douglas MacArthur about how disastrously he believed Irving and others had handled the whole affair. He expressed his contempt as well for Frank Pace and General Collins. He told MacArthur of the opportunity he had to take his arguments on behalf of the dismissed cadets to President Truman, but that Truman had told him it was too late for him to intervene even with an honorable discharge. Blaik wrote to MacArthur that he wished he had told Truman instead that it was Collins and Marshall who had rescued the president in the MacArthur investigation ". . . and that we are all small men together." He then pleaded with MacArthur to consider running for president with Robert Taft as his running mate and told the general that, "you will lick that crowd in Washington and after this season you may count on me to support actively your position, whatever it may be." Red Blaik was evidently looking ahead as well.

Part Six

The Harder Right

Twenty-Three

Life Goes On

The Brave Old Army Team was broken apart. Sportswriters and analysts, even Douglas MacArthur, predicted that it would take a decade or more to rebuild the football program at West Point to even get close to being nationally competitive. Rival football programs saw opportunity in Army's misfortune and recruited shamelessly.

Kansas State University got themselves a new offensive line by landing Ray Malavasi, Bob Volonnini, Ed Stahura, John McShulskis, and Gerald Hart. Rival University of Kansas won the allegiance of promising backup quarterback Richard Hunt. Offensive lineman James Jackson went to the University of Houston and enrolled in their ROTC program. Gene Filipski remembered many discussions with Jake and found himself attracted to the football program at Villanova.

Bob Blaik went to Colorado College.

Al Pollard probably would not make it at another major college because of academic ability, but it turned out he did not need to consider another school. In 1950 the football team New York Yankees, along with two other teams from the defunct All-America Football Conference, joined the established National Football League. In 1951 Al Pollard signed with the Yankees.

Pollard would get three years of professional football. In 1951 the Yankees had four wins and eight losses with Pollard playing halfback, fullback, and sometimes even defensive back. He was the Yankees' top yard gainer before the franchise was moved and Pollard found himself playing for the Philadelphia Eagles. The 1952 season was Pollard's best, with more than five hundred yards to his credit and one touchdown. His performance dropped off in 1953, and that was the last year of his professional football career.

At West Point, the Bartlett Board released its report on 7 September. It was the most thorough and deliberate of the many groups to look at the cheating scandal. The Bartlett Board documented further abuses of West Point's administrative and honor systems and reaffirmed the Collins and Hand Board findings that the honor code was in trouble. The Bartlett Board placed the blame for this situation squarely on the football program. The board recommended a wide range of changes in academy policies and practices relating to recruiting athletes, preparing candidates for admission, the method of awarding appointments, cadet activities and privileges, organization for athletics, the aptitude for the service system, and more. It was especially harsh in its criticism of Red Blaik, "The cause of the incident was a misalignment of values . . . [and] . . . over emphasis on football. . . . Blaik's loyalties to the football program transcended his loyalties to the corps and its traditions. . . . the football player is physically and spiritually separate from the corps. . . . he is . . . inclined to think he is doing West Point a favor rather than the reverse. . . ." Since those individual players were now gone, no serious consideration was given to making any fundamental changes in the athletic, academic, or honor systems for decades.

UNDER THE GOLDEN DOME

Bill Jackomis did not care about West Point anymore. He was on his way to Notre Dame. It was only an hour-and-a-half flight to Chicago from New York City but Jake slept most of the way. He was not sure how he was going to get to South Bend once he got to Chicago, but he did not worry about that for the moment. He just wanted to sleep. The air conditioning in the plane was quite a luxury. Nothing at West Point was air conditioned in 1952, so the cool inside of the aircraft seemed to Jake a technological marvel. It had been a long, hot summer, and for the first time since that evening back in May when he appeared before the Collins Board, he slept well.

He woke up as the plane was taxiing to the terminal in Chicago. He hitched a ride to the South Bend train station, about two hours away. The priest at St. Patrick's had told him only that once he got to South Bend he was to ask for Father Norton. Jake stood with his one blue bag filled with about a week's worth of clothing at the outside entrance to the train station and just looked around. He saw that he was just down from an intersection where a main road crossed the railroad tracks. On the opposite side of the intersection there were a few stores and a café. In front of the café there was a group of about five or six men milling around, obviously waiting for a bus.

Jake strode across the intersection, intending to go up to one of the guys in the group and ask which way he should go to get to the Notre Dame campus, intending to walk there no matter how far away it was. He figured he would establish his credibility with the group simply by asking the question, since they would realize that he was on his way to the famous university and they would instantly recognize him as a big college man. They might even look at his build and guess that he was on his way to play football there on Frank Leahy's nationally famous team.

As he approached the group, a priest emerged from the center of the men and walked right up to Jake. He extended his right hand to greet Jake and said, "Hello, young man, I can tell by looking at you that you are one of the men from West Point. Let me welcome you to Notre Dame." He ushered Jake into a school bus along with the other men for the brief ride through town to the university campus. While the other men went to the registration area with hundreds of other new students for in-processing, Jake was taken into an office, where he met with Father Norton.

Father Norton spoke to Jake for about an hour, learning about

Jake's family, his feelings, and his academic potential. Then the discussion shifted to a more administrative tone, "Do you have any money?" asked Father Norton.

"No, just a couple of bucks left," answered Jake, a little embarrassed to admit he was broke.

Father Norton took no notice of Jake's discomfort with the subject, "Here is your room and board for the next two weeks," he said, handing Jake forty-two dollars in cash. "We will take care of your tuition and books; this has to take care of the rest. You should be able to find suitable accommodations near the campus. Let me know if you have any difficulty finding a place." With that, the priest told him to go out and register for class and get ready to start the academic year.

This certainly was a far cry from "R Day," thought Bill Jackomis. He felt pretty good about things now. He went out to a housing bulletin board to see if he could locate a rooming house; he had heard that lots of folks in South Bend opened their homes up and even provided meals for Notre Dame students. On his way he ran into Jim Guardino. Jake could not believe his luck; here was another man from West Point, a football player, here at Notre Dame on the same scholarship from that anonymous donor. Guardino had made the A squad in yearling year and had been slated to see plenty of action in the 1951 season. He, too, had resigned on 17 August, and now he found himself taking up the opportunity to accept the full scholarship to Notre Dame.

Guardino had been in South Bend for a day or so and had already found himself a room. He was at the bulletin board looking for a third roommate and latched on to Jackomis, "Jake, old man, how are you doing? Need a room? I found a little old lady in South Bend who only takes boarders by recommendation. I can get you in for six bucks a week. Come with me and meet the nice woman."

Bill liked the sound of it. Not only was it pretty cheap, but it sounded like it would suit him. He followed Guardino to the house, five miles away at 702 Rush Street. The lady was in her eighties, but she was sharp and spry as a cat. Her husband was bedridden, and she was renting out space to make extra money to care for him. She had one room remaining, a small one that was not much more than a dormer over the porch. It was sparsely furnished with just a small bunk, a dresser, and a card table. Jake thought it was just great for six dollars a week. The other real room in the house was rented out by Jim Stein. Stein was also going to Notre Dame and was working as an engineer for Bendix.

The three of them made out well on Rush Street. Usually they ate out because they were out of the house most of the time. The five-mile walk to campus got them out early in the morning and kept them away well into the evening. On weekends she enjoyed fixing meals for the men as if they were her own sons. Jake and Guardino did not have much money left over for entertainment on weekends, and neither of them had transportation anyway, so they welcomed the attention she gave them. They reciprocated by helping around the house.

What entertainment they were able to enjoy was whatever came to Notre Dame, which in the fall of 1951 was not much because the Korean War was going on. But because of his age and completion of basic military training at West Point, he was eligible for the armed services' Reserve Officer Training Corps (ROTC) program. In fact, most of Jake's free time went to the ROTC battalion. Jake still wanted to be a paratrooper. Now, after his dismissal and his estrangement from his family, Jake wanted more than ever to get into the Army and show them all what he was made of. He had been allowed to transfer only some of his academy credits to Notre Dame and essentially had to start over as a sophomore.

Jake thought he could get into Notre Dame's Army ROTC program and get his commission that way. He could still try for jump school and perhaps get into the airborne infantry. He went to the Army ROTC Department and asked to see the professor of military science.

Jake had no clue that he was about to walk into a hornet's nest. The ROTC battalion at Notre Dame was a fairly popular place. In the 1950s it was fashionable among young American men to demonstrate their patriotism while deferred from the draft because of their student status by entering the ROTC program.

It involved spending additional time on campus after normal classes, going through military drill and training, and spending the summer between junior and senior years in an intense training camp at an Army post. Upon completion of the program and when your student deferment was lifted upon graduation, you were commissioned in the reserves and placed on active duty for a short time, usually about two years. Notre Dame's ROTC program was particularly popular. You did not evade military service, but you at least got the opportunity to become an officer after you graduated. For most men that seemed like a better path than taking your chances on the draft and letting the Army decide what enlisted position you would get.

The professor of military science at a large campus was more powerful than any West Point tactical officer was. He was the legal equivalent of the commandant of cadets, and he reported directly to the Army staff rather than to the university president, although the campus relationship was always a complicated one. Whatever the colonel said was generally the way things went in an ROTC battalion. This one had heard about the former cadets and had determined that they had no place in the same Army he served in. He told Jake that he had already denied a similar request from the other twelve ex-cadets and had no intention of letting him into the ROTC program. He was, after all, a cheater. In fact, the colonel pointed out to Jake, the truly professional officer corps should have no interaction whatsoever with the dismissed cadets; as violators of the honor code they were to be "silenced" for the rest of their lives. If they ever showed up in the military, the only contact they were supposed to have with other officers was strictly in the performance of official duties. Otherwise they were to be professionally ostracized and socially isolated.

Jake could not believe what he had been told. He knew he could serve well in the Army, and after all, he had not cheated, he had not even really been tried by a board of officers, he had simply chosen to resign rather than go through the process. Jake suddenly realized he was branded probably for the rest of his life. He went to some of the other men and asked about their experiences with the ROTC program and to see what they intended to do. Jake wanted to try anything that might work to get into the program. Maybe they had some creative ideas or knew of ways to use regulations in their favor.

Another former West Point cadet, John McDonald, who had been dismissed for cheating along with Jackomis, was also trying to get into the Notre Dame ROTC. McDonald called his father in Florida. John McDonald, Sr., had graduated in the Class of 1920 and was one of Red Blaik's teammates on the Army football team. He also knew well the chief of staff of the Army, Gen. J. Lawton Collins. The elder McDonald had been retired in 1925 because of physical disability but was recalled to active duty during World War II in 1942. He retired again as a colonel in 1947 after serving at West Point on the faculty. Colonel McDonald called General Collins and asked that the chief of staff personally intervene on behalf of his son and the others to allow them the opportunity to serve in the ROTC detachment. Collins agreed to do it.

In the meantime, the U.S. Air Force had formed several ROTC detachments of its own across the country to fill the growing demand for officers in the ranks of this newest of the armed services. At the time, the Air Force was becoming increasingly popular as the branch of the future, with its jet fighters and strategic bombers. American jet fighter pilots were scoring some spectacular tactical victories in the Korean War and became the first jet aces in the world, with several having shot down Soviet-made MiGs over North and South Korea. The Notre Dame Air Force ROTC detachment recruited vigorously for the best and brightest men on campus. The Air Force program was so popular that they could afford to be choosy.

When they were rejected by the Army, Jake and a few others, including John McDonald, went over to see the Air Force ROTC colonel. He, too, knew about their dismissal from the academy but told them he would give them a chance to make it in the Air Force ROTC program. He warned them sternly not to let other cadets at the university know that they had been dismissed from the academy. If they screwed up and were found out, he would discharge them from the program and they would automatically lose their student deferments and be eligible to be drafted. Jake did not know if that was correct, but he did not check it out. He took the chance and enrolled in the Air Force program. A few days later the Army colonel relented and told them he would allow them into the Army ROTC program. A couple of them signed up, but Jake stayed with the Air Force. It would turn out to be the best career decision he would ever make.

In the summer between his sophomore and junior years, Bill Jackomis got a summer job at the Inland Steel Company mill in South Bend. Steel was still king in America at the time, and this was a good job. Jake worked the blast furnace at Inland; he was able to land it because he already knew the steelworking trade from his high school days back in Gary. He saved his summer wages to pay for things like a coat for the winter and other necessities not covered by his scholarship. The only indulgence he allowed himself was to spend twenty-five cents every Friday night for one beer at the joint across from the steel mill.

Although he was not permitted to try out for football or even track, Jake stayed in shape during the school year at Notre Dame because he had to walk everywhere he went. The five miles to and from campus were tolerable until winter came. Jake did not have a heavy coat, but he managed to get by without one that year. He cut financial corners wherever he could in order to save up enough to get some things, such as a coat, the following year. He saved on food by using up other students' meal tickets when they preferred to eat off campus. Because he walked everywhere he went, and hardly went anywhere besides class, he had no transportation expenses. By the end of his junior year his hard work and discipline paid off by propelling him to the top of his ROTC detachment.

PORK CHOP HILL

The big news the summer of 1953 was that the peace talks had started in Korea. The Chinese had entered the war in late 1950 and pushed the United Nations south of Seoul by February 1951. Counteroffensives had re-established U.N. lines along the 38th parallel by April 1951, when MacArthur had been relieved of command for undermining the Truman administration's attempts to begin negotiating with the Chinese and North Koreans. General Matthew B. Ridgway was given MacArthur's command. Ridgway marshaled several attempts to regain the initiative, but the Chinese simply outnumbered the U.N. forces. Two years of stalemate ensued until both sides, wearied by war and unwilling to make the commitment to total war, engaged in cease-fire talks at Panmunjom.

But the war dragged on at a stalemate even as the Panmunjom talks proceeded. In fact, the Communists launched an offensive in July 1953 that was to take the life of Bill Jackomis's friend and role model, Dick Shea, at the Battle of Pork Chop Hill.

Shea had continued to display uncommon valor in his pursuit of excellence at West Point. In his senior year, 1952, he set Academy records for the mile (4:10) and two-mile (9:05.8) that stood for more than ten years. He had an open door to go with the U.S. Olympic team to the 1952 summer Olympics in Helsinki, Finland, but turned down that opportunity to go instead into the infantry. During his pre–West Point enlisted time, Shea had been an infantryman. By the summer of 1953 he found himself serving as the executive officer of A Company, 17th Infantry Regiment, assigned to the 7th Infantry Division on the high ground outside the Korean village of Sokkogae. We know the area now as Pork Chop Hill.

On 6 July 1953, A Company took the ridgeline from the Communists in a fierce fight. Lieutenant Shea was leading a reinforcing column to the position, trying to arrive before the Communists could mount their counterattack, which was sure to come. On their way the enemy attacked Shea's column. Rather than let his column get bogged down in a defensive battle, the energetic track star led his men in a hasty counterassault right back at the enemy. The two columns collided in close combat of the fiercest kind. Dick Shea killed two enemy soldiers with his bare hands and trench knife as the executive officer repelled the assault and reached A Company positions before dark. At dawn on 7 July the enemy hurled another column at Pork Chop Hill, again closing to hand-to-hand range. Shea was severely wounded but refused medical evacuation. His men were pinned down by heavy machine-gun fire. The fastest long-distance runner from West Point then stood up from his position, cried out to his men "Follow me!," and led a charge on the machine-gun nest, firing his carbine and hurling grenades into the enemy position. He killed three of the Communists in eliminating their position. By that time A Company had only twenty men left, but Lieutenant Shea would not let the enemy rest. He inspired his soldiers to follow him in an assault on the enemy's positions that solidified their own tactical advantage. On 8 July the 17th Regiment fought off another Communist assault, and Shea once again led his men in a counterattack. He was last seen again in a death grip with enemy soldiers. When the battle was over, Dick Shea lay dead on Pork Chop Hill. Bill Jackomis found out about it when he read about Shea's exploits in being awarded the Congressional Medal of Honor posthumously. On 27 July the warring sides signed the Korean Armistice at Panmunjom. In Shea's memory, the north athletic field, where Dick Shea and Bill Jackomis had excelled in track, was renamed Shea Stadium. Like Dennis Michie, Shea had been a leader at West Point and an outstanding athlete—and he had fallen in battle in the full vigor of youth.

In his senior year at Notre Dame, Bill Jackomis was appointed cadet battalion commander of the 1700-man Notre Dame Air Force ROTC detachment, the top man in the entire outfit. It looked like the war in Korea would drag on, and Jake began to realize that he would soon be in combat. It had lost its appeal to glory by now, but Jake was ready to go to Korea to prove that he was as capable an officer as any man who had graduated from West Point. In fact, he was determined to prove to them that he was better than they were.

The fall of 1953 Jake went with the Notre Dame students who traveled with the football team to see the Fighting Irish play the Purdue Boilermakers. It would turn out to be Frank Leahy's last year as head coach at Notre Dame, and Jake was glad that he went to see at least one game away from Notre Dame's stadium. The night after the game he took advantage of the fact that the train carrying the Notre Dame student body passed through Gary on its way back to South Bend from the Purdue campus at Lafayette,

Indiana. He hopped off at his hometown with a promise to make his way back to campus in time for class on Monday.

Jake had briefly talked only with his mother once or twice since that day in August 1951. He made his way to his home to find the family in the middle of a wake for an older relative who had passed away. He waited around for a while, and called a few other relatives. No one wanted to see him or talk to him. He just left. The only sign of his relationship still there was the stenciled wooden box he had shipped from West Point when he resigned. He had nowhere to put it now so he just left it there, figuring he would send for it once he got into the Air Force after graduation.

Jake was an excellent engineering student at Notre Dame. He majored in the new field of aero-mechanical engineering, figuring that would fit in well with an Air Force career, although he hoped that he could qualify to be a pilot. Jake was wise enough now to realize that even if he did succeed to become a hotshot fighter pilot, the ambition that had come to replace his boyhood dream of being an airborne trooper, he would eventually get old and need to have something else to fall back on. The Cold War was in full swing and a missile race was on with the Soviets, so aero-mechanical engineering seemed to have a bright future. He did well enough to land a full-time job in his last semester as an assemblyman on the line at the Bendix plant. He worked the 4:00 P.M. to midnight shift putting together brakes for the F-86 jet fighter while he carried an overload of twenty hours at Notre Dame.

The hard work paid off. Bill Jackomis finished his studies in January 1954 from the University of Notre Dame as the top Air Force ROTC cadet in academics. He marched at the front of the detachment's graduation review as its commander. He had earned the distinction of being an ROTC "distinguished military graduate," a status few were granted and that would have allowed him to enter the Air Force on an equal level, in terms of priority assignments, with West Pointers. Jake declined that award because he realized it would bring him into close contact with his former classmates who were now two years ahead of him in date-of-rank. Since Jake was branded by them as a cheater, they were bound by the tradition of the honor code to "silence" him—that is, they could have no contact with him at all except that minimally required to complete their own military duties. Jake could take whatever they were going to dish out, but he wanted above all to put that behind him and fly jets.

While waiting for call-up by the Air Force, he worked for Du Pont Chemical Company, as a petroleum sales engineer. He was picked to go to flight school and was soon off to basic pilot school at Bartow Air Force Base in Florida, learning to handle the T-6 and the Piper Supercub training aircraft. Du Pont placed him in their management training program and promised to keep his job available to him for the duration of his active duty service.

Bill Johnson had plenty to prove, too. The second-generation West Pointer, and former mascot for the academy's soccer team, left West Point a bitter man. Like Bill, he had not cheated, although he knew about the cheating ring. In fact, he had told his roommate Ralph Martin about the ring, and it was Martin who turned in Johnson's name. The Collins Board had no toleration for men like Johnson, who were B squad football players, and they did not believe him when he told them he had not cheated. Board members Collins, Irving, and Harrington judged that if a football player knew about the ring he was himself guilty. In fact, their approach was to question the roommates of football players to determine if they could incriminate the player; then they would call in the football man and confront him with evidence he could not refute. Johnson had admitted his knowledge of the cheating, and the Collins Board convicted him of "guilty knowledge." Martin was allowed to remain, claiming he had only heard from Johnson the week the investigation became known in late May 1951.

But Bill Johnson had none of Bill Jackomis's fire to prove himself. He just wanted to get away from everything associated with West Point. His father practically coerced him into enrolling in another school, and he went immediately to Rutgers University in late August 1951. He got himself into a fraternity there and wound up spending too much time with the modern Greeks rather than the classics. He left Rutgers after a semester and enrolled in the Air Force Aviation Cadet Program, a nine-month course that produced commissioned officer pilots. In 1953 he went to Korea and flew the F-86 fighter in combat for the 330th Fighter Interceptor Squadron.

Bill's good friend from L-2 Company, Fred Jones, had several offers of football scholarships when it became known that he was leaving among the honor victims. He wanted to play football at the University of Oklahoma, but coach Bud Wilkinson was not allowed to let Jones play because the Big Eight Conference had declared that all expelled cadets would have a year's eligibility taken away. Wilkinson offered to take Jones into the university's program as an assistant coach.

Meanwhile, Jones heard that the Skelly Oil Company provided special awards to young men with demonstrated leadership potential to attend the University of Tulsa Petroleum Engineering School. Two conditions went with the scholarship: The student had to meet regularly with Mr. Skelly himself in a mentorship program, and upon graduation he had to work for Skelly Oil. Jones was approached by a representative of the company and took him up on the offer to study petroleum engineering at the University of Tulsa. Jones was allowed to play football there and played for their nationally ranked Gator Bowl team. He also joined the Air Force ROTC program.

Jones scored among the highest on all of his Air Force aptitude tests; in fact the officer in charge accused him of cheating, his scores were so high. Jones was branded among students and faculty as one of the "cheaters" from West Point, but he endured the censure and graduated as student commander of the Air Force ROTC at Tulsa. He went to work for Skelly but soon was called to active duty by the Air Force. Jones was not interested in becoming a pilot, and he hoped the Air Force would exploit his degree and training in petroleum engineering. Instead they sent him off to electronics officer school in Biloxi, Mississippi, at Keesler Air Force Base.

To his dismay, his commander there turned out to be the same officer who had been Jones's company tactical officer at West Point. Jones's former tac was an Air Force officer at the academy and found himself running the electronics school for the Air

Force at the air base at Keesler. He told Jones he would be in big trouble if he did not play football for the base football team. He wanted Jones to delay his graduation from electronics school so the Keesler team could have a shot at the armed forces championship that year. But Jones did not really want to play football, he wanted to graduate with his class and get on to his military service so he could perform his duty, then return to his now very promising career in the petroleum industry for Skelly Oil. Jones did not play at Keesler and found himself assigned to a remote station in the Far East after graduation. To this day, Jones is convinced that the assignment was his former tac's retribution for refusing to play football for the base team.

Jones reported initially to Korea, but after the armistice he was reassigned to Tokyo and became the head of maintenance and engineering for a secret electronics outfit working out of a remote base in Misawa, Japan. His airplanes led the entire Far East Command in operational readiness, and he actually enjoyed playing football for the Japan team in the interservice football competition. In fact, Misawa won the Far East championship in 1953. When his time was up, Fred Jones returned to Tulsa, expecting to work again for Skelly Oil.

WHEN YE SUFFER FOR RIGHTEOUSNESS SAKE

Jim Pfautz was an unhappy cadet. He had resented the role that Colonel Harkins had beguiled him into serving. He had done it anyway because he believed it was the right thing to do. Afterward, when he saw how many lives were shattered by the Collins Board, he positively hated the way the commandant had deceived him into believing that things would turn out all right for everyone. It certainly did not turn out all right for the eighty-three men who had to leave. Pfautz was convinced that many of them were outright cheaters and deserved to be court-martialed for what they had done, but not all those guys were in the same category. Harkins just threw them all out, and that was not fair. The system was at fault for many of those guys, and in some cases it was the faculty that was asleep at the wheel, aiding and abetting the cheating. It should not have been the cadets who took the blame all by themselves. But that is what the academy had said, and the Army agreed. Everything at West Point was okay; there was something wrong with these men, not the system.

Many of them blamed him. Pfautz had been able to keep his role as informant hidden from all but those closest to him. But word got around. West had threatened his life; another classmate blamed Pfautz for the death of his mother, who had a heart attack at about the time she learned of her son's involvement in the cheating incident. One newspaper, referring to the informant without knowing his identity, called him "a judicious little prig."

Jim Pfautz kept his anger and resentment from making him bitter. He turned his energies to his swimming. He was very good at it his plebe year, and as a cow he set an academy record in the individual medley. In his senior year Pfautz broke more swimming records than any previous cadet had ever done. He was captain of Army's nationally competitive team, which ended its season with a record of six wins, four losses, and a tie. Pfautz went into the Air Force after he graduated and immediately went off to pilot school, then transitioned into jet fighters.

Jim Pfautz had carried the swimming team a long way from 1950, when he was a plebe and the team went 1–5. Jeffery Rich had been on that plebe team with Pfautz, but in December 1952, after his first semester of cow year, Rich was turned back to the Class of 1954 because of his grades in solids and in social sciences. He was not on Pfautz's winning squad of 1953, and he graduated as the last man in the Class of 1954.

Red Blaik found a release from the anxiety of the cheating incident in politics. He continued to encourage his mentor, General MacArthur, to make a real run for the Republican nomination and for the presidency in the 1952 election. In the fall of 1951 Blaik's attention was at least partially diverted from the enormous task of beginning to rebuild the Brave Old Army Team by the drawing room maneuvers required of a presidential campaign in the United States in the 1950s.

MacArthur did not declare his candidacy after his rousing speech to Congress in April, but he acted as if he were a candidate. After a congressional hearing on the stalemate in Korea he set off on a cross-country speaking tour filled with criticism of the Truman administration's handling of foreign affairs. It apparently had a pronounced effect on public support for Truman as the president began a slide in the polls from which he never recovered. In March 1952 MacArthur practically called Truman a Communist. Truman announced shortly after that he would not run for reelection.

MacArthur then was chosen to deliver the Republican convention keynote speech and began to direct his maneuvering against Dwight Eisenhower for the Republican nomination. Whoever won the GOP nomination in July would likely win the election in November. Blaik continued to encourage MacArthur to engage in the preconvention maneuvering needed to win, but if the general did want the nomination he did not heed the advice being offered from people such as Blaik. In fact, Blaik was serving as a go-between with MacArthur for the rival forces of Ohio Republican senator Robert Taft. Blaik never let his family political connections to his native Ohio wither away, and the Taft forces were working through the convention season trying to broker a MacArthur-Taft ticket if they could not manage a Taft-MacArthur billing. They used Blaik's good offices to keep open their lines of communication with the general.

In the primary season the voters clearly signaled their preference for Eisenhower. He won in New Hampshire and came in a close second to Harold Stassen in the Minnesota GOP race. MacArthur the crowd pleaser was not much of a vote getter. At the convention MacArthur and Taft had an opportunity to cut a last-minute deal and perhaps take the convention away from Eisenhower. Red Blaik was working party politics in New York City until well past midnight for the hopefuls, who never quite gave up trying to convince MacArthur to cut a deal with Taft. In the end no deal could be arranged and Eisenhower took the nomination and the presidency.

In the meantime Blaik "could not . . . coach with [his] normal enthusiasm, drive, and patience." The rebuilding of the Brave Old Army Team did not fully capture his attention in 1951. There were no returning lettermen, and they went 2–7. Rumors again abounded that he would resign, but he had signed a five-year contract in January 1951 and was determined to stick with it long enough to rebuild Army's football program to some level of respectability. When Army lost to Northwestern, 20–14, Vince Lombardi broke down and cried. The 1952 season was better at 4–4–1 and even Red Blaik allowed himself to be a little optimistic. In a dramatic end to a spectacular season, Army beat Navy 20–7 in 1953, with a team of mostly seniors that had been the same team to lose to the midshipmen 42–7 in 1951. The 1953 Army team ended the year at 7–1–1 and was picked as Eastern champions, winning the Lambert Trophy, and Blaik was selected by the Washington Touchdown Club as Coach of the Year. Blaik was offered the head coaching job of the New York Giants that year, but turned it down. The Giants then picked Lombardi as an assistant coach.

The 1954 Army team featured an explosive offense that presented equally capable threats from the running game and the passing of quarterback Peter Vann to receiver Don Holleder. By the end of the 1954 season Blaik's boys had fought their way back to the national rankings, with a season record of 7–2, and the Associated Press writers placed them seventh in the country. The only disappointment was the 27–20 defeat at the hands of Navy.

Don Holleder epitomized the spirit of the new Brave Old Army Team. He was not the nationally recruited star on the order of Davis and Blanchard, but by his junior year season in 1954 he was one of the country's best pass receivers. Holleder had to serve punishment tours, and he sat out the first two games of the 1954 season. He thus earned something of a dubious reputation with the Tactical Department, but he returned to lead the cadets to a first ranking in the national polls on offense by midseason.

But the next year, Army lost most of its starters to graduation, and Red Blaik moved Holleder from end to quarterback. He was terrible at the position, initially, mainly because the team as a whole was not nearly as competitive as it had been the previous two years. Everyone at the academy second-guessed Blaik's move putting Holleder in at quarterback, and Don himself came to Blaik at midseason intending to ask to be put back to his familiar position at end. But Blaik told Holleder that he was the quarter-back, that he had faith in the man even when no one else seemed to. Holleder responded with inspirational play to the end of the season, including an upset victory over heavily favored Navy.

Although Holleder had run into some disciplinary problems early in his cadet career, and struggled with academics, he had overcome doubts about his leadership to be appointed as company commander of M-2 in his senior year. A natural leader on the athletic field and in the Corps of Cadets, he went into the infantry and served with conspicuous distinction until being killed in combat in Vietnam. The building housing Army's basketball and hockey facilities, which some had wanted to name for Red Blaik, is today called Holleder Center.

Twenty-Four

The Wonder Years

Douglas MacArthur did not accept defeat well. He thought he should be president of the United States and believed he could maneuver his way into the position. Until he ran afoul of Harry Truman, MacArthur had never lost any campaign he had set out on, and even when temporary setbacks looked to others to be final, MacArthur always found a way to return. This time his defeat was no temporary setback. There would be no return, no alternative to defeat on the battlefield of politics.

Once Dwight Eisenhower was in office, MacArthur offered a foreign policy proposal that he claimed would bring about general world peace. He met with the president-elect in December 1952 and told Ike that he should deliver an ultimatum to Red China. MacArthur told Ike he should tell the Chinese to pull back out of Korea, and if they did not, then he would order nuclear bombs be dropped on North Korea and China, he would send the four-hundred-thousand-man Chinese Nationalist Army deep into Manchuria to surround the Chinese forces in Korea while attacking with U.S. troops from the south. Then, argued MacArthur to the man who twenty years earlier had been his aide, the president should insist on an amendment to the U.S. and Soviet Union constitutions that would outlaw war as a means of foreign policy. Eisenhower listened politely, then never again asked Mac-Arthur for advice.

The Korean War's end in July 1953 came too soon for Bill Johnson and Fred Jones to make it to the war zone. When Jones completed his tour as engineering officer at Misawa, his term of active duty service was up and although the commander of the Air Force in the Pacific asked him to stay, Jones decided to start his new career sooner rather than later. He had developed quite a reputation as a football player in the interservice leagues, and he even caught the eye of professional scouts. He played one season in the Canadian Football League before he came back to Oklahoma to pick up his engineering career where he had left it off. There he discovered better prospects for the future in the growing aerospace engineering field, so he left Skelly Oil to join a small new firm working on ramjets for the Air Force. His design skills advanced and he grew with the industry into nuclear propulsion design, small rockets for space flight controls—he built the attitude control engines for the Apollo service and lunar modules—and small jet engines that would eventually be used in secret advanced weapons being developed by the Air Force.

His good friend Bill Johnson found that Air Force service suited him well after all. Bill qualified for pilot training and made it into jet school, eventually winning an assignment at the 330th Fighter Interceptor Squadron. In 1956 he caught the attention of the commander of the Eastern Air Defense Command and was selected to be the general's aide. From 1956 to 1959 he served in the Eastern Air Defense Command and sometimes even flew transports out of Stewart Air Force Base in New York, just outside of West Point. From there, he occasionally flew the superintendent of the military academy on executive transport missions. After that assignment, in 1960, Johnson went back to an interceptor squadron until it was his turn to go to Vietnam in 1963.

The Army football team in 1956 was incurably bad. Earlier, Blaik had lost his superb line coach, Vince Lombardi, who went to be an assistant coach with the New York Giants in 1953. By 1956 Vince had become discouraged with the Giants and he called his old boss to ask if he could come back. Blaik tried to move fast; he needed something new to shore up the ailing cadet football program, but in the meantime, the Green Bay Packers offered Lombardi the job as head coach. The rest, as they say, is history.

Blaik needed Lombardi's toughness and fire. Army ball handlers committed forty fumbles in 1956. They even arrived late to the Navy game and were nearly locked out of the stadium. The 1957 team showed some promise with young players who would later become stars in the likes of Bill Carpenter, Pete Dawkins, and Bob Anderson. But 1957 was a disappointment despite Army's 7–2 record, because of losses to the Irish and the renewal of the rivalry with Notre Dame and Navy. Blaik may have been distracted by the fact that in 1956 Gar Davidson had taken over as superintendent of the Military Academy. Davidson had been head coach before Blaik and now as superintendent had particular ideas about the role of football at West Point, views that were not in consonance with Blaik's.

A GOOD PILOT

Bill Jackomis lost touch with Army football after graduating from Notre Dame and entering the Air Force. But he never was far from the reach of academy graduates who remembered him as one of the men dismissed for cheating. Even his flight instructor in jet school at Greenville, Mississippi, Air Force Base had known Jake at the academy.

Because Jake was a full year behind his ex-cadet colleagues, Bob Kendall, who graduated from West Point in 1952, was already completely flight-qualified and had seen combat in Korea. He was now an instructor pilot, and he was grading Jake in his check ride in a T-28 jet trainer.

Back at the academy Jake had wrestled Kendall in physical education class. In fact, Jake pinned him and got a superior grade. Jake worried throughout the entire flight school that Kendall would remember him. But Kendall never said a word about it during flight training, although he seemed to be giving Jake a hard time with his evaluations. He kept complaining that Jake's maneuvers in the cockpit were too slow. During Jake's final check ride in the jet, which would determine if he would qualify for assignment to high-performance aircraft, Kendall was silent as Jake went through his paces. At the end of the flight, Kendall finally acknowledged that he remembered all along who Jake was and that he had been one of the men dismissed for cheating. While they were still in the air and no one could overhear them— West Pointers were not supposed to be talking to any of the men who had been dismissed—Kendall asked how he was doing, then told him that he had passed with flying colors.

Bill Jackomis was a good pilot, one of the Air Force's better flyers, in fact. When he transitioned to the T-33 trainer for interceptor high performance flying at Williams Air Force Base in Arizona, he was one of the first to be allowed to fly solo. One of the final tests for interceptor training was to demonstrate the ability to fly in formation. For this exercise, one of those who had already qualified to fly solo took off first; then the instructor would teach the others how to approach and join up in a formation.

For his group's test, Jake was the only man who thus far qualified for solo flight, so the instructor told him to take off and circle to the left over the white water tanks until he arrived with the other student pilot. These water tanks were easily recognizable features in the normally clear blue skies around the training site at Kirtland Air Force Base in New Mexico; Jake had plenty of confidence he could handle this until the instructor arrived at his side. In fact, he had grown pretty proud of his flying skills by this time.

The only problem was that the weather had no respect for Jake's talents as a pilot, and by the time he had climbed to the designated altitude of four thousand feet and had reached the distance from the airfield that should have placed him over the tanks, an overcast had set in below him that completely prevented him from seeing anything on the ground. He did not see his instructor yet, so he figured he must not have quite reached the rally point, and he kept flying in his left turn but climbed to ten thousand feet, hoping to catch a glimpse of the ground through the occasional hole in the ceiling that appeared below. He was too proud to call out on the radio that he did not see the tanks.

Then he heard a call on his radio, "Jackomis, are you over the tanks yet? You should be here by now, but I don't see you." The instructor must already be there and I must have missed it, Jake thought. He dared not answer for at least a few seconds until he could get his bearings. He certainly did not want to tell the instructor that he was lost. He wasn't really lost anyway—not yet, at least. He started his descent, figuring at worst he had overshot a little and the turn would bring him back over the tanks at some point.

"Okay, Jackomis, I know you're there somewhere," crackled the voice again in his radio. "If you are circling at four thousand like you were supposed to then just drop down to three thousand through the clouds, at a hundred and eighty knots, and I'll pick you up." Jake continued to drop and turn, but by the time he reached 3,000 feet his airspeed indicator showed 350 knots.

Suddenly Jake heard a panicked voice in his headphones, "Break! Break!" As Jake broke through the overcast, there were the white tanks straight ahead. And there was his instructor's aircraft directly in front of him, obviously moving at only 180 knots. Jake's instructor pulled up out of his way and said only, "Now go home, Jackomis." Jake managed to recover from this one incident and in fact finished interceptor school as a top pilot.

Bill Jackomis was the number one graduate in his interceptor school class. But because he was not regular Air Force he had to wait to receive his first assignment until the West Point graduates and the distinguished military graduates first chose theirs from among the available stations. Then the Air Force parceled out the remaining assignments to the reservists, like Jake, who would serve for only three years full-time, then revert to weekend and summer duty for the rest of their careers. Jackomis drew an assignment as the adjutant at Scott Air Force Base in Illinois.

That was not very appealing, so he asked to be considered for an overseas job, figuring he at least should have a better shot at getting into a cockpit on foreign duty. An added benefit was that he would go overseas without the new wife he had just married, not that he wanted to get away from her, but for a married man an unaccompanied tour for one year counted toward his service obligation as if it were a three-year tour. That meant that when his overseas assignment was over he could leave the Air Force. His plan then was to return to work for Du Pont, since they were holding his management position open for him until he completed his military service.

The Air Force sent him orders to Resolution Island, a remote site inside the Arctic Circle and the nearest land base to the North Pole, to be personnel officer. Jake figured the assignments officer must have been a West Pointer who found out Jake had been thrown out for cheating. He could not believe what the Air Force was doing to him, wasting all that flight training to send him to be a personnel officer. He decided he had sufficient grounds to make a complaint to the base inspector general. He figured the worst that could happen to him was that he would be thrown out of flight school, and that had already happened to him once. They certainly could not find a worse assignment to send him to than Resolution Island.

When he walked into the IG's office he tossed his pilot's wings on the colonel's desk and told him that even the guys who washed out from pilot school got better assignments than that, so why should he bother to keep his wings? Was there someone at Air Force headquarters out to get him because he was a newlywed? The IG was sympathetic to Jake's plea and managed to get him posted to Northeastern Air Defense Command to be the personnel officer for the interceptor squadron at Goose Bay, Labrador. But it would still be a nonrated job, one in which he would have to fly a desk.

Jackomis figured there was no way the Air Force was going to give him a flying assignment, so he gave the IG his signed resignation from the service. The IG told him the service would not accept his resignation and that Jake would have to go where they told him to go, but he would try one more time to get him a better assignment. He came back with a three-year accompanied tour to Harmon Air Force Base in Newfoundland, where there was an interceptor squadron, but he simply could not get him into a rated pilot's slot. Those were all taken by the West Pointers and indefinite reservists (officers from among the highest ROTC graduates). Jake accepted his fate; it sure beat the North Pole, and at least he would have his wife along with him for the three years. Maybe in that time he could work his way over to a flying job.

At Harmon, conditions were austere; in Bill Jackomis's judgment, they might as well have been at the North Pole. The first thing he had to do was find a place to live, which was not an easy thing to do in Stevenville, Newfoundland, the nearest town to the base. There was no base housing for junior officers, so Jake took all the money he had saved, about twenty-five hundred dollars, and bought a used thirty-six-foot house trailer. It was just as well that it was small, since they had no furniture to move into the place.

And there was no heater. He had bought the trailer from a technical sergeant who was leaving the base to go back to the States with his family. It was in pretty good shape, but the heater that had come with the unit was incapable of protecting humans from the frigid Arctic cold, so the sergeant had rigged up a fifty-five-gallon drum and some pipes that fed heating oil into a large furnace that provided central heating for the entire trailer. Things would stay toasty warm for the Jackomis family all winter.

Their thirty-six feet were cramped but cozy for Bill and his wife. Their daughter was born in Stevenville that first year, and they needed more space than the trailer could ever provide. But Bill had no money for a bigger place, and he still did not qualify for on-base housing. He decided he would build an extension on the side of the trailer; he certainly had plenty of free time for carpentry, since his duties as personnel officer left plenty of off-duty time for that sort of thing. Jake borrowed a truck from an Army detachment on base and drove up to the top of a mountain where the Air Force had just finished building a radar shack. There he knew he would find plenty of salvageable lumber, insulation, and even roofing materials for his project, and he hauled a truckload down to his trailer. The only shortcoming in his ambition was that he had never built anything before. Eventually he completed construction of a living room and an entryway the entire length of the trailer. The Jackomis family then used the rest of the trailer as bedrooms and were indeed quite proud of their humble home. It withstood the weather the entire three years there, and when they left to return to the States Jake sold the place to another Air Force officer for six thousand dollars.

It did not take long for Jake to work his way into a flying job either. After about six months of plugging away at the administrative chores that came his way as squadron adjutant, the commanding officer of the 61st Fighter Interceptor Squadron, Lt. Col. Phillip Parr, could sense that Jake was itching to fly. He figured the man was probably a pretty good pilot in school, but would he be able to withstand the rigors of a real-live interceptor squadron?

Those rigors were very real. The mission of the 61st Fighter Interceptor Squadron was to fly up to and shoot down Soviet bombers that were on their way to drop nuclear bombs on American cities. There would not be much time left to accomplish this by the time the Soviets reached Harmon Air Force Base. The 61st's state-of-the-art F-89 fighters were armed with 104 2.75-inch rockets. Their tactic was to roll down on the bombers from above and release all their rockets at once into the Soviet formation, which intelligence told them would probably be six airplanes. If that did not stop the bombers, they were to ram them with their F-89s. A pilot would be a small but honorable sacrifice to save an entire city from nuclear annihilation.

Time was so critical that the squadron always kept two aircraft on strip alert, with the pilots suited up and in the cockpit, ready to launch. Four other aircraft would be in the hangar with pilots ready to run out and crew chiefs standing by to start them up and get them on their way. The entire first flight of six aircraft had to be airborne within two minutes or the Soviet bombers would be out of range of the F-89s. Not only did the interceptors have to catch up to the bombers, they also had to make up altitude rapidly to reach the Soviets, who probably would be flying at upwards of thirty-five thousand feet. And that burned up a lot of fuel in the F-89, which was one of the first operational aircraft to have an afterburner on its engine exhaust to give it far greater acceleration than a conventional jet engine.

A HEAVY TOLL

The strip alert, the constant training, the frequent readiness drills, and the not infrequent Soviet bomber attempts to penetrate North American air space took a high toll on the pilots of the 61st FIS. In fact, the 61st had developed a reputation in the Air Force, by the time Jake got on to flight status there in 1955, as one of the worst in the service. They were losing on average a pilot every three months to fatal crashes of aircraft. Everyone attributed their record to the combination of the intensity of the duty with the really crappy weather there, and meteorological conditions that combined the worst of mountains and ocean to produce frequent precipitation and nearly constant overcast. But the Air Force could not afford to lose pilots at the rate the 61st was losing them, and when the loss rate went up to two pilots every three months, equating to eight pilots per year, every pilot's chance of surviving his three-year assignment to Harmon went down to zero. Colonel Parr had his flight surgeon look into possible physical causes to recommend action the commander could take to ease the burden of the duty.

The flight surgeon quickly discovered a more simple reason for the crashes than stress and weather, one that the commander could readily affect. He noted that most of the crashes were occurring in the morning hours among unmarried pilots. Most of the pilots at Harmon were single. They lived in the bachelor officers' quarters. When the surgeon observed their living habits he learned that for breakfast they subsisted on a cup of coffee and a doughnut. The result of this habit was that when they got up, they gulped down their coffee and doughnut on the way to the flight line; by the time they were airborne they were alert and energetic from a sugar-and-caffeine jolt. But a couple of hours later, when they were ready to return to base, their body metabolisms had slowed to accommodate the rapid drop in sugar level just when the pilots needed more energy for their landing approaches or during their intercept missions. The 61st was losing pilots because they did not eat a decent breakfast.

Parr ordered his executive officer, Major Newcomb, to open up a snack bar in the BOQ to serve breakfast to all pilots. Newcomb hired local "Newfies" to operate a grill and served ham and eggs with pancakes every morning. He even turned a profit on the operation by charging the pilots out of their Air Force food allowance for the service. Parr ordered them all to eat every morning. He also called in all the base wives and told them that if they wanted their husbands to come home alive every day, to make sure they got a good morning meal before sending them to the base. To this day, Bill Jackomis has a hearty breakfast every morning, served up by his wife whenever he is at home.

The squadron practiced frequently, both the interception and the shooting parts of their mission. Jake sat many a cold winter morning in the cramped cockpit of his fighter jet, warmed by the heating tube fed into the half-opened canopy. The tube led down into the floor so his feet and legs toasted while his head froze. He could often see the contrails of U.S. B-47s on practice runs up to the Soviet border. After turning parallel to the Soviet Union for a time to test the Communists' defenses, the B-47s would return to the United States and overfly the interceptor bases to give them practice in scrambling to meet an incoming bomber.

Jake nearly shot down a B-47 in one of these drills. The procedure for the exercise was that a radar in the Distant Early Warning (DEW) system would alert the interceptors to an incoming flight. At Harmon Air Force Base the radar station was known to the pilots as "Pinetree X," and it was somewhere up in northern Canada. It was up to the pilots to get airborne and make the identification of friend or foe before engaging their targets or breaking off from friendly B-47s. The B-47s were given the radio frequency to contact the 61st so that they could talk to the interceptor pilots as well. The big bombers had enough radios to be able to keep one tuned to the fighters' assigned frequency, while the interceptor squadron would have retune to switch to the bombers' frequency. It was the bomber crews' job to call the interceptors to make sure they had made the identification as friendly and break off the rocket run.

During one drill in particular it almost went badly for one U.S. bomber crew. Jake sat on strip alert that day and watched the contrails of a flight of B-47s make their way north toward the Soviet Union. He figured they would be back in time for the end of his shift and, sure enough, he could see the white streaks off in the distance on this particularly clear day before the radar alert even came from Pinetree X. The order to scramble came, and ground control intercept gave Jake his vector, clearing him to intercept for positive identification. Standing orders for the interceptor squadron were, of course, that once a pilot made positive identification of an enemy bomber he was cleared to fire, since there was no time to get another pilot to confirm his identification, and no other way to do it in those days.

When Jake got to an altitude above the bombers he could see clearly that they were B-47s, and he waited for the radioman to call him on the 61st's radio frequency to wave him off. The call did not come, and Jake continued to shadow the flight of six big bombers from about five thousand feet above them. He reached a point where he had either to get them on the radio or go back to the base without contacting them, which would have been technically a violation of intercept procedure. Jake had no idea what their frequency was, so he tried a different tactic to get their attention.

"GCI, this is Typhoon One-seven, request firing pass on six bogeys, look like Bears," Jake said into his own radio.

"Check ID again," was the response from his ground control intercept operator.

"Roger, I have a clear view down low, request firing pass."

This time there was no response from GCI. Jake could see them in his mind, scrambling to look up the B-47s' radio frequency to tell them to come up on the intercept frequency because there is this guy up there who will do exactly what he says he'll do and doesn't always wait for instructions to take aggressive action.

Jake called again to his controller, "I'm on approach to the bogies now, they're at my twelve, request firing pass." If they were listening to him now and playing games with him, Jake had just told them that he was directly in front of them and ready to drop down in altitude, head straight for their noses, and unload his rockets their way.

"Negative! Negative!" came the frantic voice in his earpiece, obviously not belonging to anyone in the 61st, as Jake blew right by the bombers without firing a shot except with his saluting hand as he went by.

Occasionally Jake's flying would not be so adventuresome. He would take the executive officer up to give him enough stick time to keep his flight rating. Holcomb was in his forties, had been an outstanding combat pilot, but was now reaching the end of his physical ability to fly a high-performance airplane. Jake would fly rear seat in a T-33 trainer for Holcomb whenever the major wanted to pilot the aircraft. These were pleasant flights for Jake, who looked forward to the time just to relate to Holcomb, who had a kind of grandfatherly affection for all the young pilots in the squadron.

At the end of one of these flights, however, Jake had the unhappy chore of landing the aircraft for the major. The final approach to Harmon Air Force Base was always difficult. You had to begin your descent at twenty thousand feet altitude at four thousand feet per minute to fly around the two mountains that guarded the approach to the single runway there. In the descent, you had to take an easy right turn until the mountains were visible, then roll into the final approach, turning along the way to avoid the terrain. On this flight, visibility was low, but Holcomb and Jackomis knew the pattern well enough to feel comfortable taking the sleek T-33 up. On the landing approach, however, Jake was distraught when Holcomb failed to pull up from the descent after going through minimum altitude of four thousand feet still in the fog. He called to the exec, "Major Holcomb! Major Holcomb!" but there was no response. Jake looked ahead and saw his pilot's head slumped over the control panel; he obviously had passed out.

Jake grabbed the stick and rather than finish the landing, not knowing exactly where the mountains were, he climbed up out of the weather back to twenty thousand feet and shot the approach again. He hoped that Holcomb would come to and feel up to making the landing himself and no one would be the wiser. But Holcomb never did wake up on that flight. Jake made the landing and called the control tower for an ambulance. After they took Holcomb away, Jake learned that the exec had been carrying a nervous disorder for some time and was hoping to get a few more flying hours in to make it to permanent flight status so he could draw flight pay for the rest of his career. Holcomb did recover but he did not make it back to fly, and Jake never saw Holcomb again.

SOME PLAYED PRO FOOTBALL

Even from far north in Canada, Jake was able to watch the exploits of some of their other former classmates. By 1956 two former Army football players who had been dismissed in the cheating incident made the big time in the National Football League. Jackson surpassed the potential that Blaik had seen in him as a yearling playing for Army. He played in the 1950s for the Washington Redskins and the Baltimore Colts, then in 1958 Jackson played for Lombardi at Green Bay.

Gene Filipski made it to the NFL championships. In 1955 he played halfback, running behind Lombardi's blockers for the New York Giants. He was outstanding for the Giants, gaining eighty-five yards rushing, thirty-seven yards receiving, and returning kickoffs for a total of 390 yards in his first year as a pro.

Flip had his fifteen minutes of glory at the end of a stellar 1956 season with New York. He scored a touchdown rushing during the Giants' 8–3–1 regular season and nearly doubled his yardage total that year, but his greatest contribution was the tone he set for the NFL championship game at Yankee Stadium against the Chicago Bears. Gene Filipski ran the opening kickoff back fifty-three yards to the Chicago thirty-eight, and four plays later took the ball in for the Giants' first score as they rolled on to a 47–7 victory to win football's top crown.

Red Blaik may not have noticed the performances of his former players because he was enjoying the fruits of success in his rebuilding efforts at Army. He had a good backfield in the persons of yearling Bob Anderson and second classman Pete Dawkins. In 1957 Anderson broke Glenn Davis's rushing record by more than fifty yards by running up a total of 983 yards rushing for the season. That year West Point and Notre Dame renewed their home-and-away series, but Army's lack of depth resulted in Army giving up a third-quarter two-touchdown lead to lose to the Irish, 23–21.

Blaik placed the blame for this loss squarely on the reforms in recruiting that had been instituted by Superintendent Davidson, reducing the number of recruited football players Blaik's coaches could bring in under unfilled appointments to the academy.

Actually Davidson did not reduce the total number of athletic appointments; he told Blaik that as athletic director he had to distribute the appointments proportionately among all varsity intercollegiate sports, in effect cutting the number that went to football players to about two dozen. Given historical attrition rates, Blaik argued in his response to the supe, that would result in fewer than half a dozen quality players who would make it through Beast, plebe year, and yearling academics to become solid Army football team players. Davidson said that was the policy and that Blaik had to implement it.

The 1958 season was quite promising if Army's players could stay healthy. Dawkins was the paragon of West Point virtue: He was elected president of his class, he was selected by the Tactical Department to be the first captain, and he was an outstanding football player who would win the Heisman Trophy. Because of his all-round superiority he was awarded a Rhodes scholarship and went to Oxford after graduating from West Point. For the 1958 football season Blaik had developed another very special player who would play a new role, capitalizing on this man's special talents.

In considering how to set up Army's offense for 1958, Blaik had to deal with the problem of a lack of depth in his line and the continued lack of a superior passer at quarterback. His inspired solution was to return to an old football strategy known as the far flanker, in which the end set wide. This would give him several steps ahead of the pass rush or before the backfield blockers could come in to make their move for a reception. In 1958, Army would add to the old far flanker strategy two twists that would make the innovation the rival of the two-platoon system or the T formation that Army had advanced for football in previous years.

The far flanker would set up very far on the flank—so far, in fact, that the defensive end would dare not risk pulling out to block him and the defensive backfield would have no idea which way he might run his pass pattern. The other twist came to Blaik as he realized that he had the end so far out on the flank that he would use up precious time on the clock and energy in the end going back and forth from the huddle. Blaik developed a set of secret signals that permitted the Army team to call the play without the end ever coming to the huddle. That not only saved time, it also took time away from the defense in setting up their formation from scrimmage. To run this new offense, Blaik needed a big, fast man with a lot of brains. That was Bill Carpenter, who would earn the title role in what became Army's "lonely end" offense.

It worked. Army was undefeated that year, failing to win only against Pittsburgh, who fought Army to a 14–14 tie. The Brave Old Army Team was ranked third in the nation for the 1958 season and was invited to the Cotton Bowl for post-season play. Blaik had always opposed playing in bowl games; he felt it was too much for his players to keep up with their studies during first semester term-end exams while preparing for the rigors of a New Year's Day bowl game. Besides, he felt that playing in a postseason contest would diminish the importance of the Army–Navy game, something he did not wish to see happen to the nation's greatest football rivalry.

But at the beginning of the 1958 season, some of the players sensed that they might get a bid to a big bowl game, and Dawkins asked Blaik on behalf of the team if he would consent to them accepting this time if they were invited to the Cotton Bowl. Blaik relented and promised the players that he would accept if they were invited. As the season drew to a close the Cotton Bowl selection committee inquired of Blaik if Army would consider a bid this year, and Blaik told them he would. But ten days before bowl bids were to be announced, the superintendent issued a directive that stated that Army would not accept any bowl bid. The move prompted Blaik to complain that "Old coaches never die, they just write directives." When the bid came, Blaik took it to the Athletic Board, which voted to accept it, but the superintendent's policy made it a moot point.

COACH BLAIK RETIRES
At the end of the 1958 season, Blaik took warm satisfaction in the fact that he had rebuilt the Brave Old Army Team back to what it once had been, a nationally competitive program. But he was get-

ting sick more frequently with West Point's bitter winters, and he was losing more policy battles than he was winning under Gar Davidson. The final blow came for Blaik when Davidson approved a staff recommendation to split the position of athletic director from that of head football coach. Davidson was genuinely convinced that football had grown to dominate the academy's programs and that a new balance needed to be struck with other sports and activities. Blaik had always believed, even during his Dartmouth days, that football was the most important sport in the nation and that it was the one contest that most closely prepared men for combat. It was clear that there could be no compromise with Davidson.

When an offer came from his old Ohio friend and political mentor Victor Emmanuel to come to Avco Corporation as an executive, Blaik decided that the time was ripe to leave. He spent December getting his assistant coaches' contracts renewed. Then he discussed his plans with his family and made his final decision in early January. On 13 January 1959 he walked into Superintendent Davidson's office and submitted his resignation. The Red Blaik era of Army football, which had spanned seventeen seasons, was over.

Blaik had become one of football's greatest innovators and was one of its toughest taskmasters. His record at Army was 121 wins, 32 losses (7 of them coming in the postcheating incident season of 1951), and 10 ties. His record against Navy was 8 wins, 8 losses, and 2 ties. Red Blaik is still the winningest coach in the history of Army football.

He did not fade away from public service after his retirement. He made some money and tried to join with a group of investors to buy a professional football team. That did not work out, but his generosity continues today with large gifts to worthy causes from his family estate. He answered the call of politics when President John F. Kennedy asked him to help when the dispute between the Amateur Athletic Union and the National Collegiate Athletic Association late in 1962 nearly ruined amateur sports in America. Blaik worked as a behind-the-scenes assistant to Douglas MacArthur as the general forced the feuding sides to work out a compromise in a marathon weekend negotiating session just before the 1964 Olympic trials season opened. In 1963 Blaik served on a panel of dignitaries dispatched by President Kennedy to Birmingham, Alabama, to help resolve racial disputes there in an attempt to avoid sending in federal troops.

MacArthur did not fade away from the Brave Old Army Team either. From his Waldorf Astoria apartment he kept up his correspondence with Blaik on the joys and tribulations of the team. Blaik frequently brought game films over and patiently heard the old man out when he offered his advice on how to improve the team's performance.

When Douglas MacArthur came to West Point in May 1962 to receive the Thayer Award for service to the country reflecting the principles of duty, honor, and country, there was no question as to the source of the powerful force that had made West Point what it had become. Douglas MacArthur had shaped the academy's very definition of integrity at his congressional testimony on hazing back in 1899; he had created its honor system as superintendent in 1918; he had imparted to Red Blaik the dictum that "there is no substitute for victory" during the war years and now he presented a benediction on the values of West Point that would ring true into the twenty-first century.

MacArthur's "Duty, Honor, Country" speech in accepting the Thayer Award remains the most eloquent expression of what West Point should be:

> Duty, honor, country: Those three hallowed words reverently dictate what you ought to be, what you can be, what you will be. They are your rallying point to build courage when courage seems to fail, to regain faith when there seems to be little cause for faith, to create hope when hope becomes forlorn. . . .
>
> Yours is the profession of arms, the will to win, the sure knowledge that in war there is no substitute for victory, that if you lose, the nation will be destroyed, that the very obsession of your public service must be duty, honor, country. . . .
>
> The Long Gray Line has never failed us. Were it to do so,

a million ghosts in olive drab, in brown khaki, in blue and gray would rise from their white crosses, thundering those magic words: duty, honor, country. . . .

In my dreams I again hear the crash of guns, the rattle of musketry, the strange, mournful mutter of the battlefield. But in the evening of my memory always I come back to West Point. Always there echoes and reechoes: duty, honor, country.

Today marks my final roll call with you, but I want you to know that, when I cross the river, my last conscious thoughts will be of the Corps, and the Corps, and the Corps.

I bid you farewell.

It has become the most inspired description of West Point and its values. One of MacArthur's biographers, William Ganoe, wrote that if Sylvanus Thayer was the father of West Point, then MacArthur was its savior. Red Blaik believed it was so. He joined the entire nation in mourning the death of his mentor on 5 April 1964 and helped Robert Kennedy upstage President Johnson at MacArthur's Washington funeral motorcade. The general had taught Blaik well.

Twenty-Five

Fight On to Victory

After three years of enduring the cold and hazardous flying conditions of Harmon Air Force Base, Bill Jackomis was reassigned to Suffolk Air Force Base on Long Island, New York, to the 52d Fighter Group. Jake was a very good pilot and while he was on Long Island managed to transition to rotary wing aircraft after learning how to fly helicopters. His squadron's primary mission was airborne search and rescue.

On one occasion, several convicts escaped from the famous "Sing Sing" prison in Ossining, New York, and the air base was called on to help provide search assistance. The helicopters on Long Island were there for search and rescue duty, so they were quite well suited to the task of looking for escaped convicts. Jake went out on this mission, figuring it would provide some real mission experience without someone shooting back at him. Well into the flight his helicopter developed mechanical problems and he had to cut its engines and crash-land it in a clearing in the midst of a large wooded area, using a technique known to helicopter pilots as "autorotation," in which the momentum of the blades continues to provide a little bit of aerodynamic lift as the bird circles to the ground. It is a very difficult maneuver for a pilot to execute, since it requires great physical strength and an exquisite sense of timing. For Bill Jackomis it was a lot like taking a toss from the quarterback on an option play. He saved his aircraft and walked away from it without a scratch. The crooks got away.

Bill had another close call later in a navigation training mission, leading a flight of three on a long flight to practice skills required for long-distance flight. Once or twice a year the squadron would fly north into Canada to a remote small base near a town called Bagotville. The challenge was not only in finding the way to Bagotville, but once there the Canadian forces and air controllers, as did all the local population, spoke only French. The squadron was to rest overnight, then fly back to Suffolk via different individual routes to recovery fields elsewhere in and around New York State.

Bill's flight was the second to leave in a timed departure sequence for the trip north and was to recover at Hancock Field, near Syracuse, New York. The weather was good, and when they reached their assigned altitude of thirty-seven thousand feet they took up their heading and relaxed a little. After about an hour Jake realized that his magnetic compass had been drifting and was now forty-five degrees off true north. He had no idea how long it had been drifting, but he knew he was far from where he was supposed to be and probably far west of Bagotville. He estimated that they should be somewhere near Montreal and ought to be able to pick up their air control tower to get their bearings and regain their course.

The only trouble was that part of the training for the mission was to maintain radio listening silence the whole way to touchdown at Bagotville. They would automatically fail the mission if he tried to raise Montreal. He looked up the Montreal approach frequency and dialed it but heard nothing. Jake decided they had been flying north long enough and had probably flown beyond Montreal, so he told his flight to turn back south. He then broke radio silence himself and began trying to raise Montreal tower on "guard" frequency, which was reserved to all pilots for in-flight emergencies. He heard nothing from Montreal.

By this time they were low on fuel. They had exhausted their wing tanks and were now burning up their last ninety-five gallons in the rear tank. That did not leave much time to find a runway to land on. And now clouds had rolled in under them and they had no way of locating an emergency field to land on. Jake decided it was time to declare an emergency and get some help. He had no idea that his radio was indeed working, he was transmitting loud and clear. Montreal was responding, and the entire squadron, now on the ground in Bagotville, was listening to the entire episode. But no one could talk to Jake; his radio was not receiving at all.

"May day, May day," spoke Jake calmly into his microphone, hoping that someone out there could hear his declaration of emergency. "I am at thirty-seven thousand feet on a heading of one-eight-oh magnetic, am out of fuel. Can someone come up and guide me in?"

No response.

Jake called on the intercom to his backseat man and told him to tighten his chute and be prepared to eject.

"May day, May day, this is Angels three-seven. We are coming down to lower altitude to look for an airfield." Jake looked at the approach maps for Montreal and saw that the minimum initial approach altitude was forty-five hundred feet. He told his front seat, "We'll go down to forty-five hundred and if we haven't broken out of the weather we'll just climb back up till flameout, then slow to one-three-five knots and punch out."

Meanwhile, the entire Northeastern Search and Rescue system was looking for him. As he descended, they could all hear Jake call out his altitude: "ten, nine, seven, four thousand feet . . ." Suddenly Jake was through the cloud cover and he could see in front of him over at about three o'clock a C-47 dropping its wheels. He knew that it must be on short final approach and there had to be an airport close by. Jake's T-33 was still moving faster than the lumbering transport, so he pulled under and in front of him. All the while the C-47 pilot was screaming at him on the approach frequency, but of course Jake was oblivious to it all. Jake landed, and as he taxied toward the apron, just under the control tower itself, his engine flamed out with the last drop of fuel in his system. He read the location on a sign on the hangar, "Syracuse." He climbed out, walked into the tower building, and called back to Long Island. They already knew what had happened.

The investigation cleared Jake, and in fact he had done a nifty job of dead reckoning in his navigation. In October 1959 Jackomis was cited for a daring rescue of two downed crew members from an F-101B that had plunged into the stormy waters off Montauk Point, Long Island. Despite heavy winds and high seas, which exceeded the flight envelope of his H-19 helicopter, Jackomis braved the elements and managed to save the pilot of the jet. Bill continued as a senior instructor pilot to the end of his second three-year tour. When his assignment at Long Island was complete, Jackomis applied for the new astronaut program and was selected to be among the first group of men to enter that very special training program.

Jackomis did not make the final cut to be with that first group of astronauts; instead he went on to get a graduate degree in aerospace engineering from the Air Force Institute of Technology. In fact, Jake took so well to the program of study that he completed a doctoral dissertation and won his Ph.D. while he was at Oklahoma State University working on his masters. For his graduate engineering project Jackomis developed an award-winning design for a new solid rocket motor thrust control. The Air Force then sent him to its secret weapons laboratory in the desert in the Southwest, where he was test director for two nuclear weapons underground test detonations.

In 1964 Jackomis received a most unusual letter. It was from the Notre Dame University president, Father Cavanaugh, informing him that the anonymous donor who had provided him the scholarship to Notre Dame in 1951 was none other than Joseph P. Kennedy. Ted Kennedy, while recovering from a nearly fatal airplane crash during a campaign trip, was editing a book of reminiscences about his father. Would Jackomis be so kind as to write a letter of a page or two in length telling what it meant to him to have received the scholarship so that Ted could put it into the book he was preparing for his family's use?

Jake could not believe it. Joseph Kennedy had been his benefactor at Notre Dame. Jake wondered why one of the wealthiest men in America had taken an interest in the plight of those cadets so many years ago. Jake wrote the letter and sent it off. Others wrote, too. *The Fruitful Bough* was published by Ted Kennedy in September 1965 to memorialize his father. Ray Bara's letter was the only one Kennedy chose to publish, and it was representative of all the expressions of gratitude. Ted Kennedy inscribed a copy of the book for Bill Jackomis on 6 September 1965.

By the mid-1960s Jackomis was in Southeast Asia, flying combat missions in support of operations in Vietnam. He was based in Udorn, Thailand, and saw more than a hundred hours of combat flying in his one-year tour. Mostly he flew the AC-130 gunship in support of ground troops. But he also managed to qualify himself in the F-4 Phantom jet fighter, and on one mission he shot down a North Vietnamese MiG fighter that came up to take them on, although the kill could not be officially confirmed and credited.

He returned from the Vietnam War in 1970, and was assigned to an Air Force laboratory directing classified experimental work. His lab was visited by the commanding general of Air Force Systems Command, who was stationed at another air base. It was a command review visit, the kind that made or broke the careers of the officers conducting the kind of research Jackomis was heading. These inspections were in fact elaborate briefings, where the visiting general and his entourage were briefed by the scientists and their lab directors on the status of their various research programs. It was at this briefing that Bill Jackomis met the man he was convinced had turned him in for cheating at West Point.

The lights were down so that all could see the slides being presented on the projection screen and the briefing had been under way for some time when Lieutenant Colonel Jackomis gave his pitch on the project, which was then highly classified and even now remains under a cloak of secrecy. He was the final briefer, and the lights came up as he finished. The general had no questions, rose from his seat, and turned to leave. Immediately Jake caught the eye of the general's executive officer in the back of the room, and he could see a countenance of concern come over the lieutenant colonel—it was Jim Pfautz. Jackomis signaled to Pfautz on his way to his place at the general's side and stopped to speak to his former classmate. "I need to talk to you before you leave this room," said Pfautz. "Stick around for a minute."

"Okay," Bill replied. Jake had heard the rumors that Pfautz had been one of the informants who had turned in some names of the cheaters. They had been classmates in neighboring companies and lived just a few divisions apart in old south barracks. But Jake had no idea who had turned his name in because once the Collins Board got started, several men turned in names. Jake figured he would never know, and it did not matter anymore because he was getting on with his Air Force career just fine without the knowledge. He wanted his Air Force colleagues to know him as a good pilot, and that was working out so far. Even those who knew him from the academy, such as Kendall, could warm up to him because of his flying abilities. Jake had no desire to get into it with Pfautz because he would rather not draw any further attention to his status as a former cadet. If Pfautz wanted to make something of that, Jake was determined to make it difficult for him to do so and avoid any public altercation with the general's aide.

For his part, Jim Pfautz did not even know Bill Jackomis at West Point and now only vaguely recalled him as one of the men who had resigned after the Collins Board hearings. This was the first time they had met face to face, and Pfautz had no inkling of what Jackomis might do in front of his boss. Would Jackomis jump up and accuse Pfautz in public of being a mole, a squealer, or a rat? To Jim Pfautz the only thing more odious than a cheater was a squealer. He still felt angry at Colonel Harkins for putting him in the untenable dilemma during the cheating scandal, but Jim still could not figure any respectable way out other than to choose the harder right* as he had done back in 1951.

After the briefing, Jake discovered he had it all wrong about Pfautz's motivation to speak to him.

---

*The Cadet Prayer in Pfautz's and Jackomis's day was replete with entreaties to God on behalf of the honor system, including the line "Help us choose the harder right instead of the easier wrong, and never to be content with a half truth when the whole can be won."

"Jake, I know that you must hate me because you probably think I turned you in to the commandant back at West Point," said the man with the general, "but I want you to know that I had no choice in what I did."

So who turned my name in? wondered Jake.

"I wouldn't blame you for taking a poke at me," said Pfautz with an evident look of concern. "I want you to know that ever since that June Week of 1951, I have felt betrayed by Colonel Harkins, the commandant. He put me in the position of either informing on Davidson or being thrown out myself for toleration, just as he did to one of my classmates earlier who refused to serve as an informant. I turned Davidson in; the others started adding names to the list."*

Bill Jackomis could not believe what he had just heard. He had long since put behind him his departure from West Point. In fact, he realized he probably did better academically at Notre Dame and certainly came out higher in military standing through Notre Dame's Air Force ROTC program than he ever would have done at West Point. In many ways Pfautz may have done him a favor. But he was not going to tell him that.

"Let's just let bygones be bygones, Jim. I'm doing well enough here, and few people know about my past. I'd just as soon keep it that way if you don't mind," said the scientist, whose technicians were at that moment undergoing their evaluation by Pfautz's boss.

"That's fine with me, too, Bill. If you ever need anything and I can help, you call me," said the general's exec. Then Pfautz departed the conference room to catch up with his general.

Jackomis was reassigned early in the 1970s to the Pentagon to serve on the air staff. He was a full colonel now and took over the directorate that prepared analyses in support of the Air Force's annual budget request to Congress for funding for research, development, testing, and evaluation. In that role he often had to get highly classified briefings from Air Force intelligence on what

*Pfautz and Jackomis differ slightly in their recollection of this melodramatic encounter.

the Soviets were doing to provide justification for those budget requests to do the research needed to stay ahead of them. His main contact on the air staff was another colonel by the name of Jim Pfautz.*

Like Bill Jackomis, Jim Pfautz had a highly successful early career as a pilot. He was a jet pilot and served initially in France. Pfautz was picked to go to graduate school as well and served as the assistant professor of military science at a major university while he worked in his free time to get his masters degree. Pfautz found himself in the Military Assistance and Advisory Group to Vietnam in 1964–65 where he, too, logged plenty of combat flying hours. He then spent four years at Air Force Systems Command. Then he went to the Pentagon to serve on the Air Staff in 1971. For three years he was an Air Force expert for a wide range of Air Staff activities, including Bill Jackomis's RDT&E budget committee.

Jake stayed at the Pentagon, but in 1976 the head of the U.S. delegation to the Strategic Arms Limitations Talks, James Wade, selected him to be on his staff for negotiating the implementation review of the Strategic Arms Limitations Treaty (SALT I) with the Soviets. Jackomis's analysis covered the implications of this treaty on antiballistic missiles for all foreseeable future possibilities on Soviet offensive and defensive nuclear missile programs. Jim Wade had graduated from West Point in the Class of 1953 but early in his career got an advanced degree in physics and went into the nuclear weapons program. He knew all about Bill Jackomis. Jake would stay with Wade as a staff officer for several subsequent negotiations with the Soviets until Jake's retirement from the Air Force in 1980. He followed Wade when he was appointed by President Ronald Reagan to be assistant secretary of defense in 1984, in charge of negotiations on Strategic Arms Reduction Treaty (START) and the Comprehensive Nuclear Test Ban Treaty.

Meanwhile, Jim Pfautz left the Air Staff in 1974 to be a fellow at the prestigious Council on Foreign Relations, then was brought

---

*Pfautz and Jackomis differ slightly on this point.

back to the Defense Department as military assistant to the assistant secretary of defense for international security affairs. In 1977 Pfautz was chosen to be the defense attaché to Egypt to handle the especially sensitive issues surrounding the implementation of the Egypt-Israeli peace treaty that settled the 1973 Arab-Israeli War. Pfautz demonstrated his ability to handle matters of high policy with great intelligence and sensitivity and was promoted by the Air Force to brigadier general in 1978 to be the assistant chief of Air Force intelligence. He sometimes met with Jackomis to provide Wade with intelligence briefings related to the negotiations with the Soviets. When Jake retired in 1980, Pfautz went off for three years to serve on the staff of the commander-in-chief, Pacific.

SOME THINGS JUST TAKE MORE TIME

While Pfautz and Jackomis and many of the others involved in the 1951 cheating incident worked their way down the roads life had thrown at them, West Point changed very little in the fundamental systems that had created the conditions for the cheating incident. The academy did change, to be sure. It doubled its enrollment in the midst of the Vietnam War and greatly expanded its physical plant. But by 1973 the honor and academic systems were much the same as they were in 1953.

One history professor, who was selected to be a White House fellow, looking at the difficulties in the honor system that were going untouched, predicted that ". . . this bedrock of academy life is in danger of irremediable erosion or its alternative—scandalous, painful, embarrassing, and public rehabilitation." He went on to cite four specific examples of cadets caught in the act of cheating or lying in the late 1960s who were acquitted by the Honor Committee. In 1973 there was a nationally prominent case of a cadet convicted of an honor code violation who chose not to resign. Because of legal rules and procedures academy officials could not dismiss the man. He was silenced by the Corps of Cadets.

In 1976 West Point's honor system reached a new crisis when more than a hundred cadets were caught cheating on an electrical engineering examination. The incident nearly caused the academy to be shut down in a scandal of national proportions. The entire honor system was finally reformed after several investigations and reviews. In 1951 the academy and the Army blamed only the cadets and Red Blaik for choosing the easier wrong rather than the harder right. But in 1976 the academy had to face the fact that the problems also stemmed from flaws in the institution as well.

Red Blaik's prediction of the demise of Army football came true, too. By the 1973 season Army football had reached a new low, deeper even than the depths it had reached in 1940. The 1973 Army team lost all eleven of its games, including a 77–7 shelling by Nebraska on national television and an ignominious loss to Navy, 55–0. Army football needed an overhaul, too.

Several of the other dismissed cadets continued to do well. Bill Johnson served a second tour in Southeast Asia as the commander of an airborne command and control squadron in 1975. He organized the evacuation of the remaining U.S. troops from the Republic of Vietnam as the North overran that country in 1975. On his return from that assignment, Johnson went to the National Defense University, where he retired in 1982. He is now a nationally respected business executive.

The officer in charge of the investigation, Ace Collins, would go on to a distinguished career as a combat arms commander in Europe during the Cold War and Vietnam. He retired in 1974 as a three-star general and in 1978 published a book titled *Common Sense Training* (Presidio Press), which became highly influential in restoring a sense of integrity in military training and an abiding commitment to realism in the preparation of soldiers and units for war.

In the decade of the 1980s, West Point the institution finally began to move to catch up with the progress that its graduates had made since 1951. The honor system reforms that came out of the 1976 cheating scandal were fully implemented by 1980, and cadets began to share the responsibility for development of the virtues associated with integrity with the academy administration and with graduates who had trod that ground before. Bill Johnson began a campaign to get the members of his class who had been dismissed admitted as associate members of the USMA Association of Graduates, the alumni organization for West Pointers. Former cadets who left for a variety of reasons were permitted to join the alumni group as associate members, but not those who were dismissed for violating the honor code. Johnson felt that the changes in the honor system vindicated the eighty-three who resigned in 1951 and that if those changes had been in place at the time, very few of them would have been dismissed. In 1993 his former classmates agreed and permitted those from the Class of 1952 who had been dismissed to join their class as associate members.

One of the former cadet football players reached the epitome of the football world in 1980, the Super Bowl. Ray Malavasi had left the academy in 1952 and gone to Kansas State to play football. After graduating, Malavasi could not break into professional football, so he became a college assistant coach. He coached at several schools until 1966, when Denver in the American Football League hired him as an assistant. Denver's head coach quit after only two games, and Malavasi took over as head coach for the rest of the season. The Los Angeles Rams hired him as an assistant coach, and in 1978, when George Allen was fired after the first two games of the season, Malavasi found himself propelled to the head coach position.

The 1978 season was a tough one for the Rams, but in 1979 they had the talent to win the National Football Conference championship and make it into the Super Bowl for 1980. To many sportswriters, Malavasi seemed out of place in the Super Bowl. He was not one for glamor and glitz. In fact, he held a prebowl party for reporters at his home outside Los Angeles and one reporter remarked at how working class it was. Malavasi was "sausage and beer, not champagne and canapés," and he seemed so out of place at Super Bowl XIV.

At midseason, Malavasi's Rams were sporting a 5–6 record, and Ray thought for sure he would soon be looking for a job. His big problem was at quarterback. Ray finally put Vince Ferragamo in the position, and he turned out to be a winner. Vince took the Rams to the NFC championship and the Super Bowl with a 9–7 regular-season record and impressive playoff wins over Dallas and Tampa Bay.

The football world did not give the Rams a chance against Terry Bradshaw and the Steelers. Malavasi took his team in as heavy underdogs. But he also took to his team the kind of fight he had learned as a player under Red Blaik and Vince Lombardi. Malavasi never quit. He sent in the plays to his rookie quarterback, and the lead went back and forth between the Rams and the Steelers no fewer than six times. At the half Los Angeles was ahead, 13–10. In the end the Rams lost, but the Steelers knew they had earned this one against a tough team under a scrappy coach. Malavasi coached the Rams until 1982, when he moved to the U.S. Football League and the L.A. Express. He retired in 1987 when that league folded.

The 1980s brought the return of football to the place that Douglas MacArthur wanted it at West Point. In the early 1980s West Point hired a new coach, Jim Young, who had coached Purdue's nationally ranked teams. Young soon brought winning back to the program. He took the Army team into national prominence and even got them into the academy's first bowl game in 1985. All the while he kept the academy's mission as his own, the development of the nation's officers, and did not let football become an end unto itself.

Bill Jackomis retired from the Air Force in 1980 and went to work for General Electric Aerospace in Valley Forge, Pennsylvania. After less than a year he was hired by Fred Jones, who was working as a senior vice president for Williams International Corporation. Jones needed a strategic planner who knew the Air Force customer well and who had access to the top secret programs Williams was working on at the time, including the then-classified cruise missile.

At the same time, Jim Pfautz got his second star and was chief of Air Force intelligence. Jackomis arranged a meeting between his company president, Sam Williams, who was the inventor of the cruise missile, and Major General Pfautz on developments in Soviet cruise missile programs. In a further gesture of goodwill,

Pfautz also wrote a letter to Jackomis's mother describing to her the good character her son had displayed to him.

Pfautz was the last of those involved in the cheating incident to leave the uniformed service. The incident leading up to his retirement reflected the same courage of conviction that had motivated him back in 1951. As chief of Air Force intelligence in 1983 he had access to most of the highest sources of intelligence collection available to the nation. In many cases he was the first senior official to get access to raw intelligence data collected by electronic means, because several Air Force platforms were the collectors of information that went to the president and his top national security advisers.

When the Soviets shot down Korean Air Lines Flight 007 in 1983, Pfautz's staff was among the first to piece together the separate electronic indicators of what had happened. He concluded, based on the evidence, that there was a good probability that the Soviets had honestly mistaken the identity of the Korean Boeing 747 for a U.S. spy plane. Pfautz tried for several hours to convince Secretary of Defense Weinberger and the joint chiefs chairman, Gen. John Vessey, not to accuse the Soviets publicly of a deliberate shoot-down of an innocent airliner. Pfautz was not able to convince them, but Weinberger agreed to present Pfautz's views to CIA director Casey and to Vice President Bush. They went with Weinberger's view. Although he was offered the opportunity to head the Defense Intelligence Agency, Pfautz retired in 1985.

One of the last chapters on the 1951 cheating incident was closed in May 1989 when Red Blaik was laid to rest at the West Point cemetery. Dignitaries from all over the world attended the services, and Army football great Pete Dawkins read from Scripture at his graveside. With the burial of Red Blaik and the sunset of the careers of so many of those who had been involved in the incident, it seemed that the whole affair might finally be laid to rest and forgotten.

That same month a commission on the West Point honor code and system issued its final report to the Army chief of staff, Gen. Carl Vuono. The report signaled the final healing of the academy's honor code. The commission found that many of the problems of 1951 were still present. It recommended a total of twenty-five changes to the honor system to correct those tendencies, ". . . intended to simplify enforcement of the code; to remove excess and trivial detail; to endorse flexibility of sanctions, enabling rehabilitation of an offender when that is feasible; to reaffirm that enforcement of the code is the responsibility of every participant; to amplify the favorable effect of the code in later careers and throughout the Army; and to support the code as an exemplar for all public service."

West Point now has an honor system that can help the academy to maintain the honor of the corps untarnished and unsullied. Football has been restored to its proper place in the life of cadets, balancing the will to win with the demand for integrity. And the men who had been involved in the cheating incident have contributed much to their country and to their families and have brought much credit upon themselves and to West Point.

The Brave Old Army Team, in the end, has won the battle.

Epilogue

It was typically cool, gray, and damp that day in March 1986 in Germany. Major General Dave Palmer was waiting in his office at the headquarters of 1st Armored Division. Palmer was not an office general; he spent most of his career training soldiers, leading them in battle, or educating them. He would rather be with them in the field, but for now he had to wait in his office for an important visitor.

He had been in command less than a year when he was notified that he was to be reassigned that summer to become the fifty-third superintendent of the U.S. Military Academy at West Point. It was bittersweet news. On the one hand, he would join the company of a gallery of great Americans who preceded him as "the supe," including the likes of Robert E. Lee, Douglas MacArthur, Maxwell Taylor, and William C. Westmoreland. Palmer was one of a very few line commanders in the U.S. Army who was also a scholar, and as a published historian he knew that he was about to enter the ranks of the truly elite in American history.

On the other hand, he would have to leave his first love, command of American soldiers in a combat unit. The Army had only sixteen divisions in 1986, and Dave Palmer had been selected from out of thousands of his peers over the years to earn the trust of the Army's senior leaders to command the twenty-five thousand men and women of the 1st Armored Division. He had survived two tours in Vietnam, and commanded at battalion and brigade levels in the 1960s and 1970s in the very difficult times of the "hollow" Army. By the mid-1980s the Army was once again a well-honed, highly professional fighting force, and Palmer was just reaching his stride as a division commander when the call came from Washington to go to West Point.

He accepted his lot, as all true professionals do, and readied himself to do his duty by going to West Point. It meant a third star, but the promotion was less important to him than the challenge of molding the young men and women of the next generation of officers. Indeed, among many other changes, women were now a well-established element of the Corps of Cadets, and it would be a very different West Point he would return to than the one he left when he graduated in 1956. It would also be even more different than the West Point where he taught military history in the 1960s. In fact, one of the women in his divison would soon offer her advice to him: "Some people are always running down the cadets. I don't know why," she told General Palmer. "You should always remember that they are fine young Americans." Palmer looked forward to returning to his alma mater, which, in spite of dramatic change, remained constant in its development of leaders of character to serve the nation in the common defense.

For now the assignment was not yet known publicly. He would first meet with the current superintendent, Willard Scott, for an exchange of views. He would be given a short time to collect his thoughts about how he would guide the academy before moving back to the States early in the summer of 1986. As he waited in his office for Scott to arrive that dreary March day, Palmer wondered what it would have been like if he had been permitted to serve out his command tour in Germany. Dave and his wife, Lu, whom he had known since before their high school days, had endeared themselves to German locals over the years of previous assignments, and they felt as much a part of their community as they did their own hometowns in Texas. Parting with such dear foreign friends and close American professionals would be very sad.

Scott arrived promptly and, after exchanging formalities, he told Palmer that he would very soon face a most difficult decision as supe, one that Scott himself did not want to face and that indeed he would leave for Palmer to decide. For several years a major construction project had been under way at the academy, drawing a lot of attention. It was a very large athletic building and had been opened earlier that year. Scott warned Palmer that naming it would not be a trivial matter. It was built in space that had been blasted out of the side of a mountain adjacent to Michie Stadium, where the football team played. It housed a new hockey rink and basketball arena, among other sites, and was intended to be the center of cadet athletic activity for indoor sports. Scott informed Palmer that there was a strong move afoot to name the facility after famed Army football coach and athletic director Red Blaik, but that many West Point graduates opposed the move. He warned the incoming supe that he had better have a way to deal with the issue before he got to West Point because it was sure to boil over and cause him serious difficulty if he did not settle the issue in a most judicious manner.

Soon after he arrived at West Point, Palmer received a letter that opened the door on the controversy that would soon come virtually to consume him and nearly cause him to be relieved of his command. In September of 1986 Palmer received a letter from another former superintendent, Garrison "Gar" Davidson. Davidson was Blaik's contemporary, and it was clear from his letter that he held great contempt for Army's greatest football coach of all time.

Davidson believed that Blaik's attitude was the antithesis of America's national spirit and that of the military academy. This was based on his belief that Blaik evaded wartime service during World War I. He wrote, "My blood boils and I see red when my mind drifts to the possibility of a draft dodger memorialized at West Point." This statement exemplified the dilemma facing the new supe. Graduates were at opposite poles of opinion on a potentially divisive issue that Palmer could not avoid. The new facility had to be named, and he could not possibly achieve a compromise between the two views they voiced.

Instead of choosing between the two views and the considerable followings that each side commanded, Palmer instead took a larger approach to the issues they represented. Palmer had taught military history at West Point, and he knew that names on buildings had a far-reaching impact beyond their sentimental value. When you carved something in stone it was going to be around for a long time. Douglas MacArthur had composed the verse now engraved on the wall of the Cadet Gymnasium that had become so firmly imbedded in the spirit of West Pointers for decades, "Upon the fields of friendly strife are sown the seeds that, upon other fields on other days, will bear the fruits of victory." He decided not to decide on memorializing just one building and one man. Rather, Palmer decided to create a policy to guide all such memorializations.

In a memorandum he signed on 22 June 1987, less than a year after taking command at West Point, Lt. Gen. Dave Palmer established the policy still in effect at West Point on the naming of athletic facilities. That policy holds that any facility in which cadets compete will be named for a West Point graduate who had gained distinction in sports, who was a leader in the Corps of Cadets, and who had fallen in battle in the full vigor of youth. This, Palmer believed, would add meaning to the naming of facilities far beyond mere remembrance. It would also be a policy that only the most callous of critics would oppose publicly. The new facility was named for Don Holleder, a hero—and one of Blaik's former players—who had been killed in the Vietnam War. Palmer hoped that would defuse the issue of naming something for Blaik.

It did not.

Red Blaik died on 5 May 1989. His funeral at West Point on 13 May was an impressive ceremony and was attended by former president Richard Nixon. After a long and successful career as a football coach, Blaik continued to serve the country, for a while as an active board member of a major defense corporation, and later as a personal adviser to Presidents Kennedy, Nixon, and Ford. Although he was well known as a conservative Republican—Blaik had worked the 1948 Republican National Convention for Douglas MacArthur—in 1963 Democratic president John F. Kennedy appointed Blaik to a commission sent to Birmingham, Alabama, to relieve racial tensions there during the early days of desegregation. Later, Vice President George Bush nominated Blaik for the Presidential Medal of Freedom, which was awarded by Ronald Reagan in 1986.

Palmer was beginning to think that Red Blaik was larger than life, and this funeral did nothing to dispel the thought. When Blaik's headstone was revealed it became clear just how much clout the man had. Early in the twentieth century, rules had to be imposed at West Point National Cemetery concerning the size of grave markers. For decades during the nineteenth century, families of the departed memorialized their loved ones—heroes and rogues alike—with ever larger and more ornate headstones. The twentieth-century rules required all grave markers to conform to size, shape, and color restrictions that would impose the gravity and seriousness demanded of the site as well as conserve the diminishing space available. Blaik's headstone, a tall, black football shape, flagrantly violated these proscriptions and stands today in testimony to his still divisive character.

The dirt had barely settled over Blaik's grave when the controversy again came to afflict Dave Palmer. Seizing on the emotion of the funeral, a number of Blaik partisans, some of whom had been generous campaign supporters of the Republican Party, convinced Gerald Ford and Richard Nixon to write directly to President George Bush, appealing to him to memorialize Blaik more distinctively by renaming the football stadium for him. Former Air Force Academy superintendent and West Point football player Winfield Scott contacted Palmer, also urging him to rename Michie Stadium for Blaik, reporting that many of Blaik's former players would be supporting that position. Soon an active campaign developed calling for the renaming of the football field to "Blaik Stadium," or at least "Michie-Blaik" stadium.

A countermovement emerged just as quickly to oppose the attempt. Another former superintendent wrote to Palmer, "I trust that we will succeed in killing this outrageously asinine notion before it does real damage." Palmer was once again caught in a dilemma.

Palmer decided to contact the Blaik family directly, placing a call in June 1989 to Red Blaik's son Robert Blaik. Palmer told Bob Blaik that he could not now change the policy on naming of athletic facilities, nor could he make an exception. He did offer to rename a different building on the post for Red Blaik or to designate the soon-to-be-built Administration Building for the Office of the Director of Intercollegiate Athletics to be named "Blaik Hall." That would be in addition to several other ways in which the famous coach had already been memorialized at the military academy. Bob Blaik declined the offer. He told the superintendent that he sincerely believed that the football stadium should be renamed Blaik Stadium and that he would continue to work to that end.

President Bush initially saw no reason not to go along with the apparently straightforward request of two of his predecessors. He had not been informed by those pushing for the renaming of the stadium that it would reverse academy policy or that Blaik himself was a very controversial figure among West Pointers. But by early July 1989 the White House had learned of the hornet's nest that had been stirred up, and presidential adviser Andrew Card became involved on behalf of President Bush. Card wrote a memo to Secretary of the Army John Marsh, delegating him the responsibility to solve the problem. For Dave Palmer, the historian, the situation resembled the one the secretary of the Army found himself in back in 1951 when President Truman ordered young Frank Pace, the thirty-four-year-old lawyer who was then secretary of the Army, to relieve General MacArthur of his command in Korea.

However, Marsh was quite politically astute, having served five terms in the House of Representatives. He did not act precipitously. He first wrote back to the White House urging a more diplomatic solution than what would amount to a presidential decree overriding the policy of the academy and the judgment of military leaders. Meanwhile, after learning of the intense controversy between the pro- and anti-Blaik factions, Marsh wrote to a number of retired generals asking for their opinion on the issue. A solid body of opinion one way or the other would provide the president with some political cover.

But Marsh did not get the chance to provide the stratagem to solve this increasingly vexing political problem for the president. President Bush asked him to head a special panel on Defense Department management reforms, and Undersecretary Michael Stone stepped up to become secretary of the Army. One of the first things to hit Stone's desk was a terse message from Andrew Card telling him the White House would not take direct action, and to get on with finding an appropriate way to memorialize Blaik at West Point. Palmer thoroughly briefed Secretary Stone of the full and divisive ramifications of the move to rename Michie Stadium, including the fact that some opponents of the action threatened to reveal publicly very embarrassing information about Blaik and the 1951 cheating incident if the stadium were to be renamed for Blaik in any way.

Michael Stone had been senior enough for long enough in appointive bureaucratic positions that he could sense a serious political threat when it came. The football stadium could not be renamed. In April 1990 he wrote a memorandum through the Army chief of staff to the superintendent, USMA. In the memo he stated that the president had asked the secretary of the Army to determine the appropriate memorial to Blaik and that he—Stone— had decided to name the new Administration Building for the Office of the Director of Intercollegiate Athletics after Red Blaik. He ordered Palmer to proceed to make the announcement and to establish a construction program to complete the project in time for West Point's Bicentennial celebration in 2002. Stone then wrote to Bob Blaik to inform him of the decision. He also told Blaik that he had directed Palmer to keep Blaik informed as the project proceeded.

It was clear from the tone of the correspondence that Stone did not appreciate the fact that Palmer had given him such a hot political potato. But Stone's attention was quickly diverted to other issues as Congress slashed the Army's budget in the aftermath of the Cold War. He soon had to respond to a serious move to reduce the role of West Point, and the other military academies as well, from Senator John Glenn and others in Congress. Dave Palmer also became preoccupied with justifying West Point's programs and budgets in response to a stream of critical questions emanating from Senator Glenn's Senate sub-committee. General Palmer had assumed the superintendency of West Point believing that there was a window of opportunity, for the first time in perhaps decades, for the superintendent to shape the future of the institution without much outside inter-ference. In July 1990 Palmer wrote to the Army chief of staff, Carl Vuono, that the window had slammed shut. The Blaik issue be-came part of a larger concern for the very survival of the military academy in its traditional form.

Meanwhile, intrigued by the mention of Blaik's involvement in the 1951 cheating scandal, General Palmer assigned one of his senior faculty members to explore the incident more fully as a case study that might prove to be instructive in approaching honor code issues of the 1990s. Colonel Anthony Hartle, profes-sor of philosophy in the English Department, was given access to the archives of the academy to explore the nature and causes of the 1951 incident to assess its relevance and to build case studies for faculty and staff instructional purposes. Palmer felt that one thing the academy lacked was adequate preparation for incom-ing officers for their role in the honor system.

Hartle was not to bring any old skeletons out of the closet; he was required to maintain strict anonymity in his final report. Palmer did not want to rub any salt into old wounds; as a histo-rian he believed that values such as integrity had timeless rele-vance to professional soldiers and that appropriate principles of integrity could be dramatically illustrated by way of case studies from the past. Hartle soon found that there was indeed much to be learned about the 1951 affair.

For one thing, he discovered that not much had been written about the scandal once it disappeared from the headlines in the summer of 1951. A large cheating ring had been uncovered and eighty-three cadets were dismissed from the academy. Many of them were football players, and the dismissals devastated Army's nationally powerful team. It would take years for West Point to regain its winning ways, yet there was little to be found in print about the incident outside of Blaik's memoirs and a few passing remarks in sports histories. When he delved into the academy's records, Hartle discovered that many of the official records of the time had been mysteriously misplaced. General Palmer himself found some important documents hidden away in a little-known corner of the archives, filed under a strange title and apparently untouched for nearly forty years.

As he continued to study the reports, Hartle realized he would need to talk to the former cadets themselves. Bringing into his project a number of additional faculty members sworn to protect the confidentiality of their subjects, Hartle directed more than thirty interviews in the project and in the end painted a comprehensive picture of what had happened in 1951. As a case study it promised to be a very effective teaching tool for the present day because many of the roots of trouble that led to the scandal of 1951 were still in place when a second cheating scandal rocked the academy in 1976. Palmer was convinced that teaching the details of both events would be a vital step toward not repeating the mistakes of the past.

But word soon got out from the many interviews that Palmer was resurrecting the 1951 affair. Since Bob Blaik had been involved, and had been interviewed by one of the academy's instructors, it appeared to the pro-Blaik faction that this was a backhanded attempt to smear the name of Red Blaik. They reached Secretary Stone, who in turn told the Army staff to have West Point halt the case study effort immediately. Somehow Dave Palmer never got the word, and Colonel Hartle completed the case study.

When the pro-Blaik faction learned that, they complained again to Secretary Stone. As far as he was concerned his direct order had been disobeyed, and he was prepared to relieve Palmer of his command at West Point. The Army vice chief of staff, Gen. Gordon Sullivan, called Palmer and learned the facts of the matter. The two then had to decide what to do. Palmer proposed to Sullivan that he would halt further distribution of the study and that it would be used strictly internally at West Point. He agreed to submit the final version of the study to Army headquarters for clearance and would invite any comments on the case study to be sent directly to Colonel Hartle. He then committed the entire train of events to a memorandum for the record.

The Army's official review of the case study was conducted by the Center for Military History, under the direction of Col. Hal Nelson. Nelson's response, in letter form, was scathing in its criticism of the study and its interpretation of events of forty years before. But it did admit that the case study raised valid questions, both about the institutional stories held forth by West Point and the Army about the incident and about some of the people who were central to that tale.

For whatever reason, the entire intrigue soon faded from sight. Perhaps the Persian Gulf War gave Army leaders more pressing matters to deal with. But the scandal did not fade from the memory of those involved in the incident. Some still speak of it, though only in hushed tones or under cover of anonymity. A few refuse to speak of it at all. Several told me all I wanted to know about it and then some. Some told me much, then asked that I not reveal their identities.

Although failing to have the new athletic building or the football stadium named for Red Blaik, the Blaik family was gratified with the considerable recognition accorded to him; at West Point he is one of the most repeatedly honored academy graduates, standing behind only Sylvanus Thayer, Douglas MacArthur, Dwight D. Eisenhower, Robert E. Lee, Ulysses S. Grant, and John J. Pershing. On Red Blaik's gravestone is engraved a simple phrase: "On, Brave Old Army Team."

Sources

DOCUMENTS

Hand, The Honorable Learned, Lt. Gen. Troy H. Middleton, U.S.A. (Ret) and Maj. Gen. Robert L. Danford, U.S.A. (Ret). 25 July, 1951. *Report of Board to the Secretary of the Army.* U.S. Military Academy Archives.

Hartle, Col. Anthony E. 10 September, 1990. *Honor Violations at West Point, 1951: A Case Study.* Final Draft.

Headquarters, 3rd Infantry Division. 1950. *3d Infantry Division in Korea.* The Pentagon Library.

Headquarters, United States Military Academy. 30 June, 1951. *Official Register of the Officers and Cadets of the United States Military Academy.* The Pentagon Library.

Headquarters, United States Military Academy. 30 June, 1951. *Superintendent's Report.* The Pentagon Library.

Headquarters, United States Military Academy. 28 May, 1951. *Proceedings of a Board of Officers Convened Pursuant to Letter Orders, Hq USCC, West Point, New York.* Lt. Col. Arthur S. Collins, President of the Board. U.S. Military Academy Archives.

Headquarters, United States Military Academy. 7 September, 1951. *Report of a Board of Officers to Review Present Procedures and Practices at the USMA, with Particular Emphasis on Those Having a Bearing on Conditions Brought Out in the Recent Investigation of Honor Violations.* Col. B. W. Bartlett, Col. F. M. Greene, and Col. C. H. Miles.

The Military History Institute. 28 April, 1974. *The Paul O. Harkins Oral History.* U.S. Army Military History Research Collection, Senior Officers Debriefing Program. U.S. Army War College, Carlisle Barracks, Penn.

The Military History Institute. May, 1982. *The Arthur S. Collins Oral History.* U.S. Army Military History Research Collection, Senior Officers Debriefing Program. U.S. Army War College, Carlisle Barracks, Penn.

Posvar, Wesley W. May, 1989. *Final report of the Special Commission of the Chief of Staff on the Honor Code and Honor System at the United States Military Academy.*

U.S. House. 17 February 1909. Committee on Military Affairs. Hazing at the United States Military Academy, 60th Cong., 2d sess. Letter from the secretary of war, transmitting a response to the inquiry of the House in relation to hazing at the U.S. Military Academy. Referred to the committee and ordered to be printed.

ARTICLES

Associated Press. 1946. Army–Notre Dame Suspension Is Laid to Ticket Speculation. *New York Herald Tribune,* 31 December.

Brean, Herbert and Luther Conant. 1952. The Mystery of the Missing Cadet. *Life,* 14 April.

Bryant Edward Moore Obituary. 1951. *Assembly,* October.

Ferguson, Louise Trent. 1951. John Charles Trent Obituary. *Assembly,* July 1955.

Hall, Charles W. and Jeff Leeds. 1994. U-Va Upholds Its Honor Code. *Washington Post,* 4 March.

The New York Times Magazine. 9 August, 1951.

Rendel, John. 1946. Break Is Declared in Classic Rivalry. *The New York Times,* December 31.

Rothe, Anna, ed. 1946. Blaik, Earl H(enry). In *Current Biography: Who's News and Why 1945.* New York: H.W. Wilson.

Tuition at Notre Dame Offered Needy Cadets: Must Shun Sports. 1951. *Boston Herald,* 22 August.

Whalen, James D. Blaik, Earl Henry "Red". In David L. Porter. 1987. *Biographical Dictionary of American Sports: Football.* New York: Greenwood Press.

BOOKS

Ambrose, Steven E. 1966. *Duty Honor Country: A History of West Point.* Baltimore: The Johns Hopkins Press.

Blaik, Earl H. 1974. *The Red Blaik Story.* New Rochelle, N.Y.: Arlington House Publishers.

Blaik, Earl H., and Tim Cohane. 1960. *You Have to Pay the Price.* New York: Holt, Rinehart and Winston.

Bugle Notes. 1950. N.p.

Connor, Jack. 1995. *Leahy's Lads: The Story of the Famous Notre Dame Football Teams of the 1940s.* South Bend, Indiana: Diamond Communications.

David, Lester. 1995. *Good Ted, Bad Ted: The Two Faces of Edward M. Kennedy.* New York: Birch Lane Press.

Davidson, Garrison H. 1974. *Grandpa Gar: The Saga of One Soldier as Told to his Grandchildren.* Unpublished Manuscript. Carlisle Barracks, Pennsylvania. Military History Insitute, U.S. Army War College.

Dineen, Joseph E. 1988. *The Illustrated History of Sports at the United States Military Academy.* Norfolk, Va.: Donning.

Edson, James S. 1954. *The Black Knights of West Point.* New York: Bradbury, Sayles, O'Neil.

Sources 409

Eichelberger, Robert. 1989. *Our Jungle Road to Tokyo*. Nashville: Battery Classics.

Esposito, Vincent. 1968. *West Point Atlas of American Wars*. Vol. II. New York: Frederick Praeger Publishing.

Fleming, Thomas J. 1969. *West Point: The Men and Times of the United States Military Academy*. New York: William Morrow.

Greene, Jerry. 1991. *Super Bowl Chronicles*. Grand Rapids, Mich. Masters Press.

Gunther, Gerald. 1995. *Learned Hand: The Man and the Judge*. New York: Knopf.

Hersh, Seymour. 1986. *The Target Is Destroyed: What really Happened to Flight 007 and What America Knew About It*. New York: Random House.

Howitzer. 1917. N.p.

Howitzer. 1920. N.p.

Howitzer. 1927. N.p.

James, D. Clayton. 1970. *The Years of MacArthur*. Vol. I. *1880–1941*. Boston: Houghton Mifflin.

James, D. Clayton. 1985. *The Years of MacArthur*. Vol. III. *Triumph and Disaster, 1945–1964*. Boston: Houghton Mifflin.

Johnson, Otto., ed. 1993. *Information Please Almanac Atlas and Yearbook*. 46th ed. Boston: Houghton Mifflin.

Kennedy, Edward M. 1965. *The Fruitful Bough: A Family Memorial Tribute to Joseph P. Kennedy*. N.p.

Krause, Moose and Stephen Singular. 1993. *Notre Dame's Greatest Coaches*. New York: Simon & Schuster.

MacArthur, Douglas A. 1964. *Reminiscences*. New York: McGraw Hill.

MacArthur, Douglas. 1965. *A Soldier Speaks: Public Papers and Speeches of General of the Army Douglas MacArthur*. New York: Frederick A. Praeger.

Manchester, William. 1978. *American Caesar: Douglas MacArthur, 1880–1964*. Boston: Little Brown.

Martin, Ralph G. 1995. *Seeds of Destruction: Joe Kennedy and His Sons*. G.P. Putnam's Sons.

Neft, David S. 1977. *The Encyclopedia of Professional Football*. New York: A.S. Barnes.

O'Brien, Michael. 1987. *Vince: A Personal Biography of Vince Lombardi*. New York: William Morrow.

Pappas, George S. 1993. *To The Point: The United States Military Academy, 1802–1902*. Westport, Conn: Praeger.

Schoor, Gene. 1989. *100 Years of Army–Navy Football*. New York: Henry Holt.

Sperber, Murray. 1993. *Shake Down the Thunder: The Creation of Notre Dame Football*. New York: Henry Holt.

Taylor, Maxwell D. 1972. *Swords and Plowshares*. New York: W. W. Norton.

Treat, Roger. 1977. *The Encyclopedia of Football*. 15th rev. ed. Ed. Pete Palmer. New York: A.S. Barnes.

Valtin, Jan. 1988. *Children of Yesterday: The Twenty-fourth Division in World War II*. Nashville: The Battery Press.

LETTERS

Blaik, Earl H. 10 November, 1932. Letter to Gen. Douglas MacArthur. U.S. Military Academy Library Special Collections.

Blaik, Earl H. 16 December, 1940. Letter to Maj. Gen. Robert Eichelberger. U.S. Military Academy Library Special Collections.

Blaik, Earl H. 14 May, 1946. Letter to Douglas A. MacArthur. U.S. Military Academy Library Special Collections.

Blaik, Earl H. 28 December, 1948. Letter to Douglas A. Mac-Arthur. U.S. Military Academy Library Special Collections.

Blaik, Earl H. 29 December, 1949. Letter to Douglas A. MacArthur. U.S. Military Academy Library Special Collections.

Blaik, Earl H. 9 May 1950. Letter to Douglas A. MacArthur. U.S. Military Academy Special Collections.

Blaik, Earl H. 4 September, 1951. Letter to Douglas A. MacArthur. U.S. Military Academy Library Special Collections.

Irving, F. A. 23 August, 1952. Letter to Brig. Chauncy L. Fenton, U.S.A. (Ret.).

Taylor, Maxwell D., Superintendent U.S. Military Academy. 8 January, 1946. Letter to Dwight. D. Eisenhower, Chief of Staff, U.S. Army.

Woodmansee, Lt. Col. John W. 1968. Letter to Col. Thomas E. Griess.

VIDEO

Army Football Classics 1948–49–50 Seasons. 1987. Produced by the Army Athletic Association. 55 min. SPI. Videocassette.